Sirt Food Diet

2 Books in 1

Definitive Guide to Activate Your "Skinny Gene" and start burning fat fast + 600 Tasty Recipes Cookbook For Simple, Quick and Easy Meals + a 7-day Healthy Weight Loss Plan

Serena Baxter

TABLE OF CONTENTS

Sirt
Food
Diet

A Definitive guide to losing weight with a 7-day Healthy, Foolproof Weight Loss Plan + 200 Tasty Recipes

INTRODUCTION

The official Sirtfood Diet combines a short calorie restriction phase with a long-term commitment to nutrient-dense sirtuin-activating foods.

How you eat is your diet; restricting how you eat is dieting. Aside from the first week, Stage 1, the Sirtfood diet is not a traditional diet in that, instead of merely restricting calories, you focus on increasing nutrition and improving quality.

There are only 2 stages in the Sirtfood Diet, which take up 3 weeks of your life. Still, those 3 weeks are designed to set the stage for incorporating sirtfoods into your lifelong diet, eliminating your need to ever resort to dieting again.

The average American consumes many solid fats and sugars, refined grains, sodium, and saturated fat. They also under-consume vegetables, fruits, whole grains, and the nationally recommended intake of dairy and oils.

If this sounds like it matches your current eating patterns, don't be too hard on yourself, you're certainly not alone. And you've been practically brainwashed into adopting these poor nutrition habits. The number of fast-food restaurants continues to grow, as do your options for pre-made, packaged foods full of empty calories, and misleading promises. When you live on a diet of these foods devoid of all nutrition for too long, you find yourself getting sick and overweight. So, you turn to the industry that profits off of your poor health, the diet industry.

Sirtfood Diet is the newest approach to fast weight loss without extreme diet by stimulating the same 'skinny gene' mechanisms, typically just through fasting and exercise. Other foods varieties contain chemical substances known as polyphenols that stress our cells lightly, allowing genes to replicate the effects of fasting and exercise. The Sirtuin pathways, which affect metabolism, age, and mood, are guided by the food rich in polyphenols, like broccoli, dark chocolate, and red wine. However, a diet sufficient in these Sirtfoods starts to lose weight without sacrificing muscle while maintaining excellent health.

Combine healthy Sirtfoods with efficient and sustained weight loss, great energy, and bright health to your diet. Switch on the fat-burning strength, overburden weight loss, and help stave off disease with this easy-to-follow diet that nutritional, medical experts have established who have demonstrated the impact of Sirtfoods. Dark chocolate, coffee, and kale – they are all menus that enable Sirtuin and switch to what is known as the 'skinny gene' in the body. Sirtfood Diet presents you with a fast and safe way to eat for weight reduction, delicious easy-to-make recipes, and a long-term performance management program. The Sirtfood Diet is an inclusion diet with no exclusion, and Sirtfood is extensively affordable and available. However, this is a diet that encourages you to get a better version of yourself.

One of the significant advantages of the Sirtfood Diet is that we can achieve significant benefits with no long-term calorie restriction. The very first week of diet is the process of hyper-success, where we combine mild fasting with an abundance of strong Sirtfoods for a double blow to fat. And we expected some signs of hunger here, as with all the fasting regimens. But we have had none!

All thanks to the body's primary appetite-regulating hormone, leptin, called the "satiety hormone." As we feed, leptin rises, signaling the hypothalamus inhibiting desire to a part of the brain. Conversely, leptin signaling to the mind decreases when we fly, which makes us feel hungry. Leptin is so effective in controlling appetite that early expectations could be used as a "magic bullet" for treating obesity.

It is effortless to start the Sirt food diet. It only takes a little preparation. If you don't know what kale is or where you can find green tea, you may have a learning curve, albeit a tiny one.

1. Healthy Coffee Cookies

Preparation Time: 20 minutes
Cooking Time: 12 minutes
Servings: 20
Ingredients:
For dry ingredients:
- ½ cup cocoa, unsweetened
- 6 tablespoons all-purpose flour
- ½ cup whole-wheat flour
- ¾ tablespoon finely ground coffee beans or instant coffee
- ½ teaspoon baking soda
- ¾ teaspoon ground cinnamon
- ¼ teaspoon kosher salt

For wet ingredients:
- 3 small eggs, lightly beaten
- ¼ cup nonfat or low-fat plain Greek yogurt
- ½ tablespoon olive oil
- ½ + 1/8 cup blueberries
- ½ ripe banana
- ¼ cup honey
- 1 teaspoon pure vanilla extract
- ¼ cup dark or semi-sweet chocolate chips

Directions:
1. Preheat the oven to 350°F.
2. Brush baking sheet by spraying with nonstick cooking spray. Set it aside.
3. Combine all the dry ingredients i.e. whole-wheat flour, all-purpose flour, cocoa, cinnamon, salt, baking soda, and coffee in a mixing bowl.
4. Place banana in a microwave-safe bowl and cook on high for about 50 seconds.
5. Mash the banana and add into a bowl. Also add eggs, yogurt, oil, honey, and vanilla. Mix until well incorporated.
6. Fill wet ingredients into the dry ingredients and mix until just combined, making sure not to over-mix.
7. Add chocolate chips and blueberries and fold gently.
8. Make 20 equal portions of the mixture and place it on the baking sheet. It should be approximately 1-½ tablespoons per portion.
9. Press the cookies lightly. You can use a fork to do so.
10. Place the baking sheet in the oven and bake for about 12 – 14 minutes.
11. Cool on the baking sheet for 10 minutes. Loosen the cookies by pushing a metal spatula underneath the cookies. Transfer onto a wire rack
12. Cool before transferring into an airtight container.

Nutrition 60 Calories 1.5g Fat 2g Protein

2. Healthy Strawberry Oatmeal Bars

Preparation Time: 18 minutes
Cooking Time: 34 minutes
Servings: 8
Ingredients:
For strawberry bars:
- ½ cup old-fashioned rolled oats
- 3 tablespoons light brown sugar
- 1/8 teaspoon kosher salt
- 1 cup small-diced strawberries, divided
- ½ tablespoon fresh lemon juice
- 6 tablespoons white whole wheat flour
- 1/8 teaspoon ground ginger
- 3 tablespoons unsalted butter, melted
- ½ teaspoon cornstarch
- 3 teaspoons granulated sugar, divided

For the vanilla glaze: Optional
- ¼ cup powdered sugar, sifted
- ½ tablespoon milk
- ¼ teaspoon pure vanilla extract

Directions:
1. Preheat the oven to 350°F.
2. Situate rack in the center of the oven.
3. Prepare a small square or rectangular baking pan by lining it with a large sheet of parchment paper such that the extra sheet is hanging from 2 opposite sides.
4. Add oats, brown sugar, flour, salt, and ginger into a bowl and stir well.
5. Mix butter and mix until sort of crumbly.
6. Take out about 4 tablespoons of the mixture into a bowl and set it aside.

7. Transfer the rest of the mixture into the baking pan. Press it well onto the bottom of the baking pan.
8. Spread ½ cup chopped strawberries over the crust—dust cornstarch over it.
9. Drizzle lemon juice over the strawberries. Sprinkle 1 ½ teaspoons sugar.
10. Spread remaining strawberries and 1 ½ teaspoons sugar over it.
11. Scatter the retained crumb mixture on top.
12. Place the baking dish in the oven and bake for about 30 – 35 minutes or until golden brown on top.
13. Take out the baking dish and place it on the wire rack to cool.
14. Meanwhile, make the glaze. For this, add powdered sugar, milk, and vanilla into a bowl and whisk well.
15. Lift the bars along with the parchment paper and place it on your cutting board.
16. Pour glaze on top. Cut into 8 equal bars and serve.

Nutrition 100 Calories 5g Fat 2g Protein

3. Parsley Cheese Balls

Preparation Time: 13 minutes
Cooking Time: 0 minutes
Servings: 12
Ingredients:
- ¼ cup shredded, Kraft 2% milk sharp cheddar cheese
- 1 package (8 ounces) Philadelphia Neufchatel cheese, softened
- ½ tablespoon finely chopped green onion
- ½ tablespoon finely chopped red pepper
- ¼ cup finely chopped parsley
- 1 teaspoon Dijon mustard
- 6 stalks celery, cut each into 4 equal pieces crosswise
- 60 whole-wheat Ritz crackers

Directions:
1. Add Neufchatel and cheddar cheeses into a bowl. Beat with an electric hand mixer until well combined.
2. Stir in green onion, red pepper, and Dijon mustard.
3. Place the bowl in the refrigerator for an hour.
4. Split mixture into 12 equal portions and shape into balls.

5. Place parsley on a plate. Dredge the balls in parsley.
6. Place on a plate. Chill until use.

Nutrition 130 Calories 7g Fat 3g Protein

4. Baked Kale Chips

Preparation Time: 8 minutes
Cooking Time: 13 minutes
Servings: 3
Ingredients:
- ½ bunch kale (hard stems and ribs discarded)
- ½ tablespoon olive oil
- Spices of your choice to taste (optional)

Directions:
1. Preheat the oven to 350°F.
2. Prep baking sheet by lining it with parchment paper.
3. Dry the kale using a salad spinner.
4. Place kale on the baking sheet. Trickle oil over it. Sprinkle salt over the kale and spread it evenly.
5. Place the baking sheet in the oven and bake for about 12 – 14 minutes or until crisp.
6. Cool completely and serve. Store the leftovers in an airtight container.

Nutrition: 58 Calories 2.8g Fat 2.5g Protein

5. Chocolate Covered Date with Almonds

Preparation Time: 23 minutes
Cooking Time: 8 minutes
Serving: 12
Ingredients:
- 12 Medjool dates
- ¾ cup semi-sweet chocolate chips
- ½ teaspoon ground cinnamon
- 12 unsalted roasted almonds
- ½ teaspoon canola oil
- 1 teaspoon crushed almonds
- 1 teaspoon crushed pistachios

Directions:
1. Insert an almond in each date. The dates should completely cover the almond. Situate on a tray that has been lined with parchment paper.
2. Add cinnamon, canola oil, and chocolate chips into a heatproof bowl. Place the bowl in a double boiler. For setting a double

boiler, pour some water into a pot. The heatproof bowl should just fit on the top of the pot. Place the pot over medium flame. The chocolate will slowly melt. Stir often until chocolate melts.

3. Put off the heat and take out the heatproof bowl from the double boiler.
4. Dunk the almond stuffed date in the melted chocolate, one at a time. Lift it out with a spoon and place it back on the tray.
5. Mix pistachios and almonds in a small bowl.
6. Sprinkle almond and pistachios on the chocolate-coated dates. Put tray in the freezer and freeze until the chocolate sets, about an hour.
7. Take out the tray from the freezer and place it on your countertop for 10 minutes before serving.
8. Serve.

Nutrition: 152 Calories 5.4g Fat 2g Protein

6. Sticky Date and Walnut Pudding

Preparation Time: 25 minutes
Cooking Time: 60 minutes
Servings: 4
Ingredients:

- ½ cup chopped dried, pitted dates
- ¼ cup reduced-salt margarine
- 1 egg, lightly beaten
- 1/8 teaspoon ground cinnamon
- ¼ cup chopped, toasted walnuts
- 2 tablespoons low-fat milk
- ¼ cup brown sugar
- ½ cup self-rising flour
- ¼ teaspoon ground ginger

For pineapple and marmalade sauce:

- ½ can (from 14.1 ounces can) pineapple in natural juice
- 2 ½ tablespoons fine cut orange marmalade
- ½ teaspoon arrowroot

Directions:

1. Preheat the oven to 350°F.
2. Prepare a small pudding basin by lining it with parchment paper (cut into a circle to fit the bottom of the basin).

3. Add dates and a tablespoon of milk into a bowl and stir well. Set aside.
4. Add sugar, margarine, a tablespoon of milk and egg into another bowl and whisk well.
5. Add flour, ground ginger, and cinnamon into a third bowl and stir well.
6. Add the flour mixture into the bowl of egg mixture and beat until smooth.
7. Add walnuts and the soaked dates and fold gently.
8. Pour the mixture into the pudding basin.
9. Place the pudding basin in a baking pan. Take some boiling water and pour it all around the pudding basin up to ½ inch.
10. Tent the baking pan as well as the pudding basin with foil.
11. Place the baking pan and the pudding basin, in the oven. Bake for about 50 minutes
12. Take out the baking dish and place it on the wire rack to cool.
13. While the pudding is baking, make the pineapple and marmalade sauce. Use most of the juice of the pineapple (about 2/3). The rest can be used in some other recipe like a smoothie.
14. Add arrowroot and about a teaspoon of the pineapple juice in a small saucepan. Whisk well.
15. Add the rest of the juice and place the saucepan over medium flame. Bring to a boil, stirring constantly. It will be slightly thick.
16. Add pineapple pieces and marmalade. Stir well. Let it cook on low heat for a couple of minutes. Stir occasionally. Turn off the heat.
17. Invert the pudding onto a plate. Spread some of the sauce over it.
18. Slice into 4 equal portions and serve with some of the remaining sauce. It can be served warm or at room temperature.

Nutrition: 282 Calories 16g Fat 6g Protein

7. Healthy Chocolate Pudding

Preparation Time: 9 minutes
Cooking time: 0 minutes
Servings: 3
Ingredient:

- 2 ripe bananas, sliced
- ½ cup peanut butter

- ½ cup oats
- 1/8 teaspoon salt
- ½ cup cocoa powder
- ½ cup honey
- 1 teaspoon vanilla extract

Directions:
1. Blend bananas, peanut butter, oats, salt, cocoa, honey, and vanilla in a blender until smooth.
2. Divide equally into 4 dessert bowls. Cover the bowls with cling wrap.
3. Chill until it sets.
4. Serve chilled.

Nutrition: 454 Calories 18g Fat 11g Protein

8. Layered Frozen Chocolate Coffee Pops

Preparation Time: 13 minutes
Cooking Time: 0 minutes
Servings: 4

Ingredients:
- ½ package (from a 4-serving size package) low calorie white instant chocolate pudding mix
- 1 cup fat-free milk
- 3 tablespoons fat-free sweetened condensed milk
- 1 teaspoon instant espresso coffee powder or more to taste
- ¾ cup water
- 2 tablespoons cocoa powder, unsweetened
- ¼ teaspoon vanilla extract

Directions:
1. For the first layer: Add pudding mix, ¾ teaspoon espresso powder, and milk into a bowl.
2. Whisk constantly for 2 minutes or until it is thick.
3. Take 4 paper cups or plastic drinking cups and divide the mixture equally into the paper cups.
4. Cover the cups with plastic wrap and place it in the refrigerator.
5. While the first layer is chilling, prepare the second layer.
6. Add condensed milk, vanilla extract, the rest of the espresso powder, and the cocoa powder into a bowl and whisk well. Add more espresso powder to taste if desired.

7. Add water and whisk until well combined.
8. Pour the condensed milk mixture over the chilled first layer.
9. Cover the paper cups with foil. Make a slit in each of the foil. Insert Popsicle sticks through the slit, into the cup.
10. Place the pudding pops in the freezer. Freeze for 10 – 12 hours.
11. Just before serving, discard the foil and the paper cup as well.

Nutrition: 78 Calories 0.4g Fat 3.2g Protein

9. Ultimate Tofu Burrito Bowls

Preparation Time: 12 minutes
Cooking Time: 27 minutes
Servings: 2

Ingredients:
For tofu scramble:
- 2 tablespoons olive oil
- Salt to taste
- 9.4 ounces extra-firm tofu, drained, cubed
- Pepper to taste
- 1 teaspoon garlic powder
- 1 teaspoon onion powder
- 2 teaspoons fresh lemon juice

For beans:
- 2/3 cup finely diced red onion
- ¾ tablespoon olive oil
- Salt to taste
- ¼ teaspoon turmeric powder
- 1 jalapeño pepper, deseeded, chopped
- 2 cloves garlic, peeled, minced
- 1 teaspoon ground cumin
- 1 1/3 cups chopped tomatoes
- A handful fresh cilantro, chopped
- 2/3 can (15.5 ounces can) black beans

Directions:
1. Place a heavy skillet over medium-high flame. Add 1 ½ tablespoons of oil. Once the oil is heated, add tofu, salt, and pepper and cook until brown. Stir often.
2. Stir in turmeric powder, garlic powder, and onion powder—cook for a couple of minutes.
3. Add ½ tablespoon oil and lemon juice and mix well. Turn off the heat after 5 minutes. Stir frequently during this time.

4. To make beans: Place another pan over medium-high heat. It is better to place a heavy-bottomed pan.
5. Pour oil into it. When the oil is heated, add onion, salt, and jalapeños and cook until onion turns pink.
6. Stir in garlic and sauté for a few seconds until you get a nice aroma in the air.
7. Stir in cumin and tomatoes. Add some salt to taste. Cook until tomatoes are soft.
8. Stir in lemon juice and cilantro—cook for a couple of minutes.
9. Stir in the beans and heat thoroughly, stirring often.
10. To assemble: Divide hash browns into 2 serving bowls. Divide the beans into the bowls and place it over the hash browns.
11. Scatter avocado on top. Drizzle lemon juice and hot sauce on top. Garnish with cilantro and serve.

Nutrition: 579 Calories 39.6g Fat 22g Protein

10. Kale Egg Cups

Preparation Time: 11 minutes
Cooking Time: 33 minutes
Servings: 6
Ingredients:

- ½ tablespoon olive oil
- 2 cloves garlic, peeled, minced
- 4 ounces hot chicken sausage
- Salt to taste
- 1 cup chopped kale
- 3 eggs or ¾ cup egg substitute
- ½ medium red onion, finely chopped
- 4 ounces mushrooms, thinly sliced
- ½ ounce sun-dried tomatoes, finely chopped
- 4 ounces feta cheese, crumbled
- Pepper to taste

Directions:

1. Preheat the oven to 350°F.
2. Prepare 6 muffin cups by spraying with cooking spray.
3. Place a skillet over medium flame. Add oil. Once heated, cook onion until it turns pink.
4. Stir in the garlic and cook for about a minute.
5. Stir in the mushrooms. Cook until slightly brown.

6. Stir in the sausage and cook until brown, breaking it simultaneously as it cooks.
7. Now add sundried tomatoes and kale and cook for a couple of minutes.
8. Remove the pan from heat. Add feta and mix well.
9. Divide the mixture into the prepared muffin cups.
10. Add one beaten egg into each muffin cup. Season well and stir lightly.
11. Place the muffin cups in an oven and bake for about 25 – 30 minutes.
12. Once baked, remove the muffin cups from the oven and set aside to cool for a few minutes.
13. Remove the muffins from the cup.
14. Serve warm.

Nutrition 146 Calories 8g Fat 10g Protein

11. Rosemary Toasted Walnuts

Preparation Time: 13 minutes
Cooking Time: 18 minutes
Servings: 8
Ingredients:

- 2 cups raw walnuts
- 2 tablespoons fresh rosemary, finely chopped
- ¼ cup olive oil
- ½ teaspoon salt
- 1 teaspoon pepper

Directions:

1. Preheat oven to 350° F. Line a baking sheet with parchment paper.
2. In a bowl, whisk together olive oil, rosemary, salt, and pepper.
3. Add in walnuts and toss until completely covered in olive oil mixture.
4. Bake the walnuts for 10-15 minutes in the oven, tossing every 4-5 minutes until they're golden brown. Enjoy!

Nutrition: 223 Calories 23g Fat 4g Protein

12. Dark Chocolate Pretzel Cookies

Preparation Time: 26 minutes
Cooking Time: 12 minutes
Servings: 4
Ingredients:

- 1 cup yogurt

- 1/2 tsp baking soda
- 1/4 tsp. salt
- 1/4 tsp cinnamon
- 4 tbsp. butter
- 1/3 cup brown sugar
- 1 egg
- 1/2 tsp vanilla
- 1/2 cup dark chocolate chips
- 1/2 cup pretzels

Directions:
1. Set oven to 350 degrees.
2. Scourge sugar, butter, vanilla, and egg.
3. Mix flour, baking soda, and salt.
4. Incorporate bread mixture with all the moist components, chocolate chips and pretzels
5. Scoop large spoonful of dough on an unlined baking sheet.
6. Bake for 16 minutes.
7. Cool in wire rack.

Nutrition: 133 Calories 9g Fat 29g Carbohydrates

13. Strawberry Buckwheat Tabbouleh

Preparation Time: 8 minutes
Cooking Time: 4 minutes
Servings: 3

Ingredients:
- 50 g buckwheat
- 1 tbsp. ground turmeric
- 80 g avocado
- 65 g tomato
- 20 g red onion
- 25 g Medjool dates, pitted
- 1 tbsp. capers
- 30 g parsley
- 100 g strawberries, hulled
- 1 tbsp. extra virgin olive oil
- Juice from 1/2 lemon
- 30 g rocket

Directions:
1. Cook the buckwheat with the turmeric as guided by the package. Drain to cool and keep to one side.
2. Chop the tomato, avocado, dates, red onion, capers, and parsley thinly.
3. Mix them with the cool buckwheat.

4. Slice the strawberries, and mix the oil and lemon juice gently into the salad. Serve up on a rocket bed.

Nutrition: 226 Calories 8.3g Fat 12.4g Protein

14. Artichoke with Three Cheeses

Preparation Time: 23 minutes
Cooking Time: 36 minutes
Servings: 4

Ingredients:
- 2 cups artichoke hearts
- ½ cup vegetable broth
- 3 Tbsp extra virgin olive oil
- 1 tsp lemon juice
- 2 garlic cloves, minced
- Fresh parsley, chopped
- Fresh basil, chopped
- ½ cup shredded Fontina cheese
- ½ cup of shredded Swiss cheese
- ½ cup shredded Parmesan cheese

Directions:
1. Preheat oven to 400F
2. Arrange artichokes in single layer of a deep baking dish.
3. Drizzle oil, lemon juice, garlic, vegetable broth over the artichokes.
4. Start with fontina cheese, then Swiss cheese, parmesan cheese last.
5. Cover baking dish with aluminum foil. Bake 15 minutes.
6. Remove foil. Bake an additional 15 minutes.
7. Remove from oven. Let it cool to room temperature. Serve.

Nutrition: 57 Calories 14g Fat 4g Protein

15. Raw Vegan Coffee Cashew Cream Cake

Preparation Time: 12 minutes
Cooking Time: 37 minutes
Servings: 4

Ingredients:
- Coffee cashew cream
- 2 cups raw cashews
- 1 tsp of ground vanilla bean
- 3 tbsp. melted coconut oil
- ¼ cup raw honey

- 1/3 cup very strong coffee or triple espresso shot

Directions:

1. Blend all ingredients for the cream, pour it onto the crust and refrigerate.
2. Garnish with coffee beans.

Nutrition: 153 Calories 1g Fat 2g Protein

16. Blackberry Peach Compote

Preparation Time: 8 minutes
Cooking Time: 24 minutes
Servings: 12

Ingredients:

- ¼ cup Sauvignon Blanc wine
- 2 Tbsps. Xylitol
- 1 tsp ground ginger
- 1 tsp Cinnamon
- 3 medium peaches
- ¼ cup blackberries
- ½ tsp thick it up

Directions:

1. In a large saucepan, combine the wine, Xylitol, ginger, peaches, and cinnamon.
2. Simmer for 15 minutes.
3. Add the blackberries. Simmer another 5 minutes, until berries are tender.
4. Stir in the thick it up. Simmer approximately 5 minutes.
5. Remove from heat. Cool to room temperature. Serve.

Nutrition: 35 Calories 0.2g Fat 0.5g Protein

17. Chicken with Broccoli & Mushrooms

Preparation Time: 13 minutes
Cooking Time: 26 minutes
Servings: 6

Ingredients:

- 3 tablespoons olive oil
- 1-pound skinless, boneless chicken breast, cubed
- 1 medium onion, chopped
- 6 garlic cloves, minced
- 2 cups fresh mushrooms, sliced
- 16 ounces small broccoli florets
- ¼ cup water
- Salt and ground black pepper, to taste

Directions:

1. Heat the oil in a large saucepan over medium heat and cook the chicken cubes for about 4–5 minutes.
2. With a slotted spoon, transfer the chicken cubes onto a plate.
3. In the same wok, add the onion and sauté for about 4–5 minutes.
4. Add the mushrooms and cook for about 4–5 minutes.
5. Stir in the cooked chicken, broccoli, and water, and cook (covered) for about 8–10 minutes, stirring occasionally.
6. Stir in salt and black pepper and remove from heat.
7. Serve hot.

Nutrition: 197 Calories 10g Fat 21g Protein

18. Dark Chocolate Mousse

Preparation Time: 7 minutes
Cooking Time: 0 minute
Servings: 6

Ingredients:

- 16 ounces (2 cups) cream cheese
- 3-6 tablespoons of the desired sweetener
- 1/2 cup unsweetened cocoa powder
- 1/2 cup heavy whipped cream
- One large avocado
- 90% dark chocolate, to garnish
- 1/4 teaspoon vanilla extract

Directions:

1. Beat cream cheese until it becomes smooth and creamy, slowly mix cocoa powder.
2. Add avocado and beat it nicely for 5 minutes until it becomes creamy.
3. Add vanilla and sweetener, and then hit it again until it becomes creamy and smooth.
4. Place the whipped cream in the chocolate mixture and fold gently. Place the chocolate mousse in the desired containers. Garnish with dark chocolate chips.

Nutrition: 333 Calories 35g Fat 1g Protein

19. Chocolate Chia Pudding with Almonds

Preparation Time: 12 minutes
Cooking Time: 0 minute
Servings: 2

Ingredients:

- 4 tablespoons of chopped almonds
- 1 cup of water

- Sweetener
- ½ cup heavy cream
- 2 tablespoons of cocoa powder
- 6 tablespoons of chia seeds
- 2 tablespoons of MCT oil

Directions:
1. Add chia seeds, heavy cream, water, MCT oil, cocoa powder, and sweetener in a bowl.
2. Mix them. Allow sitting for 7-11 hours. After 11 hours, add almonds. Your dish is ready.

Nutrition: 288 Calories 28g Fat 8g Fiber

20. Coconut Macadamia Chia Pudding

Preparation Time: 12 minutes
Cooking Time: 0 mins
Servings: 3

Ingredients:
- 4 tablespoons of macadamia nuts (chopped)
- 1 cup of water
- Sweetener
- ½ cup coconut cream
- 2 tablespoons of MCT oil
- 6 tablespoons of chia seeds

Directions:
1. Add chia seeds, coconut cream, water, MCT oil and sweetener in a bowl. Mix them.
2. Allow sitting for 7-11 hours.
3. After 11 hours add macadamia nuts.

Nutrition: 250 Calories 9g Fat 2g Protein

21. Chocolate Mug

Preparation Time: 8 minutes
Cooking Time: 0 minute
Servings: 1

Ingredients:
- 2 tablespoons of butter
- 1 teaspoon sweetener
- 1/4 cup almond powder
- 1/2 teaspoon baking powder
- Two tablespoons of cocoa powder
- Pinch of salt
- 1 big beaten egg
- 1/4 cup whipped cream, to serve

- 2 tablespoons of Keto-based chocolate chips

Directions:
1. Melt butter in a microwaveable cup.
2. Stir in remaining ingredients except for whipped cream.
3. Microwave for 45 seconds to 1 minute. Serve with cream.

Nutrition: 500 Calories 50g Fat 7g Protein

22. Vanilla Chia Pudding

Preparation Time: 6 minutes
Cooking Time: 0 minute
Servings: 1

Ingredients:
- 1/2 cup strawberries
- 2 cups of water
- Sweetener
- ½ cup heavy cream
- Vanilla extract (few drops)
- ½ cup chia seeds
- 2 tablespoons MCT oil

Directions:
1. Add chia seeds, heavy cream, water, MCT oil, vanilla extract, and sweetener in a bowl.
2. Mix them. Allow sitting for 7-11 hours.
3. After 11 hours, add strawberries.

Nutrition: 550 Calories 57g Fat 2g Protein

23. Choco Lava Cake

Preparation Time: 23 minutes
Cooking Time: 0 minute
Servings: 4

Ingredients:
- ounces of dark chocolate
- 1tablespoon almond flour
- 1/4 cup coconut oil
- 1/4 teaspoon Vanilla extract
- 2 eggs
- Cocoa powder for garnish
- 2 tablespoons of sweetener

Directions:
1. Preheat oven to 375 ° C.
2. Grease two molds with coconut oil and sprinkle them with cocoa powder.
3. Melt chocolate, coconut oil and add vanilla to it.
4. Beat eggs and sweetener together in a different bowl.

5. Slowly add the chocolate mixture with egg mixture and beat until well mixed.
6. Add the almond flour and mix until incorporated.
7. Fill the molds evenly with the dough.
8. Bake for 10 minutes. Serve immediately.

Nutrition: 247 Calories 24g Fat 3g Protein

24. Celery Juice

Preparation Time: 11 minutes
Cooking Time: 0 minutes
Servings: 2

Ingredients:

- 8 celery stalks with leaves
- 2 tablespoons fresh ginger, peeled
- 1 lemon, peeled
- ½ cup filtered water
- Pinch of salt

Direction:

1. Situate all the ingredients in a blender and pulse until well combined.
2. Through a fine mesh strainer, strain the juice and transfer into 2 glasses.
3. Serve immediately.

Nutrition: 32 Calorie 0.5g Fat 1g Protein 1 g

25. Kale & Orange Juice

Preparation Time: 14 minutes
Cooking time: 0 minutes
Servings: 1

Ingredients:

- 5 large oranges, peeled and sectioned
- 2 bunches fresh kale

Directions:

1. Add all ingredients into a juicer and extract the juice according to the manufacturer's method.
2. Pour into 2 glasses and serve immediately.

Nutrition: 315 Calories 0.6g Fat 10.3g Protein

26. Smoked Sirt Salmon Omelet

Preparation Time: 9 minutes
Cooking Time: 28 minutes
Servings: 2

Ingredients

- 4 medium-size eggs
- 200g smoked salmon, sliced
- 1 teaspoon Capers
- 20g arugula (Rocket), chopped
- 2 teaspoon chopped parsley
- 2 teaspoon Extra virgin olive oil.

Direction:

1. Crack eggs into a bowl and beat very well.
2. Add the salmon, rocket, capers, and parsley.
3. Cook olive oil in a non-stick frying pan
4. Add the egg mixture around the pan until it is even.
5. Reduce the heat and let the omelet cook through.
6. Flip the omelet with a spatula to the other side to cook properly.
7. Roll up or fold the omelet in half to serve.

Nutrition: 259 calories 11.9g fat 12.2g protein

27. Green Tea Smoothie-Sirtfood

Preparation Time: 9 minutes
Cooking Time: 0 minute
Serving: 2

Ingredients

- 1 banana
- 1 cup milk
- ¼ tsp. vanilla bean paste
- 3 ice cubes
- 1 tsp honey

Direction:

1. Situate all the ingredients together in a blender, pulse well and serve.

Nutrition 101 Calories 4g Fat 0.4g Protein

28. Sirt Muesli

Preparation Time: 11 minutes
Cooking Time: 0 minute
Servings: 1

Ingredients

- 1/4 cup buckwheat flakes
- 2/3 cup buckwheat puffs
- 3 tablespoons coconut flakes
- 1/4 cup Medjool dates, pitted and chopped
- 1/8 cup walnuts chopped
- 10 g cocoa nibs
- 100g strawberries, hulled and chopped
- ½ cup plain Greek yogurt (soy or coconut yogurt, for vegan)

Direction:

1. Incorporate all the ingredients together except the strawberries and yogurt if you are not serving immediately.

Nutrition 98 Calories 2g Fat 4g Protein

29. Bacon Sirtfood Omelet

Preparation Time: 9 minutes
Cooking Time: 13 minutes
Serving: 2

Ingredients

- 100g sliced smoked bacon
- 5 medium eggs
- 50g red endive sliced
- 20g red onions
- 10g parsley, finely chopped
- 2 teaspoon turmeric
- 2 teaspoon extra virgin olive oil

Direction

1. Break eggs into a bowl and whisk, add the onions, endive, parsley, and turmeric.
2. Chop the smoked bacon into cubes, add to the egg mixture and mix properly.
3. Heat up olive oil in a non-stick frying pan.
4. Add the egg mixture, using a spatula, move it around the pan to start cooking the egg. Kip the bits of cooked egg moving and swirl the raw egg around the pan until the omelet level is even.
5. Reduce the heat and let the omelet cook properly.
6. Ease the spatula around the edges and roll up or fold the omelet to serve.

Nutrition 148 Calories 7g Fat 11g Protein

30. Sirtfood Mushroom Scramble Eggs

Preparation Time: 4 minutes
Cooking Time: 13 minutes

Serving: 1

Ingredients

- 2 medium eggs
- I teaspoon turmeric
- 20g kale
- 1 tsp. olive oil
- 1/2 chili
- 10g red onions
- 5g parsley
- A handful of button mushrooms

Direction

1. Steam the kale for 2-3 minutes.
2. Mix the turmeric powder with water to form a light paste.
3. Break into a bowl and whisk, add the turmeric paste, parsley, and mix properly.
4. Cook olive oil in a non-stick frying pan over medium heat and fry the onion, chili, and mushroom until they have started to brown and soften.
5. Add the steamed kale to the mixture in the frying pan and stir.
6. Pour the egg mixture into the frying pan and stir.
7. Reduce the heat and allow the egg to cook and stir.

Nutrition 151 Calories 9g Fat 7g Protein

31. Sirtfood Smoothie

Preparation Time: 7 minutes
Cooking Time: 0 minute
Servings: 1

Ingredients

- 100g plain Greek yogurt
- 6 walnut halves
- 8 to 10 medium strawberries, hulled
- A handful of kale stalks removed
- 20g dark chocolate (85 percent cocoa solids)
- 1 Medjool date pitted
- 1/2 teaspoon ground turmeric
- 1 small size chili
- 7/8 cup (200ml) unsweetened almond milk.
- 1 teaspoon honey

Direction:

1. Incorporate all the ingredients in a blender until smooth and serve.

Nutrition 151 Calories 6g Fat 9g Protein

32. Strawberry and Blackcurrant Jelly

Preparation Time: 12 minutes
Cooking Time: 6 minutes
Servings: 4

Ingredients

- 200g strawberries, hulled and chopped
- 200g blackcurrants washed and stalks removed
- 400ml water
- 3 tablespoon granulated sugar.
- 4 gelatin leaves

Direction

1. Arrange the strawberries in 4 serving dishes.
2. Soften gelatin leaves in a bowl of cold water.
3. Situate blackcurrants in a small pan with sugar and 200ml of water and boil. Simmer for 5 minutes then remove from heat. Leave to stand for 2 minutes
4. Squeeze out excess water from the gelatin leaves and add them to the blackcurrant mixture. Let it dissolve, then mix in the rest of the water. Fill liquid into the prepared dishes and refrigerate till it set.

Nutrition 143 Calories 6g Fat 7g Protein

33. Nutty Yogurt with Mixed Berries

Preparation Time: 13 minutes
Cooking Time: 0 minute
Servings: 2

Ingredients

- 250g mixed berries
- 250g plain Greek yogurt
- 50g walnuts, finely chopped
- 20g dark chocolate (85 percent cocoa solids), grated

Direction:

1. Simply add your preferred berries into a bowl and top with the yogurt.
2. Sprinkle with the walnuts and chocolate.

Nutrition 156 Calories 9g Fat 11g Protein

34. Turmeric Tea

Preparation Time: 12 minutes
Cooking Time: 0 minute
Serving: 1

Ingredients

- 1 ½ heaped tsp turmeric powder
- ½ tablespoon fresh ginger, grated
- 1 small lemon
- Orange zest
- 1 teaspoon honey.

Direction
1. Boil 200ml of water in the kettle
2. Situate turmeric, ginger, and orange zest in a teapot or jug. Transfer over the boiling water and allow to stand for 5 minutes.
3. Use tea strainer into a cup, add lemon juice or a slice of lemon and sweeten with honey.

Nutrition 94 Calories 3g Fat 4g Protein

35. Stir-Fried Mushroom
Preparation Time: 13 minutes
Cooking Time: 6 minutes
Servings: 2

Ingredients
- 1/2 Pound mushroom, wiped clean with a wet paper towel
- 2 tablespoon extra-virgin olive oil
- 2 teaspoon fresh lemon juice
- ¼ cup chopped parsley
- 1 small chili, finely chopped.
- ½ teaspoon turmeric

Direction
1. Cut off mushroom stems. With a small sharp knife, cut grooves on each mushroom that spiral out from the center to edges.
2. Heat the olive oil in the skillet until hot, add mushrooms, fluted side down, veins up. Add lemon juice and turmeric, cook gently for 4 to 5 minutes, then turn over and cook briefly. Sprinkle with parsley and the chili, stir. Serve immediately.

Nutrition 141 Calories 7g Fat 9g Protein

36. Apple Pancakes with Blackcurrant Compote
Preparation Time: 14 minutes
Cooking Time: 7 minutes
Servings: 2

Ingredients
- 40g porridge oats
- 65g plain flour
- 1 tbsp. caster sugar
- ½ tsp. baking powder
- 1 big green apple
- 2 cups semi-skimmed milk
- 1 egg white
- 1 teaspoon light olive oil.

For the compote:
- 60g blackcurrants washed and stalks removed.
- 1 tablespoon caster sugar
- 2 tablespoon water.

Direction
1. Make the compote first. Simmer blackcurrants, sugar, and water in a small pan for 14 minutes.
2. Place the Oats, flour, baking powder, and caster sugar in a large bowl and mix properly.
3. Stir the apple into the powder mixture and then whisk in the milk a little at a time until you have a smooth mixture.
4. Whisk the egg white to a stiff peak and then fold into the pancake batter.
5. Heat ½ teaspoon olive oil in a non-stick frying pan on medium heat and pour ½ of the batter. Reduce heat and allow the pancake to cook properly, flip to the other side with a spatula. Cook both sides until golden brown. Remove and repeat to make 2 pancakes.
6. Topped with the blackcurrant compote

Nutrition 136 Calories 6g Fat 12g Protein

37. The Sirtfood Diet's Date and Walnut Porridge
Preparation Time: 14 minutes
Cooking Time: 7 minutes
Serving: 1

Ingredients
- 200 ml Milk or dairy-free alternative
- 1 Medjool date, chopped
- 4 chopped walnut halves
- 50 g Strawberries, hulled
- 35 g Buckwheat flakes

Direction
1. Place the milk and date in a pan, heat gently, then add the buckwheat flakes and cook the porridge to your desired consistency.

2. Stir in the walnuts, top with the strawberries and serve.

Nutrition 126 Calories 10g Fat 9g Protein

38. Mushroom and Tofu Scramble

Preparation Time: 8 minutes
Cooking Time: 9 minutes
Servings: 2

Ingredients

- 200g extra firm tofu
- 2 teaspoon turmeric powder
- 1 teaspoon black pepper
- 40g kale, roughly chopped
- 2 teaspoon extra virgin olive oil
- 40g red onion, thinly sliced
- 1 Thai chili, thinly sliced
- 100g mushrooms, thinly sliced
- 4 tablespoons (10g) parsley, finely chopped

Direction

1. Cover tofu in paper towels and put something heavy on top to help it drain.
2. Mix the turmeric with a little water until you achieve a light paste.
3. Steam the kale for 2 to 3 minutes.
4. Cook olive oil in a frying pan over medium heat fry onion, chili, and mushrooms for 2 to 3 minutes.
5. Crumble the tofu into bite-size pieces and add to the pan, pour the turmeric paste over the tofu, and mix thoroughly. Add the black pepper and stir. Cook over medium heat for 2 to 3 minutes.
6. Add the kale and continue to cook over medium heat for another minute. Finally, add the parsley, mix well, and serve.

Nutrition 138 Calories 6g Fat 9g Protein

39. Sirt Fruit Salad- Sirtfood Recipes

Preparation Time: 14 minutes
Cooking Time: 0 minute
Servings: 2

Ingredients

- 1 cup freshly made green tea
- 1 fresh orange juice
- 1 orange, chopped
- 2 green apples, cored and roughly chopped
- 20 red seedless grapes

- 10 blueberries
- 2 teaspoon honey

Direction

1. Stir the honey into a cup of green tea. When dissolved, add the orange juice. Leave to cool.
2. Place the chopped orange, chopped apple, grapes, and blueberries together in a bowl. Pour the cool green tea over it and leave too steep for some minutes before serving.

Nutrition 151 Calories 11g Fat 7g Protein

40. Spiced Scrambled Eggs

Preparation Time: 13 minutes
Cooking Time: 4 minutes
Servings: 2

Ingredients:

- 2 teaspoon extra virgin olive oil
- 1/4 cup (40g) red onion, finely chopped
- 1/2 bell pepper, finely chopped
- 6 medium eggs
- 1/2 cup (100ml) milk
- 1 teaspoon ground turmeric
- 4 tablespoons (10g) parsley, finely chopped

Direction

1. Pre-heat oil in a frying pan and cook red onion and bell pepper until soft but not browned.
2. Whisk the eggs, milk, turmeric, and parsley. Add to the hot pan and continue cooking over low to medium heat, constantly moving the egg mixture around the pan to scramble it and stop it from sticking/burning.
3. When you have achieved your desired consistency, serve.

Nutrition 143 Calories 11g Fat 8g Protein

41. Mushroom Scramble Eggs

Preparation Time: 11 minutes
Cooking Time: 6 minutes
Serving: 2

Ingredients

- 2 tbsp
- 1 teaspoon ground garlic
- 1 teaspoon mild curry powder
- 20g lettuce, approximately sliced
- 1 teaspoon extra virgin olive oil

- 1/2 bird's eye peeled, thinly chopped
- a couple of mushrooms, finely chopped
- 5g parsley, finely chopped

Direction

1. Mix the curry and garlic powder and then add just a little water till you've achieved a light glue.
2. Steam the lettuce for two -- 3 minutes.
3. Heat the oil in a skillet over a moderate heat and fry the chili and mushrooms 2-- three minutes till they've begun to soften and brown.
4. Insert the eggs and spice paste and cook over moderate heat, then add the carrot and then proceed to cook over a moderate heat for a further minute. In the end, put in the parsley, mix well, and function.

Nutrition 148 Calories 7g Fat 9g Protein

42. Blue Hawaii Smoothie

Preparation Time: 9 minutes
Cooking Time: 0 minutes
Serving: 1

Ingredients

- 2 tablespoons rings or approximately 4-5 balls
- 1/2 cup frozen tomatoes
- two Tbsp ground flaxseed
- 1/8 cup tender coconut (unsweetened, organic)
- few walnuts
- 1/2 cup fat-free yogurt
- 5-6 ice cubes
- dab of water

Direction

1. Throw all of the ingredients together and combine until smooth.

Nutrition 89 Calories 3g Fat 4g Protein

43. Turkey Breakfast Sausages

Preparation Time: 17 minutes
Cooking Time: 9 minutes
Serving: 3

Ingredients

- 1 lb. extra lean ground turkey
- 1 Tbsp EVOO, and a little more to dirt pan
- 1 Tbsp fennel seeds

- 2 teaspoons smoked paprika
- 1 teaspoon red pepper flakes
- 1 teaspoon peppermint
- 1 teaspoon chicken seasoning
- A couple of shredded cheddar cheese
- A couple of chives, finely chopped
- A few shakes garlic and onion powder
- Two spins of pepper and salt

Direction

1. Pre Heat oven to 350F.
2. Utilize a little EVOO to dirt a miniature muffin pan.
3. Combine all ingredients and blend thoroughly.
4. Fill each pit on top of the pan and then cook for approximately 15-20 minutes. Each toaster differs; therefore, when muffin fever is 165, then remove.

Nutrition 156 Calories 9g Fat 13g Protein

44. Banana Pecan Muffins

Preparation Time: 11 minutes
Cooking Time: 34 minutes
Serving: 6

Ingredients

- 3 Tbsp butter softened
- 4 ripe bananas
- 1 Tbsp honey
- 1/8 cup OJ
- 1 teaspoon cinnamon
- 2 cups all-purpose pasta
- 2 capsules
- a couple of pecans, sliced
- 1 Tbsp vanilla

Direction

1. Set oven to 350°F.
2. Grease bottom and sides of the muffin tin, and then dust with flour.
3. Dust the surfaces of the tin gently with flour then tap to eradicate any excess.
4. Peel and insert the batter to a mixing bowl and with a fork, mash the carrots; therefore, that you've got a combination of chunky and smooth, then put aside.
5. Insert the orange juice, melted butter, eggs, vanilla, and spices and stir to combine.
6. Roughly chop the pecans onto a chopping board, when using, then fold throughout the mix.

7. Spoon at the batter 3/4 full and bake in the oven for approximately 40 minutes, or until golden and cooked through.

Nutrition 167 Calories 9g Fat 12g Protein

45. Banana and Blueberry Muffins - SRC

Preparation Time: 13 minutes

Cooking Time: 42 minutes

Serving: 8

Ingredients

- 4 large ripe bananas, peeled and mashed
- 3/4 cup of sugar
- 1 egg, lightly crushed
- 1/2 cup of butter, melted
- 2 cups of blueberries
- 1 teaspoon baking powder
- 1 teaspoon baking soda
- 1/2 teaspoon salt
- 1 cup of coconut bread
- 1/2 cup of flour
- 1/2 cup applesauce
- dab of cinnamon

Direction

1. Situate mashed banana to a large mixing bowl.
2. Insert sugar & egg and mix well.
3. Add peanut butter and strawberries.
4. Sift all the dry ingredients together, then add the dry ingredients into the wet mix and mix together lightly.
5. Set into 12 greased muffin cups
6. Bake for 20-30min in 180C or 350 F.

Nutrition 161Calories 11g Fat 15g Protein

46. Morning Meal Sausage Gravy

Preparation Time: 12 minutes

Cooking Time: 22 minutes

Serving: 4

Ingredients

- 1 lb. sausage
- 2 cups 2 percent milk
- 1/4 cup entire wheat bread

Direction

1. Cook sausage from skillet.
2. Add flour and blend cook for about a minute.
3. Insert two cups of milk.

4. Whisk Whilst gravy thickens and bubbles.
5. Add pepper and salt and keep to taste until flawless.
6. Let stand a minute or so to ditch and function over several snacks.

Nutrition 159 Calories 7g Fat 13g Protein

47. Easy Egg-white Muffins

Preparation Time: 13 minutes

Cooking Time: 22 minutes

Serving: 8

Ingredients

- Language muffin 7 grain
- egg-whites - 6 tbsp or two large egg whites
- turkey bacon or bacon sausage
- sharp cheddar cheese or gouda
- green berry
- discretionary - lettuce, and hot sauce, hummus, flaxseeds, etc.

Direction

1. At a microwavable safe container, then spray entirely to stop the egg from adhering, then pour egg whites into the dish.
2. Lay turkey bacon or bacon sausage paper towel and then cook.
3. Subsequently, toast your muffin, if preferred.
4. Then put the egg dish in the microwave for 30 minutes. Afterward, with a spoon or fork, then immediately flip egg within the dish and cook for another 30 minutes.
5. Whilst dish remains hot sprinkle some cheese while preparing sausage.
6. The secret is to get a paste of some kind between each coating to put up the sandwich together, like a very small little bit of hummus or even cheese.

Nutrition 153 Calories 11g Fat 16g Protein

48. Sweet Potato Hash

Preparation Time: 19 minutes

Cooking Time: 23 minutes

Serving: 4

Ingredients

- 1 Sweet-potato
- 1/2 red pepper, diced
- 3 green onions, peppermint
- leftover turkey
- 1 Tbsp of butter

- carrot powder - a few shakes
- Pepper
- pepper and salt to flavor

Direction

1. Stab a sweet potato and microwave for 5 minutes.
2. Remove from microwave, peel the skin off, and foliage.
3. At a skillet, on medium-high warmth, place peppers and butter and sauté to get a few minutes.
4. Insert potato bits and keep sautéing.
5. Whilst sauté, add sweeteners, leafy vegetables, and green onions.
6. Insert a dab of cheddar and Revel in!

Nutrition 152 Calories 7g Fat 12g Protein

49. Asparagus, Mushroom Artichoke Strata

Preparation Time: 9 minutes
Cooking Time: 21 minutes
Serving: 4

Ingredients

- 1 little loaf of sourdough bread
- 4 challah rolls
- 8 eggs
- 2 cups of milk
- 1 teaspoon salt
- 1/4 teaspoon black pepper
- 1 cup Fontina cheese, cut into little chunks
- 1/2 cup shredded Parmesan cheese
- 1 Tbsp butter
- 1 teaspoon dried mustard
- 1/2 can of artichoke hearts, sliced
- 1 bunch green onions, grated
- 1 bunch asparagus
- 1 10oz package of baby Bella

Direction

1. Clean mushrooms and slice and trim asparagus and cut in 1-inch pieces. Reserve in a bowl and scatter 1/2 teaspoon salt mixture.
2. Drain and dice 1/2 may or modest artichoke hearts.
3. Melt butter in a pan over moderate heat, also sauté the asparagus and mushrooms before the mushrooms start to brown, about 10 minutes.

4. Blend the artichoke core pieces into a bowl with all a mushroom/asparagus mix. Set aside.
5. Cut or split a tiny sourdough loaf into 1-inch bits.
6. Grease a 9x13 inch baking dish and generate a base coating of bread at the dish. Spread 1/2 cup of Fontina cheese bread, at a coating, and disperse half an apple mixture on the cheese.
7. Lay-down a different layer of these vegetables and bread and high using a 1/2 cup of Fontina cheese.
8. Whisk together eggs, salt, milk, dry mustard, and pepper into a bowl and then pour the egg mixture on the vegetables and bread.
9. Cover the dish, and then simmer for 3 weeks.
10. Pre Heat oven to 375 degrees.
11. Eliminate the casserole from the fridge and let stand for half an hour.
12. Spread All the Parmesan cheese at a coating within the strata.
13. Bake for 45 minutes. Let stand 5 to 10 minutes before cutting into squares.

Nutrition 171 Calories 9g Fat 16g Protein

50. Egg White Veggie Wontons with Fontina

Preparation Time: 8 minutes
Cooking Time: 19 minutes
Serving: 6

Ingredients

- 1 cup egg whites
- butter
- fontina cheese
- mixed shredded cheddar cheese
- broccoli
- tomatoes - diced
- salt and pepper
- prosciutto - two pieces

Direction

1. Remove Won Ton wrappers out of the freezer.
2. Pre Heat oven to 350.
3. Spray miniature cupcake tin with cooking spray.

4. After wrappers begin to defrost, peel off them carefully - apart, one at a time and press cupcake tin lightly.
5. Slice the wrappers having a little bit of peanut butter. (optional)
6. set a chunk of cheese in every bottom.
7. Satisfy desired lettuce
8. Pour egg whites all toppings.
9. Sprinkle each with some of those shredded cheddar cheese.
10. Cook for approximately 15 minutes, but get started watching them afterward 10 - whenever they poof up - assess them poking the middle with a fork.
11. While eggs are cooking, then spray a sheet of foil with cooking spray and then put 2 pieces of prosciutto onto it and then cook at exactly the exact same period as the egg whites. After 8 minutes, then take and let sit once it cools it becomes crispy and chop and high eggs!

Nutrition 201 Calories 9g Fat 15g Protein

51. Crunchy and Chewy Granola

Preparation Time: 9 minutes
Cooking Time: 1 hour
Serving: 3
Ingredients
- Two 1/4 cup old-style yogurt
- 1 Tbsp flax seeds
- 1/4 tsp kosher salt
- 1/2 tsp cinnamon
- 1/4 ground ginger
- 1/2 cup honey
- two Tbsp packaged splendid brown-sugar
- 3/4 cup ounces raw peppers
- 1/2 cup sliced peppers
- 1/2 cup golden raisins
- 1/2 cup dried cranberries
- 1 Tbsp vanilla

Direction
1. Pre Heat oven to 300.
2. Line baking sheet with parchment paper.
3. Mix 9 components together.
4. Insert 1 cup hot tap water, then mix together with hands and spread into a thin coating over a baking sheet.
5. Bake for 60 minutes

6. Remove from the oven and let cool.
7. Stir in dried fruit.
8. Dust with sugar.

Nutrition 218 Calories 10g Fat 17g Protein

52. Blueberry Pancakes

Preparation Time: 7 minutes
Cooking Time: 6 minutes
Serving: 5
Ingredients
- 2 capsules
- 1 cup milk
- 1 Tbsp vegetable oil
- 1.5 tsp butter melted
- 1 1/4 cup All-purpose flour 3 tsp baking powder
- 3 tsp sugar
- 1/2 tsp salt
- 2 cups frozen blueberries

Direction
1. Put a nonstick griddle or a skillet over moderate heat.
2. Independent eggs yolks and whites, moving whites to some medium mixing bowl.
3. Whisk functions well with milk, butter, and oil.
4. Gradually fold dry ingredients to liquid with a wooden spoon.
5. In yet another bowl, sift together dry skin.
6. Working with an electric beater, whip egg whites until frothy.
7. Pour egg whites into the batter until just combined
8. When skillet is hot, brush the skillet with melted butter.
9. Pour 1/4 cup batter onto the skillet for each pancake, leaving space.
10. Top each pancake using 5 6 blueberries, even if using.
11. When bubbles form inside the batter, then flip the pancake.
12. Keep on cooking until golden at the ground, about two minutes.
13. Drink instantly.

Nutrition 210 Calories 7g Fat 13g Protein

53. Power Balls

Preparation Time: 19 minutes
Cooking Time: 7 minutes
Serving: 8

Ingredients

- 1 cup old fashion ginger
- 1/4 cup quinoa cooked
- 1/4 cup unsweetened coconut
- 1/3 cup cranberry/raisin blend
- 1/3 cup dark chocolate chips
- 1/4 cup almonds
- 1 tbsp. peanut butter

Direction

1. Simmer quinoa in orange juice for 3 minutes. Let cool.
2. Mix chilled quinoa and the remaining ingredients
3. Incorporate ingredients and form into golden ball sized chunks.
4. Chill until the firm.

Nutrition 214 Calories 18g Fat 16g Protein

54. Cinnamon Crescent Rolls

Preparation Time: 19 minutes
Cooking Time: 24 minutes
Serving: 8

Ingredients

- 2 cans refrigerated crescent rolls
- 1 stick butter, softened
- 1/2 cup brown or white sugar
- 1 tbsp cinnamon

Glaze

- 1/2 cup powdered sugar
- 1 tsp vanilla
- 2 tbsp milk

Direction

1. Heat oven to 350°F.
2. Scourge sugar, butter, and cinnamon
3. Separate dough into rectangles.
4. Spread each rectangle about two tbsp cinnamon butter mix.
5. Roll-up starting at the broadest side, as you'll ordinarily do to crescent rolls. Firmly press ends to seal.
6. Put each cinnamon filled crescent roll on a parchment lineup baking sheet.
7. Bake for 10 to 15 minutes or until golden brown.
8. In a small bowl, combine all glaze ingredients, adding enough milk for desired drizzling consistency. Drizzle over hot rolls.

Nutrition 217 Calories 11g Fat 23g Protein

55. Fresh Fruit Pizza

Preparation Time: 16 minutes
Cooking Time: 0 minute
Serving: 8

Ingredients

- 4 crescent rolls (Rolled-out and poked with a fork)
- Two spoonsful of moderate Cream-cheese
- 1 teaspoon of sugar
- 1 teaspoon Vanilla extract
- Handful berries
- Sliced almonds

Direction

1. Place crescent rolls nonstick pan and then poke a few times with a fork. Cook at 375 for approximately 14 minutes. Let cool.
2. At a bowl, combine cream, Vanilla infusion & sugar stir with a spoon.
3. Spread onto crescent rolls, then add almonds and fruit.

Nutrition 161 Calories 9g Fat 13g Protein

56. Turkey Mole Tacos

Preparation Time: 8 minutes
Cooking Time: 16 minutes
Servings: 3

Ingredients:

- 75-pound lean ground turkey
- 4 stalks green onion, chopped
- 2 garlic cloves, minced
- 1 rib celery, chopped
- ounces roasted sweet peppers, chopped and drained
- 7 ounces diced tomatoes
- 6 corn tortillas 6 inches
- 1 red onion, thinly sliced
- 2 tablespoons walnuts, roasted, chopped
- 2 ounces dark chocolate, chopped
- .25 teaspoon sea salt
- 4 teaspoons chili powder
- .5 teaspoon cumin
- .125 teaspoon ground cinnamon,

Directions:

1. In a large skillet that is non-stick cook the ground turkey with the green onions, celery, and garlic over medium heat. Cook until there is no pink remaining, the turkey has reached a temperature of one-hundred and sixty-five degrees, and the vegetables are tender.
2. Into the skillet with the cooked turkey add the canned tomatoes, roasted red peppers, cinnamon, chocolate, chili powder, cumin, and sea salt. Allow the liquid from the tomatoes to come to a boil before reducing the heat to medium-low, covering the skillet with a lid, and simmering for ten minutes. Stir occasionally to prevent sticking and burning.
3. Remove the cooked ground turkey from the heat and stir in the walnuts.
4. Divide the taco meat between the corn tortillas, topping it off with the sliced red onion. Serve while warm.

Nutrition: 475 Calories 3g Fat 30g Protein

57. Sweet and Sour Tofu

Preparation Time: 8 minutes
Cooking Time: 17 minutes
Servings: 4

Ingredients:

- Tofu, firm – 14 ounces
- Cornstarch – 8 tablespoons, divided
- Egg white – 1
- Pineapple, chopped – 1 cup
- Bell pepper, chopped – 2
- Rice vinegar – 6 tablespoons
- Date sugar – 6 tablespoons
- Tamari sauce – 2 tablespoons
- Sea salt – 1 teaspoon
- Tomato paste – 2 tablespoons
- Water – 2 teaspoons
- Cornstarch – 2 tablespoons
- Sesame seeds, toasted – 1 teaspoon

Directions:

1. Line an aluminum baking sheet with kitchen parchment or a silicone sheet and set the oven to Fahrenheit three-hundred and fifty degrees.
2. Begin by pressing your tofu and then slicing it into bite-sized cubes. Sprinkle two of the eight divided tablespoons of cornstarch over the tofu, tossing it until the tofu is evenly coated.
3. Place the remaining six tablespoons of divided cornstarch in one bowl and the egg white (or aquafaba) in another.
4. Dip a few tofu cubes at a time first in the egg white and then in the cornstarch. Transfer the breaded cubes to the prepared baking sheet and continue the process until all the cubes are prepared. Arrange the tofu cubes on the pan evenly so that they don't touch, and then bake until crispy, about fifteen to twenty minutes.
5. While the tofu cooks, whisk together the rice vinegar, date sugar, tamari sauce, sea salt, tomato paste, water, two tablespoons of corn starch, and the sesame seeds.
6. Add the peppers and pineapple to a large skillet and sauté them until slightly tender. Add in the mixed sauce and deglaze the skillet. Add the cooked tofu to the skillet and continue to cook it in the sauce until it is coated and sticky and the sauce has thickened.

7. Serve while warm over brown rice or buckwheat.

Nutrition: 366 Calories 4g Fat 28g Protein

58. BBQ Tempeh Sandwiches

Preparation Time: 12 minutes

Cooking Time: 44 minutes

Servings: 4

Ingredients:

- Barbecue sauce - .75 cup
- Tempeh, sliced into long strips – 8 ounces
- Liquid smoke - .5 teaspoon
- Red cabbage, shredded – 1.5 cups
- Red onion, diced - .5 cup Date sugar - .5 teaspoon
- Sea salt – 1.5 teaspoons Carrots, shredded - .5 cup
- Apple cider vinegar – 1 tablespoon
- Garlic powder - .5 teaspoon
- Mayonnaise 2 tablespoons Whole wheat buns - 4
- Black pepper, ground - .25 teaspoon

Directions:

1. Place the sliced tempeh in a glass baking dish and coat it in the barbecue sauce and the liquid smoke. While you don't have to add the liquid smoke, it is a great addition that makes it taste as if it has come freshly off the grill.
2. Allow the dish to marinate for at least forty-five minutes. When the tempeh is nearly done marinating begin to preheat your oven to Fahrenheit four-hundred and fifty degrees. Cover the tempeh in a sheet of aluminum and allow it to bake for first thirty minutes, and then remove the aluminum and bake it for an additional five minutes.
3. Meanwhile, prepare the slaw by combining the remaining ingredients (except for the buns) in a bowl. Once combined, cover the bowl and allow it to meld in the fridge until the tempeh is done cooking. To serve divide the tempeh strips between the buns and then top them off with the slaw.

Nutrition: 382 Calories 6g Fat 27g Protein

59. Tofu Tikka Masala

Preparation Time: 13 minutes

Cooking Time: 24 minutes

Servings: 4

Ingredients:

- Cumin – 1 teaspoon
- Tofu, extra-firm, sliced into bite-sized cubes – 14 ounces
- Ginger, peeled and grated – 2 teaspoons
- Sweet paprika - .5 teaspoon
- Turmeric - .5 teaspoon Garlic, minced – 2 cloves
- Garam masala – 1.5 teaspoons
- Coriander powder - .5 teaspoon
- Cayenne - .25 teaspoon
- Tomato passata (if not available use puree) – 1 cup
- Coconut milk, full-fat – 14 ounces
- Olive oil – 2 tablespoons Red onion, diced – 1
- Sea salt – 1 teaspoon

Directions:

1. Add the olive oil, red onion, and salt to a skillet and allow it to cook over medium until the onions have become soft, about five minutes. Add in the grated ginger and minced garlic, cooking for a minute before adding in all the spices. Cook for 3 minutes
2. Keep a close eye on the spices, stirring constantly to avoid burning. Stir the tomato passata or puree into the skillet and allow it to continue cooking until thickened and reduced, about ten to fifteen minutes.
3. Add the tofu and canned coconut milk to the skillet and bring the pan to a boil. Reduce the stove to low and allow the tikka masala to simmer for ten minutes. Serve warm over brown rice or buckwheat.

Nutrition: 344 Calories 9g Fat 26g Protein

60. Tempeh Vegan Chili

Preparation Time: 13 minutes

Cooking Time: 26 minutes

Servings: 4

Ingredients:

- Tempeh, roughly grated – 8 ounces
- Extra virgin olive oil – 2 tablespoons
- Red onion, diced – 1
- Celery, diced – 1 rib
- Bell pepper, diced – 1
- Garlic, minced – 4 cloves

- Black beans, drained and rinsed – 15 ounces
- Kidney beans, drained and rinsed – 15 ounces
- Tomato sauce - .75 cup
- Water – 1.25 cups
- Chili powder - 1 tablespoon
- Crushed red pepper flakes - .25 teaspoon
- Cumin, ground – 2 teaspoons
- Sea salt – 1 teaspoon
- Cocoa powder – 1 tablespoon

Directions:

1. Add the extra virgin olive oil and grated tempeh to a large pot and allow it to brown over medium heat for five minutes.
2. Add the celery, garlic, bell pepper, and onions to the pot, cooking until slightly tender, about five more minutes.
3. Stir in the remaining ingredient and allow the chili to simmer and the flavors to meld for approximately fifteen more minutes. Serve warm with your favorite chili toppings.

Nutrition: 455 Calories 7g Fat 22g Protein

61. Eggroll in a Bowl

Preparation Time: 9 minutes
Cooking Time: 17 minutes
Servings: 6
Ingredients:

- Chicken broth - .25 cup
- Extra virgin olive oil – 2 tablespoons, divided
- Ground turkey – 1 pound
- Garlic, minced – 3 cloves Sea salt - .5 teaspoon
- Red cabbage, shredded – 5 cups
- Ginger, minced - .5 teaspoon
- Carrots, shredded – 1 cup
- Tamari sauce – 2 tablespoons
- Onion, finely diced – 1.5 cups
- Sesame seed oil – 1 teaspoon
- Apple cider vinegar – 2 teaspoons
- Black pepper, ground - .25 teaspoon

Directions:

1. Situate one tablespoon of the extra virgin olive oil to a large pot and brown the ground turkey over medium heat until cooked nearly all the way cooked through, about five minutes.
2. Push the turkey to the side of the pan and then add the remaining olive oil and the diced onion to the center.
3. Sauté the onion until translucent, about five minutes. Stir in the ginger, garlic, and carrots, cooking for two minutes until fragrant. Stir the vegetables and turkey all together.
4. Pour the chicken broth into the large pot and scrape the bottom of the pot with a wooden spoon to deglaze it. Stir in the sea salt, tamari sauce, red cabbage, and ground pepper until well combined.
5. Cover the pot with a lid and reduce the heat to medium-low. Continue cooking the ingredients until the red cabbage is tender, about twelve to fifteen minutes. Remove the large pot from the heat of the stove and stir in the sesame seed oil.

Nutrition: 208 Calories 11g Fat 33g Protein

62. Beef and Red Cabbage

Preparation Time: 13 minutes
Cooking Time: 37 minutes
Servings: 6
Ingredients:

- Beef broth – 4 cups
- Fire roasted crushed tomatoes – 28 ounces
- Ground beef – 1 pound
- Celery, chopped – 2 stalks Onion, diced – 1
- Carrot, chopped – 1 Bell pepper, diced – 1
- Garlic, minced – 3 cloves
- Red cabbage, chopped – 1 head
- Italian herb seasoning – 1 tablespoon
- Fresh thyme – 2 sprigs Sea salt – 1.5 teaspoons
- Spicy brown mustard – 1 tablespoon
- Black pepper, ground - .25 teaspoon

Directions:

1. Add the ground beef to a large steel soup pot and brown it over medium-high heat until fully cooked. Once done cooking, drain off most of the excess fat, leaving only about two tablespoons in the pot.
2. Set the ground beef aside. Into the now empty soup pot add the reserved beef fat

along with the carrot, celery, onion, and bell pepper. Cook until the vegetables are tender, about six minutes. Add in the garlic and cook until fragrant, about one more minute.

3. Return the cooked ground beef to the soup pot along with the beef broth, crushed tomatoes, seasonings, and spicy brown mustard, stirring it all together to combine.

4. Bring the pot of beef and tomatoes to a boil and then reduce to a simmer, cooking for fifteen to twenty minutes. Stir the cabbage into the soup, allowing it to cook until tender, about ten to fifteen minutes. Serve alone or over either cooked rice or buckwheat.

Nutrition: 362 Calories 9g Fat 28g Protein

63. **Parmesan Chicken and Kale Sauté**

Preparation Time: 12 minutes
Cooking Time: 18 minutes
Servings: 6
Ingredients:

- Chicken breasts, boneless and skinless – 1.5 pounds
- Extra virgin olive oil – 2 tablespoons
- Sea salt – 1 teaspoon Onion, diced – 1
- Red pepper flakes - .25 teaspoon
- Lemon juice – 1 tablespoon
- Black pepper, ground - .25 teaspoon
- Garlic, minced – 3 cloves Chicken broth – .5 cup
- Parmesan cheese, grated - .5 cup
- Kale, chopped – 12 ounces

Directions:

1. Slice the chicken breasts into long strips, each half an inch thick. Add the extra virgin olive oil to a large skillet and set the stove to medium heat. Allow the olive oil to heat until it shimmers, but don't let it smoke. Add the chicken, sea salt, and black pepper, sautéing it until the chicken is fully cooked through, about five to seven minutes.

2. The chicken breasts are ready when they reach an internal temperature of Fahrenheit one-hundred and sixty-five degrees. Transfer the cooked chicken

breast to a plate and cover it with aluminum or a lid to keep it warm. Add the minced garlic, diced onion, and red pepper flakes to the now empty skillet, sautéing for about two minutes until the onions soften.

3. Add the kale and broth to the skillet and then cover with a lid. Stir occasionally, allowing the kale to cook until tender, about five minutes. Add the cooked chicken breast back into the skillet along with the lemon juice and Parmesan cheese. Stir everything to combine and then remove the skillet from the heat before serving.

Nutrition: 361 Calories 13g Fat 34g Protein

64. **Parsley Pesto Pasta**

Preparation Time: 16 minutes
Cooking Time: 13 minutes
Servings: 5
Ingredients:

- Parsley, fresh, packed – 2 cups
- Garlic – 3 cloves Pine nuts - .25 cup
- Sea salt – 1 teaspoon Lemon juice – 2 tablespoons
- Coconut cream – 5 tablespoons
- Nutritional yeast – 3 tablespoons
- Black pepper, ground - .25 teaspoon
- Almonds - .5 cup Nutritional yeast – 1 tablespoon
- Sea salt - .25 teaspoon Pasta of choice – 200 grams

Directions:

1. In a food processor mix together the parsley, garlic, pine nuts, teaspoon of sea salt, lemon juice, coconut cream, three tablespoons of nutritional yeast, and the black pepper to create the parsley pesto.

2. In a blender combine the almonds and one tablespoon of nutritional yeast until it forms a fine meal. This will be your vegan Parmesan cheese.

3. Meanwhile, cook the pasta according to the instructions on the packaging until it is al dente. Drain the water off of the cooked pasta and return it back to the pot.

4. Pour the pesto over the pasta and allow it to cook together over medium heat while constantly stirring for one to two minutes. Remove the pot from the heat.

5. Serve the pasta, topping it off with the vegan Parmesan cheese you previously prepared.

Nutrition: 348 Calories 7.4g Carbohydrates 3.2g Fat

65. Spicy Garlic Soba Noodles with Bok Choy

Preparation Time: 6 minutes
Cooking Time: 3 minutes
Servings: 4

Ingredients:
- Soba noodles – 6 ounces
- Baby bok choy – 6 ounces
- Bean sprouts – 1 cup
- Green onions, diced, white and greens separated – 3
- Garlic, minced – 3 cloves
- Sesame seed oil – 3 teaspoons, divided
- Tahini paste – 2 tablespoons
- Rice wine vinegar – 1 tablespoon
- Chili garlic sauce – 1 tablespoon
- Sriracha sauce – 1 tablespoon
- Tamari sauce – 3 tablespoons
- Peanuts, roasted, chopped – .25 cup
- Red pepper, flakes - .25 teaspoon

Directions:
1. In a bowl create a sauce for the soba by whisking together the tahini paste, tamari sauce, chili garlic sauce, sriracha sauce, red wine vinegar, and two teaspoons of sesame seed oil. After combining, set the sauce aside.
2. Bring a large steel pot of water to a boil. Once boiling, stir in soba noodles to the pot, and cook until tender, about seven minutes. Strain the boiling water and rinse the noodles with cold water.
3. While the noodles cook, prepare the bok choy by adding it to a large skillet along with the sesame seed oil and red pepper flakes. Cook over medium-high heat while flipping frequently, until the bok choy has begun to wilt. Pull out bok choy from the pan and set aside.
4. Add the whites of the green onions and the garlic to the skillet, cooking for thirty seconds until fragrant. Pour the bean sprouts and half of the prepared sauce into the skillet with the onion and garlic, heating for an additional thirty seconds. Reduce the heat to medium-low and add the remaining sauce and cooked noodles. Toss until the soba noodles are coated in the garlic sauce and then add the bok choy back to the pan, continuing to cook until all the ingredients are heated through. Top the dish with the greens of the onions and the peanuts before serving.

Nutrition: 313 Calories 11g Fat 23g Protein

66. Chicken with Balsamic Onions and Mushrooms

Preparation Time: 6 minutes
Cooking Time: 36 minutes
Servings: 6

Ingredients:
- Chicken thighs, boneless and skinless – 3
- Sea salt – .5 teaspoon
- Chicken broth - .25 cup
- Mushrooms, sliced – 4 ounces
- Extra virgin olive oil – 1.5 tablespoon, divided
- Onion, thinly sliced – 1
- Heavy cream – .5 tablespoon
- Balsamic vinegar – 1 tablespoon
- Black pepper, ground - .25 teaspoon

Directions:
1. Add one tablespoon of the extra virgin olive oil to a large skillet and sear the chicken thighs on each side over medium-high heat for four minutes on each side. Remove the cooked chicken thighs from the large skillet and set it aside.
2. Into the skillet add the remaining olive oil with the onions and sauté them over medium-low heat until they caramelize, about fifteen minutes.
3. Stir the mushrooms into the skillet, cooking for five-minute minutes until browned. Mix in the chicken broth, balsamic vinegar, and heavy cream. Nestle the chicken thighs into the mixture and continue to cook over medium heat until the chicken is cooked all the way through, about ten more minutes. The chicken is done when the internal temperature

reaches Fahrenheit one-hundred and sixty-five degrees.

Nutrition: 164 Calories 6.3g Fat 7.9g Protein

67. Red Wine Risotto with Kale and Mushrooms

Preparation Time: 7 minutes

Cooking Time: 18 minutes

Servings: 6

Ingredients:

- Arborio rice – 1.5 cups
- Vegetable broth – 4 cups
- Dried porcini mushrooms, loosely packed - .75 cup
- Maitake mushrooms - .75 pound
- Extra virgin olive oil – 2 tablespoons
- Onion, diced – 1
- Sea salt – 1 teaspoon
- Allspice, ground - .25 teaspoon
- Garlic, minced – 4 cloves
- Red wine – 1 cup
- Butter, cut into pieces – 3 tablespoons
- Parmesan, grated – .5 cup
- Baby kale, packed – 2 cups
- Black pepper, ground - .25 teaspoon

Directions:

1. Set the oven to Fahrenheit four-hundred and fifty degrees and line a baking sheet with kitchen parchment.
2. In a small saucepan, simmer the porcine mushrooms in a cup of water over medium-low heat. Do this until the porcini have softened and infused the water with their flavor, about five minutes.
3. Pull the mushrooms into thin florets and place them on the prepared baking sheet. Spray them with a little non-stick cooking spray and sprinkle them with a small amount of the sea salt and black pepper. Roast the mushrooms until crispy and browned, about twenty to twenty-five minutes, tossing them once halfway through the cooking time.
4. In a large pot add the extra virgin olive oil and set the heat to medium. Cook the onion for about four minutes, until softened. Add in the garlic and cook for an additional minute, until fragrant.

5. Stir the rice into the pot, cooking for one minute while stirring. Add in the allspice and the remaining sea salt and black pepper. Stir in the red wine, continuing to stir until the rice absorbs all of the liquid, about two minutes.
6. Slowly add the liquid from the porcini mushrooms into the rice, stirring after each addition. Don't add the next addition until the previous one has been fully absorbed. When you are done adding in the porcini broth, start adding in the vegetable broth.
7. Coarsely chop the porcini and add them to the risotto. During the last five minutes of cooking the risotto, add in the kale so that it can wilt.
8. Lastly, stir in the butter and the Parmesan, cooking for one last minute before removing the risotto from the heat.
9. Garnish with the roasted mushrooms.

Nutrition: 392 Calories 14g Fat 23g Protein

68. Sausage Stuffed Eggplant

Preparation Time: 8 minutes

Cooking Time: 33 minutes

Servings: 8

Ingredients:

- Onion, finely diced – 1
- Eggplants, slice din half lengthwise – 2
- Extra virgin olive oil – 2 tablespoons
- Garlic, minced – 5 cloves
- Italian sausage, removed from casing – 1 pound
- Sea salt – 1 teaspoon Oregano, dried - .5 teaspoon
- Thyme, dried - .5 teaspoon
- Parsley, fresh, chopped - .25 cup
- Black pepper, ground - .25 teaspoon
- Mozzarella, part-skim, shredded – 1 cup
- Hot water – 1 cup

Directions:

1. While you preheat your oven to Fahrenheit four-hundred degrees prepare the eggplant. To do this, use a spoon to scoop out a portion of the flesh from the eggplant halves. Scoop out the middle portion of the flesh, leaving a half-inch border of flesh around the eggplant's shell.

2. Set the eggplant shells in a baking dish and sprinkle the inside with half of the sea salt. Chop up the eggplant you scooped out.

3. Add the extra virgin olive oil to a large skillet along with the chopped eggplant and the onion. Cook for two minutes.

4. Use your hands to break the sausage into pieces, adding it to the skillet along with the herbs, garlic, black pepper, and remaining sea salt. Continue to cook until the sausage is evenly browned, about six minutes. Remove the skillet from the heat.

5. Using a couple clean kitchen towels or paper towels dab at the prepared eggplant shells, removing any liquid that formed. This happens to eggplant when it comes into contact with salt, and it is important to not skip this step.

6. Divide the sausage mixture between the four eggplant shells, stuffing them full. Into the baking dish, along with the eggplant, pour the hot water. Don't pour the water over the top of the eggplant, which will mess up the filling. Instead, pour it around the outer portion of the shells.

7. Roast the eggplant until tender, about twenty-five to thirty minutes. Drizzle cheese over the top and cook for an additional five minutes. Remove the eggplant from the oven and serve.

Nutrition: 314 Calories 23g Fat 31g Protein

69. **Super-Speedy Prawn Risotto**

Preparation Time: 17 minutes
Cooking Time: 22 minutes
Servings: 4
Ingredients:
- 100g diced onion
- Two x 250g packs whole grain rice & quinoa
- 200g frozen garden peas 1/285g tote water-cress
- Two x 150g packs cooked and peeled king prawns

Directions:
1. Heating 1 tablespoon coconut oil in a skillet on a medium-high heat and then put in 100g diced onion; cook 5 mins. Insert 2

x 250g packs whole grain rice & quinoa along with 175ml hot vegetable stock (or plain water), together side 200g suspended garden peas.

2. Gently split using rice using a wooden spoon. Cover and cook 3 mins, stirring occasionally Add two x 150g packs cooked and peeled king prawns. Cook for 12 mins before prawns, peas and rice have been piping hot and the majority of the liquid was consumed.

3. Remove from heat. Chop 1/2 x 85g tote water-cress and stir throughout; up to taste. Top with watercress leaves and pepper to function.

Nutrition: 484 Calories 20g Fat 25g Protein

70. **Bacon and Egg Fried Rice**

Preparation Time: 18 minutes
Cooking Time: 34 minutes
Servings: 4
Ingredients:
- 350g long-grain rice, well rinsed
- 1 1/2 tablespoon olive oil
- 100g streaky bacon, diced 2 eggs
- Two peppers, finely chopped
- 2 red onions, finely chopped
- 200g carrots, peeled and coarsely grated
- 5cm slice ginger, peeled and grated
- 1 red chili, finely chopped (optional)
- 2 tsp soy sauce
- 2 garlic cloves, crushed

Directions:
1. Cook the rice in a big bowl of warm water for 10 mins until not quite tender. Drain, rinse with warm water and drain. Set aside.

2. Meanwhile, warm 1/2 tablespoon oil in a skillet on a high heat and fry the bacon for 5 - 7 mins until golden and crispy. Remove from the pan using a slotted spoon and place a side. Add 1 tablespoon oil and fry the peppers for 10 mins until lightly bubbling. Add the carrots, onions, ginger, garlic and chili and fry over a moderate - high temperature for 5 mins more.

3. Insert the rice and bacon and simmer for 5 mins, stirring often. Push the rice mix to a single side of this pan and then crack the eggs to the gap. Beat the eggs with a wooden spoon, then stir throughout the

rice. Cook for 2 mins, then add the soy sauce and then remove from heat. Split between 4 shallow bowls to function.

Nutrition: 309 Calories 20g fat 45g Protein

71. Lentil, Kale, and Red Onion Pasta

Preparation Time: 8 minutes
Cooking Time: 35 minutes
Serving: 2

Ingredients

- 2 ½ cups vegetable broth
- ¾ cup dry lentils
- 1 bay leaf
- ¼ cup olive oil
- 1 large red onion, chopped
- 1 teaspoon fresh thyme, chopped
- ½ teaspoon fresh oregano, chopped
- 8 ounces ground turkey, (optional)
- 1 bunch kale
- 1 (12 oz) package buckwheat pasta
- 2 tablespoons nutritional yeast

Directions

1. Rinse the lentils using fine mesh sieve under cold water until the water runs clear
2. Boil vegetable broth, lentils, ½ teaspoon of salt, and bay leaf over high heat. Set heat to medium-low, cover, and cook for 20 minutes. Pour additional broth if needed to keep the lentils moist. Take out the bay leaf once done.
3. As it simmers, cook olive oil in a skillet over medium-high heat. Stir in the onion, thyme, oregano, and season well.
4. Cook for a minute, stirring frequently, then stir ground turkey, if using. Reduce the heat to medium-low, and cook until the onion has softened, about 10 minutes.
5. Meanwhile, bring a large pot of lightly salted water to a boil over high heat. Add the kale and pasta. Cook until the pasta is al dente, about 8 minutes.
6. Remove some of the cooking water and set aside. Drain the pasta, then return to the pot.
7. Stir in the lentils, and onion mixture.
8. Use the reserved cooking liquid to adjust the sauciness of the dish to your liking. Sprinkle with nutritional yeast to serve

Nutrition: 319 Calories 23g fat 42g Protein

72. Arugula Linguine

Preparation Time: 7 minutes
Cooking Time: 25 minutes
Serving: 2

Ingredients

- 12 ounces linguine or other dried pasta
- 3 tablespoons extra virgin olive oil
- 3 - 4 cloves garlic, sliced thinly
- 2 large handfuls baby arugula
- 2 tablespoons capers, drained
- ½ cup Parmesan, shredded or shaved
- 1/3 cup pine nuts, toasted

Directions

1. Cook the pasta in a large pot of boiling salted water until al dente, about 8 minutes.
2. While pasta is cooking, heat oil in a large pan and sauté the garlic over medium heat for 2 – 3 minutes until just turning golden.
3. When your pasta is ready, drain and immediately add the remaining ingredients, including the garlic and toss to combine well.

Nutrition: 321 Calories 21g fat 40g Protein

73. Potato Casserole

Preparation Time: 38 minutes
Cooking Time: 1 hour
Serving: 7

Ingredients

For the Potato Crust:

- 5 russet potatoes, peeled
- 1 clove garlic, crushed
- 1 stalk celery, chopped
- 1 bunch fresh parsley, chopped
- 1 yellow onion, chopped
- 1 tablespoon light Miso paste

For the Filling:

- 1 tablespoon extra-virgin olive oil
- ¾ cup diced red onion
- 1 clove garlic, minced
- ½ pound fresh mushrooms, sliced
- 1 cup kale, chopped
- 1 (12 oz) package of firm tofu, crumbled
- 1 tablespoon nutritional yeast
- 1 teaspoon paprika

For the Gravy:

- 2 tablespoons olive oil

- 1/8 cup whole wheat flour
- 2 teaspoons nutritional yeast
- 1 tablespoon Miso broth

Directions

1. Preheat oven to 400 degrees F.
2. Skin and quarter potatoes. Situate medium size pot with water to cover. Add garlic, celery, parsley, and yellow onion. Boil, then simmer over medium-low heat for 18 minutes, covered.
3. To Make Filling: While potatoes are cooking, heat 1 tablespoon oil in a large skillet and sauté onion and garlic over medium heat for 1 minutes, then add mushrooms and kale and sauté for 2 additional minutes.
4. Crush tofu in chunks into the skillet and sauté briefly, mixing well. Stir in, yeast, thyme and paprika. Mix well and sauté, stirring frequently, for 20 minutes over medium heat.
5. To Make Potato Crust: When they're cooked, transfer potatoes from water to a large bowl, reserving 3 ½ cups of the remaining stock. Whisk the miso paste and oil, to 1 cup of the potato stock and add to the potatoes simultaneously, as you mix the stock. Pour only enough water to moisten potatoes adequately.
6. Assemble Casserole: Scoop filling into an oiled, deep ovenproof casserole dish. Press down with back of a large spoon.
7. Spread potato crust evenly over filling, smoothing top with a spoon or spatula. Dust evenly with paprika.
8. Bake for 30 to 40 minutes, or until crust is golden.
9. To Make the Gravy: While casserole bakes, cook oil in a large frying pan. Whisk flour and yeast, over medium heat. Slowly stir in remaining 2 ½ cups of reserved potato water, whisking as you stir to allow gravy to thicken. Stir in instant miso paste and continue whisking until gravy is thick and smooth; add additional potato water, if necessary.
10. Serve casserole inverted, with crust on the bottom and filling on top. Spoon gravy over top.

Nutrition: 289 Calories 18g fat 36g Protein

74. Harvest Nut Roast

Preparation Time: 11 minutes
Cooking Time: 90 minutes
Serving: 4

Ingredients

- ½ cup celery, chopped
- 2 red onions, chopped
- ¾ cup walnuts
- ¾ cup pecan or sunflower meal
- 2 ½ cups soy milk
- 1 teaspoon dried basil
- 1 teaspoon dried lovage
- 3 cups breadcrumbs
- Salt and pepper to taste

Direction

1. Prep oven to 350 degrees F and lightly oil a loaf pan.
2. In a medium size skillet, sauté the chopped celery and onion in 3 teaspoons water until cooked.
3. In a large mixing bowl combine the celery and onion with walnuts, pecan or sunflower meal, soy milk, basil, lovage, breadcrumbs, and salt and pepper to taste; mix well.
4. Place mixture in the prepared loaf pan.
5. Bake for 60 to 90 minutes; until the loaf is cooked through.

Nutrition: 309 Calories 20g fat 45g Protein

75. Quick Spaghetti Sauce

Preparation Time: 9 minutes
Cooking Time: 30 minutes
Serving: 4

Ingredients

- 1 (29 ounce) can tomato sauce
- 1 cup mushrooms, chopped
- ½ cup chopped celery
- ¼ cup diced red onion
- ¼ cup Medjool dates, chopped
- ¼ cup walnuts, chopped
- 1 tomato, quartered
- 1 large orange, quartered
- 1 tablespoon garlic, minced

Directions

1. Using huge, heavy saucepan combine tomato sauce, mushrooms, celery, red onion, dates, walnuts, tomato, orange and

garlic. Cook on medium-high for 30 minutes.
   2. Side with pasta or vegetable noodle alternative.

Nutrition: 317 Calories 30g fat 42g Protein

76. Shepherd's Pie

Preparation Time: 22 minutes
Cooking Time: 80 minutes
Serving: 4

Ingredients
For the mashed potatoes:
- 6 large potatoes, peeled and cubed
- ½ cup soy milk
- ¼ cup extra virgin olive oil
- 2 teaspoons salt

For the bottom layer:
- 1 tablespoon extra-virgin olive oil
- 1 yellow onion, chopped
- 3 carrots, chopped
- 3 stalks celery, chopped
- ½ cup frozen peas
- 1 tomato, chopped
- 1 teaspoon dried parsley
- 1 teaspoon dried lovage
- 1 teaspoon dried oregano
- 3 cloves garlic, minced
- 1/2 cup kasha (toasted buckwheat groats)
- 2/3 cup bulgur
- 2 cups fresh mushrooms, diced

Directions
   1. Preheat oven to 350 degrees F and spray a 2-quart baking dish with cooking spray.
   2. Place the potatoes into a large pot with enough cold water to cover them completely. Bring the water to a boil and then reduce heat to a low boil for 20 minutes. Drain and transfer to a large bowl.
   3. Using a hand blender, mix the soy milk, olive oil, and salt into the potatoes, and blend until smooth. Cover and set aside until your bottom layer are ready.
   4. At the same time, in a saucepan, boil 1 ½ cups water with ½ teaspoon salt. Mix in kasha. Reduce heat and simmer uncovered, for 15 minutes.

   5. Add 1 ½ cups more water and bring back to a boil. Add bulgur, cover, and remove from heat. Let stand for 10 minutes.
   6. Cook olive oil in a large pan, and sauté the onion, carrots, celery, frozen peas, and tomato on medium heat until they start to soften, about 5 minutes. Cook mushrooms for another 3 minutes.
   7. Dust flour over vegetables; stir constantly for 2 minutes. Pour remaining 1 ½ cups milk over the vegetables and increase heat to high. Stir until sauce is smooth. Reduce heat and simmer for 5 minutes. Stir in parsley, lovage, oregano, garlic, and salt and pepper to taste.
   8. Combine vegetable mixture and kasha mixture in a large bowl and mix well.
   9. Spoon into a greased 10" pie pan, and smooth with a spatula. Lay out mashed potatoes over top, leaving an uneven surface.
   10. Bake for 30 minutes.

Nutrition: 401 Calories 31g fat 47g Protein

77. Spinach and Turkey Lasagna

Preparation Time: 36 minutes
Cooking Time: 27 minutes
Serving: 4

Ingredients
- 9 whole-wheat lasagna noodles
- 1 teaspoon extra virgin olive oil
- ½ cup red onion, chopped
- 1-pound ground turkey breast
- 3 cups tomato sauce
- 1/2 cup mushrooms, sliced
- 1 teaspoon dried parsley
- 1 teaspoon dried lovage
- 1 teaspoon dried oregano
- ¼ teaspoon garlic powder
- Salt and pepper to taste
- 6 cups fresh spinach, chopped
- 2 cups ricotta cheese
- ¼ teaspoon ground nutmeg
- 2 cups shredded mozzarella cheese

Directions
   1. Preheat an oven to 375 degrees F.
   2. Boil lightly salted water. Cook lasagna noodles until al dente, approximately 8

minutes. Drain noodles and rinse under cold water.

3. Preheat olive oil in a skillet at medium heat. Cook onion for 2 minutes.

4. Cook ground turkey for 6 minutes more, stirring to break up any large chunks of meat.

5. Stir in tomato sauce, mushrooms, parsley, lovage, oregano, black pepper, and garlic powder. Simmer for 3 minutes and season well.

6. Mix spinach, ricotta, and nutmeg.

7. To assemble, arrange 3 noodles lengthwise in the bottom of a greased 9x13 inch baking dish. Spread with 1/3 the spinach-ricotta mixture, 1/3 of the turkey mixture, and 1/3 of the mozzarella. Repeat layers, ending with remaining mozzarella.

8. Bake in preheated oven for 25 minutes. Cool for 5 minutes before serving.

Nutrition: 341 Calories 19g fat 43g Protein

78. Thai Curry with Chicken and Peanuts

Preparation Time: 42 minutes
Cooking Time: 26 minutes
Serving: 4

Ingredients

- 2 Bird's Eye chili peppers
- 2 tablespoons ginger root, chopped
- 1 tablespoon fresh turmeric root, chopped
- ½ teaspoon cumin
- ½ teaspoon dried coriander
- 1/2 teaspoon ground nutmeg
- 2 tablespoons lemongrass, thinly sliced
- 1 shallot, chopped
- 2 cloves garlic, chopped
- 2 teaspoons fermented shrimp paste
- 2 tablespoons fish sauce
- 3 tablespoons brown sugar
- 2/3-pound skinless, boneless chicken breast, cut into cubes
- 2 tablespoons extra virgin olive oil
- ½ cup roasted peanuts

Directions

1. Place the chili peppers in a bowl; pour enough water over the chili peppers to cover. Allow the peppers to soak until

softened, about 10 minutes. Drain, chop the peppers finely and set aside.

2. In a large bowl, add the ginger and turmeric root, cumin, coriander, lemongrass, shallot, garlic, shrimp paste, and chopped chili peppers and mash into a paste. Stir the fish sauce and sugar into the paste.

3. Toss chicken to the paste to coat the evenly.

4. Cover bowl and marinate for at 25 minutes.

5. Cook oil in a large skillet over medium heat and cook for 6 minutes.

6. Stir 2 cups of water into the pan and add the peanuts.

7. Simmer for 30 minutes. You can also cook this at a lower temperature for up to 2 hours.

Nutrition: 321 Calories 19g fat 43g Protein

79. Red Lentil Curry

Preparation Time: 13 minutes
Cooking Time: 24 minutes
Serving: 4

Ingredients

- 2 cups whole red lentils
- 1 large red onion, diced
- 1 tablespoon extra-virgin olive oil
- 1 ½ tablespoons curry paste
- 2 tablespoons curry powder
- 1 teaspoon chili powder
- 1 teaspoon ground turmeric
- 1 teaspoon ground cumin
- 1 teaspoon salt
- 1 teaspoon sugar
- 3 cloves garlic, minced
- 1" section of fresh ginger root, peeled and minced
- 1 (14.25 ounce) can crushed tomatoes

Directions

1. Rinse the lentils with a fine mesh sieve under cold water until the clear

2. Transfer the lentils to a medium-sized pot with enough water to cover completely and simmer covered until they're just starting to become tender, about 15 – 20 minutes. Add additional water as necessary.

3. In the meantime, warm the oil in a large skillet and sauté the onions until they're golden.
4. In a separate bowl, combine the curry paste, curry powder, chili powder, turmeric, cumin, salt, sugar, garlic, and ginger and mix well.
5. When the onions are translucent, add the curry mixture and cook on high, stirring constantly for 2 - 3 minutes.
6. Add in the crushed tomato and reduce the heat. Let the curry blend simmer until the lentils are ready.
7. When the lentils are cooked to your liking, drain well and add to the curry sauce, mixing well.
8. Serve immediately.

Nutrition: 322 Calories 23g fat 47g Protein

80. Spiced Fish Tacos with Fresh Corn Salsa

Preparation Time: 13 minutes
Cooking Time: 21 minutes
Serving: 4
Ingredients
- 1 cup corn
- 1/2 cup red onion, diced
- 1 cup jicama, peeled and chopped
- 1/2 cup red bell pepper, diced
- 1 cup fresh cilantro leaves, finely chopped
- 1 lime, zested and juiced
- 2 tablespoons sour cream
- 2 tablespoons cayenne pepper
- Salt and pepper to taste
- 8 (4 ounce) fillets tilapia
- 2 tablespoons olive oil
- 8 corn tortillas, warmed

Directions
1. Preheat grill for high heat.
2. For the Corn Salsa: Scourge corn, red onion, jicama, red bell pepper, and cilantro. Stir in lime juice and zest.
3. Grease each fillet with olive oil, and season with the cayenne, salt and pepper.
4. Arrange fillets on grill and cook for 3 minutes per side. For each fish taco, top two corn tortillas with fish, sour cream, and corn salsa.

Nutrition: 329 Calories 21g fat 39g Protein

81. Greek Pizza with Arugula, Feta and Olives

Preparation Time: 18 minutes
Cooking Time: 15 minutes
Serving: 4
Ingredients
- 2 tablespoons extra virgin olive oil
- 4 cloves garlic, minced
- 3 tablespoons All Purpose flour
- 1 cup milk
- 1 teaspoon dried oregano
- ½ cup Parmesan, grated or shredded
- 1 cup feta cheese, crumbled
- 1 (12 inch) pre-baked pizza crust
- ½ cup oil-packed sun-dried tomatoes
- 2 cups arugula
- ¼ cup pitted Kalamata olives
- 1/2 small red onion
- 1 tablespoon oil from the sun-dried tomatoes
- ¼ teaspoon chili pepper flakes

Direction
1. Situate oven rack to lowest position, and set oven to 450 degrees.
2. For the white sauce: Heat oil in a saucepan and sauté the garlic until it's fragrant, about 2 minutes.
3. Add the flour and stir well until it's browned, another 2 – 3 minutes.
4. Add the milk, oregano, Parmesan, and half the Feta and stir continuously until the cheese is well combined and the sauce has thickened, about 5 minutes. Transfer to a small dish.
5. Assemble the Pizza: Situate pizza crust on a cookie sheet; spread white sauce evenly and generously over the crust.
6. Top with arugula, tomatoes, onions and olives, in that order. Bake for 11 minutes.
7. Pull out from oven, and garnish with the remaining feta cheese and drizzle 1 tablespoon of the oil from the sun-dried tomatoes over top.
8. Put back to the oven and bake for 2 minutes longer. Cut into 8 slices and serve

Nutrition: 401 Calories 23g fat 34g Protein

82. Pesto Goat Cheese Kale Pizza

Preparation Time: 16 minutes
Cooking Time: 10 minutes
Serving: 4

Ingredients

- 1 (12 inch) pre-baked pizza crust
- 6 tablespoons prepared
- 3 Roma tomatoes, thinly sliced
- 8 ounces goat cheese
- 2 cloves garlic, thinly sliced
- 1 cup fresh baby kale
- 1 teaspoon olive oil

Direction

1. Place oven rack to lowest position, and adjust oven to 450 degrees.
2. Pour pesto onto the center of the pizza base and spread toward the outer edges.
3. Situate goat cheese into thin coins and spread or crumble across the pizza.
4. Place the kale and then tomato slices over goat cheese and top with garlic. Rub crust edges lightly with olive oil.
5. Place pizza directly on preheated oven rack. Bake for 10 minutes
6. Once cooked, allow to cool to set before slicing into 8 equal pieces.

Nutrition: 297 Calories 18g fat 41g Protein

83. Tuscan Garlic Chicken

Preparation Time: 17 minutes
Cooking Time: 31 minutes
Serving: 4

Ingredients

- 1½-pounds boneless skinless chicken breasts, thinly sliced
- 1 cup heavy cream
- 2 tablespoons extra virgin olive oil
- ½-cup chicken broth
- ¼ teaspoon dried parsley
- ¼ teaspoon dried oregano
- ¼ teaspoon dried lovage
- 1 teaspoon garlic powder
- ½ cup Parmesan cheese
- 1 cup arugula, chopped
- ½ cup sun-dried tomatoes
- 1/3 cup capers, drained

Directions

1. Pre-heat olive oil in a big pan on medium heat. Add the chicken and cook for 3-5 minutes until brown all over.
2. When the chicken is no longer pink in the center, remove it from heat and set aside on a plate.
3. Add the chicken broth, heavy cream, garlic powder, parsley, oregano, lovage, and Parmesan cheese to the pan. Whisk on medium heat until it thickens.
4. Add the arugula, sundried tomatoes and capers, allowing them to simmer, until the arugula starts to wilt.
5. Then add the chicken back to the mixture in the pan to reheat for 1 minute before serving.

Nutrition: 341 Calories 17g fat 41g Protein

84. Baked Walnut Chicken Breast

Preparation Time: 7 minutes
Cooking Time: 20 minutes
Serving: 4

Ingredients

- ¼ cup of walnuts, chopped
- 2 tablespoons of extra virgin olive oil.
- 2 boneless, skinless chicken breasts

Directions

1. Pre-heat the oven to 350 degrees F.
2. Slice a deep groove into the middle of each chicken breast using a sharp knife and place the chopped walnuts in this groove, pouring the olive oil over top.
3. Put the chicken breasts on a baking tray and bake for 20 minutes.

Nutrition: 327 Calories 21g fat 35g Protein

85. Roast Duck with Apple Dressing

Preparation Time: 15 minutes
Cooking Time: 80 minutes
Serving: 4

Ingredients

- 1 (4 pound) whole duck
- Salt and pepper to taste
- 1 teaspoon poultry seasoning
- 2 tablespoon extra-virgin olive oil
- 3 tablespoons red onion, chopped
- 5 stalks celery, chopped
- 3 cups, chopped

- 3 cups cornbread crumbs

Directions

1. Preheat oven to 350 degrees F.
2. Rinse the duck and pat dry. Rub with salt, pepper, and poultry seasoning, to taste.
3. Warm half (1 tablespoon) of the olive oil in a small skillet over medium heat. Sauté onion and celery until tender.
4. In a medium bowl, combine with apple and cornbread crumbs with the onion-celery mixture. Mix together to make stuffing, adding a little water to moisten if necessary.
5. Fill the duck's cavity with the stuffing and sew shut with kitchen twine. Rub the outside of bird lightly with the remaining tablespoon of olive oil, and place in a shallow roasting pan or 9x13 inch baking dish.
6. Bake in preheated oven for 60 to 80 minutes, or until internal temperature reaches 180 degrees F.

Nutrition: 341 Calories 19g fat 38g Protein

86. Ginger Mushrooms

Preparation Time: 12 minutes
Cooking Time: 23 minutes
Servings: 4
Ingredients:
- 1-pound mushrooms, sliced
- 1 yellow onion, chopped
- 1 tablespoon ginger, grated
- 1 tablespoon olive oil
- 2 tablespoons balsamic vinegar
- 2 garlic cloves, minced
- A pinch of salt and black pepper
- ¼ cup lime juice
- 2 tablespoons walnuts, chopped

Directions:
1. Preheat pan with the oil over medium-high heat, cook onion and the ginger for 5 minutes.
2. Cook mushrooms and the other ingredients over medium heat for 18 minutes and serve.

Nutrition: 120 calories 9g fats 7g protein

87. Bell Pepper Sauté

Preparation Time: 7 minutes
Cooking Time: 22 minutes
Servings: 4
Ingredients:
- 1 red bell pepper, cut into strips
- 1 yellow bell pepper, cut into strips
- 1 green bell pepper, cut into strips
- 1 orange bell pepper, cut into strips
- 3 scallions, chopped
- 1 tablespoon olive oil
- 1 tablespoon coconut aminos
- A pinch of salt and black pepper
- 1 tablespoon parsley, chopped
- 1 tablespoon rosemary

Direction:
1. Warm up pan with the oil over medium-high heat, cook scallions for 5 minutes.
2. Toss bell peppers and the other ingredients, then cook over medium heat for 15 minutes more, and serve.

Nutrition: 120 calories 1g fat 6g protein

88. Kale and Tomatoes

Preparation Time: 8 minutes
Cooking Time: 23 minutes
Servings: 4
Ingredients:
- 1 cup cherry tomatoes, halved
- 1-pound baby kale
- 1 yellow onion, chopped
- 2 tablespoons olive oil
- 1 tablespoon balsamic vinegar
- 1 tablespoon cilantro, chopped
- 2 tablespoons vegetable stock
- A pinch of salt and black pepper

Direction:
1. Preheat pan with the oil over medium heat, add the onion and sauté for 5 minutes.
2. Cook kale, tomatoes and the other ingredients, over medium heat for 17 minutes, portion and serve.

Nutrition: 170 calories 6g fat 4g protein

89. Chili Artichokes

Preparation Time: 12 minutes
Cooking Time: 28 minutes
Servings: 4
Ingredients:
- 2 artichokes, trimmed and halved
- 1 teaspoon chili powder
- 2 green chilies, mined
- 2 tablespoons olive oil
- 1 teaspoon garlic powder
- 1 teaspoon sweet paprika
- A pinch of salt and black pepper
- Juice of 1 lime

Directions:
1. In a roasting pan, combine the artichokes with the chili powder, the chilies and the other ingredients, toss and bake at 380 degrees F for 25 minutes.
2. Divide the artichokes between plates and serve.

Nutrition: 132 calories 2g fat 6g protein

90. Brussels Sprouts Mix

Preparation Time: 13 minutes
Cooking Time: 21 minutes
Servings: 4

Ingredients:
- 2 tablespoons olive oil
- 1-pound Brussels sprouts, trimmed and halved
- 1 tablespoon ginger, grated
- 2 garlic cloves, minced
- 1 tablespoon pine nuts
- 1 tablespoon olive oil

Direction:
1. Warm up a pan with the oil over medium heat, add the garlic and the ginger and sauté for 2 minutes.
2. Add the Brussels sprouts and the other ingredients, toss, cook for 18 minutes more, divide between plates and serve.

Nutrition: 160 calories 2g fat 5g protein

91. Cauliflower Mix

Preparation Time: 13 minutes
Cooking Time: 28 minutes
Servings: 4

Ingredients:
- 1-pound cauliflower florets
- 2 tablespoons avocado oil
- 1 teaspoon nutmeg, ground
- 1 teaspoon hot paprika
- 1 tablespoon pumpkin seeds
- 1 tablespoon chives, chopped

Directions:
1. Arrange cauliflower florets on a baking sheet lined with parchment paper, add the oil, the nutmeg and the other ingredients, toss and bake at 380 degrees F for 25 minutes.
2. Divide the cauliflower mix between plates and serve as a side dish.

Nutrition: 160 calories 4g fat 6g protein

92. Baked Broccoli and Pine Nuts

Preparation Time: 16 minutes
Cooking Time: 31 minutes
Servings: 4

Ingredients:
- 2 tablespoons olive oil
- 1-pound broccoli florets
- 1 tablespoon garlic, minced
- 1 tablespoon pine nuts, toasted
- 1 tablespoon lemon juice

- 2 teaspoons mustard
- A pinch of salt and black pepper

Directions:
1. In a roasting pan, combine the broccoli with the oil, the garlic and the other ingredients, toss and bake at 380 degrees F for 30 minutes.
2. Divide everything between plates and serve as a side dish.

Nutrition: 220 calories 6g fat 6g protein

93. Quinoa and Peas

Preparation Time: 12 minutes
Cooking Time: 34 minutes
Servings: 4

Ingredients:
- 1 yellow onion, chopped
- 1 tomato, cubed
- 1 cup quinoa
- 3 cups vegetable stock
- 1 tablespoon olive oil
- 1 cup peas
- 1 tablespoon cilantro, chopped
- A pinch of salt and black pepper

Directions:
1. Heat up a pot with the oil over medium heat, add the onion, stir and sauté for 5 minutes.
2. Add the quinoa, the stock and the other ingredients, toss, bring to a simmer and cook over medium heat for 25 minutes.
3. Divide everything between plates and serve as a side dish.

Nutrition: 202 calories 3g fat 6g protein

94. Basil Green Beans

Preparation Time: 14 minutes
Cooking Time: 23 minutes
Servings: 4

Ingredients:
- 1 yellow onion, chopped
- 1-pound green beans, trimmed and halved
- 1 tablespoon avocado oil
- 2 teaspoons basil, dried
- A pinch of salt and black pepper
- 1 tablespoon tomato sauce

Direction:
1. Warmup a pan with the oil over medium-high heat, add the onion and sauté for 5 minutes.

2. Add the green beans and the other ingredients, toss, and cook for 15 minutes more.
3. Divide everything between plates and serve as a side dish.

Nutrition: 221 calories 5g fat 8g protein

95. Apples and Cabbage Mix

Preparation Time: 7 minutes
Cooking Time: 0 minute
Servings: 4

Ingredients:
- 2 cored and cubed green apples
- 2 tbsps. balsamic vinegar
- ½ tsp. caraway seeds
- 2 tbsps. olive oil
- Black pepper
- 1 shredded red cabbage head

Directions:
1. Mix and toss cabbage with the apples and the other ingredients, then serve.

Nutrition: 165 Calories 7.4g Fat 2.6g Protein

96. Baked Mushrooms with Thyme

Preparation Time: 11 minutes
Cooking Time: 34 minutes
Servings: 4

Ingredients:
- 1 tbsp. chopped thyme
- 2 tbsps. olive oil
- 2 tbsps. chopped parsley
- 4 minced garlic cloves
- Black pepper
- 2 lbs. halved white mushrooms

Directions:
1. Using a baking pan, mix mushrooms with the garlic and the other ingredients, introduce in the oven and cook at 400 0F for 30 minutes.
2. Divide between plates and serve.

Nutrition: 251 Calories 9.3g Fat 6g Protein

97. Baked Endives

Preparation Time: 13 minutes
Cooking Time: 21 minutes
Servings: 4

Ingredients:
- 2 tbsps. olive oil
- 1 tsp. dried rosemary
- 2 halved endives
- ¼ tsp. black pepper
- ½ tsp. turmeric powder

Directions:
1. In a baking pan, toss endives with the other ingredients and oil, and bake at 400 F for 20 minutes.
2. Divide between plates and serve.

Nutrition: 66 Calories 7.1g Fat 0.3g Protein

98. Braised Leek with Pine Nuts

Preparation Time: 41 minutes
Cooking Time: 19 minutes
Servings: 3

Ingredients:
- 20g Ghee
- 2 tsp. Olive oil
- 2 pcs. Leek
- 2 cups Vegetable broth
- 1 tbsp. fresh oregano
- 1 tbsp. Pine nuts (roasted)

Directions:
1. Slice leek into thin rings and finely chop the herbs. Roast the pine nuts at medium heat.
2. Cook ghee together with the olive oil in a pan.
3. Fry leek for 5 minutes, stirring constantly.
4. Cook vegetable broth for 10 minutes
5. Mix in the herbs and drizzle the pine nuts before serving.

Nutrition: 97 Calories 2g Protein 6g Fat

99. Casserole with Spinach and Eggplant

Preparation Time: 1 hour
Cooking Time: 40 minutes
Servings: 2

Ingredients:
- 1-piece Eggplant
- 2 pieces Onion
- Olive oil 3 tablespoon
- Spinach (fresh) 450 g
- Tomatoes 4 pieces
- Egg 2 pieces
- 60 ml Almond milk
- 2 teaspoons Lemon juice
- 4 tablespoon Almond flour

Directions:

1. Preheat the oven to 200 ° C.
2. Cut the eggplants, onions and tomatoes into slices and sprinkle salt on the eggplant slices.
3. Brush the eggplants and onions with olive oil and fry them in a grill pan.
4. Shrink the spinach in a large saucepan over moderate heat and drain in a sieve.
5. Put the vegetables in layers in a greased baking dish: first the eggplant, then the spinach and then the onion and the tomato. Repeat this again.
6. Whisk eggs with almond milk, lemon juice, salt and pepper and pour over the vegetables.
7. Sprinkle almond flour over the dish and bake in the oven for about 30 to 40 minutes.

Nutrition: 446 Calories 13.9g Protein 31.8g Fat

100. Mexican Bell Pepper Filled with Egg

Preparation Time: 57 minutes
Cooking Time: 21 minutes
Servings: 2

Ingredients:

- 1 tablespoon Coconut oil
- 4 pieces Egg
- 1-piece Tomato
- 1 pinch Chili flakes
- 1/4 teaspoon Ground cumin
- 1/4 teaspoon Paprika powder
- 1/2 pieces Avocado
- 1-piece green peppers
- 2 tablespoon fresh coriander

Directions:

1. Cut the tomatoes and avocado into cubes and finely chop the fresh coriander.
2. Melt the coconut oil in a pan over medium heat, beat the eggs in the pan and add the tomato cubes.
3. Keep stirring until the eggs solidify and season with chili, caraway, paprika, pepper, and salt.
4. Finally add the avocado.
5. Place the egg mixture in the pepper halves and garnish with fresh coriander.

Nutrition: 497 Calories 21g Protein 41g Fat

101. Tuna Balls on Zucchini Salad

Preparation Time: 13 minutes
Cooking Time: 21 minutes
Servings: 2

Ingredients:

- 100 Grams of sheep's cheese
- 1 Tin of tuna (tuna salad, 160 g)
- Pepper (freshly ground)
- 1 Clove of garlic
- 1 Juice orange
- 4th Tsp olive oil
- 1 Tablespoons apple cider vinegar (mild)
- 1 Tsp Dijon mustard
- 2nd Tablespoons pumpkin seeds
- 0.5 Lettuce (125 g)
- 150 Grams of carrot
- 150 Grams of zucchini
- Basil leaves

Directions:

1. Chop the sheep's cheese into small pieces, mix with the tuna salad and pepper well. Cut small cams from the mass or roll them into balls with moistened hands.
2. Peel and crush garlic. Squeeze orange. Mix the orange juice, garlic, olive oil, vinegar, mustard and pepper.
3. Roast the pumpkin seeds then clean lettuce, rinse and cut into strips. Peel the carrot, rinse the zucchini, dry and grate into long strips. Mix all the ingredients.
4. Arrange the lettuce and tuna balls on 2 plates, sprinkle pumpkin seeds over them and sprinkle with basil leaves if necessary.

Nutrition: 471 calories 28g Protein 17g Fat

102. Papaya Bowl with Tuna

Preparation Time: 8 minutes
Cooking Time: 0 minute
Servings: 2

Ingredients:

- 40 Grams of iceberg lettuce (cut)
- 1 Tin of tuna (tuna salad, 160 g,
- 140 Grams of papaya (papaya pulp, sliced)
- 1 Tbsp papaya (papaya seeds)
- 50 Grams of cucumber (sliced)
- 0.5 red peppers (finely sliced)
- 2nd Tablespoons of lime juice
- 1 Tsp camelina oil
- Pepper (freshly ground)
- Salt
- 40 Grams of bread

Directions:

1. Fill iceberg lettuce, tuna salad, papaya, papaya seeds, cucumber and bell pepper into a storage box or lunch box.
2. Mix lime juice, camelina oil, pepper, salt and 1-2 teaspoons of water and drizzle over the vegetables. Close the can. Pack the bread strips separately.

Nutrition: 646 Calories 30g Protein 10g Fat

103. Sweet Potato and Salmon Patties

Preparation Time: 12 minutes
Cooking Time: 23 minutes
Servings: 4

Ingredients:

- Rice flour or buckwheat flour
- 225g/8oz wild salmon, cooked or tinned
- 225g/8oz sweet potato cooked and mashed
- Herb salt and pepper to taste

Directions:

1. Preheat the oven up to 160C / gas mark 3.
2. Mix the sweet potato, salmon, herbal salt and pepper together. Take a small size handful of the mixture and shape it into a ball. Flatten into a shape of burger then dip into the flour on each side. Place it on a lined baking tray. Repeat until the blend is used up.
3. Bake only turning once for 20 minutes. Serve with a sizeable green salad.

Nutrition: 482 calories 15g Protein 1.1g Fat

104. Trout with Roasted Vegetables

Preparation Time: 13 minutes
Cooking Time: 21 minutes
Servings: 2

Ingredients:

- 2 turnips, peeled and cut into segments
- Olive oil

- Dried dill
- Juice of 1 lemon
- 2 carrots, cut into batons
- 2 parsnips, peeled and cut into wedges
- Tamari
- 1 trout fillet per person

Directions:

1. Put the sliced vegetables into a baking tray. Sprinkle with a dash of tamari and olive oil. Set on gas mark 7 in the oven. Take the vegetables out of the oven after 25 minutes, and stir well.
2. Put the fish over it. Sprinkle with the dill and lemon juice. Cover with foil, and go back to the oven. Turn down the oven to gas mark 5/190C/375F and cook till the fish is cooked through for 20 minutes.

Nutrition: 455 calories 23.7g Protein 6.71g Fat

105. Baked Salmon with Stir Fried Vegetables

Preparation Time: 13 minutes
Cooking Time: 60 minutes
Servings: 2

Ingredients:

- Grated zest and juice of 1 lemon
- 1 teaspoon toasted sesame oil
- 2 teaspoon olive oil
- 2 carrots, cut into matchsticks
- Bunch of kale, chopped
- 2 teaspoon of root ginger, grated
- 2 wild salmon fillets
- 1 tin of water chestnuts, drained, rinsed & chopped

Directions:

1. Mix the lemon juice and ginger and zest together. Place the salmon in a shallow, oven proof dish and pour over the lemon ginger mixture. Cover with foil and leave for 30-60 minutes to marinate.
2. Bake the salmon on gas mark 5/190C in the oven for 15 minutes while cooking heat up a wok or frying pan then add the toasted sesame oil and olive oil. Cook vegetables, stirring constantly for a few minutes.
3. Once the salmon are cooked spoon some of the salmon marinade onto the

vegetables and cook for a few more minutes.
4. Serve the vegetables onto a plate and top with salmon.

Nutrition: 836 calories 95g Protein 33g Fat:

106. Shrimp Pasta

Preparation Time: 47 minutes
Cooking Time: 12 minutes
Servings: 2

Ingredients:

- 8 ounces linguine
- 1/4 cup mayonnaise
- 1/4 cup bean stew glue
- Two cloves garlic, squashes
- 1/2-pound shrimp, stripped
- One teaspoon salt
- 1/2 teaspoon cayenne pepper
- One teaspoon garlic powder
- One tablespoon vegetable oil
- One lime, squeezed
- 1/4 cup green onion, slashed
- 1/4 cup cilantro, minced
- Red bean stew chips, for embellish

Directions:

1. Cook pasta still somewhat firm as per box guidelines. In a little bowl, consolidate mayonnaise, stew glue and garlic. Race to join.
2. Put in a safe spot. In a blending bowl, include shrimp, salt, cayenne and garlic powder. Mix to cover shrimp. Oil in a heavy skillet at medium warmth. Include shrimp and cook for around 2 minutes at that point flip and cook for an extra 2 minutes.
3. Add pasta and sauce to the dish. Mood killer the warmth and combine until the pasta is covered. Include lime, green onions and cilantro, and topped with red bean stew pieces.

Nutrition: 283 Calories 26g Protein 18g Fat

107. Asian King Prawn Stir-Fry with Buckwheat Noodles

Preparation Time: 18 minutes
Cooking Time: 34 minutes
Serving: 1

Ingredients

- 150g shelled raw king prawns, deveined
- Two tsp tamari
- Two tsp additional virgin olive oil
- 75g soba (buckwheat noodles)
- One garlic clove, finely chopped
- One bird's eye chili, finely chopped
- One tsp finely cut fresh new ginger
- 20g red onions, sliced
- 40g celery, clipped as well as sliced
- 75g eco-friendly beans, chopped
- 50g kale, about chopped
- 100ml chicken stock
- 5g lovage or even celery actually leaves

Direction

1. Heat the frying pan at high temperature, then simply prepare the prawns inside one teaspoon of the tamari as well as one teaspoon of the oil for 2-3 mins.
2. Transfer the prawns to a plate. Clean the pan as you are likely to use it once again.
3. Cook the noodles for 5-8 mins or perhaps as instructed on the package. Set and drain aside.
4. Meanwhile, fry the garlic, ginger and chili, celery, red onion, kale, and beans within the leftover oil at more than a medium-high temperature for 2-3 mins. Include the inventory and carry into the boil, subsequently simmer for per minute or even 2 before veggies are prepared, however leafy.
5. Add the prawns, noodles, and lovage/celery actually leaves towards the pan, bring back the boil after that eliminate at the temperature, and fulfill.

Nutrition: 291 Calories 23g Protein 17g Fat

108. Fragrant Asian Hotpot-Sirt Food Recipes

Preparation Time: 19 minutes
Cooking Time: 34 minutes
Serving: 2

Ingredients

- One tsp tomato puree
- One-star anise, crushed
- Little handful (10g) parsley, stalks finely chopped
- Little handful (10g) coriander, stalks finely chopped
- Juice of 1/2 lime
- 500ml chicken stock, new or even made out of one cube
- 1/2 carrot, peeled as well as bring down or cut into matchsticks
- 50g broccoli, slice directly into modest florets
- 50g beansprouts
- 100g raw tiger prawns
- 100g tight bean curd, chopped
- 50g grain noodles prepared based on package instructions
- 50g prepared water chestnuts, drained
- 20g ginger sushi, chopped
- One tbsp. good quality miso paste

Direction

1. Situate tomato purée, star anise, parsley stalks, coriander stalks, lime juice, and chicken stock in a big pan and simmer for 10 minutes.
2. Simmer carrot, broccoli, prawns, tofu, noodles, and water chestnuts until the prawns are cooked through, and stir in the sushi ginger and miso paste.
3. Place the tomato puree, chicken stock, lime juice, coriander stalks, parsley stalks, and star anise within a big pan and bring to a simmer for ten mins.
4. Pour the carrot, tofu, prawns, broccoli, noodles, liquid chestnuts, and simmer gently until the prawns are prepared through.
5. Take from the heat as well as add within the sushi ginger as well as miso paste.
6. Fulfill sprinkled with the parsley as well as coriander foliage.

Nutrition: 301 Calories 28g Protein 14g Fat

109. Angry Prawn

Preparation Time: 38 minutes
Cooking Time: 28 minutes
Serving: 1

Ingredients

- 125-150g Raw or even prepared prawns
- 65g Buckwheat pasta
- One tbsp. Extra virgin olive oil
- Forrabbiata sauce

- 40g red onion, finely chopped
- One Garlic clove, finely chopped
- 30g Celery, finely chopped
- One Bird's eye chili, finely chopped
- One tsp dried mixed herbs
- One tsp Extra virgin olive oil
- Two tbsp. White wine (optional)
- 400g Tinned cut tomatoes
- One tbsp. Chopped parsley

Direction

1. Fry the onion, garlic, chili, and celery plus dehydrated/dried herbal plants in the oil at more than a medium low high temperature for 1-2 mins. Switch the high temperature to moderate, pour some of the wine, and cook for one second. Include the tomatoes and leave the marinade to simmer more than a medium-low high temperature for 20-30 mins, until it's a pleasant abundant consistency. In case you're feeling the marinade is becoming overly heavy, just put in just a little drinking water.
2. Even though the marinade is preparing to take a pan of water on the boil and also prepare the pasta based on the package guidelines. When prepared to the liking of yours, empty, toss together with the coconut oil as well as hold within the pan before necessary.
3. If you're utilizing raw prawns, put them with the marinade and also cook for an additional 3-4 mins; before they've switched opaque and pink, pour some of the parsley as well as fulfill. In case you're utilizing prepared prawns, put them together with the parsley, take the marinade on the boil, and also fulfill.
4. Add the prepared pasta into the marinade, blend extensively, but carefully as well as fulfill.

Nutrition: 297 Calories 21g Protein 16g Fat

110. Pan-Fried Turmeric Salmon

Preparation Time: 17 minutes
Cooking Time: 11 minutes
Serving: 1

Ingredients

- 125-150g Skinned Salmon
- One tsp Extra virgin olive oil
- One tsp Ground turmeric
- 1/4 Juice of a lemon

For that spicy celery

- 40g Red onion, finely chopped
- 60g Tinned purple lentils
- One Garlic clove, finely chopped
- 1cm Fresh ginger, finely chopped
- One Bird's eye chili, finely chopped
- 150 g Celery, slice into 2cm lengths
- One tsp Mild curry powder
- 130g Tomato, slice into 8 wedges
- 100ml Chicken or even veggie stock

Direction

1. Heat the oven to 200C or gasoline mark six.
2. Start together with the spicy celery. Heat at high temperature a frying pan more than a medium-low temperature, pour some of the organic olive oil, subsequently the onion, ginger, garlic, celery, and chili. Fry carefully for 2-3 mins then pour the curry powdered in addition to cooking for another second.
3. Add the tomatoes subsequently, then the stock as well as lentils and simmer carefully for ten mins.
4. Meanwhile, blend the turmeric, lemon juice, and oil and also rub with the salmon.
5. Holding a baking paper tray as well as cook for 8-10 mins.
6. To end, add the parsley with the celery as well as perform together with the salmon.

Nutrition: 283 Calories 26g Protein 18g Fat

111. Sage Carrots

Preparation Time: 9 minutes
Cooking Time: 31 minutes
Servings: 2
Ingredients:

- 2 tsps. Sweet paprika
- 1 tbsp. chopped sage
- 2 tbsps. Olive oil
- 1 lb. peeled and roughly cubed carrots
- ¼ tsp. black pepper
- 1 chopped red onion

Directions:

1. In a baking pan, combine carrots with the oil and the other ingredients, toss and bake at 380 degrees F for 30 minutes. Divide between plates and serve.

Nutrition: 204 Calories 16g Protein 8g Fat

112. Pesto Green Beans

Preparation Time: 12 minutes
Cooking Time: 66 minutes
Servings: 2
Ingredients:

- 2 tbsps. Olive oil
- 2 tsps. Sweet paprika
- Juice of 1 lemon
- 2 tbsps. Basil pesto
- 1 lb. trimmed and halved green beans
- ¼ tsp. black pepper
- 1 sliced red onion

Direction:

1. Preheat pan with the oil over medium-high heat; add the onion, stir and sauté for 5 minutes. Add the beans and the rest of the ingredients, toss, cook over medium heat for 10 minutes, divide between plates and serve.

Nutrition: 254 Calories 19g Protein 13g Fat

113. Rosemary Endives

Preparation Time: 18 minutes
Cooking Time: 32 minutes
Servings: 2
Ingredients:

- 2 tbsps. Olive oil
- 1 tsp. dried rosemary
- 2 halved endives
- ¼ tsp. black pepper
- ½ tsp. turmeric powder

Directions:

1. In a baking pan, throw gently endives with the oil and the rest of ingredients, then bake at 400 F for 20 minutes. Divide between plates and serve.

Nutrition: 207 Calories 18g Protein 15g Fat

114. Scallops with Almonds and Mushrooms

Preparation Time: 11 minutes
Cooking Time: 16 minutes
Servings: 4
Ingredients:

- 1 lb. scallops
- 2 tbsps. olive oil
- 4 scallions, chopped
- ½ c. mushrooms, sliced
- 2 tbsps. almonds, chopped
- 1 c. coconut cream

Directions:

1. Warm up a pan with the oil at medium heat; add the scallions and the mushrooms and sauté for 2 minutes.
2. Add the scallops cook over medium heat for 8 minutes more, divide into bowls and serve.

Nutrition: 217 Calories 24g Protein 16g Fat

115. Arugula with Apples and Pine Nuts

Preparation Time: 8 minutes
Cooking Time: 18 minutes
Servings: 4
Ingredients:

- 2 tbsps. extra virgin olive oil
- 2 cloves garlic, slivered
- 2 tbsps. pine nuts
- 1 apple, peeled, cored and chopped
- 10 oz. arugula
- Salt and pepper to taste

Directions:

1. Heat the olive oil in a large skillet or wok over low heat.
2. Cook the pine nuts, garlic and apple. Cook for 3 to 5 minutes until the nuts and garlic

are crispy, and the apple just starts softening.

3. Turn the heat to medium and add the arugula. Stir and cook another 2 to 3 minutes. Season with salt and pepper to taste.

Nutrition: 247 Calories 21g Protein 11g Fat

116. Kale Green Bean Casserole

Preparation Time: 13 minutes
Cooking Time: 46 minutes
Servings: 4
Ingredients:

- 1 ½ c. milk
- 1 c. sour cream
- 1 c. mushrooms, chopped
- 2 c. green beans, chopped
- 2 c. kale, chopped
- ¼ c. capers, drained
- ¼ c. walnuts, crushed

Directions:

1. Preheat the oven to 375 degrees F and lightly grease a casserole dish.
2. Whisk the milk and sour cream together in a large bowl.
3. Add mushrooms, green beans, kale, and capers. Pour into the casserole dish and top with the crushed walnuts.
4. Bake uncovered in the preheated oven until bubbly and browned on top, about 40 minutes.

Nutrition: 271 Calories 20g Protein 14g Fat

117. Rice with Lemon and Arugula

Preparation Time: 14 minutes
Cooking Time: 41 minutes
Servings: 4
Ingredients:

- 1 small red onion, chopped
- 1 c. fresh mushrooms, sliced
- 2 cloves garlic, minced
- 1 tbsp. extra-virgin olive oil
- 3 c. long-grain rice, steamed
- 10 oz. fresh arugula
- 3 tbsps. lemon juice
- ¼ tsp. dill weed
- Salt and pepper to taste

- 1/3 c. feta cheese, crumbled

Directions:

1. Pre-heat and oven to 350°F. In a skillet, sauté the onion, mushrooms and garlic in oil until tender. Stir in the rice, arugula, lemon juice, dill and salt and pepper to taste.
2. Reserve 1 tbsp. cheese and stir the rest into skillet; mix well. Transfer to an 8-in. square baking dish coated with nonstick cooking spray. Sprinkle with reserved cheese. Cover and bake for 25 minutes.
3. Uncover and bake for an additional 5-10 minutes or until heated through and cheese is melted.

Nutrition: 307 Calories 21g Protein 16g Fat

118. Cucumber Bites with Salmon and Avocado

Preparation Time: 22 minutes
Cooking Time: 13 minutes
Servings: 2
Ingredients:

- Black pepper for garnish
- 6 oz. Smoked salmon
- ½ tbsp. Lime juice
- ¼ c. Red onion, chopped
- 1 Cucumber
- 1 Avocado peel and remove the pit

Directions:

1. Peel the cucumber if and then slice it into slices that are about one-fourth inch thick, and then put the slices on a plate for serving.
2. Cream together the lime juice and avocado until they are creamy and smooth. Put a teaspoon of the mashed avocado on each slice of cucumber, and then top the avocado with a slice of the smoked salmon.
3. Use the onions and black pepper to garnish as you like.

Nutrition: 278 Calories 27g Protein 19g Fat

119. Crunchy Green Beans

Preparation Time: 16 minutes
Cooking Time: 27 minutes
Servings: 2
Ingredients:

- 2 tbsps. each chunky-style peanut butter
- 2 tbsps. sherry

- 2 tsps. oyster sauce
- 1 garlic clove, minced
- 1/2 tsp. minced pared ginger root
- 2 c. cooked frozen French-style green beans (hot)

Directions:

1. Using saucepan, boil peanut butter, sherry, oyster sauce, garlic, and ginger.
2. Reduce heat and let simmer, continually stirring until mixture is creamy about 1 minute.
3. Pour peanut butter mixture over hot green beans and serve immediately.

Nutrition: 311 Calories 28g Protein 16g Fat

120. Cottage Cheese and Vegetables

Preparation Time: 9 minutes
Cooking Time: 13 minutes
Servings: 1

Ingredients:

- 6 cherry tomatoes
- ½ c. cottage cheese
- 2 tbsps. chopped scallion (green onion)
- 2 pimiento-stuffed green olives, sliced
- 1 tbsp. chopped fresh parsley (optional)
- Lettuce leaves

Directions:

1. Cut five tomatoes into quarters; reserve remaining tomato for garnish.
2. Mix all ingredients except lettuce and garnish.
3. Arrange salad plate with lettuce leaves, garnish with cheese mixture, and reserved cherry tomato.

Nutrition: 291 Calories 31g Protein 14g Fat

121. The Bell Pepper Fiesta

Preparation Time: 8 minutes
Cooking Time: 10 minutes
Servings: 4

Ingredients:

- 2 tbsps. dill, chopped
- 1 yellow onion, chopped
- 1 lb. multi colored peppers
- 3 tbsps. organic olive oil
- 2 ½ tbsps. white wine vinegar
- Black pepper to taste

Directions:

1. Take a bowl and mix in sweet pepper, onion, dill, pepper, oil, vinegar and toss well.
2. Divide between bowls and serve.

Nutrition: 286 Calories 22g Protein 11g Fat

122. Courgette Risotto

Preparation Time: 14 minutes
Cooking Time: 19 minutes
Servings: 8

Ingredients:

- 2 tbsps. olive oil
- 4 cloves garlic, finely chopped
- 1.5 lb. Rice (Arborio)
- 6 tomatoes, chopped
- 2 tsps. chop rosemary
- 6 courgette, finely diced
- 1 ¼ c. peas, fresh or frozen
- 12 c. hot vegetable stock
- 1 c. chopped
- Salt and ground black pepper to taste

Directions:

1. Situate large, heavy-bottomed pan over medium heat. Add oil.
2. Once heated, cook onion until translucent.
3. Cook the tomatoes until soft. Next, stir in the rice and rosemary. Mix well. Add half the stock and cook until dry. Stir frequently.
4. Add remaining stock and cook for 3-4 minutes.
5. Add courgette and peas and cook until rice is tender.
6. Add salt and pepper to taste.
7. Stir in the basil and let it sit for 5 minutes.
8. Serve warm and enjoy

Nutrition: 267 Calories 27g Protein 14g Fat

123. Potato Bites

Preparation Time: 18 minutes
Cooking Time: 33 minutes
Servings: 4

Ingredients:

- 1 potato
- 2 bacon
- 1 avocado

Directions:

1. Lay out potato slices on a lined baking sheet, grease with cooking oil, bake at 350 degrees F for 20 minutes, place on a

platter, garnish each slice with avocado and crumbled bacon.

Nutrition: 285 Calories 27g Protein 12g Fat

124. Carrots and Cauliflower Spread

Preparation Time: 18 minutes
Cooking Time: 51 minutes
Servings: 4

Ingredients:

- 1 c. carrots, sliced
- 2 c. cauliflower florets
- ½ c. cashews
- 2 ½ c. water
- 1 c. almond milk
- 1 tsp. garlic powder
- ¼ tsp. smoked paprika

Directions:

1. In a small pot, mix the carrots with cauliflower, cashews and water, stir, cover, bring to a boil over medium heat, cook for 40 minutes, drain and transfer to a blender.

2. Add almond milk, garlic powder and paprika, pulse well, divide into small bowls and serve

Nutrition: 291 Calories 28g Protein 14g Fat

125. Italian Veggie Salsa

Preparation Time: 11 minutes
Cooking Time: 21 minutes
Servings: 4

Ingredients:

- 2 red bell peppers, cut into medium wedges
- 3 zucchinis, sliced
- ½ c. garlic, minced
- 2 tbsps. olive oil
- 1 tsp. Italian seasoning

Direction:

1. Warmup a pan with the oil over medium-high heat, cook bell peppers and zucchini for 5 minutes.

2. Add garlic, black pepper and Italian seasoning, toss, cook for 5 minutes more, divide into small cups and serve as a snack.

Nutrition: 278 Calories 21g Protein 17g Fat

126. Cauliflower and Walnut Soup

Preparation Time: 17 minutes
Cooking Time: 21 minutes
Servings: 5
Ingredients:

- 450g (1lb) cauliflower, chopped
- 8 walnut halves, chopped
- 1 red onion, chopped
- 900mls (1½ pints) vegetable stock (broth)
- 100mls (3½ Fl. oz.) double cream (heavy cream)
- ½ teaspoon of turmeric
- 1 tablespoon of olive oil

Directions:
1. Cook olive oil in a saucepan, add the cauliflower and red onion and cook for 4 minutes, stirring continuously.
2. Pour in the stock (broth), bring to the boil and cook for 15 minutes.
3. Stir in the walnuts, double cream, and turmeric.
4. With a food processor, puree the soup until smooth and creamy.
5. Serve into bowls and top off with a dash of chopped walnuts.

Nutrition: 212 Calories 17g Fat 3.3g Protein

127. Celery and Blue Cheese Soup

Preparation Time: 10 minutes
Cooking Time: 30 minutes
Servings: 4
Ingredients:

- 125g (4oz) blue cheese
- 25g (1oz) butter
- 1 head of celery (approx. 650g)
- 1 red onion, chopped
- 900mls (1½ pints) chicken stock (broth)
- 150mls (5fl oz.) single cream

Directions:
1. Bring to heat the butter in a saucepan, add the celery and onion and cook until the vegetables have softened.
2. Pour in the stock, bring to the boil then reduce the heat and simmer for 15 minutes.

3. Pour in the cream and stir in the cheese until it has melted.
4. Serve.

Nutrition: 216 Calories 17g Fat 10g Protein

128. Sweet Potato and Kale Soup

Preparation Time: 11 minutes
Cooking Time: 36 minutes
Servings: 4
Ingredients:

- 1 medium red onion
- 1 garlic clove
- 2 medium carrots
- 1 pound of sweet potatoes
- 1 celery stalk
- 2 tbsp. of extra virgin olive oil
- Chili powder to taste
- 4 cups of vegetable
- ½ pound of kale
- 6 walnuts

Directions:
1. Peel and cut in small cubes the onions, garlic, carrots, sweet potatoes, and celery stalk.
2. Heat the oil in the pan. Add the cubed vegetables and simmer for 3 minutes.
3. Add chili and salt, if needed
4. Add the stock and let the soup simmer for 20 minutes
5. In the meantime, wash and destem the kale.
6. Blanch the kale for about 1 to 2 minutes in boiling salted water
7. Heat up oil in a pan and add the kale. Fry it for 5 minutes.
8. Cut the walnuts
9. Puree the soup with a stab mixer. Add yogurt and chili powder to taste
10. Ladle the soup in 4 bowls and top each bowl with kale and walnuts.

Nutrition: 308 Calories 13g Fat 6.4g Protein

129. Lentil Soup

Preparation Time: 14 minutes
Cooking Time: 70 minutes
Servings: 4
Ingredients:

- 175g (6oz) red lentils
- 1 red onion, chopped
- 1 clove of garlic, chopped
- 2 sticks of celery, chopped
- 2 carrots, chopped
- ½ birds-eye chili
- 1 teaspoon of ground cumin
- 1 teaspoon of ground turmeric
- 1 teaspoon of ground coriander (cilantro)
- 1200mls (2 pints) vegetable stock (broth)
- 2 tablespoons of olive oil
- Sea salt
- Freshly ground black pepper

Directions:
1. Bring to heat the oil in a saucepan and add the onion and cook for 5 minutes.
2. Add in the carrots, lentils, celery, chili, coriander (cilantro), cumin, turmeric, and garlic and cook for 5 minutes.
3. Pour in the stock (broth), bring it to the boil, reduce the heat and simmer for 45 minutes.
4. Puree the soup until smooth.
5. Season with salt and pepper. Serve.

Nutrition: 284 Calories 7.9g Fat 16g Protein

130. Spicy Pumpkin Soup

Preparation Time: 13 minutes
Cooking Time: 47 minutes
Servings: 4

Ingredients:
- 150g (5oz) kale
- 1 butternut squash, peeled, de-seeded and chopped
- 1 red onion, chopped
- 3 bird's-eye chilies, chopped
- 3 cloves of garlic
- 2 teaspoons of turmeric
- 1 teaspoon of ground ginger
- 600mls (1 pint) vegetable stock (broth)
- 2 tablespoons of olive oil

Directions:
1. Prep all the ingredients and cook olive oil in a saucepan, add the chopped butternut squash and onion and cook for 6 minutes until softened.

2. Stir in the kale, garlic, chili, turmeric, and ginger and cook for 2 minutes, stirring constantly.
3. Pour in the vegetable stock (broth) bring it to the boil and cook for 20 minutes.
4. Using a food processor, process until smooth.
5. You can also use a hand blender.
6. Serve on its own or try with a swirl of cream or crème Fraiche. Enjoy.

Nutrition: 249 Calories 8.8g Fat 25g Protein

131. Creamy Broccoli and Kale Soup

Preparation Time: 14 minutes
Cooking Time: 34 minutes
Servings: 4

Ingredients:
- 250g (9oz) broccoli
- 250g (9oz) kale
- 1 potato, peeled and chopped
- 1 red onion, chopped
- 600mls (1 pint) vegetable stock
- 300mls (½ pint) milk
- 1 tablespoon of olive oil
- Sea salt
- Freshly ground black pepper

Directions:
1. Prepare a saucepan, heat the olive oil then add the onion and cook for 5 minutes.
2. Add in the potato, kale, and broccoli and cook for 5 minutes.
3. Pour in the stock (broth) and milk and simmer for 20 minutes.
4. Using a food processor or hand blender, process the soup until smooth and creamy.
5. Season with salt and pepper.
6. Re-heat if necessary and serve.

Nutrition: 165 Calories 5.2g Fat 7.4g Protein

132. Mushroom, Avocado, and Tomato Creamy Soup

Preparation Time: 17 minutes
Cooking Time: 3 hours
Servings: 3

Ingredients:
- 1 yellow onion
- 1 tablespoon of agave nectar
- 1 tablespoon of balsamic vinegar

- 4 tablespoons of extra-virgin olive oil
- 1 teaspoon of olive oil
- 12 ounces mushrooms, sliced
- 1 tomato, chopped
- 1 avocado, pitted, peeled and roughly chopped
- 1 garlic clove, minced
- A pinch of salt and black pepper
- 1½ cups water

Directions:
1. In a bowl, mix mushrooms with agave, vinegar, garlic, salt, pepper, and 3 tablespoons of olive oil.
2. Toss well, then transfer this to your dehydrator and dehydrate the mushrooms for 3 hours.
3. Pour the mushrooms in your blender; add onion, 1 tablespoon oil, tomato, avocado, salt, pepper, and the water.
4. Pulse very well until smooth.
5. Divide into soup bowls, drizzle 1 teaspoon oil on top and serve.

Nutrition: 382 Calories 35g Fat5.5g Protein

133. Creamy Tomato Soup

Preparation Time: 7 minutes
Cooking Time: 13 minutes
Servings: 2

Ingredients:
- 3 sun-dried tomato sliced
- 2 celery stalks, chopped
- 3 big tomatoes, chopped
- ½ teaspoon of powdered onion
- 2 basil springs, chopped
- ½ teaspoon of garlic powder
- 1 small avocado, pitted and peeled
- A pinch of sea salt
- Pinch white pepper

Directions:
1. In your blender, add the tomatoes with celery, onion powder, garlic powder, basil, avocado, salt, pepper, and pulse really well.
2. Add sun-dried tomatoes and blend again until smooth.
3. Divide into soup bowls and serve.

Nutrition: 322 Calories 25g Fat 7g Protein

134. Chard and Lentil Soup

Preparation Time: 11 minutes

Cooking Time: 42 minutes
Servings: 4

Ingredients:
- 1 yellow onion, chopped
- 2 tablespoons olive oil
- 2 carrots, chopped
- 2 garlic cloves, minced
- 1 teaspoon of ground cumin
- ½ teaspoon of ground ginger
- ½ teaspoon of ground turmeric
- ½ teaspoon of red chili flakes
- A pinch of salt and black pepper
- 15 ounces canned tomatoes, chopped
- 1 cup red lentils
- 2 quarts veggie stock
- 1 bunch chard, roughly chopped

Directions:
1. Over medium heat, heat up a pot with the oil.
2. Add the onion and carrot, stir and cook for 7 minutes.
3. Add chili flakes, garlic, cumin, ginger, turmeric, salt, and pepper, stir and cook for 1 more minute.
4. Add tomatoes, stir and cook for another 5 minutes.
5. Add the lentils and stock, stir, bring to a boil, reduce heat to medium-low and simmer for 10 minutes.
6. Add the chard, toss, cook for 5 minutes, ladle into bowls and serve.

Nutrition: 286 Calories 9g Fat 14g Protein

135. Grape Gazpacho

Preparation Time: 7 minutes
Cooking Time: 13 minutes
Servings: 4

Ingredients:
- 1 cup white grapes, seedless and halved
- 1 teaspoon of sesame oil
- 2 cups almond milk, unsweetened
- 1 small cucumber, chopped
- A pinch of salt and white pepper
- 1 tablespoon of chives, chopped for garnish
- Ice cubes for serving

Directions:

1. In your blender, mix grapes with cucumber, almond milk, sesame oil, salt, and pepper.
2. Pulse really well.

Nutrition: 313 Calories 30g Fat3.4g Protein

136. Kale, Apple, and Fennel Soup

Preparation Time: 14 minutes
Cooking Time: 22 minutes
Servings: 4

Ingredients:
- 450g (1lb) kale, chopped
- 200g (7oz) fennel, chopped
- 2 apples, peeled, cored and chopped
- 2 tablespoons of fresh parsley, chopped
- 1 tablespoon of olive oil
- Sea salt
- Freshly ground black pepper

Directions:
1. Bring to heat the olive oil in a saucepan, add the kale and fennel and cook for 5 minutes until the fennel has softened.
2. Stir in the apples and parsley.
3. Cover with hot water, bring it to the boil and simmer for 10 minutes.
4. Blitz until the soup is smooth, using a hand blender or food processor.
5. Season with salt and pepper.

Nutrition: 160 Calories 4g Fat 4g Protein

137. Fresh Onion Soup

Preparation Time: 7 minutes
Cooking Time: 62 minutes
Servings: 4

Ingredients:
- 750g (1¾ lbs.) red onions, thinly sliced
- 50g (2oz) Cheddar cheese, grated (shredded)
- 12g (½ oz.) butter
- 2 teaspoons of flour
- 2 slices whole meal bread
- 900mls (1½ pints) beef stock (broth)
- 1 tablespoon olive oil

Directions:
1. In a large pan, heat and add the olive oil and butter.
2. Add the onions and gently cook on a low heat for 25 minutes, stirring occasionally.

3. Add in the flour and stir well. Pour in the stock (broth) and keep stirring.
4. Boil then decrease the heat and simmer for 30 minutes.
5. Cut the slices of bread into triangles, sprinkle with cheese and place them under a hot grill (broiler) until the cheese has melted.
6. Serve the soup into bowls and add 2 triangles of cheesy toast on top. Enjoy.

Nutrition: 205 Calories 11g Fat 6.4g Protein

138. Creamy Asparagus Soup

Preparation Time: 7 minutes
Cooking Time: 12 minutes
Servings: 2

Ingredients:
- 12 asparagus spears, trimmed
- 1 avocado, pitted and peeled
- A pinch of salt and white pepper
- 1 yellow onion, peeled and chopped
- 3 cups of water

Directions:
1. In your blender, add the mushrooms with asparagus, avocado, onion, water, salt, and pepper.
2. Pulse well, divide into soup bowls, and serve right away. Heat if desired.

Nutrition: 246 Calories 19g Fat 4.6g Protein

139. Mushroom Creamy Soup

Preparation Time: 8 minutes
Cooking Time: 17 minutes
Servings: 2

Ingredients:
- 2 tablespoons of coconut aminos
- 1 tablespoon of lime juice
- A pinch of white pepper
- A pinch of sea salt
- 1 cup white mushrooms
- 1 garlic clove, peeled
- 1 small yellow onion, chopped
- 2 cups cashew milk, unsweetened

Directions:
1. In your blender, mix mushrooms with garlic, onion, cashew milk, salt, pepper, lime juice, and coconut aminos and pulse really well.
2. Divide into soup bowls and serve right away.

Nutrition: 72 Calories 4g Fat 2g Protein

140. Crockpot Senate Bean Soup

Preparation Time: 9 minutes
Cooking Time: 9 hours
Servings: 7

Ingredients:

- 1 lb. small white beans, dry
- 8 cups of water
- 2 cups of ham, diced
- 1 cup of white onion, diced
- 1 cup of celery, chopped
- 2 tablespoons of parsley, chopped
- Salt and pepper to taste
- 1 bay leaf

Directions:

1. Add all ingredients to crockpot.
2. Cover it and cook on low 8 to 10 hours or until beans are tender.

Nutrition: 127 Calories 4.2g Fat 11g Protein

141. Vegetable Omelet

Preparation Time: 7 minutes
Cooking Time: 11 minutes
Servings: 2
Ingredients:

- 4 eggs, preferably
- 1 small onion, chopped
- Pepper to taste
- 2 handfuls fresh kale leaves
- 4 tablespoons olive oil, divided
- 1 medium red bell pepper, chopped
- Salt to taste

Directions:

1. Place a skillet over medium-high flame. Add 2 tablespoons of olive oil. Once heated, cook onion and bell pepper for a couple of minutes. Stir in the kale and cook for another couple of minutes.
2. Turn off the heat. Transfer the vegetable mixture into a bowl.
3. Add eggs into another bowl and beat well.
4. Place the pan over medium flame.
5. Add 1 tablespoon oil and let it heat.
6. Pour half the eggs into the pan. Swirl the pan to spread the egg. When the omelet is slightly cooked, spread half the vegetable mixture on one half of the omelet. Fold the other half of the omelet over the filling.
7. Carefully remove the omelet onto a plate and serve right away.
8. Repeat steps 5 – 7 and make the other omelet.

Nutrition: 90 Calories 5g Fat 8g Protein

142. Kale Stir Fry with Crispy Curried Tofu

Preparation Time: 12 minutes
Cooking Time: 16 minutes
Servings: 4
Ingredients:
For crispy curried tofu:

- 2 blocks (7 ounces each) firm tofu
- 2 tablespoons soy sauce
- 3 teaspoons curry powder
- ½ red cabbage, thinly sliced
- Olive oil as required

For stir-fry:

- 8 large kale leaves
- 2 cloves garlic, peeled, minced
- 4 tablespoons soy sauce
- 2 carrots, thinly sliced
- 2 inches piece fresh ginger, peeled, minced
- 4 portions whole-wheat noodles
- Olive oil, as required

Directions:

1. Combine 1 ½ teaspoons curry powder and soy sauce in a bowl.
2. Stir in the tofu. Make sure that tofu is well coated with the sauce mixture. Cover and set aside for 15 minutes.
3. Follow the directions on the package and cook the noodles.
4. Place 2 pans with a little oil in each, over medium flame on 2 different burners on your stovetop.
5. Add tofu into one pan and cook until golden brown all over. Stir frequently. Remove the tofu with a slotted spoon and place on a plate lined with paper towels.
6. Simultaneously, add ginger and garlic into the other pan and cook for a few seconds until aromatic.
7. Stir in kale and cabbage, cooking until slightly limp.
8. Stir in carrot and soy sauce and cook for a couple of minutes.
9. Divide noodles into 4 plates. Divide the stir fry vegetables over the noodles. Scatter tofu on top and serve right away.

Nutrition: 190 Calories 7g Fat 9g Protein

143. Kale, Pumpkin Seed and Potato One Pot Dinner

Preparation Time: 14 minutes
Cooking Time: 17 minutes
Servings: 8
Ingredients:

- 1-pound potatoes, peeled, cut into bite size cubes
- 2 green bell peppers
- 2 orange bell peppers
- 2 large eggplants, sliced
- 2 large red onions, sliced
- 7 ounces curly kale, sliced

- 10.5 ounces baby spinach
- 4 large carrots, cut into matchsticks
- 1 can (28 ounces) plum tomatoes
- ½ cup olive oil
- 2 vegetable stock cubes
- ¼ cup ground pumpkin seeds
- 2 teaspoons sea salt or to taste

Directions:

1. Blend the plum tomatoes in a blender until smooth.
2. Season eggplant with some salt and immerse in a bowl of hot water for a couple of minutes. Rinse well.
3. Place a Dutch oven over medium flame. Add oil. When the oil is heated, add potatoes and cook for 8 – 10 minutes, stirring occasionally.
4. Stir in the carrots and eggplant and cook for about 2 minutes. Stir in the bell peppers, pumpkin seeds and plum tomatoes. Stir occasionally and cook for about 6 – 7 minutes.
5. Crumble the vegetable stock cubes and add into the pot along with salt to taste. Cook covered, on low heat until the potatoes are fork tender. Stir occasionally.
6. Stir in the kale and cook for 3 – 4 minutes. Remove from heat.
7. Stir in the spinach and keep the pot covered.
8. Serve hot.

Nutrition: 116 Calories 6g Fat 11g Protein

144. Springtime Buckwheat Risotto

Preparation Time: 8 hours
Cooking Time: 23 minutes
Servings: 2

Ingredients:

- ½ cup vegetable stock
- ½ big bunch asparagus, halved, trim the tough ends
- ½ small red onion, finely chopped
- ½ tablespoon dried Italian herbs
- Juice of ½ lemon
- Zest of ½ lemon, grated
- 1 tablespoon nutritional yeast
- Pepper to taste
- 1 cup chopped spinach

- Extra-virgin olive oil, to drizzle
- 1 tablespoon olive oil
- 1 clove garlic, peeled, minced
- 4.4 ounces buckwheat, soaked in water overnight, drained, rinsed
- ½ tablespoon apple cider vinegar
- ¼ cup peas
- 1 cup mixture of fresh parsley, basil and oregano + extra to garnish
- Salt to taste

Directions:

1. Boil stock in a saucepan. Lower the heat and let it simmer.
2. Place a pan over medium flame. Add ½ tablespoon of oil. Once heated, sauté asparagus
3. Take out the asparagus from the pan and place it on a plate.
4. Add ½ tablespoon oil into the pan. Once oil is heated, add onion and garlic and sauté until onion turns translucent.
5. Stir in the buckwheat, apple cider vinegar, dried herbs and lemon juice.
6. Once well, combined, add the simmering stock and mix well. When the stock is absorbed, add a little more stock and repeat this process of adding stock until all of it is added, making sure that the stock is absorbed each time, before adding more stock.
7. When buckwheat is well cooked, add spinach and peas and mix well. Cook for a couple of minutes.
8. Add fresh herbs, nutritional yeast, lemon zest, pepper and salt. Mix well.
9. To serve: Divide risotto into bowls. Place asparagus on top. Trickle some extra-virgin olive oil on top. Garnish with some fresh herbs and serve.

Nutrition: 141 Calories 10g Fat 18g Protein

145. Miso & Sesame Glazed Tofu Stir-Fry

Preparation Time: 23 minutes
Cooking Time: 28 minutes
Servings: 4

Ingredients:

- 4 tablespoons mirin
- 1.1 pounds tofu

- 2 red onions, thinly sliced
- 4 bird's eye chilies
- 4 teaspoons minced ginger
- 8 teaspoons sesame seeds
- 2 cups water
- 8 teaspoons extra-virgin olive oil
- 4 tablespoons brown miso paste
- 2 sticks celery, trimmed, finely chopped
- 2 courgettis, thinly sliced
- 4 cloves garlic, peeled, finely chopped
- 2 ½ cups chopped kale
- 1 cup buckwheat groats or buckwheat noodles
- 4 teaspoons turmeric powder
- 4 teaspoons soy sauce or tamari

Directions:
1. Prep a roasting pan by lining it with parchment paper.
2. Combine miso and mirin in a large bowl. Add tofu and stir until tofu is well coated with the mixture. Let it marinate for 20 minutes.
3. Transfer the tofu into the roasting pan and spread it evenly. Scatter sesame seeds over the tofu.
4. Bake tofu in an oven preheated to 400° F, for about 15 to 20 minutes brown.
5. Meanwhile, boil water in a saucepan with turmeric and salt, over high flame.
6. As the water begins to boil, stir in the buckwheat and cook until it comes to a boil.
7. Lower the heat and cook covered until dry. Turn off the heat and set aside.
8. If you are using buckwheat noodles, cook the noodles following the directions on the package and add turmeric in step 11.
9. 5 minutes before removing the tofu from the oven, place a pan over medium – high flame.
10. Add oil and let it heat. Add onion and cook for a minute.
11. Stir in ginger, garlic, celery, courgette and bird's eye chili and mix well. Once the mixture turns fragrant (in about a minute), lower the flame to medium flame. Cook until vegetables are tender.
12. Stir in kale and tamari and cook until kale wilts.
13. Serve tofu with vegetables and buckwheat.

Nutrition: 157 Calories 13g Fat 19g Protein

146. Veggie Sandwich

Preparation Time: 17 minutes
Cooking Time: 0 minutes
Servings: 2
Ingredients:
- 4 slices whole grain bread
- 4 Romaine lettuce leaves
- ½ cup thinly sliced red bell peppers
- 1 medium red onion
- 1 small cucumber, thinly sliced
- 4 teaspoons pumpkin seeds
- Salt to taste
- 4 tablespoons hummus
- ½ cup microgreens
- 2 tablespoons shredded carrots
- ½ large apple, cored, thinly sliced
- 4 teaspoons pumpkin seeds
- Pepper to taste

Directions:
1. Smear hummus on one side of each of the bread slices.
2. Place 2 lettuce leaves on 2 of the bread slices.
3. Place onion slices, cucumber slices, red bell pepper slices and apple over the lettuce. Scatter microgreens, carrots and pumpkin seeds. Place a lettuce leaf on top of each stack.
4. Cover with the remaining 2 bread slices, with the hummus side facing down.

Nutrition: 110 Calories 8g Fat 12g Protein

147. Ricotta Sandwiches with Walnut-Parsley Pesto

Preparation Time: 22 minutes
Cooking Time: 28 minutes
Servings: 4
Ingredients:
For carrots:
- 2 cups thinly sliced carrots
- tablespoon maple syrup
- 4 tablespoons olive oil
- Salt to taste
For ricotta:

- 2 cups ricotta
- Salt to taste
- 1 teaspoon grated lemon zest
- Chili flakes, to taste

For vinaigrette:

- ½ cup olive oil
- ½ cup canola oil
- ½ cup maple syrup
- ½ cup sherry vinegar
- 2 small shallots, finely minced

For walnut parsley pesto:

- 2 bunches parsley
- 2 cups parmesan cheese
- 2 tablespoons lemon juice
- 2/3 cup walnuts, toast if necessary
- Olive oil, as required
- Salt to taste

Directions:

1. To roast carrots: Combine carrots, salt, maple syrup and oil on a baking sheet lined with parchment paper and spread it evenly, in a single layer.
2. Bake carrots in an oven preheated to 360° F, for about 25 to 30 minutes or until tender.
3. For ricotta: Combine lemon zest, ricotta, chili flakes and salt in a bowl. Cover and set aside in the refrigerator until use.
4. For pesto: add walnuts, lemon juice and parsley into the food processor bowl and process until well combined.
5. Using food processor running, fill oil in a thin drizzle until smooth and the consistency you desire is achieved.
6. Pour into a bowl and refrigerate until use.
7. For vinaigrette: Add vinegar, maple syrup, oil and shallot in a small glass jar. Fasten the lid and shake the jar vigorously until well combined. Refrigerate until use.
8. To serve: Toast the bread slices to the desired doneness.
9. Add kale into a bowl and pour required amount of dressing over it. Refrigerate the remaining and use in some salads.
10. Spread pesto on 4 of the bread slices and set it aside.

11. Spread a generous amount of ricotta on the other 4 slices of bread. Place carrot slices over it. Spread kale over the carrot slices.
12. Cover with the remaining bread slices, with the pesto side facing down.
13. Cut into desired shape and serve.

Nutrition: 170 Calories 14g Fat 21g Protein

148. Squash and Kale Gratin Casserole

Preparation Time: 16 minutes
Cooking Time: 23 minutes
Servings: 4
Ingredients:

- 2 cups thinly sliced butternut squash
- 1 teaspoon olive oil
- 4 cups roughly chopped kale
- ½ cup roughly chopped red onion
- ¼ cup grated gruyere cheese
- A pinch ground nutmegs
- 3 cloves garlic, minced
- Kosher salt to taste
- 1/3 cup whole milk
- Pepper to taste
- 6 tablespoons water or more if required
- ¼ teaspoon ground cumin
- A pinch cayenne peppers
- 1 tablespoon cornstarch or all-purpose flour
- ½ cup whole-wheat panko breadcrumbs
- ½ teaspoon butter

Directions:

1. Prepare a small casserole dish by spraying some cooking spray.
2. Place a nonstick pan over medium-high flame. Add oil. Once hot, sauté onion and garlic and cook until golden. Add kale and cook until it wilts. Turn off the heat.
3. Add cornstarch and a tablespoon of milk in a bowl. Pour remaining milk into a saucepan. Place the saucepan over low heat. When the milk is heated, add the flour mixture and stir constantly until thick.
4. Stir in cheese, salt and all the spices. Cook until the cheese melts. Turn off the heat. Pour the sauce into the pan of kale and mix well.

5. Place a layer of squash slices in the casserole dish. Spread half the kale mixture over the squash.
6. Repeat the previous step once more.
7. Sprinkle breadcrumbs on top. Keep the dish covered with foil.
8. Bake at 350° F, for 34 minutes.
9. Take out from the oven and cool before serving.

Nutrition: 116 Calories 8g Fat 16g Protein

149. Three-Bean Chili with Spring Pesto

Preparation Time: 12 minutes
Cooking Time: 17 minutes
Servings: 8
Ingredients:

- ½ cup + 2 tablespoons extra- virgin olive oil, divided
- 2 carrots, diced
- Pepper to taste
- 1 large red onion, chopped
- 2 cans (15.5 ounces each) diced tomatoes with its liquid
- 2 cans (15.5 ounces each) chickpeas, rinsed, drained
- 2 cans (15.5 ounces each) kidney beans, rinsed, drained
- 2 cans (15.5 ounces each) cannellini beans, rinsed, drained
- 6 tablespoons chopped pine nuts
- 2 small cloves garlic, peeled, minced
- ½ cup fresh flat leaf parsley, chopped
- Salt to taste
- 4 cups water
- Crusty bread to serve (optional)

Directions:
1. Place a soup pot over medium-high flame. Add 2 tablespoons oil and wait until it is heated.
2. Stir in the onions and carrots and sauté until onions are translucent.
3. Add tomatoes, water, salt, pepper, chickpeas, kidney beans and cannellini beans and stir. Heat thoroughly.
4. To make spring pesto: In a small bowl, mix garlic, ½ cup oil, salt, pepper, pine nuts and parsley.

5. Serve soup in bowls. Divide the spring pesto among the bowls and serve with crusty bread if desired.

Nutrition: 117 Calories 11g Fat 17g Protein

150. Apple Glazed Vegetable & Edamame Stir-Fry

Preparation Time: 13 minutes
Cooking Time: 32 minutes
Servings: 8
Ingredients:

- 8 cups cubed vegetables of your choice
- 1 large red onion
- 1 cup water
- 1 teaspoon Old Bay seasoning
- ½ cup brown (optional)
- 1 cup applesauce
- 2 teaspoons ground ginger
- 6 tablespoons rice wine vinegar or apple cider vinegar
- 4 tablespoons soy sauce or hoisin sauce
- 1 cup cooked edamame beans
- Salt to taste
- ½ teaspoon red pepper flakes
- 1 teaspoon minced garlic
- Pepper to taste
- Cooking spray

Directions:
1. Place a large nonstick pan or wok over high flame and let the pan heat. Grease the pan by spraying some cooking spray.
2. Sauté onion and garlic. Add all the vegetables except edamame and mix well. Cook covered, until tender.
3. Add water, seasonings, spices, applesauce, vinegar and soy sauce into a bowl and stir. Pour into the pan and mix until well coated.
4. Lower the heat to medium-low and cook until tender.
5. Add edamame and mix well. Heat thoroughly and serve.

Nutrition: 119 Calories 12g Fat 22g Protein

151. Kale, Edamame and Tofu Curry

Preparation Time: 18 minutes
Cooking Time: 21 minutes
Servings: 8

Ingredients:

- 2 tablespoons olive oil
- 8 cloves garlic, peeled, grated
- 2 bird's eye chilies, deseeded, thinly sliced
- ½ teaspoon cayenne pepper
- 1 teaspoon ground cumin
- 1 teaspoon turmeric powder
- 2 teaspoons paprika
- 2 teaspoons salt or to taste
- 1.1 pounds dry red lentils, rinsed
- 3.5 ounces frozen edamame beans
- 4 tomatoes, chopped
- 2 bunches kale, discard hard stems and ribs, torn
- 8 cups boiling water
- 14 ounces firm tofu, cubed
- Juice of 2 limes

Directions:

1. Place a heavy pot over medium-low flame. Add oil. Once hot, cook onions. Stir in ginger, garlic and chili and cook for a few seconds until aromatic.
2. Stir in the spices and salt. Cook for a few more seconds and add red lentils.
3. Add boiling water and cook for 10 minutes. Lower the heat and cook covered until lentils are tender.
4. Stir in edamame, tomatoes and tofu. Cook until tomatoes are soft. Stir in lime juice and kale and cook until kale wilts.
5. Serve hot over hot cooked rice or quinoa or buckwheat.

Nutrition: 108 Calories 7g Fat 13g Protein

152. Shirataki Noodles with Kale and Chickpeas

Preparation Time: 13 minutes
Cooking Time: 11 minutes
Servings: 2

Ingredients:

- 1 tablespoon extra-virgin olive oil
- ½ large bunch kale, discard hard stems and ribs
- 1 package (8 ounces) shirataki noodles
- Salt to taste
- 2 cloves garlic, peeled, minced
- Freshly ground pepper to taste

- ½ can (15 ounces can) chickpeas, rinsed, drained
- 2 ounces shiitake mushrooms, thickly sliced
- 2 tablespoons chopped parsley
- ¼ cup marinara sauce

Directions:

1. Situate cast iron skillet over medium flame. Add oil and let it heat. Once heated, sauté garlic
2. Cook kale for a few minutes.
3. Stir in chickpeas, mushrooms, shirataki noodles and marinara sauce and heat thoroughly. Add salt and pepper and toss well.
4. Sprinkle parsley on top and serve.

Nutrition: 106 Calories 9g Fat 14g Protein

153. Buckwheat Granola

Preparation Time: 14 minutes
Cooking Time: 21 minutes
Servings: 9

Ingredients:

For granola:

- ¾ cup buckwheat groats
- ½ cup chopped walnuts
- ¾ cup gluten-free rolled oats
- ¼ cup unsweetened coconut flakes
- 1 ½ tablespoons coconut sugar
- ½ teaspoon ground cinnamon
- ¼ cup maple syrup or more to taste
- 3 tablespoons dried blueberries
- 1 tablespoon chia seeds
- ¼ teaspoon sea salt
- 2 tablespoons coconut oil or avocado oil or olive oil
- 1 ½ tablespoons nut butter or seed butter (optional)

Directions:

1. Combine buckwheat groats, coconut, coconut sugar, cinnamon, oats, chia seeds and salt in a bowl.
2. Heat oil and maple syrup over medium flame, until well combined and smooth.
3. Stir in nut butter if using. Put off the heat and pour over the buckwheat mixture.
4. Stir until well combined.
5. Transfer the mixture on a baking sheet and spread it evenly.

6. Bake in an oven preheated to 325° F until nice and aromatic and golden brown, about 20 – 25 minutes. Stir after about 10 – 12 minutes of baking.
7. Cool for a few minutes. Add blueberries if using and stir. If you want to add chocolate, let it cool to room temperature before adding the chocolate.
8. Once cooled, transfer into an airtight container. It can last for about 2 weeks.
9. Serving it with fruits and milk will make it a filling breakfast.

Nutrition: 127 Calories 7g Fat 16g Protein

154. Sirtfood Bites

Preparation Time: 13 minutes
Cooking Time: 0 minutes
Servings: 9

Ingredients:

- ½ cup walnuts
- 4.5 ounces medjool dates, pitted
- ½ tablespoon turmeric powder
- ½ teaspoon vanilla extract
- ½ ounce dark chocolate, chopped
- ½ tablespoon cocoa powder
- ½ tablespoon extra-virgin olive oil
- ½ - 1 tablespoon water

Directions:

1. Add walnuts and dark chocolate into the food processor bowl and pulse until finely powdered.

2. Add dates, turmeric powder, vanilla, cocoa and oil and process until well incorporated.
3. If the mixture sticks together and doesn't crumble, transfer the mixture into a bowl. If not, add ½ tablespoon water and process until well combined.
4. Divide the mixture into 8 – 10 equal portions and shape into balls.

Nutrition: 120 Calories 9g Fat 12g Protein

155. Dark Chocolate Cherry Energy Bites

Preparation Time: 8 minutes
Cooking Time: 27 minutes
Servings: 7

Ingredients:

- ½ cup almonds
- ¼ cup dried cherries
- 1/8 teaspoon ground cinnamon
- ¼ cup dark chocolate morsels
- 1 cup pitted dates

Directions:

1. Situate almonds in the food processor and process until chopped into slightly smaller pieces.
2. Add chocolate, cherries, dates, salt and cinnamon and process until the texture you desire is achieved.
3. Transfer into a bowl. Divide the mixture into 7 – 8 equal portions and shape into balls.

Nutrition: 111 Calories 3g Fat 9g Protein

156. Eggplant Salsa

Preparation Time: 11 minutes
Cooking Time: 13 minutes
Servings: 4
Ingredients:

- 1 ½ cups tomatoes, chopped
- 3 cups eggplant, cubed
- A drizzle of olive oil
- 2 tsp. capers
- 6 oz. green olives, pitted and sliced
- 4 garlic cloves, minced
- 2 tsp. balsamic vinegar
- 1 tbsp. basil, chopped
- Black pepper to the taste

Directions:

1. Heat a pan with the oil over medium-high heat, add eggplant, stir and cook for 5 minutes.
2. Add tomatoes, capers, olives, garlic, vinegar, basil, and black pepper, toss, cook for 5 minutes more, divide into small cups and serve cold.

Nutrition: 120 Calories 6g Fat 7g Protein

157. Mung Beans Salad

Preparation Time: 13 minutes
Cooking Time: 0 minute
Servings: 6
Ingredients:

- 2 cups tomatoes, chopped
- 2 cups cucumber, chopped
- 3 cups mixed greens
- 2 cups mung beans, sprouted
- 2 cups clover sprouts
- For the salad dressing:
- 1 tbsp. cumin, ground
- 1 cup dill, chopped
- 4 tbsp. lemon juice
- 1 avocado, pitted, peeled and roughly chopped
- 1 cucumber, roughly chopped

Directions:

1. In a salad bowl, mix tomatoes with 2 cups cucumber, greens, clover, and mung sprouts.

2. In your blender, mix cumin with dill, lemon juice, one cucumber, and avocado, blend well
3. Add the blend to your salad, toss well and serve as a snack

Nutrition: 120 Calories 1g Carbohydrates 6g Protein

158. Sprouts and Apples Salad

Preparation Time: 13 minutes
Cooking Time: 0 minute
Servings: 4
Ingredients:

- 1 lb. Brussels sprouts, shredded
- 1 cup walnuts, chopped
- 1 apple, cored and cubed
- 1 red onion, chopped

For dressing:

- 3 tbsp. red vinegar
- 1 tbsp. mustard
- ½ cup olive oil
- 1 garlic clove, minced
- Black pepper to the taste

Directions:

1. In a salad bowl, mix sprouts with apple, onion and walnuts.
2. In another bowl, mix vinegar with mustard, oil, garlic, and pepper, whisk well, add this to your salad, toss well and serve.

Nutrition: 120 Calories 2g Fat 6g Protein

159. Salsa Verde

Preparation Time: 12 minutes
Cooking Time: 0 minute
Servings: 4
Ingredients:

- ½ cup fresh parsley, finely chopped
- 3 tbsp. fresh basil or fresh cilantro, finely chopped
- 2 cloves garlic, crushed
- ¾ cup olive oil
- 2 tbsp. small capers
- Juice from ½ a lemon
- ½ tsp. ground black pepper
- 1 tsp. sea salt

Directions:

1. Situate all of the ingredients to a deep bowl and blend with an immersion blender until desired consistency.
2. Chill in the refrigerator for up to 4-5 days or in the freezer.

Nutrition: 323 Calories 37g Fat 1g Protein

160. Dijon Celery Salad

Preparation Time: 16 minutes
Cooking Time: 0 minute
Servings: 4

Ingredients:

- 5 tsp. stevia
- ½ cup lemon juice
- 1/3 cup Dijon mustard
- 2/3 cup olive oil
- Black pepper to taste
- 2 apples, cored, peeled and cubed
- 1 bunch celery and leaves, roughly chopped
- ¾ cup walnuts, chopped

Directions:

1. In a salad bowl, mix celery and its leaves with apple pieces and walnuts.
2. Add black pepper, lemon juice, mustard, stevia, and olive oil, whisk well, add to your salad, toss, divide into small cups and serve as a snack.

Nutrition: 125 Calories 2g Fat 7g Protein

161. Cabbage Slaw

Preparation Time: 14 minutes
Cooking Time: 0 minute
Servings: 4

Ingredients:

- ½ cup red bell pepper
- 1 carrot, grated
- 4 cups Napa cabbage, shredded
- 3 green onions, chopped
- 1 tbsp. olive oil
- 2 tsp. Ginger, grated
- ½ tsp. red pepper flakes, crushed
- 3 tbsp. balsamic vinegar
- 1 tbsp. coconut aminos
- 3 tbsp. low-Fat - peanut butter

Directions:

1. In a salad bowl, mix bell pepper with carrot, cabbage, and onions and toss.

2. Add oil, ginger, pepper flakes, vinegar, aminos, and peanut butter, toss, divide into small cups and serve.

Nutrition: 160 Calories 10g Fat 5g Protein

162. Tomatoes and Corn Salad

Preparation Time: 7 minutes
Cooking Time: 0 minute
Servings: 4

Ingredients:

- 2 cups of corn
- 1 tbsp. rosemary
- 1 tbsp. vinegar
- 2 tbsps. chopped mint
- 1 lb. Sliced tomatoes
- ¼ tsp. black pepper
- 2 tbsps. olive oil

Directions:

1. In a salad bowl, combine the tomatoes with the corn and the other ingredients, toss and serve.

Nutrition: 230 Calories 7.2g Fat 4g Protein

163. Apples and Cabbage Salad

Preparation Time: 8 minutes
Cooking Time: 0 minute
Servings: 4

Ingredients:

- 2 cored and cubed green apples
- 2 tbsps. Balsamic vinegar
- ½ tsp. caraway seeds
- 2 tbsps. olive oil
- Black pepper to taste
- 1 shredded red cabbage head

Directions:

1. Incorporate cabbage with the apples and the other ingredients, toss then serve.

Nutrition: 165 Calories 7.4g Fat 2.6g Protein

164. Salmon and Shrimp Salad

Preparation Time: 9 minutes
Cooking Time: 0 minute
Servings: 4

Ingredients:

- 1 cup smoked salmon, boneless and flaked
- 1 cup shrimp, peeled, deveined and cooked
- ½ cup baby arugula
- 1 tbsp. lemon juice
- 2 spring onions, chopped

- 1 tbsp. olive oil

Directions:
1. In a salad bowl, combine the salmon with the shrimp and the other ingredients, toss and serve.

Nutrition: 210 Calories 6g Fat 12g Protein

165. Kale & Raspberry Salad

Preparation Time: 14 minutes
Cooking Time: 0 minute
Servings: 2

Ingredients:
Salad
- 3 cups fresh baby kale
- ½ cup fresh raspberries
- ¼ cup walnuts, chopped

Dressing
- 1 tbsp. extra-virgin olive oil
- 1 tbsp. apple cider vinegar
- ½ tsp. pure maple syrup
- Salt and ground black pepper, to taste

Directions:
1. For the salad: in a bowl, situate all ingredients and mix.
2. For the dressing: place all ingredients in another bowl and beat until well combined.
3. Place dressing on top of the salad and toss to coat thoroughly.
4. Serve immediately.

Nutrition: 228 Calories 16.4g Fat 7.1g Protein

166. Arugula & Berries Salad

Preparation Time: 12 minutes
Cooking Time: 0 minute
Servings: 4

Ingredients:
- 1 cup fresh strawberries
- ½ cup fresh blackberries
- ½ cup fresh blueberries
- ½ cup fresh raspberries
- 6 cups fresh arugula
- 2 tbsp. extra-virgin olive oil
- Salt and ground black pepper, to taste

Directions:
1. Toss all the ingredients to coat thoroughly.
2. Serve immediately.

Nutrition: 105 Calories 7.6g Fat 1.6g Protein

167. Nutty Green Beans

Preparation Time: 12 minutes

Cooking Time: 8 minutes
Servings: 2

Ingredients:
- 2 tbsp. each chunky-style peanut butter
- 2 tbsp sherry
- 2 tsp. oyster sauce
- 1 garlic clove, minced
- 1/2 tsp. minced pared ginger root
- 2 cups cooked frozen French-style green beans (hot)

Directions:
1. With a small saucepan, mix peanut butter, sherry, oyster sauce, garlic, and ginger; then boil.
2. Reduce heat and let simmer, continually stirring until mixture Is creamy about 1 minute.
3. Pour peanut butter mixture over hot green beans and serve immediately.

Nutrition: 157 Calories 8g Fat 7g Protein

168. Vegetable-Cottage Cheese

Preparation Time: 12 minutes
Cooking Time: 0 minute
Servings: 1

Ingredients:
- 6 cherry tomatoes
- ½ cup cottage cheese
- 2 tbsp. chopped scallion (green onion)
- 2 pimiento-stuffed green olives, sliced
- 1 tbsp. chopped fresh parsley (optional)
- Lettuce leaves

Directions:
1. Cut five tomatoes into quarters; reserve remaining tomato for garnish.
2. Incorporate all ingredients except lettuce and garnish.
3. Situate salad plate with lettuce leaves, drizzle with cheese mixture, and cherry tomato.

Nutrition: 187 Calories 8g Fat 20g Protein

169. Grilled Asparagus with Caper Vinaigrette

Preparation Time: 16 minutes
Cooking Time: 3 minutes
Servings: 6

Ingredients:

- 1 ½ lb. asparagus spears, trimmed
- 2 tsp. caper, coarsely chopped
- 1 tbsp. red wine vinegar
- 1 garlic clove, minced
- 3 tbsp. Extra virgin olive oil
- ¼ cup small basil leaves
- ½ tsp. Dijon mustard
- Cooking spray
- ½ tsp. Kosher salt, divided
- ¼ tsp. ground black pepper

Directions:
1. Preheat grill to medium-high heat.
2. Place asparagus in a shallow dish.
3. Add 1 tbsp: oil and ¼ tsp. Salt, tossing well to coat. Situate asparagus on grill rack coated with cooking spray.
4. Grill for 4 minutes turning after 2 minutes.
5. Combine remaining ¼ tsp: salt, vinegar, mustard, and garlic.
6. Stir with a whisk. Slowly pour the remaining 2 tbsp. of oil into vinegar mixture, continually stirring with a whisk. Stir in capers.
7. Arrange asparagus on a serving platter.
8. Drizzle with vinaigrette and sprinkle with basil.

Nutrition: 89 Calories 6.9g Fat 2.8g Protein

170. Thyme Mushrooms

Preparation Time: 14 minutes
Cooking Time: 27 minutes
Servings: 2
Ingredients:
- 1 tbsp. chopped thyme
- 2 tbsps. olive oil
- 2 tbsps. chopped parsley
- 4 minced garlic cloves
- Salt and black pepper to taste
- 2 lbs. halved white mushrooms

Directions:
1. With a baking pan, incorporate mushrooms with the garlic and the other ingredients, and cook at 400F for 30 minutes.
2. Divide between plates and serve.

Nutrition: 251 Calories 9.3g Fat 6g Protein

171. Arugula Salad with Italian Dressing

Preparation Time: 14 minutes
Cooking Time: 0 minute
Serving: 1
Ingredients:
- 2 cups of arugula
- 1 cup of shredded cabbage

Italian dressing
- Cayenne pepper (optional)
- Few sprigs of parsley
- 2 Tbsp. chopped red onions

Direction:
1. Mix all the dressing ingredients then pour it over the mixed vegetables.

Nutrition: 241 Calories 9g Fat 4g Protein

172. Cucumber, Parsley, Buckwheat Tabbouleh

Preparation Time: 13 minutes
Cooking Time: 0 minute
Serving: 2
Ingredients
- 1 cup cooked buckwheat mixed with 1 tbsp. sesame seeds
- 1/2 cup chopped tomato and green pepper
- 1 cup chopped cucumber
- 1/2 cup chopped parsley

Dressing:
- 1 tbsp. olive oil
- 1 tbsp. fresh lemon juice
- pinch of black pepper
- pinch of sea salt

Direction:
1. Mix all ingredients.

Nutrition: 211 Calories 4g Fat 8g Protein

173. Walnuts, Buckwheat, Strawberries & Arugula Salad

Preparation Time: 19 minutes
Cooking Time: 0 minute
Serving: 2
Ingredients
- 1 cup cooked buckwheat mixed with 1 tbsp. pumpkin seeds
- 1/2 cup chopped walnuts
- 1 cup chopped arugula

- 1/2 cup sliced red peppers

Dressing:
- 1 tbsp. olive oil
- 1 tbsp. fresh lemon juice
- pinch of black pepper
- pinch of sea salt

Direction:
1. Mix all ingredients.

Nutrition: 304 Calories 7g Fat 9g Protein

174. Strawberry Arugula Salad

Preparation Time: 8 minutes
Cooking Time: 0 minute
Serving: 5

Ingredients
- 2 tbsp. black sesame seeds
- 1 tbsp. poppy seeds
- 1/2 cup olive oil
- 1/4 cup lemon juice
- 1/4 tsp. paprika
- 1 bag fresh arugula - chopped, washed and dried
- 1-quart strawberries, sliced

Direction:
1. Whisk together the sesame seeds, olive oil, poppy seeds, paprika, lemon juice and onion. Refrigerate.
2. In a large bowl, combine arugula, strawberries and walnuts. Pour dressing over salad. Toss and refrigerate 15 minutes before serving.

Nutrition: 119Calories 5g Fat 10gProtein

175. Carrot, Buckwheat, Tomato & Arugula Salad in a Jar

Preparation Time: 16 minutes
Cooking Time: 0 minute
Serving: 2

Ingredients
- 1/2 cup sunflower seeds
- 1/2 cup carrots
- 1/2 cup of shredded cabbage
- 1/2 cup of tomatoes
- 1 cup cooked buckwheat mixed with 1 tbsp. chia seeds
- 1 cup arugula

Dressing:

- 1 tbsp. olive oil
- 1 tbsp. fresh lemon juice and pinch of sea salt

Direction:
1. Put ingredients in this order: dressing, sunflower seeds, carrots, cabbage, tomatoes, buckwheat and arugula.

Nutrition: 201 Calories 3g Fat 6g Protein

176. Chickpeas, Onion, Tomato & Parsley Salad in a Jar

Preparation Time: 9 minutes
Cooking Time: 0 minute
Serving: 2

Ingredients
- 1 cup cooked chickpeas
- 1/2 cup chopped tomatoes
- 1/2 of a small onion, chopped
- 1 tbsp. chia seeds
- 1 Tbsp. chopped parsley

Dressing:
- 1 tbsp. olive oil and 1 tbsp. of Chlorella.
- 1 tbsp. fresh lemon juice and pinch of sea salt

Direction:
1. Put ingredients in this order: dressing, tomatoes, chickpeas, onions and parsley.

Nutrition: 253 Calories 8g Fat 5g Protein

177. Arugula, Carrot, Corn & Spinach Salad in a Jar

Preparation Time: 11 minutes
Cooking Time: 0 minute
Serving: 2

Ingredients
- 1 cup corn
- 1 cup tomatoes
- 1/2 cup of julienned carrot
- 1/2 cup arugula

Dressing:
- 1 tbsp. olive oil
- 2 Tbsp. Greek Yogurt
- 1 tbsp. fresh lemon juice and pinch of sea salt

Direction:
1. Put ingredients in this order: dressing, tomatoes, corn, carrots, and arugula.

Nutrition: 247 Calories 8.3g Fat 4g Protein

178. Shrimp, Cucumber & Arugula Salad in a Jar

Preparation Time: 9 minutes
Cooking Time: 0 minute
Serving: 2

Ingredients

- 1 cup cooked shrimp
- 1/2 cup of cucumber
- 1 cup of arugula

Dressing:

- 1 tbsp. olive oil
- 1 tbsp. fresh lemon juice and pinch of sea salt

Direction:

1. Put ingredients in this order: dressing, cucumber, shrimp and arugula.

Nutrition: 207 Calories 6g Fat 2g Protein

179. Broccoli, Buckwheat, Shrimps & Scallops Salad

Preparation Time: 11 minutes
Cooking Time: 0 minute
Serving: 2

Ingredients

- 1 cup cooked buckwheat mixed with 1 tbsp. ground flax seeds
- 1 cup stir fried broccoli
- 1/2 cup green peas
- 1 cup stir fried shrimp and scallops

Dressing:

- 1 tbsp. olive oil
- 1 tbsp. fresh lemon juice
- pinch of black pepper
- pinch of sea salt

Direction:

1. Mix all ingredients.

Nutrition: 211 Calories 7g Fat 5g Protein

180. Tuna, Tomato, Arugula & Eggs Salad

Preparation Time: 13 minutes
Cooking Time: 0 minute
Serving: 2

Ingredients

- 1 cup tuna chunks
- 1/2 cup chopped tomato
- 2 halved eggs
- 1 cup Arugula

- 1/2 cup sliced yellow peppers

Dressing:

- 1 tbsp. olive oil
- 1 tbsp. fresh lemon juice
- pinch of black pepper
- pinch of sea salt

Direction:

1. Mix all ingredients.

Nutrition: 236 Calories 6g Fat 11g Protein

181. Avocado, Tomato, Arugula Salad

Preparation Time: 13 minutes
Cooking Time: 0 minute
Serving: 2

Ingredients

- 1 cup Orange tomatoes
- 1/2 cup chopped avocado
- 1/2 cup arugula radish
- 1 cup Red Tomatoes

Dressing:

- 1 tbsp. olive oil
- 1 tbsp. fresh lemon juice
- pinch of black pepper
- pinch of sea salt

Direction:

1. Mix all ingredients.

Nutrition: 119 Calories 5g Fat 10g Protein

182. Chicken, Tomato, Arugula & Cucumber Salad

Preparation Time: 7 minutes
Cooking Time: 0 minute
Serving: 2

Ingredients

- 1 cup grilled chicken
- 1/2 cup chopped cucumber
- 1/2 cup chopped tomato
- 1 cup arugula

Dressing:

- 1 tbsp. olive oil or avocado oil
- 1 tbsp. fresh lemon juice
- pinch of black pepper
- pinch of sea salt

Direction:

1. Mix all ingredients.

Nutrition: 207 Calories 6g Fat 4g Protein

183. Artichoke, Arugula & Lamb Salad

Preparation Time: 6 minutes
Cooking Time: 22 minutes
Serving: 2

Ingredients

- 1 cup sliced roasted lamb
- 1 cup roasted quartered artichoke hearts.
- 1/2 cup chopped red onion
- 1 cup Arugula

Dressing:

- 1 tbsp. olive oil or avocado oil
- 1 tbsp. fresh lemon juice
- pinch of black pepper
- pinch of sea salt

Direction:

1. Roast artichoke hearts for 20 minutes in the oven.
2. Mix all ingredients.

Nutrition: 207 Calories 11g Fat 7g Protein

184. Kale, Grilled Shrimp & Eggs Salad

Preparation Time: 16 minutes
Cooking Time: 8 minutes
Serving: 2

Ingredients

- 1 1/2 cup grilled shrimp
- 1 cup chopped kale leaves
- 3 hard boiled quartered eggs

Dressing:

- 1 tbsp. olive oil or avocado oil
- 1 tbsp. fresh lemon juice
- pinch of black pepper
- pinch of sea salt

Direction:

1. Grill the shrimps for 6 minutes on both sides
2. Mix all ingredients.

Nutrition: 247Calories 12g Fat 10g Protein

185. Kale, Almond & Avocado Salad

Preparation Time: 17 minutes
Cooking Time: 0 minute
Serving: 2

Ingredients

- 1 ½ cup chopped kale
- 1/2 cup almonds
- 2 chopped avocados

Dressing:

- 1 tbsp. olive oil or avocado oil
- 1 tbsp. fresh lemon juice

Direction:

1. Mix all ingredients and season well. Serve

Nutrition: 247 Calories 13g Fat 7g Protein

186. Chocolate Mousse

Preparation Time: 24 minutes
Cooking Time: 0 minute
Serving: 2

Ingredients

- 75mls (3fl oz) double cream (heavy cream)
- 50g (2oz) cream cheese
- 25g (1oz) unsalted butter
- 1 tablespoon 100% cocoa powder
- 1 teaspoon stevia (or to taste)

Direction

1. Place the butter and stevia into a bowl and mix until smooth. Stir in the cream cheese and cocoa powder and mix thoroughly. Whip the cream until thick and fold it into the mixture.
2. Spoon the mousse into long stemmed glasses or serving bowls. Chill before serving.

Nutrition: 200 Calories 7g Protein 6g Fat

187. Chocolate & Hazelnut Clusters

Preparation Time: 31 minutes
Cooking Time: 0 minutes
Serving: 8

Ingredients

- 125g (4oz) dark chocolate (min 70% cocoa)
- 125g (4oz) dates, chopped
- 50g (2oz) hazelnuts, chopped

Direction:

1. Situate chocolate into a bowl and put the bowl over a saucepan of simmering water. Once the chocolate has melted, remove it from the heat.
2. Stir in the hazelnuts and dates. Spoon the mixture into small paper cases and allow it to set. Serve and enjoy.

Nutrition: 58 Calories 4g Protein 2g Fat

188. Green Tea Tropical Fruit Salad

Preparation Time: 19 minutes
Cooking Time: 0 minute
Serving: 4

Ingredients

- 1 green tea teabag
- 225mls (8fl oz) hot water
- 225g (8oz) blueberries
- 1 cantaloupe melon, deseeded and chopped
- 1 papaya, deseeded and chopped
- 1 mango, stone removed and chopped
- 2 apples, peeled, cored and chopped
- 2 kiwi fruit, peeled and chopped
- Seeds of 1 pomegranate

Direction:

1. Transfer hot water into a cup, add the teabag and allow it to sit for 5 minutes. Set aside and allow it to cool. Place all of the fruit into a large bowl and combine it.
2. Once the tea has cooled pour it onto the fruit salad and stir. Chill before serving.

Nutrition: 205 Calories 9g Protein 8g Fat

189. Apple & Walnut Creams

Preparation Time: 22 minutes
Cooking Time: 0 minute
Serving: 4

Ingredients

- 100g (3½ oz) cream cheese
- 50g (2oz) walnuts, roughly chopped
- 4 apples
- 3 tablespoons lemon juice

Direction

1. Skin and core the apples then slice them evenly width ways to create a circular shape.
2. Lightly coat the apple slices in lemon juice and place them on a serving plate. Mix together the cream cheese and walnuts then spoon a little of the mixture onto each apple ring. Eat immediately.

Nutrition: 221 Calories 13g Protein 11g Fat

190. Blueberry Mousse

Preparation Time: 18 minutes
Cooking Time: 17 minutes
Serving: 2

Ingredients

- 200g (7oz) blueberries
- 125g (4oz) silken tofu

Direction

1. Place the blueberries in a small pan and simmer for 10-15 minutes or until they are completely soft. Set them aside to cool.
2. Place the blueberries and tofu into a blender and process until smooth. Spoon it into glasses or bowls and chill before serving.

Nutrition: 78 Calories 4g Protein 2g Fat

191. Fruit & Nut Bars

Preparation Time: 29 minutes
Cooking Time: 0 minutes
Serving: 8

Ingredients

- 75g (3oz) blueberries
- 75g (3oz) almonds, roughly chopped
- 350g (12oz) dark chocolate, minimum 70% cocoa

Direction

1. Prep shallow baking tin with greaseproof paper. Situate chocolate in a bowl and place it over a saucepan of gently simmering water. Stir gently while the chocolate melts.
2. Scatter the blueberries and almonds over the baking sheet then pour on the melted chocolate. Cover and chill in the fridge for around an hour. Cut into 16 pieces and serve.

Nutrition: 158 Calories 5g Protein 3g Fat

192. Banana & Blueberry Rice Pudding

Preparation time: 8 minutes
Cooking Time: 15 minutes
Serving: 4

Ingredients

- 150g (5oz) risotto rice
- 50g (2oz) dried bananas
- 100g (3 ½ oz) fresh blueberries
- 1 vanilla pod, split open
- 1 liter (1 ¾ pints) unsweetened soya milk

Direction:

1. Place the milk into saucepan and add the rice, bananas and vanilla pod. Bring it to the boil, reduce the heat and simmer for 15 minutes until the rice is soft.
2. Remove the vanilla pod and stir in the blueberries. Serve the pudding immediately.

Nutrition: 302 Calories 14g Protein 12g Fat

193. Brazil Nut Brittle

Preparation Time: 11 minutes
Cooking Time: 3 minutes
Serving: 6

Ingredients

- 150g (5oz) Brazil nuts, chopped
- 150g (5oz) dark chocolate (min 70% cocoa)

Direction:

1. Double-boil the chocolate in a bowl then over a saucepan of lightly simmering water and let it melt. In the meantime, place half of the chopped Brazil nuts in the bottom of a small dish or small loaf tin. When the chocolate has melted and is smooth, pour half of it over the chopped nuts.
2. Add in the remaining chopped nuts and pour over the remaining melted chocolate. Chill in the fridge until it hardens. Break the brittle into chunks and serve.

Nutrition: 322 Calories 18g Protein 15g Fat

194. Apple & Blueberry Ice Lollies

Preparation Time: 6 minutes
Cooking Time: 0 minute
Serving: 4

Ingredients

- 175g (6oz) blueberries
- 4 apples, peeled, cored and chopped

Direction:

1. Position all of the ingredients into a blender and process until smooth. Pour the fruit mixture into lolly molds and place in the freezer until frozen.

Nutrition: 69 Calories 4g Protein 1g Fat

195. Chocolate Orange Cheesecake

Preparation Time: 18 minutes
Cooking Time: 1 hour
Serving: 10

Ingredients

- 800g (1¾ lb.) cream cheese
- 4 medium eggs
- 50g (2oz) 100% cocoa powder
- 2 teaspoons stevia sweetener powder (or to taste)

- 5 tablespoons freshly squeezed orange juice

Direction

1. Situate all of the ingredients into a bowl and combine them. Test the sweetness of the mixture and add extra stevia if necessary.
2. Transfer the mixture to a pie dish and bake at 170C/325F for one hour. Remove the cheesecake and allow it to cool. Serve chilled.

Nutrition: 400 Calories 27g Protein 22g Fat

196. Baked Apples

Preparation time: 17 minutes
Cooking Time: 36 minutes
Serving: 4

Ingredients

- 4 large apples
- 2 tablespoons raisins
- 4 teaspoons honey
- ¼ teaspoon cinnamon

Direction

1. Core the apples, leaving a small piece at the bottom of the apples to retain the filling. Place the raisins inside the apple and pour a little honey and cinnamon into the center of each one.
2. Situate apples in the oven and bake at 180C/360F for 35 minutes. Serve with a sprinkling of cinnamon.

Nutrition: 145 Calories 8g Protein 5g Fat

197. Chilled Blueberry Porridge

Preparation Time: 23 minutes
Cooking Time: 0 minute
Serving: 1

Ingredients

- 100g (4oz) blueberries
- 50g (2oz) rolled oats
- 200mls (7fl oz) unsweetened soya milk
- 2 teaspoons chia seeds
- 100ml (3½ fl oz) water

Direction:

1. Place the blueberries, oats, soya milk and water into a blender and process until smooth. Mix in the chia seeds well. Chill before serving.

Nutrition: 321 Calories 11g Protein 6g Fat

198. Blueberry Compote & Cinnamon Yogurt

Preparation Time:17 minutes
Cooking Time: 11 minutes
Serving: 2

Ingredients

- 200g (7oz) blueberries
- 200g (7oz) plain Greek yogurt
- 1-star anise
- ½ teaspoon cinnamon
- 100mls (3½ oz) water

Direction

1. Place the blueberries and star anise into a saucepan, add the water and bring to the boil. Reduce the heat and simmer for 10 minutes or until the blueberries have burst open.
2. Discard the star anise, remove the saucepan from the heat and set aside to cool. Stir the cinnamon into the yogurt then serve it into bowls. Spoon the blueberry compote over the top and eat immediately.

Nutrition: 178 Calories 9g Protein 5g Fat

199. Quinoa & Berry Porridge

Preparation Time: 16 minutes
Cooking Time: 8 minutes
Serving: 1

Ingredients

- 75g (3oz) quinoa, cooked
- 50g (2oz) raspberries
- 50g (2oz) blueberries
- 250mls (8fl oz) soya milk
- 2 tablespoons pumpkin seeds
- Sprinkling of cinnamon

Direction

1. Place the quinoa and soya milk in a saucepan. Bring to the boil and cook for 5 minutes. Sprinkle in the cinnamon.
2. Serve into a bowl, topped off with raspberries, blueberries and pumpkin seeds.

Nutrition: 351 Calories 17g Protein 9g Fat

200. Quick Blueberry Porridge

Preparation Time: 19 minutes
Cooking Time: 11 minutes
Serving: 1

Ingredients

- 75g (3oz) porridge oats
- 75g (3oz) blueberries
- 200mls (7fl oz) unsweetened soya milk

Direction

1. Place the oats and soya milk into a saucepan and cook until the mixture thickens. Serve into a bowl and top it off with the berries. Enjoy.

Nutrition: 368 Calories 9g Protein 5g Fat

7-DAY WEIGHT LOSS MEAL PLAN

DAY	BREAKFAST	MAIN DISH	SIDE DISH	DESSERT
SUNDAY	Smoked Sirt Salmon Omelet	Turkey Mole Tacos	Ginger Mushrooms	Chocolate Mousse
MONDAY	Green Tea Smoothie-Sirtfood	Sweet and Sour Tofu	Bell Pepper Sauté	Chocolate & Hazelnut Clusters
TUESDAY	Sirt Muesli	BBQ Tempeh Sandwiches	Kale and Tomatoes	Green Tea Tropical Fruit Salad
WEDNESDAY	Bacon Sirtfood Omelet	Tofu Tikka Masala	Chili Artichokes	Apple & Walnut Creams
THURSDAY	Sirtfood Mushroom Scramble Eggs	Tempeh Vegan Chili	Brussels Sprouts Mix	Blueberry Mouse
FRIDAY	Strawberry and Blackcurrant Jelly	Eggroll in a Bowl	Cauliflower Mix	Fruit & Nut Bars
SATURDAY	Nutty Yogurt with Mixed Berries	Beef and Red Cabbage	Quinoa and Peas	Banana & Blueberry Rice Pudding

CONCLUSION

The Sirtfood diet is quite simple and easy to get around since it focuses on plant sources. It encourages fruit, vegetables, whole grains, legumes, seeds, and nuts to eat, which means that most of what you eat is made up of these foods. To help you, our frozen vegetables are simple yet tasty starting point if you consider adding more crops into your diet, slowly without running about completely.

Everybody expects to lose weight when following a diet, but there is extra motivation to use it if there are also health benefits involved. Some diets are focused on anti-inflammatory ingredients, while other diets promote the decrease of carbs. In the case of the Sirt food diet, it encourages sirtuin-rich foods, also known as Sirt foods. Now, you are probably wondering what sirtuins are, and I don't blame you — most people don't have too much knowledge of chemical compounds found in macronutrients. Sirtuins represent a group of seven proteins capable of regulating inflammation, metabolism, and positively impacting your life span.

The Sirtfood diet is a great approach to change your dietary patterns, feel more advantageous, and shed pounds. The underlying not many weeks may challenge you, yet it's imperative to check which nourishments are ideal for eating and which scrumptious plans suit you. Be benevolent to yourself in the initial barely any weeks while your body adjusts and takes practice simple if you decide to do it by any stretch of the imagination. If you are somebody who moderates or extreme exercise, then it might be that you can carry on as ordinary or deal with your wellness as per the adjustment in diet. Similarly, as with any diet and exercise changes, it's about the individual and how far you can propel yourself.

You may think it's a vegetarian diet or classic vegan at first. It is not a diet mainly based on plants; it is versatile and does not boycott seafood, milk, eggs, and meat. It's an easy-going and broad approach makes this diet attractive–after all, no one likes rules! Furthermore, flexitarian diets encourage the consumption of an extensive variation of plant foods, in a way that distinct health advantages are certainly attained from this form of eating. As a nation, we currently strive to keep this figure up. Still, a vegetable diet that relies heavily on fruits and vegetables will make it easier for you to consume the recommended quantity. Also, as beans and pulses are heavily promoted, increased consumption of food, vitamins, and minerals is required–perfect because most of us do not eat enough food! To give you some insights about the different nutritious benefits of humble vegetables, the peas are a source of protein, vitamin C, sugar, and folic acid.

Naturally, a diet based on plants might lead to a protein shortage, but that is far from real–plants also supply protein! If you want to go on more plant-based foods, now is a great time to get adventurous and try new flavor and recipes you've never had before! So why not taste the flexitarian lifestyle in Green Cuisine and discover how delicious plant foods can be! Simply put, protein mix implies eating an inadequate variety of vegetable protein sources to make sure you consume all the necessary amino acids. As a general rule of thumb, there are many essential amino acids in pulses and grains. The intake of a pulse and a grain produces a full supply of protein. All the essential amino acids the body wants are easy to find. E.g., a portion of peas and rice or hummus and bread will provide a full protein source. And note that the mixed proteins don't have to be consumed in one meal-they can be consumed during the day or even week at various times!

Sirt Food
Diet Cookbook

~400~

Quick & Easy Sirt Recipes To Burn Fat by Activating
Your "Skinny Gene"

INTRODUCTION

The Sirtfood Diet is named after two ingredients that form the key to maintaining a healthy weight. Sirtfoods – as they are named – are natural plant foods that contain compounds called Sirtuins which are believed to serve as 'longevity proteins', as they work within our body in a similar way as the protein that slows down the ageing process of animals. Researchers have learnt that foods rich in Sirtuins increase the likelihood of a man or woman living longer, therefore they promote a longer and happier life. As of today, there are seven known Sirtuins described in nature – these being Sirt1, Sirt2, Sirt3, Sirt4, Sirt5, Sirt6 and Sirt7. Sirtuin 1 (Sirt1) is active in the mammalian brain, liver, intestine, kidney, and heart, having the ability to regulate the body's metabolism and control energy expenditure. Sirt1 was discovered in yeast cells in 1999 and further studies conducted in mice have since revealed that Sirt1 increases the activity of other genes, thus encouraging the breakdown of body fat and an increase in the production of good cholesterol.

Sirtfood Diet – This is the only book on the market written bout sirtfoods. To view the full story, click the images above or click here

It is thought that sirtfoods are essentially a key part of the Mediterranean diet, which was recently found to be the healthiest diet in the world. Mediterranean diet foods include a number of fruits and vegetables that are rich in these longevity proteins, resulting in their energising activity on the body. More particularly, sirtfoods are thought to prolong life by reducing the likelihood of some of the diet-related killers like heart disease and prostate cancer. Sirtuins are the same longevity proteins inside yeast cells that are also found in the Greek yogurt that is included in the Sirtfood Diet. Studies that have been carried out on mice and men have found that sirtfoods increase the length of life, because Sirt1 delays the onset of various age-related diseases. The thought is that sirtfoods act as internal 'longevity proteins.' Sirt1 works by fusing to DNA, which then produces proteins that translate into healthy cells that encode longer life. The 'yoga of eating' means that the Sirtfood Diet includes a wide variety of healthy foods, which should help to form a complete natural system. Instead of following a fad diet, this book is the perfect way to start a new, long and healthy life. This book was written with the use of The American Journal of Clinical Nutrition research, as a reference of natural weight loss and longevity factors.

APPETIZER AND SNACK RECIPES

1. Fruit Salad

Preparation Time: 13 minutes
Cooking Time: 0 minutes
Servings: 1
Ingredients:

- ½ cup crisply made green tea
- 1 teaspoon nectar One orange, split
- One apple, cored and generally cleaved
- Ten red seedless grapes
- Ten blueberries

Directions:

1. Stir the nectar into a large portion of some green tea. At the point when broken up, include the juice of a large part of the orange. Leave to cool.
2. Chop the other portion of the orange and spot in a bowl together with the hacked apple, blueberries and grapes. Transfer over the cooled tea and leave to soak for a couple of moments before serving.

Nutrition: 157 Calories 1g Fiber 0.5g Protein

2. Golden Turmeric Latte

Preparation Time: 3 minutes
Cooking Time: 7 minutes
Servings: 3
Ingredients:

- 3 cups of coconut milk
- One teaspoon turmeric powder
- One teaspoon cinnamon powder
- One teaspoon crude nectar

Directions:

1. Spot of dark pepper (expands retention)
2. Modest bit of new stripped ginger root
3. Place of cayenne pepper (discretionary)
4. Mix all fixings in a fast blender until smooth.
5. Fill a little container and warmth for 4 minutes over medium heat until hot however not bubbling.

Nutrition: 50 Calories 98g carbohydrates 2.7g Fat

3. The Sirt Juice

Preparation Time: 7 minutes
Cooking Time: 0 minute
Servings: 2
Ingredients:

- Two huge bunches (75g) kale
- A huge bunch (30g) rocket
- A tiny bunch (5g) level leaf parsley
- A small bunch (5g) lovage leaves (discretionary)
- 2–3 huge stalks (150g) green celery, including its leaves
- ½ medium green apple
- Juice of ½ lemon
- ½ level teaspoon Matcha green tea

Directions:

1. Blend the greens (kale, rocket, parsley and lovage, on the off chance that was utilizing), at that point juice them.
2. Presently squeeze the celery and apple. You can strip the lemon and put it through the juicer also, however, we think that it's a lot simpler just to crush the lemon by hand into the juice.
3. Pour a limited quantity of the juice into a glass, at that point include the Matcha and mix enthusiastically with a fork or teaspoon.
4. Give it a last mix; at that point, your juice is prepared to drink. Don't hesitate to top up with plain water, as indicated by taste.

Nutrition: 75 Calories 0.6g Fat 0.4g Protein

4. Kale Pesto Hummus

Preparation Time: 12 minutes
Cooking Time: 7 minutes
Servings: 12
Ingredients:

- Chickpeas, drained and liquid reserved – 15 ounces
- Reserved chickpea liquid - .25 cup
- Sea salt - .5 teaspoon
- Tahini paste - .5 cup
- Garlic, minced – 2 cloves
- Lemon juice – 2.5 s
- Extra virgin olive oil - .33 cup
- Black pepper, ground - .5 teaspoon
- Kale, chopped and leaves packed – 2 cups
- Pine nuts – 2 s
- Basil leaves, packed – 1.25 cups
- Garlic, minced – 4 cloves
- Extra virgin olive oil - .25 cup

Directions:

1. Into a food processor add the basil, kale, pine nuts, and four cloves of minced garlic. Pulse until the leaves and garlic are finely chopped.
2. Pour in the olive oil, and once again pulse until smooth. Remove the pesto from the bowl of the food processor and set aside.
3. Into the empty food processor add the remaining ingredients to assemble the hummus, pulsing until creamy. Add in the prepared pesto, and pulse just until the two are combined.
4. Transfer the pesto hummus to a serving bowl or store in the fridge.

Nutrition: 194 Calories 2.2g Fat5.6g Protein

5. Parsley Hummus

Preparation Time: 6 minutes
Cooking Time: 7 minutes
Servings: 6
Ingredients:

- Chickpeas, drained and rinsed – 15 ounces
- Curly parsley, stems removed – 1 cup
- Sea salt – .5 teaspoon
- Soy milk, unsweetened - .5 cup
- Extra virgin olive oil – 3 teaspoons
- Lime juice – 1 s
- Red pepper flakes -.5 teaspoons
- Black pepper, ground - .25 teaspoon
- Pine nuts – 2 s
- Sesame seeds, toasted – 2 s

Directions:

1. In the food processor blend parsley and toasted sesame. Pour extra virgin olive oil in while you continue to pulse, until it is smooth.
2. Add the chickpeas, lime juice, and seasonings to the food processor and pulse while slowly adding in the soy milk. Continue to pulse the parsley hummus until it is smooth and creamy.
3. Adjust the seasonings to your preference and then serve or refrigerate the hummus.

Nutrition: 107 Calories 4.5g Fat8.6g Protein

6. Edamame Hummus

Preparation Time: 8 minutes
Cooking Time: 0 minutes
Servings: 10

Ingredients:

- Edamame, cooked and shelled – 2 cups
- Sea salt – 1 teaspoon
- Extra virgin olive oil – 1
- Tahini paste - .25 cup
- Lemon juice - .25 cup
- Garlic, minced – 3 cloves
- Black pepper, ground - .25 teaspoon

Directions:

1. Add the cooked edamame and remaining ingredients to a blender or food processor and mix on high until it forms a creamy and completely smooth mixture. Taste it and adjust the seasonings to your preference.
2. Serve the hummus immediately with your favorite vegetables or store in the fridge.

Nutrition: 88 Calories 3.8g carbohydrates 2.6g Protein

7. Edamame Guacamole

Preparation Time: 8 minutes
Cooking Time: 0 minutes
Servings: 6

Ingredients:

- Edamame, cooked and shelled – 1 cup
- Avocado, pitted and halved – 1
- Red onion, diced - .5 cup
- Cilantro, chopped - .25 cup
- Jalapeno, minced – 1
- Garlic, minced – 2 cloves
- Lime juice – 2 s Water – 3 s
- Lime zest - .5 teaspoon
- Roma tomato, diced – 2
- Cumin - .125 teaspoon
- Sea salt - .5 teaspoon

Directions:

1. Using food processor add all of the ingredients, except for the diced tomato, onion, and jalapeno. Blend the tomato mixture on high speed until it is smooth and creamy, making sure that the edamame has been completely blended.
2. Adjust the seasoning to your preference and then transfer the guacamole to a serving bowl. Stir in the tomato, onion, and jalapeno. Place the bowl in the fridge, allowing it to chill for at least thirty minutes before serving.

Nutrition: 100 Calories 6.6g Fat45g Protein

8. Eggplant Fries with Fresh Aioli

Preparation Time: 16 minutes
Cooking Time: 27 minutes
Servings: 4

Ingredients:

- Eggplants – 2
- Black pepper, ground - .25 teaspoon
- Extra virgin olive oil – 2 s
- Cornstarch – 1
- Basil, dried – 1 teaspoon
- Garlic powder - .25 teaspoon
- Sea salt - .5 teaspoon
- Mayonnaise, made with olive oil - .5 cup
- Garlic, minced – 1 teaspoon
- Basil, fresh, chopped – 1
- Lemon juice – 1 teaspoon
- Chipotle, ground - .5 teaspoon
- Sea salt - .25 teaspoon

Directions:

1. Begin by preheating your oven to Fahrenheit four-hundred and twenty-five degrees. Place a wire cooking/cooling rack on a baking sheet.
2. Remove the peel from the eggplants and then slice them into rounds, each about three-quarters of an inch thick. Slice the rounds into wedges one inch in width.
3. Add the eggplant wedges to a large bowl and toss them with the olive oil. Once coated, add the pepper, cornstarch, dried basil, garlic powder, and sea salt, tossing until evenly coated.
4. Arrange the eggplant wedges on top of the wire rack and set the baking sheet in the oven, allowing the fries to cook for fifteen to twenty minutes.
5. Meanwhile, prepare the aioli. To do this, add the remaining ingredients into a small bowl and whisk them together to combine. Cover the bowl of aioli and allow it to chill it in the fridge until the fries are ready to be served.
6. Remove the fries from the oven immediately upon baking, or allow them to cook under the broiler for an additional three to four minutes for extra crispy fries. Serve immediately with the aioli.

Nutrition: 243 Calories 0.5g Fat 5.3g Protein

9. Eggplant Caponata

Preparation Time: 13 minutes
Cooking time: 25 minutes
Servings: 4

Ingredients:

- Eggplant, sliced into 1.5-inch cubes – 1 pound
- Bell pepper, diced – 1
- Green and black olives, chopped - .5 cup
- Capers - .25 cup
- Sea salt – 1 teaspoon
- Garlic, minced – 4
- Red onion, diced – 1
- Diced tomatoes – 15 ounces
- Extra virgin olive oil – 4 s, divided
- Black pepper, ground - .25 teaspoon
- Parsley, chopped - .25 cup

Directions:

1. Preheat your oven to Fahrenheit four-hundred degrees and line a baking sheet with kitchen parchment.
2. Toss the eggplant cubes in half of the olive oil and then arrange them on the baking sheet, sprinkling the sea salt over the top. Allow the eggplant to roast until tender, about twenty minutes.
3. Meanwhile, add the remaining olive oil into a large skillet along with the red onions, bell pepper, diced tomatoes, and garlic. Sautee the vegetables until tender, about ten minutes.
4. Add the roasted eggplant, capers, olives, and black pepper to the skillet, continuing to cook together for five minutes so that the flavors meld.
5. Remove the skillet from the heat, top it off with parsley, and serve it with crusty toast.

Nutrition: 209 Calories2.3g Fat 0.3g Protein

10. Buckwheat Crackers

Preparation Time: 8 minutes
Cooking Time: 1 hour
Servings: 12

Ingredients:

- Buckwheat groats – 2 cups
- Flaxseeds, ground - .75 cup

- Sesame seeds - .33 cup
- Sweet potatoes, medium, grated – 2
- Extra virgin olive oil – .33 cup
- Water – 1 cup
- Sea salt – 1 teaspoon

Directions:

1. Soak the buckwheat groats in water for at least four hours before preparing the crackers. Once done soaking, drain off the water.
2. Preheat the oven to a temperature of Fahrenheit three-hundred and fifty degrees, prepare a baking sheet, and set aside some kitchen parchment and plastic wrap.
3. In a kitchen bowl, combine the ground flaxseeds with the warm water, allowing the seeds to absorb the water and form a substance similar to gelatin. Add the buckwheat groats and other remaining ingredients.
4. Spread the cracker dough onto a sheet of kitchen parchment and cover it with a sheet of plastic wrap. Use a rolling pen on top of the plastic wrap (so that it doesn't stick) and roll out the buckwheat cracker dough until it is thin.
5. Peel the plastic wrap off of the crackers and transfer the dough-coated sheet of kitchen parchment to the prepared baking sheet. Allow it to partially bake for fifteen minutes and then remove the tray from the oven.
6. Reduce the oven temperature to Fahrenheit three-hundred degrees. Use a pizza cutter and slice the crackers into squares, approximately two inches in width. Return the crackers to the oven until they are crispy and dry, about thirty-five to forty minutes.
7. Remove the crackers from the oven, allowing them to cool completely before storing them in an air-tight container.

Nutrition: 158 Calories 3.8g Fat3.4g Protein

11. Matcha Protein Bites

Preparation Time: 18 minutes
Cooking Time: 70 minutes
Servings: 12

Ingredients:

- Almond butter - .25 cup

- Matcha powder – 2 teaspoons
- Soy protein isolate – 1 ounce
- Rolled oats - .5 cup
- Chia seeds – 1
- Coconut oil – 2 teaspoons
- Honey – 1
- Sea salt - .125 teaspoon

Directions:

1. Using food processor, process all of the Matcha protein bite ingredients until it forms a mixture similar to wet sand, that will stick together when squished between your fingers.
2. Divide the mixture into twelve equal portions. Form into balls.
3. Chill the bites in the fridge for up to two weeks.

Nutrition: 164 Calories 4.7g Fat 4.5g Protein

12. Chocolate-Covered Strawberry Trail Mix

Preparation Time: 7 minutes
Cooking Time: 0 minutes
Servings: 10

Ingredients:

- Freeze-dried strawberries – 1 cup
- Dark chocolate chunks - .66 cup
- Walnuts, roasted – 1 cup
- Almonds, roasted - .25 cup
- Cashews, roasted - .25 cup

Directions:

1. Mix together all of the trail mix ingredients in a bowl, and then store it in a large glass jar or divide each serving into its own transportable plastic bag. Store for up to one month.

Nutrition: 164 Calories 3.2g Fat 2.2g Protein

13. Moroccan Spiced Eggs

Preparation Time: 71 minutes
Cooking Time: 42 minutes
Servings: 2

Ingredients:

- 1 tablespoon olive oil
- One shallot, stripped and finely hacked
- One red (chime) pepper, deseeded and finely hacked
- One garlic clove, stripped and finely hacked

- One courgette (zucchini), stripped and finely hacked
- 1 tablespoon tomato puree (glue)
- ½ teaspoon gentle stew powder
- ¼ teaspoon ground cinnamon
- ¼ teaspoon ground cumin
- ½ teaspoon salt
- 400g can hacked tomatoes
- 400g may chickpeas in water
- A little bunch of level leaf parsley cleaved
- Four medium eggs at room temperature

Directions:
1. Heat the oil in a pan, include the shallot and red (ringer) pepper and fry delicately for 5 minutes. At that point include the garlic and courgette (zucchini) and cook for one more moment or two. Include the tomato puree (glue), flavors and salt and mix through.
2. Add the cleaved tomatoes and chickpeas (dousing alcohol and all) and increment the warmth to medium. With the top of the dish, stew the sauce for 30 minutes – ensure it is delicately rising all through and permit it to lessen in volume by around 33%.
3. Remove from the warmth and mix in the cleaved parsley.
4. Preheat the grill to 200C/180C fan/350F.
5. When you are prepared to cook the eggs, bring the tomato sauce up to a delicate stew and move to a little broiler confirmation dish.
6. Crack the eggs on the dish and lower them delicately into the stew. Spread with thwart and prepare in the grill for 10-15 minutes. Serve the blend in unique dishes with the eggs coasting on the top.

Nutrition: 116 Calorie 6.97g Protein 5.22g Fat

14. Exquisite Turmeric Pancakes with Lemon Yogurt Sauce

Preparation Time: 43 minutes
Cooking Time: 18 minutes
Servings: 8 hotcakes
Ingredients:
For Yogurt Sauce
- 1 cup Greek yogurt

- 1 garlic clove
- 2 tablespoons lemon juice
- ¼ tsp. ground turmeric
- 10 crisp mint leaves
- 2 teaspoons lemon wedges

For Pancakes
- 2 tsp. ground turmeric
- 1½ tsp. ground cumin
- 1 tsp. salt
- 1 tsp. ground coriander
- ½ tsp. garlic powder
- ½ teaspoon naturally ground dark pepper
- 1 head broccoli, cut into florets
- 3 enormous eggs, gently beaten
- 2 tablespoons plain unsweetened almond milk
- 1 cup almond flour
- 4 teaspoons coconut oil

Directions:
1. Make the yogurt sauce. Join the yogurt, garlic, lemon juice, turmeric, mint and pizzazz in a bowl. Taste and enjoy with more lemon juice, if possible. Keep in a safe spot or freeze until prepared to serve.
2. Make the flapjacks. In a little bowl, join the turmeric, cumin, salt, coriander, garlic and pepper.
3. Spot the broccoli in a nourishment processor, and heartbeat until the florets are separated into little pieces. Move the broccoli to an enormous bowl and include the eggs, almond milk, and almond flour. Mix in the flavor blend and consolidate well.
4. Cook 1 teaspoon of the coconut oil in a nonstick dish over medium-low heat. Empty ¼ cup player into the skillet. Cook the hotcake until little air pockets start to show up superficially and the base is brilliant darker, 2 to 3 minutes. Flip over and cook the hotcake for 2 to 3 minutes more. To keep warm, move the cooked hotcakes to a stove safe dish and spot in a 200°F oven.
5. Keep making the staying 3 hotcakes, utilizing the rest of the oil and player.

Nutrition: 262 Calories 11.7g Protein 19.2g Fat

15. Sirt Chili Con Carne

Preparation Time: 82 minutes
Cooking Time: 63 minutes
Servings: 4

Ingredients:

- 1 red onion, finely cleaved
- 3 garlic cloves, finely cleaved
- 2 chilies, finely hacked
- 1 tablespoon additional virgin olive oil
- 1 tablespoon ground cumin
- 1 tablespoon ground turmeric
- 400g lean minced hamburger
- 150ml red wine
- 1 red pepper, cored
- 2 x 400g tins cleaved tomatoes
- 1 tablespoon tomato purée
- 1 tablespoon cocoa powder
- 150g tinned kidney beans
- 300ml hamburger stock
- 5g coriander, cleaved
- 5g parsley, cleaved
- 160g buckwheat

Directions:

1. Fry onion, garlic and bean stew in the oil at medium heat for 2 minutes.
2. Include the minced hamburger and dark colored at high heat. Pour in the red wine
3. Mix red pepper, tomatoes, tomato purée, cocoa, kidney beans and stock and keep aside for 1 hour.
4. Once thick, mix in the hacked herbs. Cook the buckwheat then serve with the stew.

Nutrition: 346 Calories 14.11g Protein 11.37g Fat

16. Med-Style Olives

Preparation Time: 13 minutes
Cooking Time: 9 minutes
Servings: 6

Ingredients:

- One pinch of salt One pinch of black pepper
- 1 ½ tablespoon of coriander seeds
- One tablespoon of extra-virgin olive oil
- One lemon
- 7 oz. of kalamata olives
- 7 oz. of green queen olives

Directions:

1. Pound the coriander seeds and set aside.

2. Slice long, thin of lemon rind and mix with both the green queen and kalamata olives.
3. Pour lemon juice on top of the olives and mix olive oil.
4. Add the salt, pepper, and coriander seeds, then stir and serve.

Nutrition: 477 Calories 9g Fat 35g Protein

17. Crispy Chickpeas

Preparation Time: 14 minutes
Cooking Time: 38 minutes
Servings: 6

Ingredients:

- One pinch of salt
- One pinch of black pepper
- One pinch of garlic powder
- One teaspoon of dried oregano
- Two tablespoons of extra-virgin olive oil
- juice of 1 lemon
- Two teaspoons of red wine vinegar
- 2 15 oz. canned chickpeas

Directions:

1. Preheat your oven to 42 5 F and place a sheet of parchment paper onto a baking tray.
2. Drain and rinse the chickpeas, then pour them onto the baking tray. Spread equally. Roast for 11 minutes. Pull it out then shake. Cook again for 10 minutes. Once roasted, put aside.
3. Mix remaining ingredients and stir in roasted chickpeas. Put the chickpeas back to the oven and roast for 11 minutes. Pull it out, cool, then serve.

Nutrition: 323 Calories 15.6g fat 10.4g Protein

18. Honey Chili Nuts

Preparation Time: 13 minutes
Cooking Time: 31 minutes
Servings: 4

Ingredients:

- 5oz walnuts
- 5oz pecan nuts
- 2oz softened butter
- 1 tablespoon honey
- ½ bird's-eye chili, very finely chopped and deseeded

Directions:

1. Preheat the oven to 180C/360F. Combine the butter, honey, and chili in a bowl, then add the nuts and stir them well.
2. Lay out the nuts in a lined baking sheet and roast them in the oven for 10 minutes, stirring once halfway through. Pull out from the oven and cool before eating.

Nutrition: 65g Calories 0.5g Fat 2g Protein

19. Cauliflower Nachos

Preparation Time: 7 minutes
Cooking Time: 33 minutes
Servings: 2

Ingredients:

- 2 tablespoons extra virgin olive oil
- ½ teaspoon onion powder
- ½ teaspoon turmeric
- ½ teaspoon ground cumin
- 1 medium head cauliflower
- ¾ cup shredded cheddar cheese
- ½ cup tomato, diced
- ¼ cup red bell pepper, diced
- ¼ cup red onion, diced
- ½ Bird's Eye chili pepper, finely diced
- ¼ cup parsley, finely diced
- Pinch of salt

Directions:

1. Preheat oven to 400 ° F.
2. Mix onion powder, cumin, turmeric, and olive oil. Core cauliflower and slice into ½" thick rounds. Coat the cauliflower with the olive oil mixture and bake for 15 – 20 minutes.
3. Top with shredded cheese & bake for an additional 3 – 5 minutes, until cheese is melted. In a bowl, combine tomatoes, bell pepper, onion, chili, and parsley with a pinch of salt.
4. Top cooked cauliflower with salsa and serve.

Nutrition: 195 Calories 5g Fat 3.6g Protein

20. Cheesy Cauliflower Bars

Preparation Time: 14 minutes
Cooking Time: 39 minutes
Servings: 1

Ingredients:

- ½ cauliflower head, riced
- 1/3 cup low-fat mozzarella cheese, shredded

- ¼ cup egg whites
- 1 teaspoon Italian dressing, low fat
- Pepper to taste

Directions:

1. Lay out cauliflower rice over a lined baking sheet. Preheat your oven to 375 degrees F. Roast for 20 minutes. Transfer to a bowl and spread pepper, cheese, seasoning, egg whites, and stir well.
2. Spread in a rectangular pan and press. Situate in an oven and cook for 20 minutes. Serve and enjoy!

Nutrition: 90 Calories 4g Fat 4g Protein

21. Walnut and Date Bites

Preparation Time: 7 minutes
Cooking Time: 0 minutes
Servings: 1

Ingredients:

- 3 walnut halves
- 3 pitted Medjool dates
- the ground cinnamon, to taste

Directions:

1. Cut each walnut carefully into three slices, and do the same with dates. Put a slice of walnut, brush with cinnamon, and serve.

Nutrition: 78 Calories 7g Fat1.5g Protein

22. Sirt Energy Balls

Preparation Time: 9 minutes
Cooking Time: 11 minutes
Servings: 5

Ingredients:

- 1 cup old fashion ginger, dried
- 1/4 cup quinoa cooked
- 1/4 cup shredded unsweetened coconut
- 1/3 cup dried cranberry/raisin blend
- 1/3 cup dark chocolate chips
- 1/4 cup slivered almonds
- 1 Tbsp reduced-fat peanut butter

Directions:

1. Cook quinoa in orange juice. Boil and simmer for 4 minutes. Let cool. Combine chilled quinoa and the remaining ingredients into a bowl.
2. With wet hands and combine ingredients and roll in golden ball sized chunks.
3. Set at a Tupperware and chill until the firm.

Nutrition: 80 Calories 7g Fat 2.5g Protein

23. Celery and Raisins Snack Salad

Preparation Time: 16 minutes
Cooking Time: 0 minutes
Servings: 4

Ingredients:

- ½ cup raisins
- 4 cups celery, sliced
- ¼ cup parsley, chopped
- ½ cup walnuts, chopped
- Juice of ½ lemon
- 2 tbsp. extra virgin olive oil
- Salt and black pepper to the taste

Directions:

1. In a salad bowl, mix celery with raisins, walnuts, parsley, lemon juice, oil, and black pepper, toss, divide into small cups and serve as a snack.

Nutrition: 120 Calories 1g Fat 5g Protein

24. Yogurt & Fruit Jam Parfait

Preparation Time: 6 minutes
Cooking Time: 5 minutes
Servings: 6

Ingredients:

- 3 cups Mixed Berries
- 1 tbsp. Lemon Juice
- 7/8 cup Honey
- 2 tsp. Fruit Pectin
- 1 cup Granola
- 3 cups Greek Yoghurt

Directions:

1. For making this healthy jam, you need to place the mixed berries, honey, lemon juice, and pectin in the blender pitcher.
2. Next, pulse the mixture 3 to 4 times and then press the 'sauce/ dip' button.
3. Now, transfer the jam to a safe heat container and then place it in the refrigerator for 2 to 3 hours.
4. Once the jam is chilled, layer 1/3 cup of the Greek Yoghurt into the bottom of the parfait glass.
5. After that, spoon in a jam into it and then add the granola.
6. Serve immediately.

Nutrition: 154 calories 4g fat9g protein

25. Lemon Ricotta Cookies

Preparation Time: 19 minutes
Cooking Time: 17 Minutes
Servings: 12

Ingredients:

- 2 1/2 cups all-purpose flour
- 1 tsp. baking powder
- 1 tsp. salt
- 1 tbsp. unsalted butter softened
- 2 cups of sugar
- 2 capsules
- 1 teaspoon (15-ounce) container whole-milk ricotta cheese
- 3 tbsp. lemon juice
- 1 lemon

Glaze:

- 11/2 cups powdered sugar
- 3 tbsp. lemon juice
- 1 lemon

Directions:

1. Pre heat the oven to 375 degrees F.
2. In a medium bowl combine the flour, baking powder, and salt. Set-aside.
3. Incorporate butter and the sugar levels. Scourge sugar and butter for three minutes. Pour eggs 1 at a time, while beating.
4. Beat ricotta cheese, lemon juice and lemon zest. Mix in the dry skin.
5. Line two baking sheets with parchment paper. Spoon the dough (approximately 2 tablespoons of each cookie) on the baking sheets. Bake for 14 minutes. Pull it out then set aside for 21 minutes.
6. Combine the powdered sugar lemon juice and lemon peel then stir. Scoop about 1/2-tsp on each cookie and press. Allow glaze harden for approximately two hours. Pack the biscuits to a decorative jar.

Nutrition: 24.5g Carbohydrates 13.4g Protein 2g Fat

26. Matcha Mochi

Preparation Time: 2 minutes
Cooking Time: 19 Minutes
Servings: 2

Ingredients:

- 1 cup Superfine White Rice Flour
- 1 cup of coconut milk
- 2 tablespoons Matcha powder

- 1/2 cup sugar
- 2 tablespoons butter melted
- 1 teaspoon baking powder

Directions:
1. Preheat the oven to 325.Spray baking dish with non-stick spray. Mix all dry ingredients, including sugar.
2. Whisk to blend. Add melted butter and coconut milk. Stir well. Put into a baking dish. Bake for 20 minutes.

Nutrition: 170 Calories 4.3g Fat 4.9g Protein

27. Blueberry Muffins

Preparation Time: 14 minutes
Cooking Time: 28 Minutes
Servings: 10

Ingredients:
- 1 cup Fresh blueberries
- 2 Tbsp Melted coconut oil
- 2 Tbsp Maple syrup
- 2 Eggs
- 5 cup Almond milk
- A pinch of Salt
- tsp Baking powder
- ¼ cup Arrowroot starch
- 1 cup Buckwheat flour

Directions:
1. Set oven to 350 degrees. Prepare a muffin tin.
2. Bring out a bowl and add the salt, baking powder, arrowroot starch, and buckwheat flour.
3. Using a new bowl, mix the eggs, milk, oil, and syrup together. Beat them together until well combined. Add in the flour mixture and then fold in the blueberries.
4. Move to the muffin tins and then add into the oven. Bake for 25 minutes. When these are done, take them out to cool and then serve.

Nutrition: 391 calories 19g fats 13g protein

28. Brownie Bites

Preparation Time: 2 hours
Cooking Time: 0 minutes
Servings: 12

Ingredients:
- 2 ½ cups whole walnuts
- ¼ cup almonds
- 2 ½ cups Medjool0dates

- 1 cup cacao powder
- 1 teaspoon vanilla extract
- ¼ tsp. sea salt

Directions:
1. Blend all the ingredients using food processor.
2. Form into balls and situate on a baking sheet and freeze for 30 minutes.

Nutrition: 110 Calories 2.8g Fat 5g Protein

29. Mascarpone Cheesecake

Preparation Time: 12 minutes
Cooking Time: 23 minutes
Servings: 3

Ingredients:
Crust
- 1/2 cup slivered almonds
- 8 tsp. -- or 2/3 cup graham cracker crumbs
- 2 tbsp. sugar
- 1 tbsp. salted butter melted

Filling
- 1 (8-ounce) packages cream cheese, room temperature
- 1 (8-ounce) container mascarpone cheese, room temperature
- 3/4 cup sugar
- 1 tsp. fresh lemon juice (or imitation lemon-juice)
- 1 tsp. vanilla infusion
- 2 large eggs, room temperature

Directions:
1. For the crust: prep oven at 350 degrees. Get 9-inch diameter around the pan. Pulse almonds, cracker crumbs sugar in a food processor. Mix in butter
2. Press the almond mixture on the base of the prepared pan. Bake for 2 minutes. Lower temperature to 325 degrees F.
3. For your filling: with an electric mixer, scourge cream cheese, mascarpone cheese, and sugar. Pour in the lemon juice and vanilla. Add the eggs simultaneously until combined
4. Transfer cheese mixture on the crust from the pan. Position the pan into a big skillet then put enough hot water to the roasting pan. Bake for 1 hour Transfer the cake to a stand 1 hour. Refrigerate before cheesecake is cold, at least eight hours.

5. Decorate the cake using melted chocolate

Nutrition: 5g Carbohydrates 25g Fat 5g Protein

30. Chocolate Berry Blend

Preparation Time: 32 minutes
Cooking Time: 0 minutes
Servings: 1

Ingredients:

- 2oz kale
- 2oz blueberries
- 2oz strawberries
- 1 banana
- 1 tablespoon 100% cocoa powder or cacao nibs
- 7 oz unsweetened soya milk

Directions:

1. Situate all of the ingredients into a blender with enough water to cover them and process until smooth.

Nutrition: 256 Calories 9g Fats 6g Protein

31. Monkey Trail Mix

Preparation Time: 1 hour
Cooking Time: 32 minutes
Servings: 5

Ingredients:

- One teaspoon of vanilla extract
- Three tablespoons of coconut oil
- 1/3 cup of coconut sugar
- 6 oz. of dried banana
- ½ cup of dark chocolate chips
- 1 cup of coconut flakes, unsweetened
- 1 cup of cashews, raw and unsalted
- 2 cups of walnuts, raw and unsalted

Directions:

1. Add the coconut oil, vanilla extract, coconut sugar, coconut flakes, and nuts into a crockpot.
2. Mix then cook at high for 1 hour. Stir occasionally
3. Turn the crockpot temperature to low and continue to cook for another 30 minutes.
4. Transfer the mixture out onto parchment paper and allow to dry completely.
5. Cool before adding the banana and chocolate chips.

Nutrition: 151 Calories 10g Fat 4g Protein

32. Granola with Quinoa

Preparation Time: 31 minutes
Cooking Time: 23 minutes

Servings: 6

Ingredients:

- One pinch of salt
- ¼ cup of maple syrup
- 3 ½ tablespoons of coconut oil
- One tablespoon coconut sugar
- 1 cup of rolled oats
- 2 cups of almonds, raw and unsalted
- ½ cup of quinoa, uncooked

Directions:

1. Prep your oven to 340 F and line a baking tray with parchment paper. In a large mixing bowl, add the salt, sugar, oats, almonds, and quinoa and set aside. Using small saucepan over medium heat, pour maple syrup and coconut oil.
2. Using a whisk, stir regularly until combined, then remove from the heat. Pour the syrup over the mixed nuts and quinoa and give it a thorough stir. Place the mixture onto the baking tray and, using a spatula, spread the ingredients evenly over the dish.
3. Bake for 20 minutes. Remove the tray, give it a shake, and return to the oven to bake for another 10 minutes.
4. Allow to cool, then serve.
5. As an alternative, you may use muscovado or brown sugar instead of coconut sugar.
6. Feel free to alternate the nut mixture depending on your tastes.

Nutrition: 241 Calories 6g Fat 15g Protein

33. Med-Styled Olives

Preparation Time: 17 minutes
Cooking Time: 12 minutes
Servings: 6

Ingredients:

- One pinch of salt One pinch of black pepper
- 1 ½ tablespoon of coriander seeds
- One tablespoon of extra-virgin olive oil
- One lemon
- 7 oz. of kalamata olives
- 7 oz. of green queen olives

Directions:

1. Mash the coriander seeds and set aside.
2. Cut long slices of lemon rind and situate with kalamata olives and green queen.

3. Dash with lemon juice over the top of the olives and stir olive oil.
4. Add the salt, pepper, and coriander seeds, then stir and serve.

Nutrition: 477 Calories 9g Fat 35g Protein

34. Roasted Chickpeas

Preparation Time: 13 minutes
Cooking Time: 41 minutes
Servings: 6

Ingredients:

- One pinch of salt One pinch of black pepper One pinch of garlic powder
- One teaspoon of dried oregano
- Two tablespoons of extra-virgin olive oil
- juice of 1 lemon
- Two teaspoons of red wine vinegar 2 15 oz. canned chickpeas

Directions:

1. Preheat your oven to 425 F and place a sheet of parchment paper onto a baking tray.
2. Drain and rinse the chickpeas, then pour them onto the baking tray. Spread evenly. Roast it for 10 minutes. Take it out, shake, then roast it again for 10 minutes. Pull it out then set aside.
3. Incorporate the rest of ingredients then mix in roasted chickpeas. Cook the chickpeas again into the oven and roast for 10 minutes. Remove, let it cool, and serve.

Nutrition: 323 Calories 16g fat 10.4g Protein

35. Baked Root Veg Crisps

Preparation Time: 14 minutes
Cooking Time: 29 minutes
Servings: 2

Ingredients:

- One pinch of salt
- One pinch of black pepper
- One pinch of ground cumin
- One pinch of dried thyme
- One teaspoon of garlic powder
- Two tablespoons of extra-virgin olive oil
- One parsnip, finely sliced
- One turnip, finely sliced
- One red beet, finely sliced
- One golden beet, finely sliced
- Ingredients for the dipping sauce:

- One pinch of salt
- One pinch of black pepper
- Six tablespoons of buttermilk
- 1 cup of Greek yoghurt
- One teaspoon of honey
- One teaspoon of lemon zest
- Two cloves of garlic, minced
- Two tablespoons of fresh, flat-leaf parsley, minced

Directions:

1. Combine all of the dipping sauce ingredients into a medium mixing bowl, using a whisk to ensure that the sauce is evenly combined. Set aside in the refrigerator for when needed.
2. Preheat your oven to 400 F.
3. In a small mixing bowl, combine the seasoning, herbs, and olive oil.
4. Rinse your root vegetables and dry them off using a kitchen towel. Remove all the root vegetable skins and very gently, using a mandolin slicer, slice the vegetables into thin crisps.
5. Brush each side of the crisp with the olive oil and then place onto an oven-proof wire rack. Place the wire rack onto a baking sheet and put this into the oven to bake for 20 minutes
6. Allow to cool or enjoy them warm with the sauce.

Nutrition: 457 Calories 31g Fat 12g Protein

36. Bubble and Squeak

Preparation Time: 1 hour
Cooking Time: 44 minutes
Servings: 3

Ingredients:

- One tablespoon butter 2 cups shredded cabbage
- One medium carrot, shredded
- ¼ cup chopped onion
- One batch The Ultimate Fauxtatoes
- ½ cup shredded Cheddar cheese

Directions:

1. Prepare the oven to 350 degrees Fahrenheit. Melt the butter in a large, massive fish and smooth the vegetables until the onion begins to turn translucent, and the cabbage becomes slightly soft.

Spray a 6-liter (1.4-litre) plate with colorless cooking spray.

2. Spread one-third of the Fauxtatoes on the bottom, then make a half layer of the cabbage mixture. Repeat the layers and finish with a Fauxtatoes layer. Cheese top. Bake for 45 minutes and strain through all layers.

Nutrition: 4g protein 2g carbohydrates 1g fiber

37. **Thai Cucumber Salad**

Preparation Time: 51 minutes
Cooking Time: 28 minutes
Servings: 8
Ingredients

- ½ small red onion
- One fresh jalapeno, seeds removed
- Three medium cucumbers
- 2 or 3 cloves fresh garlic, crushed
- Two tablespoons grated fresh ginger
- ½ cup (120 ml) rice vinegar
- ½ teaspoon salt
- ¼ teaspoon pepper
- Two tablespoons Splenda

Directions:

1. With a food processor with the S blade, place the onion and syrup solution in the food and press to crush both fine.
2. Remove the S blade and place it on the cutting disc. Rotate the cucumbers and then pass them through the processor.
3. Put onions, pumpkins, and cucumbers in a large bowl. In a separate bowl, combine the garlic, ginger, vinegar, salt, pepper, and splendor. Pour the vegetables and mix well.
4. Chill several hours before serving to get the best taste.

Nutrition: 6g carbohydrates 1g fiber1g protein.

38. **Mushroom Risotto**

Preparation Time: 12 minutes
Cooking Time: 3 minutes.
Servings: 5
Ingredients:

- ½ head cauliflower
- Three tablespoons butter
- 1 cup sliced mushrooms
- ½ medium onion, diced
- One teaspoon minced garlic or two cloves garlic

- Two tablespoons dry vermouth
- One tablespoon chicken bouillon granule
- ¼ cup grated Parmesan cheese
- Guar or xanthan Two tablespoons chopped fresh parsley

Directions:

1. Run the cauliflower using a food processor with a razor blade. Put the cauliflower in a microwave oven, add a few tablespoons of water, and cover the microwave for 7 minutes over high heat.
2. While the cauliflower cooks, it melts
3. Put the butter in a large fish over medium heat and add the mushrooms, onion, and garlic and mix.
4. Once ready, take it out from microwave and drain it. Mix cauliflower to the fish and mix everything. Mix in Vermouth, boil, and cheese and cook for 2 to 3 minutes.
5. Simply sprinkle some guar or xanthan on the "risotto," always mixing to give it a creamy texture. Stir in parsley and serve.

Nutrition: 4g carbohydrates 1g fiber6g protein

39. **Cauliflower-Olive Salad**

Preparation Time: 22 minutes
Cooking Time: 14 minutes.
Servings: 5
Ingredients:

- ½ head cauliflower, broken into small florets
- ½ cup diced red onion
- One can sliced ripe olives, drained
- ½ cup chopped fresh parsley
- ¼ cup lemon juice ¼ cup olive oil
- ¼ cup (mayonnaise
- ½ teaspoon salt or Vege-Sal
- About a dozen cherry tomatoes Lettuce (optional) and parsley in a bowl.

Directions:

1. Combine lemon juice, olive oil, mayonnaise, and salt in a separate bowl. Pour the vegetables and pour well.
2. When the salad is ready, cut the cherry tomatoes in half and add them to the mixture. Serve on a bed with salad, if you like, but it's great.

Nutrition: 7g carbohydrates 2g fiber 1g protein

40. Zucchini-Crusted Pizza

Preparation Time: 31 minutes
Cooking Time: 28 minutes
Servings: 4

Ingredients

- 3 ½ cups shredded zucchini
- Three eggs 1 ½ cup rice protein powder or soy powder
- 1½ cups shredded mozzarella, divided
- ½ cup grated Parmesan cheese
- A pinch or two of dried basil
- ½ teaspoon salt
- ¼ teaspoon pepper Oil
- 1 cup sugar-free pizza sauce
- Toppings as desired

Directions:

1. Preheat oven to 350 ° F
2. Sprinkle the pumpkin with a little salt and let stand 15-30 minutes. Put it in a straightener and press for extra moisture. Multiply the chopped pumpkin, eggs, protein powder, 2 cups of mozzarella, parmesan, basil, salt, and pepper. Spray (23 33 33 cm) pan with a non-stick cooking spray and spread the pumpkin mixture. Bake for 26 minutes
3. Wash the pumpkin peel with a little oil and cook for 5 minutes until golden. Then spread the pizza sauce and add 1 cup Mozzarella and other tops. Bake for another 25 minutes, then cut into squares and serve.

Nutrition: 14g carbohydrates 2g fiber22g protein

41. Broccoli Salad

Preparation Time: 22 minutes
Cooking Time: 18 minutes
Servings: 6

Ingredients:

- ½ cup (120 ml) olive oil
- ¼ cup (60 ml) vinegar
- 1 clove garlic, crushed
- ½ teaspoon Italian seasoning herb blend
- ½ teaspoon salt or Vege-Sal
- ½ teaspoon pepper
- 4 cups frozen broccoli "cuts"

Directions:

1. Multiply the olive oil, vinegar, garlic, herbs, salt, and pepper.

2. They don't even bother you
3. Broccoli - Put it in a bowl and pour the olive oil mixture over it. Stir well and let it sit in the refrigerator for a few hours. If you think and serve it as vegetables or vegetables, mix it.

Nutrition: 7g carbohydrates 4g fiber4g protein.

42. Not-Quite-Middle-Eastern Salad

Preparation Time: 22 minutes
Cooking Time: 17 minutes
Servings: 6

Ingredients:

- ½ head cauliflower
- 2/3 cup sliced stuffed olives
- Seven scallions, sliced
- 2 cups triple-washed fresh spinach, finely chopped
- One stalk celery, diced
- One small ripe tomato, finely diced
- Four tablespoons chopped parsley
- ¼ cup olive oil
- One teaspoon minced garlic or two cloves garlic, crushed
- One tablespoon red wine vinegar
- Two tablespoons mayonnaise
- Salt and pepper

Directions:

1. Run cauliflower using a food processor knife, place in a microwave oven, add a few tablespoons (30 ml) of water, cover the pan, and cook for only 5 minutes.
2. While cooking, place the olives, onions, spinach, celery, tomatoes, and parsley in a large salad bowl.
3. When the cauliflower has come out of the microwave, pour it into a rectifier and run it for a moment or two in cold water to cool.
4. Drain the cauliflower well and sprinkle with other vegetables. Add oil, garlic, vinegar and mayonnaise, and pot. Add salt and pepper to taste, bake and serve again.

Nutrition: 5g carbohydrates 2g fiber1g protein

43. Apple Cinnamon Oats Bowl

Preparation Time: 12 minutes
Cooking Time: 4 minutes

Servings: 2

Ingredients:

- One green apple (skinned, cored)
- 1 cup Instant oats
- 1 scoop Soy protein isolate (chocolate flavor)
- ¼ cup Raisins 1 tbsp. Cinnamon 2 cups Water
- Optional Toppings:
- Apple slices Raisins Cinnamon

Directions:

1. Cut the cord and skinned apple into tiny pieces and add them to a saucepan.
2. Add the water and oats to the saucepan and put it over medium heat.
3. Bring to a boil and cook the oats for about 5 minutes.
4. Turn the heat off, add the soy isolate, raisins and cinnamon, then stir thoroughly until everything is well combined. Serve warm with the optional toppings and enjoy!

Nutrition: 366 Calories4.2g Fat28g Protein

44. **Paleo Power Bread**

Preparation Time: 31 minutes

Cooking Time: 19 minutes

Servings: 8

Ingredients:

- 1 cup Almonds Seven dates (pitted)
- 1 cup Pumpkin seeds
- 1 cup Sunflower seeds 1 cup Flaxseeds
- ¼ cup Water

Directions:

1. Prep the oven to 257°F and line a bread tin with parchment paper.
2. Add all the ingredients to a food processor and blend into a chunky dough.

3. Alternatively, chop the dates into tiny bits, crush the almonds and add them to a large bowl with the remaining ingredients and knead it into a chunky dough by hand.
4. Add the mixture to the bread tin, spread it out from edge to edge and smooth out the top with a tablespoon.
5. Transfer the bread tin to the oven and bake for 20 minutes.
6. Take the bread out of the oven and allow it to cool down completely.

Nutrition: 379 Calories 30.6g Fat 16g Protein

45. **Buckwheat Protein Bread**

Preparation Time: 51 minutes

Cooking Time: 38 minutes

Servings: 6

Ingredients:

- 1 cup Buckwheat flour
- ½ cup Pea protein
- ¼ cup Chia seeds
- ¼ cup Raisins
- 3-inch piece Ginger (minced) 2 cups Water

Directions:

1. Set the oven to 190°C and line a small loaf pan with parchment paper.
2. Add all the ingredients except the raisins to a food processor and blend into a smooth and sticky dough.
3. Add the raisins to the dough in the food processor container and stir to distribute them evenly, using a spatula. Transfer the dough to the bread tin, spread it from edge to edge and smooth out the top with a tablespoon. Transfer the bread tin to the oven and bake for 40 minutes.
4. Take the bread out of the oven and allow it to cool down completely.

Nutrition: 151 Calories 9.9g Protein 4.6g Fiber

46. Strawberry Muesli

Preparation Time: 19 minutes
Cooking Time: 0 minute
Serving: 3

Ingredients

- One-quarter cup of buckwheat flakes
- Two-thirds cup of buckwheat puffs
- Three tbsp. coconut flakes
- One-quarter cup Medjool dates
- One-eighth cup of chopped walnuts
- One and a half tbsp. of cocoa nibs
- Two-thirds cup of chopped strawberries
- 3/8 cup plain Greek Yoghurt

Direction

1. Simply mix all the ingredients in a clean bowl, and enjoy the fantastic goodness of this delicacy. However, only add strawberries and yogurt when you are ready to eat.

Nutrition: 118 calories 9g fats 6g protein

47. Sirtfood Omelet

Preparation Time: 8 minutes
Cooking Time: 7 minutes
Serving: 2

Ingredients

- 2 oz. sliced bacon
- Three medium-sized eggs
- One and a one-quarter oz. sliced red endive
- 2 tbsp. chopped parsley
- One tsp. turmeric
- One tsp. extra virgin olive oil

Direction

1. Heat up a non-stick pan.
2. Cut your bacon into thin strips.
3. Cook your sliced bacon strips at high heat until they get crisp and crunchy. You do not have to add oil to the strips; the natural fat would help cook them.
4. Remove the bacon strips from the pan once they're cooked, and place them on a paper towel to drain the extra fat.
5. Wipe your pan clean and then pour in some oil – enough to cook the three eggs.
6. Beat your eggs thoroughly and add in the turmeric, parsley, and endive.
7. Chop your bacon into fine cubes and then stir the bits into the whisked eggs.
8. Pour in oil into your pan and heat at medium heat.
9. Pour the egg mixture in the hot oil and move the mixture around with a spatula
10. Swirl the mixture carefully around the pan until the omelet is even.
11. Lower the heat on your cooker and allow the omelet to firm up and even out at the edges.
12. Fold your omelet in half, roll it up and serve hot.

Nutrition: 291 calories 10g fats 6g protein

48. Sirtfood Diet Smoothie

Preparation Time: 4 minutes
Cooking Time: 0 minute
Serving: 1

Ingredients

- 3/8 cup of Greek yogurt
- Six walnut halves
- 10 hulled strawberries
- 7 – 10 kale leaves
- ¾ oz. dark chocolate
- One Medjool date
- ½ tsp. ground turmeric
- One sliver of Thai chili
- 200ml of unsweetened almond milk

Direction

1. Load up all the ingredients into your blender and grind into a smooth pulp.

Nutrition: 107 calories 6g fat 3g protein

49. Yogurt, Berries, Walnuts and Dark Chocolate

Preparation Time: 11 minutes
Cooking Time: 0 minute
Serving: 4

Ingredients

- One and twenty-five grams of mixed berries
- Two-thirds cup of plain Greek yogurt
- ¼ cup of walnuts
- 10g of dark chocolate (85% pure cocoa)

Direction

1. Get a clean bowl and add in your berries.

2. Pour the plain Greek yogurt over the berries
3. Add in your walnuts and dark chocolate, and food is ready.

Nutrition: 188 calories 9g fat 2g protein

50. Seasoned Scrambled Eggs

Preparation Time: 6 minutes
Cooking Time: 4 minutes
Serving: 3

Ingredients

- One tsp. extra virgin olive oil
- 20g chopped red onions
- ½ chopped Thai chili
- 3 eggs (medium-sized)
- 50 ml of milk
- One tsp ground turmeric
- 2 tbsp. chopped parsley

Direction

1. Place a dry, non-stick frying pan on your cooker and set to medium heat.
2. Fry your chili and red onions till they get soft without being browned.
3. Scourge eggs in a clean bowl and add in the milk, parsley, and turmeric.
4. Pour the mixture into the hot pan and allow to cook at medium heat
5. Spread egg mixture around in the pan to scramble it and prevent burning.
6. Serve once desired consistency is achieved.

Nutrition: 381 calories 16g fats 8g protein

51. Asian Shrimp Stir-Fry Along with Buckwheat Noodles

Preparation Time: 13 minutes
Cooking Time: 34 minutes
Serving: 4

Ingredients

- Two teaspoons of deveined tamari sauce
- Seventy-five grams of buckwheat noodles
- One hundred and fifty grams of shelled raw jumbo shrimp
- Two pieces of garlic cloves
- One Thai chili (it should be finely chopped)
- One teaspoon of fresh ginger (finely chopped)

- Two teaspoons of extra virgin olive oil
- Twenty grams of red onions
- Forty-five grams of celery (sliced)
- Seventy-five grams of chopped green beans
- Fifty grams of chopped kale
- Half-a-cup of chicken stock

Direction

1. Get a frying pan (non-stick) and then use a high heat setting to heat it up.
2. Proceed by frying the shrimp by using a single teaspoon of tamari sauce along with a single teaspoon of oil. Fry for four minutes.
3. Have the shrimp transferred to a plate then use a clean paper towel to wipe the pan.
4. In the hot water, cook the noodles for five to eight minutes, and strain.
5. Proceed by frying the red onion, green beans, chili, ginger, garlic, kale and celery by using the leftover oil and tamari. Avoid including the celery leaves in that mixture. By using a medium heat setting, fry the ingredients for three-to-four minutes.
6. Now include the stock to your mixture and allow it to cook till the vegs are done.
7. The celery leaves, shrimp and noodles should now be added to the pan. Boil them. Once you're done, lower the heat then serve.

Nutrition: 491 calories 24g fats 18g protein

52. Miso and Sesame Glazed Tofu with Ginger and Chili Stir

Preparation Time: 14 minutes
Cooking Time: 29 minutes
Serving: 4

Ingredients

- One tbsp mirin
- Twenty grams of miso paste
- One hundred and fifty grams of tofu
- Forty grams of celery
- Forty grams of red onion
- One hundred and twenty grams of zucchini
- One piece of Thai chili
- Two cloves of garlic

- One teaspoon of fresh ginger (finely chopped)
- Fifty grams of kale
- Two teaspoons of sesame seeds
- Thirty-five grams of buckwheat
- One teaspoon of ground turmeric
- Two teaspoons of extra virgin olive oil
- One teaspoon of tamari sauce

Direction

1. Heat your oven to four hundred degrees.
2. Get a small roasting pan and line it with parchment paper.
3. Combine the mirin and the miso.
4. Slice up your tofu lengthwise, and then make each piece out into a triangular shape.
5. Spread the miso mixture over the tofu and allow the tofu to get steeped in the mixture.
6. Cut up your celery, red onion, and zucchini.
7. Cut up the chili, garlic, and ginger.
8. Allow the kale to gently cook in a steamer for five minutes.
9. Transfer your tofu into the roasting pan and spread the sesame seeds over it. Allow the mixture to roast in the oven for twenty minutes.
10. Rinse your buckwheat, and then sieve. Bring a pan filled with water to boil and add in the turmeric.
11. Cook the buckwheat noodles and strain.
12. Allow the oil to heat in a frying pan and then add the celery, onion, zucchini, chili, garlic, and ginger. Allow the entire mix to fry on high heat for two minutes. Reduce the heat to medium for four minutes until the vegetables are cooked.
13. Add a tablespoon of water if the vegetables get stuck to the pan. Spread in the kale and tamari and allow the mixture to cook for another minute.
14. Serve the cooked tofu with the greens and the buckwheat.

Nutrition: 517 calories 26g fats 21g protein

53. Turkey Escalope with Sage, Parsley & Capers

Preparation Time: 21 minutes
Cooking Time: 42 minutes

Serving: 5

Ingredients

- One hundred and fifty grams of chopped cauliflower
- Two garlic cloves
- Forty grams of red onions
- Two garlic cloves
- One Thai chili
- One teaspoon of chopped fresh ginger
- Two tablespoons of extra virgin olive oil
- Two teaspoons ground turmeric
- Thirty grams of sun-dried tomatoes
- Ten grams of fresh parsley
- One hundred and fifty grams of turkey steak
- One teaspoon of dried sage juice
- One-quarter lemon
- One tablespoon of capers

Direction

1. Put the raw cauliflower into your food processor.
2. Chop up the cauliflower until a fine consistency is achieved.
3. Fry the ginger, garlic, chili and red onions and ginger in the extra virgin olive oil until they are all reasonably soft.
4. Put in your turmeric and cauliflower at this point, and allow the entire mixture to cook for one minute.
5. Bring the mixture down form your cooker, then add the tomatoes and half of your parsley.
6. Cover your turkey escalope with oil and sage and fry for six minutes, making sure to turn carefully to prevent burning.
7. At this point, proceed by pouring in the lemon juice, parsley, capers, and one tablespoon of water to the pan to create your sauce.

Nutrition: 391 calories 24g fats 13g protein

54. Buckwheat Pancakes, Mushrooms, Red Onions, and Kale Salad

Preparation time: 33 minutes
Cooking Time: 19 minutes
Serving: 5

Ingredients

- One buckwheat pancake
- 50g button mushrooms
- Fifteen grams of chicken
- 200g Kale
- 20g red onions
- Extra Virgin Olive Oil

Direction

1. Clean and cut the button mushrooms.
2. Clean and cut the kale into thin strips and the red onions into rings. Combine the green cabbage and onion in a bowl, season with a drizzle of olive oil, and possibly a little lemon.
3. Cut the chicken into pieces. In a pan, arrange a drizzle of olive oil and add the chicken pieces.
4. Add the mushrooms and brown them.
5. Place everything in the buckwheat pancake, and close the pancake.
6. On a plate, arrange the green cabbage / red onion salad, then place the hot buckwheat pancake next to it. Enjoy your meal!

Nutrition: 387 calories 16g fats 7g protein

55. Naan Bread with Baked Tofu and Cauliflower

Preparation Time: 17 minutes
Cooking Time: 28 minutes
Serving: 3

Ingredients

- 50 g firm plain tofu
- 50 g cauliflower
- ½ clove garlic
- ½ small onion
- 50ml of water
- 50ml coconut milk
- ½ tablespoon of tomato puree
- ½ teaspoon powdered Indian broth
- ½ tablespoon coconut oil
- ½ teaspoon curry powder
- ½ teaspoon cumin
- ½ tablespoon potato starch

Naan bread:

- 75g wheat flour
- One plain yogurt
- Two pinches of sugar
- 5g baker's yeast or 8 g dehydrated yeast
- 5g salt

- Two tablespoons extra virgin olive oil
- 5 cl lukewarm water
- One teaspoon caraway seed

Direction

1. Peel and mince the garlic and the onions.
2. In a casserole dish, sauté everything in coconut oil with the curry and cumin until lightly colored.
3. Add the coconut milk, the tomato puree, and 50 ml of water and the Indian broth. Mix well then bring to a dainty simmer.
4. Add the tofu pieces and the cauliflower.
5. Cook gently without the lid on for about 20 min until the cauliflower is slightly tender.
6. Dilute the starch with a little cooking juice, then pour back into the casserole dish and continue cooking for 5 min.
7. Serve with basmati rice and naan bread.
8. Naan Bread
9. Put the flour in your food processor.
10. Add the crumbled yeast, olive oil, sugar, yogurt, caraway seeds, and mix well.
11. Proceed by adding the water and continue mixing with the whisk
12. Now place the ball of dough in a small bowl then cover, and allow to stand for thirty minutes.
13. Heat up an empty pan, and cook the naan bread on each side for four minutes to remove moisture.
14. Enjoy your mouth-watering delicacy.

Nutrition: 399 calories 24g fats 16g protein

56. Sautéed Potatoes in Chicken Broth

Preparation Time: 19 minutes
Cooking Time: 37 minutes
Serving: 6

Ingredients

- Six medium-sized potatoes
- One onion
- Chicken broth
- 100ml of water
- One tbsp extra virgin olive oil
- Salt to taste

Direction

1. First peel the potatoes then slice it across into pieces.

2. Proceed by peeling the onions and chop into small pieces.
3. Fry minced onion pieces in oil for five minutes. Cook the potatoes for 10 minutes while stirring gently.
4. Dilute the chicken broth with water and add to the cooker, and cook for five minutes.
5. Add salt to taste and serve.

57. Classic Waldorf Salad

Preparation Time: 14 minutes
Cooking Time: 0 minute
Serving: 2

Ingredients

- One hundred and twenty-five grams of mayonnaise
- Two tablespoons white vinegar
- One apple, peeled and cut into pieces
- One celery stalk, diced
- One hundred and twenty-five grams of grapes
- One hundred and twenty-five grams of chopped walnuts
- Salt and pepper to taste

Direction

1. In a large bowl, whisk the mayonnaise and vinegar.
2. Add the apple, celery, raisins, and walnuts.
3. Sprinkle in salt and pepper. Mix everything and serve fresh.

Nutrition: 247 calories 18g fats 11g protein

58. Whole Wheat Pita

Preparation Time: 1 hour
Cooking Time: 24 minutes
Serving: 8

Ingredients

- 250g of whole wheat flour
- 2 tbsp extra virgin olive oil
- 5g salt
- 10g dry baker's yeast
- One hundred and fifty-ml hot water

Direction

1. Add the whole flour and the salt in a bowl and stir. Then add the rest of the ingredients: oil, yeast, and water. Stir thoroughly to mix.

2. Mix all the ingredients well until the pita bread dough is formed. Knead the dough for a few minutes on the table.
3. Once kneaded, make the dough into a ball and put it in a bowl. Cover and let it be there for two hours.
4. Take out the whole pita bread dough and knead again. Work the dough into balls of about 80g each. Use a roller to make the dough well-rounded. Make the pieces of bread ten-to-twelve cm wide and One cm thick.
5. Put the pitas on a tray. Preheat the oven to 200 ° C, slot in the tray, and let the pieces of bread bake for ten minutes, depending on the oven.
6. Finally, take out the pieces of bread, let them cool a little and serve!

Nutrition: 322 calories 21g fats 16g protein

59. Scrambled Tofu with Mushrooms

Preparation Time: 8 minutes
Cooking Time: 3 minutes
Serving: 4

Ingredients

- One hundred and twenty-five grams of plain firm tofu
- 100g silky tofu
- One tbsp. fresh cream
- One tbsp. sesame puree
- One tsp. Mustard
- ½ tsp. ground turmeric
- Four sprigs of fresh chives
- Half onion (optional)
- One garlic clove (optional)
- 50g mushrooms
- 2 tbsp. Extra Virgin Olive Oil
- One tbsp. Tamari soy sauce (gluten-free, organic soy sauce)
- Salt and pepper to taste

Direction

1. In a bowl, crush the firm tofu, add in the silky tofu, cream, tahini, mustard, turmeric, and chopped chives.
2. Mix thoroughly, and add salt and pepper to taste.
3. Peel and chop the onion and the garlic.

4. Rinse the mushrooms under a stream of water. Cut off the ends of the stalks and cut the mushrooms into strips. Gently fry the mushrooms, onions, and garlic over medium-high heat in a pan with a little olive oil.

5. Once the mushrooms, onions, and garlic are very tender and slightly brown in color, add the mixture to the tofu and cook over medium heat for about 5 minutes. Stir the mixture continuously with a spatula.

6. Serve hot, and enjoy.

Nutrition: 276 calories 18g fats 10g protein

60. Pasta with Smoked Salmon and Arugula

Preparation Time: 13 minutes
Cooking Time: 24 minutes
Serving: 2

Ingredients

- 250g Spaghetti
- One hundred and fifty grams of Smoked salmon
- One bunch of arugulas
- 2 tbsp. Extra virgin olive oil
- One finely chopped onion
- Salt and pepper to taste

Direction

1. Place the pasta in boiling water for ten minutes. Add salt to taste.
2. Slice the smoked salmon into strips. Rinse and wring the arugula.
3. Heat One tablespoonful of extra virgin olive oil in a frying pan and chop the onion. Add in the drained spaghetti, the salmon strips, and the arugula. Mix well and cook for 2 min.
4. Sprinkle in the rest of the olive oil, salt, and pepper.
5. Mix and serve hot.

Nutrition: 477 calories 25g fats 17g protein

61. Tofu with Cauliflower

Preparation time: 6 minutes
Cooking Time: 45 minutes
Servings 2

Ingredients

- 2 ounces of red pepper, seeded
- 1 Thai chili, cut in two halves, seeded
- 2 cloves of garlic

- 1 teaspoon of olive oil
- 1 pinch of cumin
- 1 pinch of coriander
- Juice of a 1/4 lemon
- 7 ounces of tofu
- 7 ounces of cauliflower, roughly chopped
- 1 ounce of red onions, finely chopped
- 1 teaspoon finely chopped ginger
- 2 teaspoons turmeric
- 2-ounce dried tomatoes, finely chopped
- 2 ounces of parsley, chopped

Direction

1. Preheat oven to 400 °. Slice the peppers and put them in an ovenproof dish with chili and garlic. Pour some olive oil over it, add the dried herbs and put it in the oven for 20 minutes. Let it cool down, put the peppers together with the lemon juice in a blender and work it into a soft mass.
2. Cut the tofu in half and divide the halves into triangles. Place the tofu in a small casserole dish, cover with the paprika mixture and place in the oven for about 20 minutes.
3. Chop the cauliflower until the pieces are smaller than a grain of rice.
4. Then, in a small saucepan, heat the garlic, onions, chili and ginger with olive oil until they become transparent. Add turmeric and cauliflower, mix well and heat again. Remove from heat and add parsley and tomatoes, mix well. Serve with the tofu in the sauce.

Nutrition: 298 Calories 18g fats 11g protein

62. Indulgent Yoghurt

Preparation Time: 13 minutes
Cooking Time: 24 minutes
Servings: 1

Ingredients

- 125 mixed berries
- 3.5oz of Greek yoghurt
- 25 walnuts, chopped
- 0.9oz of dark chocolate (at least 85% cocoa solids), grated

Directions

1. Toss the mixed berries into a serving bowl. Cover with yoghurt and top with chocolate and walnuts. Voila!

Nutrition: 298 Calories 11g fats 7g protein

63. Frozen Gazpacho

Preparation Time: 16 minutes
Cooking Time: 0 minutes
Servings: 2
Ingredients:

- 2 large or 6 small tomatoes, chopped
- 1 avocado, seeded, sliced and picked (wait until prompted)
- 1 medium cucumber, chopped
- 1 small red onion, chopped
- 1 cup very finely chopped arugula
- ½ celery stalk, finely chopped
- 1 garlic clove, chopped or pressed
- ½ chili or a pinch of cayenne pepper
- 1 teaspoon of lime juice pinch of sea salt
- A pinch of pepper

Direction:

1. Put the ingredients in a blender or food processor and let them beat gently. You don't want to mix too well, or you make a liquid instead of a soup. The gazpacho must be thick. After mixing, put in the refrigerator for about 1 hour. You can also leave it overnight.
2. Cut and remove the avocado just before eating. Serve half of the gazpacho in a cold bowl. Add the avocado slices and serve immediately.

Nutrition: 292 Calories 13g fat 8g protein

64. Tomato Frittata

Preparation Time: 17 minutes
Cooking Time: 22 minutes
Servings: 2
Ingredient

- 1.3oz cheddar cheese, grated
- 1.4oz kalamata olives, pitted and halved
- 8 cherry tomatoes, halved
- 4 large eggs
- 1 tablespoon fresh parsley, chopped
- 1 tablespoon fresh basil, chopped
- 1 tablespoon olive oil

Directions

1. Scourge eggs together in a large mixing bowl. Toss in the parsley, basil, olives, tomatoes and cheese, stirring thoroughly.

2. Using small skillet, cook olive oil over high heat. Fill in the frittata mixture and cook for 5-10 minutes. Pull out skillet from the hob and place under the grill for 5 minutes. Divide into portions and serve immediately.

Nutrition: 123 Calories 17g fat 6g protein

65. Chicken with Kale and Chili Salsa

Preparation Time: 7 minutes
Cooking Time: 41 Minutes
Servings 1
Ingredients

- 3 ounces of buckwheat
- 1 teaspoon of chopped fresh ginger
- Juice of ½ lemon, divided
- 2 teaspoons of ground turmeric
- 3 ounces of kale, chopped
  - ounce of red onion, sliced
- 4 ounce of skinless, boneless chicken breast
- 1 tablespoon of extra-virgin olive oil
- 1 tomato
- 1 handful parsley
- 1 bird's eye chili, chopped

Directions

1. Start with the salsa: Remove the eye out of the tomato and finely chop it. Mix it with the chili, parsley, and lemon juice.
2. Heat your oven to 220 degrees F. Marinate the chicken with a little oil, 1 teaspoon of turmeric, and the lemon juice. Let it rest for 5-10 minutes.
3. Preheat pan over medium heat until it is hot then add marinated chicken and allow it to cook for a minute on both sides until it is pale gold. Transfer the chicken to the oven and bake for 10 minutes. Get the chicken out of the oven, cover with foil, and rest for five minutes before you serve.
4. Meanwhile, in a steamer, steam the kale for about 5 minutes.
5. In a little oil, fry the ginger and red onions until they are soft but not colored, and then add in the cooked kale and fry it for a minute.
6. Cook the buckwheat in accordance to the packet Directions with the remaining

turmeric. Serve alongside the vegetables, salsa and chicken.

Nutrition: 135 Calories 15g fats 9g protein

66. Buckwheat Tuna Casserole

Preparation Time: 9 minutes
Cooking Time: 38 minutes
Servings: 2

Ingredients

- 2 tablespoons butter
- 10-ounce package buckwheat ramen noodles
- 2 cups boiling water
- 1/3 cup dry red wine
- 3 cups milk
- 2 tablespoons dried parsley
- 2 teaspoons turmeric
- ½ teaspoon curry powder
- 2 tablespoons All-Purpose flour
- 2 cups celery, chopped
- 1 cup frozen peas
- 2 cans tuna, drained

Directions

1. Dot butter into your crockpot and grease the pot.
2. Place buckwheat ramen noodles in a large bowl and pour boiling water to cover. Let sit for 5 – 8 minutes, or until noodles separate when prodded with a fork.
3. Scourge red wine, milk, parsley, turmeric and flour.
4. Fold in celery, peas, and tuna.
5. Drain the ramen and place into crockpot, pouring the tuna mixture over top. Mix to combine.
6. Close and cook at Low 8 hours, stirring occasionally.

Nutrition: 411 Calories 19g fats 11g protein

67. Tuscan Stewed Beans

Preparation Time: 21 minutes
Cooking Time: 33 minutes
Servings: 1

Ingredients

- 1 dl. extra virgin olive oil
- Salt to taste
- Pepper as needed.
- Cannellini beans
- Sage
- Garlic clove
- Water

Directions

1. Submerge beans for at least 12 hours before cooking. Pour the beans in a crockpot with water, a clove of garlic, sage, and a generous pinch of salt, adjust the flame as low as possible.
2. Once boiling, cover the pot, and continue cooking for at least 3 and a half hours, taking care that the flame remains very low, the beans in the pot must not move around.
3. Once you are done cooking, serve the beans with extra virgin olive oil, salt, and pepper on the table.

Nutrition: 145 Calories 22g fats 15g protein

68. Buckwheat Tabbouleh with Strawberries

Preparation Time: 21 minutes
Cooking Time: 33 minutes
Servings: 1

Ingredients

- Buckwheat (broken)
- Turmeric powder 2 teaspoon
- Avocado 1
- Tomatoes
- Tropia red onions
- Medjool dates (pitted)
- Parsley
- Strawberries
- 2 tablespoons extra virgin olive oil
- Lemon juice 1
- Rocket 1.3 ounce

Direction

1. Heat up the water to cook the buckwheat.
2. When it boils, add turmeric and buckwheat. Be careful not to overcook it. It is good to leave, it "al dente." When cooked, drain the buckwheat and set aside to cool. Take a large bowl to spice the tabbouleh.
3. Cut the tomatoes into cubes and let them drain for a few minutes in a colander to remove the water.

4. On a cutting board, begin to finely chop the red onion, dates, and parsley and combine them with buckwheat.

5. Skin the avocado and cut it into small cubes and add it with the tomatoes to the buckwheat. Cut the strawberries into slices and gently add them to the rest of the ingredients. Add the chopped arugula, oil, and lemon juice. Mix all the ingredients and let the buckwheat tabbouleh take on extra flavor for an hour before serving it at the table.

Nutrition: 145 Calories 26g fat 13g protein

69. <u>Scramble Tofu and Mushroom</u>

Preparation Time: 11 minutes
Cooking Time: 28 minutes
Servings: 2

Ingredients

- 7 ounces of extra firm tofu
- 2 teaspoon turmeric powder
- 1 teaspoon black pepper
- ounce of kale, roughly chopped
- 2 teaspoons extra virgin olive oil
- Oz. of red onion
- 1 Thai chili
- 100g mushrooms
- 4 tbsp. parsley

Direction

1. Drain tofu in paper towels.
2. Blend the turmeric with water.
3. Steam the kale for 3 minutes.
4. Cook olive oil at medium heat, fry onion, chili, and mushrooms for 3 minutes
5. Crush the tofu into bite-size pieces and put in the pan, mix the turmeric paste over the tofu. Season with black pepper. Cook at medium heat for 2 minutes
6. Cook kale at medium heat for 4 minutes. Sprinkle parsley and serve.

Nutrition: 122 calories 20g fat 11g protein

70. <u>Kale Scramble</u>

Preparation Time: 17 minutes
Cooking Time: 6 minutes
Servings: 2

Ingredients

- 4 eggs
- 1/8 teaspoon ground turmeric

- Salt and ground black pepper, to taste
- 1 tablespoon water
- 2 teaspoons olive oil
- 1 cup fresh kale, tough ribs removed and chopped

Directions

1. Scourge eggs, turmeric, salt, black pepper, and water and using a whisk.
2. In a wok, cook oil over medium heat.
3. Stir egg mixture and stir to combine.
4. Set the heat to medium-low and cook for 2 minutes.
5. Mix in the kale and cook for 4 minutes.
6. Remove from the heat and serve immediately.

Nutrition: 183 Calories 25g fats 13g protein

71. <u>Pancakes with Blackcurrant Compote</u>

Preparation Time: 18 minutes
Cooking Time: 21 minutes
Servings: 2

Ingredients

- 4 ounce of porridge oats
- ounce of plain flour
- 1 tablespoon caster sugar
- ½ teaspoon baking powder
- 1 large green apple
- 2/3 cup semi-skimmed milk
- 1 egg white
- 1 tsp. olive oil.

For the compote:

- ounce of blackcurrants washed and stalks removed.
- 1 tablespoon caster sugar
- 2 tablespoon water.

Direction

For compote:

1. Simmer blackcurrants, sugar, and water for 13 minutes.

For Pancake:

2. Incorporate Oats, flour, baking powder, and caster sugar in a bowl.
3. Mix apple into the powder mixture then stir in milk simultaneously.
4. Beat egg white to a stiff peak then mix into the pancake batter.
5. Pre-heat ½ teaspoon olive oil in a non-stick frying pan at medium heat and place

½ of the batter. Lower the heat then cook both sides until golden brown.

6. Drizzle pancakes with the blackcurrant compote.

Nutrition: 123 calories 20g fats 8g protein

72. Cinnamon Buckwheat Porridge

Preparation Time: 12 minutes
Cooking Time: 17 minutes
Servings: 2

Ingredients

- 1 cup buckwheat, rinsed
- 1 cup unsweetened almond milk
- 1 cup water
- ½ teaspoon ground cinnamon
- ½ teaspoon vanilla extract
- 1–2 tablespoons raw honey
- ¼ cup fresh blueberries

Directions

1. Boil all the ingredients (except honey and blueberries) at medium-high heat
2. Now, reduce the heat to low and simmer, covered for about 10 minutes.
3. Drizzle honey and take out from the heat.
4. Set aside, covered, for 5 minutes.
5. With a fork, fluff the mixture, and transfer into serving bowls.
6. Top with blueberries and serve.

Nutrition: 358 Calories 29g fats 18g protein

73. Mushroom Scramble Egg

Preparation Time: 7 minutes
Cooking Time: 13 minutes
Servings: 3

Ingredients

- Two eggs
- 1 teaspoon ground turmeric
- 1 teaspoon mild curry powder
- 20g kale, roughly chopped
- 1 teaspoon extra virgin olive oil
- ½ bird's eye chili, thinly sliced
- A handful of thinly sliced, button mushrooms
- 5g parsley, finely chopped

Directions

1. Mix the curry and turmeric powder, then add a little water until a light paste has been achieved.

2. Steam up the kale 2–3 minutes.
3. Over medium heat, cook oil in a frying pan and fry the chili and mushrooms for 2–3 minutes
4. Put the eggs and spice paste, and cook over medium heat, then add the kale and start cooking for another minute over medium heat. Add the parsley, then mix well and serve.

Nutrition: 185 Calories 27g fats 16g protein

74. Sirtfood Eggs and Mushroom

Preparation Time: 13 minutes
Cooking Time: 21 minutes
Servings: 1

Ingredients

- 2 medium eggs
- I teaspoon turmeric
- 1 ounce of kale, roughly chopped
- 1 teaspoon extra virgin olive oil
- 1/2 chili, thinly sliced
- 0.5 ounce of red onions
- Parsley, thinly chopped
- A handful of button mushrooms, thinly sliced

Direction

1. Smoke the kale for 2 minutes.
2. Dissolve turmeric powder with water.
3. Blend turmeric paste, parsley, and mix properly.
4. Warm up olive oil at medium heat then sauté onion, chili, and mushroom
5. Mix steamed kale to the mix in the frying pan.
6. Stir in egg mixture to the pan
7. Decrease heat and cook the egg.

Nutrition: 157 Calories 52g Protein 26g fats

75. Matcha Green Juice

Preparation Time: 8 minutes
Cooking time: 0 minutes
Servings: 2

Ingredients

- 5 ounces fresh kale
- 2 ounces fresh arugula
- ¼ cup fresh parsley
- ½ tsp. Matcha green tea
- 4 celery stalks
- 1 green apple, cored and chopped

- 1 (1-inch) piece fresh ginger, peeled
- 1 lemon, peeled

Direction

1. Incorporate the all ingredients then extract the juice as stated by the manufacturer's direction.
2. Fill into the glasses then serve.

Nutrition: 115 Calories 27g fat 11g protein

76. Berry Pancakes

Preparation Time: 11 minutes
Cooking Time: 4 minutes
Servings: 4

Ingredients

- ½ cup coconut milk
- 1 tablespoon coconut oil
- 1 egg, beaten lightly
- 1/3 cup buckwheat flour
- 1 teaspoon baking powder
- Pinch of salt
- ¼ cup frozen blueberries

Direction

1. Incorporate flour, baking powder, and salt.
2. Scourge coconut milk, coconut oil, and eggs.
3. Stir in flour mixture and mix well.
4. Fold in blueberries.
5. Heat up greased non-stick skillet at medium heat.
6. Place half of the mixture and spread in an even circle.
7. Cook for about 2–3 minutes.
8. Flip and cook for additional 1 minute.
9. Repeat with the remaining mixture.
10. Serve warm.

Nutrition: 181 Calories 11g Fat 5.4g Protein

77. Pumpkin Pancakes

Preparation Time: 13 minutes
Cooking Time: 41 minutes
Servings: 10

Ingredients

- 2 tablespoons ground flaxseed
- 6 tablespoons water
- 1 cup buckwheat flour
- 1 tablespoon baking powder
- 1 teaspoon pumpkin pie spice
- ½ teaspoon salt
- 1 cup pumpkin puree

- ¾ cup plus 2 tablespoons unsweetened almond milk
- 3 tablespoons pure maple syrup
- 2 tablespoons coconut oil
- 1 teaspoon vanilla extract

Direction:

1. Mix ground flaxseed well. Set aside for 5 minutes.
2. In a blender, add flaxseed mixture and remaining ingredients and pulse until well combined.
3. Situate mixture into a bowl and set aside for about 10 minutes.
4. Preheat greased non-stick skillet over medium heat.
5. Place about ¼ cup of the mixture and spread in an even circle.
6. Cook for about 2 minutes per side.
7. Repeat with the remaining mixture.
8. Serve warm.

Nutrition: 102 Calories 4g Fat 2.1g Protein

78. Simple Waffles

Preparation Time: 12 minutes
Cooking Time: 40 minutes
Servings: 4

Ingredients

- 1¼ cups unsweetened almond milk
- 1 tablespoon apple cider vinegar
- 1 tablespoon ground flaxseed
- 3 tablespoons water
- 1 cup buckwheat flour
- 1 tablespoon coconut sugar
- 1¼ teaspoons baking powder
- 1 teaspoon baking soda
- ¼ teaspoon salt
- ¼ teaspoon ground cinnamon

Direction

1. In a cup, mix together almond milk vinegar. Set aside for 5 minutes.
2. Incorporate ground flaxseed. Keep aside for 6 minutes.
3. In a separate bowl, add buckwheat flour, coconut sugar, cinnamon, baking powder, baking soda, and salt, and mix well.
4. In the bowl of flaxseed mixture, add almond milk mixture and stir to combine.
5. Mix flour mixture. Set aside for about 8 minutes.

6. Heat and grease the waffle iron
7. Place the desired amount of the mixture into the preheated waffle iron and cook for about 5 minutes per side or until golden-brown.
8. Repeat with the remaining mixture.
9. Serve warm.

Nutrition: 136 Calories 2.6g Fat 4.4g Protein

79. Green Veggies Quiche

Preparation Time: 17 minutes
Cooking Time: 17 minutes
Servings: 4

Ingredients

- 6 eggs
- ½ cup unsweetened almond milk
- Salt and ground black pepper, to taste
- 2 cups fresh baby kale, chopped
- ½ cup green bell pepper, seeded and chopped
- 1 scallion, chopped
- ¼ cup fresh parsley, chopped
- 1 tablespoon fresh chives, minced

Direction

1. Preheat the oven to 400°F.
2. Lightly grease a pie dish.
3. In a bowl, add eggs, almond milk, salt, and black pepper, and beat until well combined. Set aside.
4. In another bowl, add the vegetables and herbs and mix well.
5. In the bottom of prepared pie dish, place the veggie mixture evenly and top with the egg mixture.
6. Bake for 21 minutes.
7. Remove pie dish from the oven and set aside for about 5 minutes before slicing.
8. Cut into desired sized wedges and serve warm.

Nutrition: 123 Calories 7.1g Fat 9.8g Protein

80. Tofu & Kale Omelet

Preparation Time: 21 minutes
Cooking Time: 23 minutes
Servings: 2

Ingredients

- 10 ounces firm silken tofu, pressed and drained
- 4 tablespoons nutritional yeast
- 4 tablespoons hummus

- 2 teaspoons arrowroot powder
- 2 cups fresh kale, tough ribs removed and chopped
- ½ teaspoon paprika
- Salt and ground black pepper, to taste
- 1–2 tablespoons water
- 2 tablespoons extra-virgin olive oil

Direction

1. Preheat oven to 375°F.
2. Using a food processor, blend tofu, nutritional yeast, hummus, arrowroot powder, paprika, salt, black pepper, and water.
3. Grease a medium, ovenproof skillet with 1 tablespoon of oil and heat over medium heat.
4. Add the kale, salt, and black pepper, and sauté for about 3–5 minutes.
5. Remove from the heat and transfer the kale into a bowl.
6. Grease the same skillet with the remaining oil.
7. In the bottom of greases skillet, place the tofu mixture.
8. With a spatula, gently spread the tofu mixture in a thin and even layer.
9. Situate skillet over medium heat and cook for 5 minutes.
10. Immediately, transfer the skillet into the oven and bake for about 10–15 minutes
11. In the last 5 minutes of cooking, situate remaining cooked kale on top evenly.
12. Remove the skillet from oven and fold over the omelet.
13. Cut the omelet in 2 portions and serve.

Nutrition: 371 Calories 21.7g Fat 23.3g Protein

81. Kale, Chickpeas & Olives Salad

Preparation Time: 18 minutes
Cooking Time: 0 minutes
Servings: 4

Ingredients

Dressing

- 2 tablespoons fresh orange juice
- 2 tablespoons fresh lemon juice
- 3 tablespoons extra-virgin olive oil
- 1 tablespoon red wine vinegar
- 1 tablespoon honey

- 1 tablespoon fresh orange zest, grated
- ¾ tablespoon Dijon mustard
- Salt and ground black pepper, to taste

Salad
- 3 cups cooked chickpeas
- 2 cups mixed olives, pitted
- 1 cup red onion, chopped
- 6 cups fresh kale, tough ribs removed and torn

Direction
1. For dressing: In a small bowl, add all ingredients and beat well.
2. For salad: In a large salad bowl, mix together all ingredients.
3. Place dressing over salad and toss to coat well.
4. Serve immediately.

Nutrition: 468 Calories 20g Fat 13.1g Protein

82. Steak Salad

Preparation Time: 21 minutes
Cooking Time: 7 minutes
Servings: 2
Ingredients
Steak
- 1 (12-ounce) sirloin steak
- Salt and ground black pepper, to taste
- 2 tablespoons extra-virgin olive oil

Salad
- ¼ cup cucumber; peeled, seeded, and sliced
- ¼ cup red onion, sliced
- ¼ cup cherry tomatoes, halved
- 2 tablespoons fresh parsley, chopped
- 2 tablespoons fresh mint leaves
- 3 cups fresh kale, tough ribs removed and chopped finely

Dressing
- 1 tablespoon extra-virgin olive oil
- 1 tablespoon fresh lemon juice
- Salt and ground black pepper, to taste

Direction
1. For steak: Season the steak with salt and black pepper lightly.
2. In a heavy-bottomed sauté pan, heat 2 tablespoons of the oil over high heat and cook the steak for 8 minutes on both sides.

3. Pull out from the heat and place the steak onto a cutting board for about 10 minutes.
4. For salad: Place all ingredients in a salad bowl and mix.
5. For dressing: Place all ingredients in another bowl and beat until well combined.
6. Cut the steaks into desired sized slices against the grain.
7. Place the salad onto each serving plate.
8. Top each plate with steak slices.
9. Drizzle with dressing and serve.

Nutrition: 567 Calories 31.8g Fat 55g Protein

83. Chicken & Orange Salad

Preparation Time: 13 minutes
Cooking Time: 16 minutes
Servings: 5
Ingredients
Chicken
- 4 (6-ounce) boneless, skinless chicken breast halves
- Salt and ground black pepper, to taste
- 2 tablespoons extra-virgin olive oil

Salad
- 8 cups fresh baby arugula
- 5 medium oranges, peeled and sectioned
- 1 cup onion, sliced

Dressing
- 2 tablespoons extra-virgin olive oil
- 2 tablespoons fresh orange juice
- 2 tablespoons red wine vinegar
- 1½ teaspoons shallots, minced
- 1 garlic clove, minced
- Salt and ground black pepper, to taste

Direction
1. For chicken: Season each chicken breast half with salt and black pepper evenly.
2. Place chicken over a rack set in a rimmed baking sheet.
3. Refrigerate for at least 30 minutes.
4. Remove the baking sheet from refrigerator and pat dry the chicken breast halves with paper towels.
5. Heat the oil in a 12-inch sauté pan over medium-low heat.
6. Place the chicken breast halves, smooth-side down, and cook for about 9–10 minutes, without moving.

7. Flip the chicken breasts and cook for about 6 minutes or until cooked through.
8. Remove the sauté pan from heat and let the chicken stand in the pan for about 3 minutes.
9. Transfer the chicken breasts onto a cutting board for about 5 minutes.
10. Cut each chicken breast half into desired-sized slices.
11. For salad: Place all ingredients in a salad bowl and mix.
12. Add chicken slices and stir to combine.
13. For dressing: place all ingredients in another bowl and beat until well combined.
14. Place the salad onto each serving plate.
15. Drizzle with dressing and serve.

Nutrition: 463 Calories 22g Fat 42g Protein

84. Buckwheat Burgers

Preparation Time: 18 minutes
Cooking Time: 47 minutes
Servings: 4

Ingredients

Patties
- ¾ cup dry buckwheat
- 1½ cups filtered water
- Salt, to taste
- 2 tablespoons extra-virgin olive oil, divided
- ½ of large yellow onion, chopped finely
- ½ of large carrot, peeled and grated
- ½ of celery stalk, chopped finely
- 1 fresh kale leaf, tough ribs removed and chopped finely
- 1 cooked sweet potato
- 2 tablespoons almond butter
- 2 tablespoons low-sodium soy sauce

Salad
- 4 cups fresh baby arugula
- 2 large tomatoes, chopped

Direction
1. Preheat the oven to 350°F.
2. Line a baking sheet with parchment paper.
3. For patties: Heat a non-stick frying pan over medium heat and toast the buckwheat for about 5 minutes, stirring continuously.
4. Boil water and salt over high heat.
5. Put heat to low and cook, covered for 15 minutes.

6. Cook 1 tablespoon of the oil in a skillet over medium heat and sauté the onion for 5 minutes.
7. Cook carrot and celery for 5 minutes.
8. Stir in the remaining ingredients and remove from the heat.
9. Transfer the mixture into a bowl with buckwheat and stir to combine.
10. Set aside to cool completely.
11. Make 4 equal-sized patties from the mixture.
12. Arrange the patties onto the prepared baking sheet in a single layer and bake for about
13. Bake for about 20 minutes per side.
14. Divide the arugula and tomatoes onto serving plates.
15. Top each plate with 2 patties and serve

Nutrition: 287 Calories 21.7g Fat 8.3g Protein

85. Sautéed Mushrooms

Preparation Time: 16 minutes
Cooking Time: 11 minutes
Servings: 2

Ingredients
- 2 tablespoons extra-virgin olive oil
- 2–3 tablespoons red onion, minced
- ½ teaspoon garlic, minced
- 12 ounces fresh mushrooms, sliced
- 1 tablespoon fresh parsley
- 1 teaspoon fresh lemon juice
- Salt and ground black pepper, to taste

Direction
1. In a sauté pan, heat the oil over medium heat and sauté the onion and garlic for 3–4 minutes.
2. Cook mushrooms and cook for 9 minutes.
3. Stir in the parsley, lemon juice, salt and black pepper and remove from the heat.
4. Serve hot.

Nutrition: 163 Calories 14.5g Fat 5.6g Protein

86. Kale with Cranberries & Pine Nuts

Preparation Time: 13 minutes
Cooking Time: 17 minutes
Servings: 6

Ingredients
- 2 pounds fresh kale, tough ribs removed and chopped

- 3 tablespoons extra-virgin olive oil
- 1 tablespoon garlic, minced
- ½ cup dried unsweetened cranberries
- Salt and ground black pepper, to taste
- 1/3 cup pine nuts

Direction

1. Using a pan of boiling salted water, cook the kale for about 5–7 minutes.
2. In a colander, drain the kale and immediately transfer into an ice bath.
3. Drain the kale and set aside.
4. Preheat oil on medium heat and sauté the garlic for about 1 minute.
5. Add kale, cranberries, salt, and black pepper, and cook for about 4–6 minutes, tossing frequently with tongs.
6. Stir in the pine nuts and serve hot.

Nutrition: 196 Calories 12.2g Fat 5.6g Protein

87. Tofu with Kale

Preparation Time: 18 minutes
Cooking Time: 8 minutes
Servings: 2

Ingredients

- 1 tablespoon extra-virgin olive oil
- ½ pound tofu; pressed, drained, and cubed
- 1 teaspoon fresh ginger, minced
- 1 garlic clove, minced
- ¼ teaspoon red pepper flakes, crushed
- 6 ounces fresh kale, tough ribs removed and chopped finely
- 1 tablespoon low-sodium soy sauce

Direction

1. Pre-heat olive oil in a large non-stick wok over medium-high heat and stir-fry the tofu for about 2–3 minutes.
2. Sauté ginger, garlic and red pepper flakes, stirring continuously.
3. Stir in the kale and soy sauce and stir-fry for about 4–5 minutes.
4. Serve hot.

Nutrition: 190 Calories 11.8g Fat 12.5g Protein

88. Buckwheat Pancakes

Preparation Time: 11 minutes
Cooking Time: 17 minutes
Servings: 5

Ingredients

- 1 cup unsweetened almond milk
- 2 teaspoons apple cider vinegar

- 1 cup buckwheat flour
- 2 tablespoons ground flaxseed
- 1 tablespoon baking powder
- ¼ teaspoon sea salt
- ¼ cup maple syrup
- 1 teaspoon vanilla extract
- 1 tablespoon extra-virgin olive oil

Direction

1. Blend almond milk and vinegar. Set aside.
2. Combine flour, flaxseed, baking powder, and salt.
3. Add the coconut milk mixture, maple syrup, and vanilla extract and beat until well combined.
4. In a non-stick skillet, heat the oil over medium heat.
5. Transfer 1/3 cup of the mix in a pan and spread in an even circle.
6. Cook for about 1–2 minutes.
7. Flip and cook for additional 1 minute.
8. Repeat with the remaining mixture.
9. Serve warm.

Nutrition: 174 Calories 5.2g Fat 3.8g Protein

89. Blueberry Waffles

Preparation Time: 14 minutes
Cooking Time: 21 minutes
Servings: 2

Ingredients

- ¼ cup coconut flour
- ½ teaspoon baking powder
- Pinch of salt
- 1/8 teaspoon ground cinnamon
- 4 eggs
- ¼ cup coconut oil, melted
- 2 tablespoons maple syrup
- 1 tablespoon fresh lemon juice
- ¼ cup fresh blueberries
- 1½ teaspoons lemon zest, grated

Direction

1. Through a fine-mesh sieve, sift together the flour, baking powder, cinnamon, and salt in a bowl.
2. In another large bowl, add the eggs and coconut oil and beat until well combined.
3. Add the maple syrup and lemon juice and again beat until well combined.
4. Stir in flour mixture and combine well.
5. Lightly, stir in blueberries and lemon zest.

6. Heat waffle iron and grease, it.
7. Pour desired amount of mixture and cook for about 5 minutes or until golden-brown.
8. Repeat with the remaining mixture.
9. Serve warm.

Nutrition: 244 Calories 19g Fat 6.7g Protein

90. Tofu & Arugula Scramble

Preparation Time: 13 minutes
Cooking Time: 9 minutes
Servings: 2

Ingredients

- 1 tablespoon extra-virgin olive oil
- 1 garlic clove, minced
- ¼ pound medium-firm tofu, drained, pressed, and crumbled
- 1/3 cup homemade vegetable broth
- 2½ cups fresh arugula
- ¼ cup tomato, chopped finely
- 2 teaspoons low-sodium soy sauce
- 1 teaspoon ground turmeric
- 1 teaspoon fresh lemon juice

Direction

1. Cook olive oil in a frying pan over medium-high heat and sauté the garlic for about 1 minute.
2. Add the tofu and cook for about 2–3 minutes, slowly adding the broth.
3. Add the arugula, tomato, soy sauce, and turmeric and stir fry for about 3–4 minutes. Drizzle lemon juice and serve immediately.

Nutrition: 125 Calories 10g Fat 6.8g Protein

91. Aromatic Chicken Breast, Kale, Red Onion, and Salsa

Preparation Time: 53 minutes
Cooking Time: 32 minutes
Servings: 2

Ingredients

- 120g skinless, boneless chicken breast
- 2 teaspoons ground turmeric
- ¼ lemon
- 1 tablespoon extra-virgin olive oil
- 50g kale, chopped
- 20g red onion, sliced
- 1 teaspoon fresh ginger, chopped
- 50g buckwheat

Directions

1. To prepare the salsa, remove the tomato eye and finely chop. Add the chili, parsley, capers, lemon juice and mix.
2. Set oven to 220°C. Pour 1 teaspoon of the turmeric, the lemon juice and a little oil on the chicken breast and marinate. Allow to stay for 5–10 minutes.
3. Position an ovenproof frying pan on the heat and cook the marinated chicken for a minute on each side to achieve a pale golden color. Then transfer the pan containing the chicken to the oven and allow to stay for 8–10 minutes or until it is done. Pull out from the oven and wrap with foil, set aside for 5 minutes before serving.
4. Situate kale in a steamer for 5 minutes. Drizzle little oil in a frying pan and sauté red onions and the ginger. Stir in cooked kale and fry for another minute.
5. Cook the buckwheat following the packet's instructions using the remaining turmeric. Serve alongside the chicken, salsa, and vegetables.

Nutrition: 149 Calories 16g Protein 5g Fat

92. Kale and Red Onion Dal with Buckwheat

Preparation Time 7 minutes
Cooking Time 25 minutes
Servings: 2

Ingredients

- ½ tablespoon olive oil
- ½ small red onion, sliced
- 1 ½ garlic cloves, crushed
- 1cm ginger, grated
- ½ birds eye chili, deseeded and finely chopped
- 1 teaspoon turmeric
- 1 teaspoon garam masala
- 80g red lentils
- 200ml coconut milk
- 100ml water
- 50g kale or spinach
- 80g buckwheat or brown rice

Directions

1. Cook olive oil, stir in sliced onion and cook on a low heat for 5 minutes. Sauté ginger, garlic, and chili for extra 1 minute.
2. Add to it, the garam masala, turmeric, and a splash of water. Cook for 3 minutes before adding the coconut milk, red lentils, and 200ml water.
3. Thoroughly mix all together and cook over a gentle heat for 20 minutes with the lid closed. When the dhal starts sticking, add a little more water and stir occasionally.
4. Add the kale, after 20 minutes and thoroughly stir and still cover the lid to cook for additional 5 minutes or 1-2 minutes when you substitute with spinach.
5. Put the buckwheat in a saucepan and pour boiling water like 15 minutes before the curry gets ready. Allow the water to boil and cook for 10-12 minutes. Drain the buckwheat and serve with the dhal.

Nutrition: 355 Calories 14g Protein 5.7g Fat

93. Chargrilled Beef and Herb Roasted Potatoes

Preparation Time: 90 minutes
Cooking Time: 70 minutes
Servings: 2

Ingredients

- 100g potatoes, peeled and dice
- 1 tablespoon extra-virgin olive oil
- 5g parsley, finely chopped
- 50g red onion, sliced into rings
- 50g kale, sliced

- 1 garlic clove, finely chopped
- 120–150g beef fillet steak
- 40ml red wine
- 150ml beef stock
- 1 teaspoon tomato purée
- 1 teaspoon corn flour
- 1 tablespoon water

Directions

1. Preheat the oven to 220C (430F) and put the potatoes in a boiling water and cook for 4–5 minutes, drain. Pour 1 teaspoon oil in a roasting tin and roast the potatoes for 35–45 minutes turning the potatoes on every sides every 10 minutes to ensure they cook evenly.
2. Remove from the oven when fully cooked, sprinkle with chopped parsley and mix thoroughly.
3. Pour 1 teaspoon of the oil on a saucepan and fry the onion for 5-7 minutes to become soft and neatly caramelized. Keep it warm.
4. Place the kale in a saucepan, steam for 2–3 minutes and drain. In ½ teaspoon of oil, fry the garlic for 1 minute to become soft though not colored. Add the kale and continue to fry for extra 1–2 minutes to become tender. Maintain the warmth.
5. Over a high heat, place an ovenproof frying pan until it becomes smoking. Then use the ½ a teaspoon of the oil to coat the meat and fry over a medium–high heat. Take out the meat and set aside to rest.
6. Pour the wine to the hot pan and bubble to reduce the wine quantity by half to form syrupy and to have a concentrated flavor. Add the tomato purée and stock to the steak pan and boil. Add the corn flour paste little at a time to act as a thickener to until the desired consistency is achieved. Add any juices from the rested steak and serve with the kale, onion rings, roasted potatoes, and red wine sauce.

Nutrition: 244 Calories 14g Protein 14.4g Fat

94. Crunchy Braised Leeks

Preparation Time: 41 minutes
Cooking Time: 21 minutes
Servings: 3
Ingredients

- 20 g Ghee
- 2 teaspoon Olive oil
- 2 pieces Leek
- 150 ml Vegetable broth
- Fresh parsley
- 1 tablespoon fresh oregano
- 1 tablespoon Pine nuts

Directions

1. Cut the leek into thin rings and finely chop the herbs. Roast the pine nuts in a dry pan over medium heat.
2. Melt the ghee together with the olive oil in a large pan.
3. Cook the leek until golden brown for 5 minutes, stirring constantly.
4. Add the vegetable broth and cook for another 10 minutes.
5. Stir in the herbs and drizzle pine nuts on the dish just before serving.

Nutrition: 95 Calories 1.35g Protein 4.8g Fat

95. Sweet and Sour Pan with Cashew Nuts

Preparation Time: 31 minutes
Cooking Time: 0 minutes
Servings: 2
Ingredients

- 2 tablespoon Coconut oil
- 2 pieces Red onion
- 2 pieces yellow bell pepper
- 250 g White cabbage
- 150 g Pak choy
- 50 g Mung bean sprouts
- 4 pieces Pineapple slices
- 50 g Cashew nuts
- For the sweet and sour sauce:
- 60 ml Apple cider vinegar
- 4 tablespoon Coconut blossom sugar
- 2 tablespoon Tomato paste
- 1 teaspoon Coconut-Aminos
- 2 teaspoon Arrowroot powder
- 75 ml Water

Directions

1. Roughly cut the vegetables.
2. Mix the arrow root with five tablespoons of cold water into a paste.

3. Situate all the other ingredients for the sauce in a saucepan and add the arrowroot paste for binding.
4. Cook coconut oil in a pan and fry the onion.
5. Add the bell pepper, cabbage, Pak choy and bean sprouts and stir-fry until the vegetables become a little softer.
6. Add the pineapple and cashew nuts and stir a few more times.
7. Pour a little sauce over the wok dish and serve.

Nutrition: 573 Calories 15.2g Protein 27.8g Fat

96. <u>Eggplant and Spinach Casserole</u>

Preparation Time: 60 minutes
Cooking Time: 42 minutes
Servings: 3
Ingredients

- 1 Eggplant
- 2 Onions
- Olive oil 3 tbsp.
- Spinach 16 oz.
- 4 Tomatoes
- 2 Egg
- ¼ cup Almond milk
- 2 tsp. Lemon juice
- 4 tbsp. Almond flour

Directions

1. Set oven to 200°C
2. Slice eggplants, onions and tomatoes and rub with salt.
3. Fry eggplants and onions with olive oil in a grill pan.
4. Blanch spinach in a saucepan at medium heat and strain.
5. Arrange vegetables in layers in a greased baking dish: eggplant, spinach, onion and tomato in this order. Repeat.
6. Scourge eggs with almond milk, lemon juice, salt and pepper then drizzle over the vegetables.
7. Dust some almond flour and bake for 36 minutes.

Nutrition: 443 Calories 11g Protein 33g Fat

97. <u>Vegetarian Paleo Ratatouille</u>

Preparation Time: 71 minutes
Cooking Time: 52 minutes
Servings: 2
Ingredients

- 200 g (7 oz.) Tomato cubes (can)
- ½ pieces Onion
- 2 cloves Garlic
- ¼ teaspoon dried oregano
- ¼ TL Chili flakes
- 2 tablespoon Olive oil
- 1-piece Eggplant
- 1-piece Zucchini
- 1-piece hot peppers
- 1 teaspoon dried thyme

Directions

1. Prepare oven to 180°C and slightly grease a round dish.
2. Slice the onion and garlic.
3. Incorporate tomato cubes with garlic, onion, oregano and chili flakes, season well and situate on the bottom of the baking dish.
4. With a mandolin, cut the eggplant, zucchini and hot pepper into very thin slices.
5. Place vegetables in a bowl
6. Pour the remaining olive oil on the vegetables and season with thyme, salt and pepper.
7. Wrap baking dish with parchment paper and bake for 51 minutes.

Nutrition: 273 Calories 5.6g Protein 14.5g Fat

98. <u>Vegetarian Curry from the Crock Pot</u>

Preparation Time: 6 hours
Cooking Time: 6 hours
Servings: 2
Ingredients

- 4 pieces Carrot
- 2 pieces Sweet potato
- 1-piece Onion
- 3 cloves Garlic
- 2 tablespoon Curry powder
- 1 teaspoon Ground caraway (ground)
- ¼ teaspoon Chili powder
- ¼ TL Celtic sea salt
- 1 pinch Cinnamon
- 100 ml (3 ½ fl. oz.) Vegetable broth
- 400 g (14 oz.) Tomato cubes (can)

- 250 g (9 oz.) Sweet peas
- 2 tablespoon Tapioca flour

Directions
1. Roughly chop vegetables and potatoes and press garlic. Halve the sugar snap peas.
2. Put the carrots, sweet potatoes and onions in the slow cooker.
3. Mix tapioca flour with curry powder, cumin, chili powder, salt and cinnamon and sprinkle this mixture on the vegetables.
4. Pour the vegetable broth over it.
5. Cover the lid and simmer for 6 hours on a low setting.
6. Stir in the tomatoes and sugar snap peas for the last hour.

Nutrition: 397 Calories 9.35g Protein 6.07g Fat

99. Fried Cauliflower Rice

Preparation Time: 51 minutes
Cooking Time: 16 minutes
Servings: 2

Ingredients
- 1-piece Cauliflower
- 2 tablespoon Coconut oil
- 1-piece Red onion
- 4 Garlic cloves
- ¼ cup Vegetable broth
- 1.5 cm fresh ginger
- 1 tsp. Chili flakes
- ½ pc. Carrot
- ½ pc. Red bell pepper
- ½ pc. Lemon juice
- 2 tbsp. Pumpkin seeds
- 2 tbsp. fresh coriander

Directions
1. Cut the cauliflower into small rice grains in a food processor.
2. Finely chop the onion, garlic and ginger, cut the carrot into thin strips, dice the bell pepper and finely chop the herbs.
3. Cook 1 tablespoon of coconut oil in a pan and add half of the onion and garlic to the pan and fry briefly until translucent.
4. Add cauliflower rice and season with salt.
5. Pour in the broth and stir everything until it evaporates and the cauliflower rice is tender.
6. Pull rice out of the pan and set it aside.

7. Melt the rest of the coconut oil in the pan and add the remaining onions, garlic, ginger, carrots and peppers.
8. Cook until the vegetables are tender. Sprinkle with a little salt.
9. Add the cauliflower rice again, heat the whole dish and add the lemon juice.
10. Garnish with pumpkin seeds and coriander before serving.

Nutrition: 230 Calories 5.12g Protein 17.8g Fat

100. Fried Chicken and Broccolini

Preparation time: 10 minutes
Cooking time: 35 minutes
Servings: 2

Ingredients
- 2 tablespoon Coconut oil
- 400 g (14 oz.) Chicken breast
- 150 g (5 ¼ oz.) Bacon cubes
- 250 g (8 oz.) Broccolini

Directions
1. Cut the chicken into cubes.
2. Pre-heat coconut oil in a pan over medium heat and brown the chicken with the bacon cubes and cook through.
3. Season with chili flakes, salt and pepper.
4. Add broccolini and fry.
5. Stack on a plate and enjoy!

Nutrition: 461 Calories 72g Protein 32g Fat

101. Turkey with Cauliflower Couscous

Preparation Time: 43 minutes
Cooking Time: 12 minutes
Servings: 2

Ingredients
- 150g cauliflower, roughly chopped
- 1 garlic clove, finely chopped
- 40g red onion, finely chopped
- 1 bird's eye chili, finely chopped
- 1 tsp finely chopped fresh ginger
- 2 tbsp extra virgin olive oil
- 2 tsp ground turmeric
- 30g sun dried tomatoes, finely chopped
- 10g parsley
- 150g turkey steak
- 1 tsp dried sage
- Juice of ½ lemon

- 1 tbsp capers

Directions

1. Disintegrate the cauliflower using a food processor. Blend in 1-2 pulses until the cauliflower has a breadcrumb-like consistency.
2. In a skillet, fry garlic, chili, ginger and red onion in 1 tsp olive oil for 3 minutes. Sprinkle in the turmeric and cauliflower then cook for 2 minutes. Remove from heat and add the tomatoes and roughly half the parsley.
3. Garnish the turkey steak with sage and dress with oil. Over medium heat, fry the turkey steak for 6 minutes. Stir in lemon juice, capers and a dash of water then serve with the couscous.

Nutrition: 462 Calories 16.8g Protein 39.9g Fat

102. Chicken Thighs with Creamy Tomato Spinach Sauce

Preparation Time: 44 minutes
Cooking Time: 13 minutes
Servings: 2

Ingredients

- One tablespoon olive oil
- 1.5 lb. chicken thighs, boneless skinless
- ½ teaspoon salt
- ¼ teaspoon pepper
- 8 oz. tomato sauce
- Two garlic cloves, minced
- ½ cup overwhelming cream
- 4 oz. new spinach
- Four leaves fresh basil (or utilize ¼ teaspoon dried basil)

Directions

1. In a much skillet heat olive oil on medium warmth. Boneless chicken with salt and pepper. Add top side down to the hot skillet.
2. Cook for 5 minutes on medium heat, until the high side, is pleasantly burned. Flip over to the opposite side and heat for five additional minutes on medium heat.
3. Expel the chicken from the skillet to a plate. Step by step instructions to make creamy tomato basil sauce: To the equivalent, presently void skillet, include

tomato sauce, minced garlic, substantial cream. Bring to bubble and mix.

4. Lessen warmth to low stew. Include new spinach and new basil. Mix until spinach withers and diminishes in volume.
5. Taste the sauce and include progressively salt and pepper, if necessary. Include back cooked boneless skinless chicken thighs, increment warmth to medium.

Nutrition: 1061 Calories 66g Protein 77g Fat

103. Sirt Chili with Meat

Preparation Time: 81 minutes
Cooking Time: 63 minutes
Servings: 4

Ingredients

- 1 red onion, finely cleaved
- 3 garlic cloves, finely cleaved
- 2 Bird's Eye chilies, finely hacked
- 1 tbsp additional virgin olive oil
- 1 tbsp ground cumin
- 1 tbsp ground turmeric
- 400g lean minced hamburger (5 percent fat)
- 150ml red wine
- 1 red pepper, cored, seeds evacuated and cut into reduced down pieces
- 2 x 400g tins cleaved tomatoes
- 1 tbsp tomato purée
- 1 tbsp cocoa powder
- 150g tinned kidney beans
- 300ml hamburger stock
- 5g coriander, cleaved
- 5g parsley, cleaved
- 160g buckwheat

Directions

1. Cook onion, garlic and bean stew in the oil over a medium heat for 3 minutes
2. Include the pounded hamburger and dark colored at high heat. Stir in red wine
3. Incorporate red pepper, tomatoes, tomato purée, cocoa, kidney beans and stock and set aside for 60 minutes.
4. Cook the buckwheat and present with the stew.

Nutrition: 346 Calories 14g Protein 11.4g Fat

104. Chickpea, Quinoa and Turmeric Curry

Preparation Time: 82 minutes
Cooking Time: 1 hour
Servings: 6

Ingredients

- 500g new potatoes, split
- 3 garlic cloves, squashed
- 3 teaspoons ground turmeric
- 1 teaspoon ground coriander
- 1 teaspoon stew drops or powder
- 1 teaspoon ground ginger
- 400g (14 oz.) container of coconut milk
- 1 tbsp tomato purée
- 400g (14 oz.) container of slashed tomatoes
- Salt and pepper
- 180g (6 ¼ oz.) quinoa
- 400g (14 oz.) container of chickpeas, depleted and flushed
- 150g (6 oz.) spinach

Directions

1. Spot the potatoes in a dish of cold water and bring to the boil, at that point let them cook for around 25 minutes
2. Spot the potatoes in an enormous skillet and include the garlic, turmeric, coriander, bean stew, ginger, tomatoes, coconut milk, and tomato purée
3. Boil, season well, stir in quinoa with a cup of simply boil water (300ml - 10 fl. oz.).
4. Diminish the heat to a stew, place the top on and permit to cook. Throughout the following 30 minutes, blending at regular intervals or so to ensure nothing adheres to the base.
5. Halfway through cooking, include the chickpeas. When there are only 5 minutes left, include the spinach and mix it in until it withers. Once the quinoa has cooked and is cushioned, not crunchy, it's prepared.
6. On the off chance that you like a touch of heat, add a cut red bean stew to the cooking curry simultaneously as different flavors.

Nutrition: 609 Calories 23g Protein 22.2g Fat

105. Chargrilled Beef with a Red Wine

Preparation Time: 18 minutes
Cooking Time: 37 minutes
Servings: 2

Ingredients

- 100 grams potatoes (peeled and cut into 2cm dice)
- 1 tbsp extra virgin olive oil
- 5g parsley, finely chopped
- 50g red onion, sliced into rings
- 50g Kale, sliced
- 1 garlic clove, finely chopped
- 120-150g sirloin steak
- 40ml red wine
- 150ml beef stock
- 1 tsp tomato purée
- 1 tsp corn flour, mix with 1 tbsp water

Directions

1. Heat your oven to (430°F).
2. Situate potatoes in a saucepan with boiling water.
3. Bring back to the boil now cook for 4–5 minutes.
4. Drain.
5. Now place in a roasting tin with 1 teaspoon of the oil. Roast it in the hot oven for about 35 to 45 mins.
6. Turn the potatoes every 10 minutes.
7. When it is cooked, remove from the oven. Then sprinkle with the chopped parsley and mix well.
8. Fry the onion in 1 teaspoon oil and heat for 5 minutes. Fry till they get soft and nicely caramelized. Keep warm. Now steam the Kale for 2–3 minutes then drain.
9. Fry the garlic gently oil (1/2 tablespoon oil). Fry for one minute. It should get soft, but it should not be colored. Add the Kale and fry for 2 minutes more, until it gets tender. Keep warm.
10. Heat a frying pan over high heat. Heat until smoking.
11. Coat the meat in ½ teaspoon of the oil, fry in the hot pan over a medium to high temperature, i.e. heat according to how you like your meat cooked.

12. If you like to cook the meat on a medium level, it would be better to sear the meat. Now transfer the pan to an oven set at 220°C/gas 7(430°F). Finish the cooking that way for a specific time.
13. Remove the meat from the pan. Set aside to rest. Now add the wine to the hot pan to bring up if any meat residue is left. Bubble to reduce the wine by its half. It becomes syrupy with a thick flavor in this way.
14. Add stock and tomato purée to the steak pan to boil it. Then keep adding the corn flour paste to thicken the sauce, adding it a little at a time.
15. Stir in any of the juices from your steak.
16. Serve it with the roasted potatoes, Kale, onion rings and the red wine sauce.

Nutrition: 240 Calories 14.2g Protein 14.4g Fat

106. Creamy Beef and Shells
Preparation Time: 8 minutes
Cooking Time: 32 minutes
Servings: 3
Ingredients:
- 8 ounces medium pasta shells
- One tablespoon olive oil
- 1-pound ground meat
- One little sweet onion (diced)
- Five cloves garlic (minced)
- One teaspoon Italian flavoring
- One teaspoon dried parsley
- 1/2 teaspoon dried oregano
- Two tablespoons generally useful flour
- 1 cup meat stock
- 1 (15oz can) marinara sauce
- 3/4 cup overwhelming cream
- 1/4 cup sharp cream
- Legitimate salt and crisply ground dark pepper (to taste)
- 1/2 cups cheddar (newly ground)

Directions:
1. Cook pasta as per bundle directions in an enormous pot of bubbling salted water and channel well. W olive oil in a large skillet over medium-high warmth. Include ground meat and cook for 4 minutes.

2. With a same skillet, stir diced onion, and cook for 2minutes. Include garlic, and cook until fragrant, around one moment.
3. Speed in flour until delicately caramelized, for around one moment. Step by step rush in hamburger stock and mix. Incorporate marinara sauce, Italian flavoring, dried parsley, oregano, and paprika.
4. Heat to the boiling point, diminish warmth and stew, mixing once in a while until decreased and somewhat thickened around 6-8 minutes. Mix in cooked pasta, include back meat.
5. Mix in overwhelming cream until warmed through, about 1-2 minutes. Taste and change for salt and pepper. Mix in sour cream. Mix in cheddar until liquefied, about 1-2 minutes. Serve promptly, embellish with parsley whenever wanted.

Nutrition: 624 Calories 63g Fat 40g Protein

107. Rowdy Enchiladas
Preparation Time: 9 minutes
Cooking Time: 29 minutes
Servings: 3
Ingredients
- Two large chicken breasts (about 400g)
- 2 red peppers, thinly chopped
- 1 tablespoon olive oil
- 3/4 tsp mild chili powder
- 10g fresh coriander, roughly sliced
- For the sauce
- 1 tablespoon olive oil
- 1/2 onion, finely chopped
- 2 tsp cloves, crushed
- 500g tomato passata
- 1 tablespoon chipotle chili paste
- 400g tin black beans drained and rinsed
- 1/2 lime, juiced

Directions:
1. Preheats the oven to gas 5, 190°c, buff 170°c. Set the chicken at a 20 x 30cm skillet with all the peppers olive oil, chili powder, cumin, and paprika. Mix to coat, then cover with foil. Roast for 25-30 mins. Take out the chicken from the dish and then shred with two forks. Reserve in a bowl.

2. Meanwhile, make the sauce. Heat the oil in a saucepan on a low heat and cook the garlic and onion for 10 mins.

3. Stir from the passata and chipotle chili glue; increase heat to moderate, simmer for 10 mins. Bring the beans and carrot juice season.

4. Mix one-third of this sauce plus half of the mozzarella to the cultured broccoli and chicken.

5. To gather, spoon 4 tablespoons of this sauce in exactly the exact baking dish before. Spoon a bit of the chicken mixture down the middle of each tortilla, roll up and then put from the dish.

6. Repeat with the tortillas and filling, then placing them alongside in order that they do not shatter. Scatter together with all the coriander to function.

Nutrition: 674 Calories 57g Fat 37g Protein

108. Braised Pork Belly and Avocado Skewers

Preparation Time: 12 minutes
Cooking Time: 27 minutes
Servings: 3
Ingredients:

- 1 1/2 pounds pork belly
- One tablespoon samba
- 6 cups of water
- Two tablespoons sugar
- Two tablespoons whole-grain mustard
- 1/2 tablespoon salt
- One teaspoon cayenne
- Three tablespoons sherry vinegar
- Two avocados, cubed
- Eight skewers

Directions:
1. Preheat oven to 300°F. Place samba, water, sugar, mustard, salt, cayenne and sherry vinegar in a small saucepan, heat just until sugar and salt dissolve. Place pork in a baking dish and cover with braising liquid.

2. Cover dish with plastic wrap, followed by aluminum foil. Braise in the oven and cook for approximately 3 1/2 hours, or until tender. Remove pork belly and let cool. While the pork belly is cooling, drain liquid and place in a small saucepot.

3. Reduce until consistency has developed, then remove from heat. Once the abdomen is cold, slice into one 1/2-inch cube. Skewer one piece of pork and one piece of avocado on a skewer. Grill while basting with the sauce and serve.

Nutrition: 599 Calories 54g Fat 32g Protein

109. Chicken Ayam

Preparation Time: 14 minutes
Cooking Time: 34 minutes
Servings: 3
Ingredients:

- One sliced red chili
- One teaspoon of ginger
- One small red onion, sliced
- One teaspoon turmeric
- One teaspoon galangal
- Four cloves of garlic
- One pinch black pepper
- Three tips muscovado sugar
- Three tsp. shrimp paste
- 1/3 cup coconut milk

Directions:
1. Season the chicken legs. Put on low heat on the grill for about 10 min on one side. Bring all the ingredients together as finely as possible using a mortar and pestle or a blender.

2. Fry in some peanut oil. Put some paste on the chicken. Cook the other side for about 5 min. Add some glue to the chicken.

3. Move to the hotter side of the grill, flip, baste and cook for three additional minutes on both sides. Grill the cake on both sides.

Nutrition: 557 Calories 39g Fat 28g Protein

110. Sri Lankan-Style Sweet Potato Curry

Preparation Time: 17 minutes
Cooking Time: 39 minutes
Servings: 3
Ingredients

- 1/2 onion, roughly sliced
- 3 garlic cloves, roughly sliced
- 25g sliced ginger, chopped and peeled
- 15g fresh coriander stalks and leaves split leaves sliced

- Two 1/2 tablespoon moderate tikka curry powder
- 60g package cashew nuts
- 1 tablespoon olive oil
- 500g Red Mere farms sweet potatoes, peeled and cut into 3cm balls
- 400ml tin isle sun coconut-milk
- 1/2 vegetable stock block, as much as 300ml
- 200g grower's harvest long-grain rice
- 300g frozen green beans
- 150g Red Mere farms lettuce
- 1 sun trail farms lemon, 1/2 juiced, 1/2 cut into wedges to function

Directions:
1. Set the onion, ginger, garlic, coriander stalks, tikka powder along with half of the cashew nuts in a food processor. Insert 2 tablespoons water and blitz into a chunky paste.
2. In a large skillet, warm the oil over moderate heat. Insert the paste and cook, stirring for 5 mins. Place in the sweet potatoes, stir, then pour into the coconut milk and stock.
3. Bring to the simmer and boil for 25-35 mins before the sweet potatoes are tender.
4. Meanwhile, cook the rice, following packet directions. Toast the rest of the cashews in a dry skillet.
5. Stir the beans into the curry and then simmer for two minutes. Insert the lettuce in handfuls, allowing each to simmer before adding the following; simmer for 1 minute. Drizzle lemon juice and the majority of the coriander leaves.
6. Sprinkle on the remaining coriander and cashews. Serve with the rice and lemon wedges.

Nutrition: 571 Calories 52g Fat 37g Protein

111. Chicken Liver Along with Tomato Ragu

Preparation Time: 11 minutes
Cooking Time: 27 minutes
Servings: 3

Ingredients

- 2 tablespoon olive oil
- 1 onion, finely chopped

- 2 carrots, scrubbed and simmer
- 4 garlic cloves, finely chopped
- 1/4 x 30g pack fresh ginger, stalks finely chopped, leaves ripped
- 380g package chicken livers, finely chopped,
- 400g tin grower's harvest chopped berries
- 1 chicken stock cube, created around 300ml
- 1/2 tsp caster sugar
- 300g penne
- 1/4 sun trail farms lemon, juiced

Direction:
1. Cook 1 tablespoon oil in a skillet, over a low-medium heating system. Fry the onion and carrots to 10 minutes, stirring periodically. Stir in the ginger and garlic cloves and cook 2 minutes more. Transfer into a bowl set aside.
2. Turn the pan into high heat and then add the oil. Add the chicken livers and simmer for 5 mins until browned. Pour the onion mix to the pan and then stir in the tomatoes, sugar, and stock. Season well, boil, then simmer for 20 mins. Meanwhile, cook pasta to package guidelines.
3. Taste the ragu and put in a second pinch of sugar or more seasoning, if needed. Put in a squeeze of lemon juice to taste and stir in two of the shredded basil leaves. Divide the pasta between four bowls, then spoon across the ragu and top with the rest of the basil.

Nutrition: 497 Calories 39g Fat 21g Protein

112. Minted Lamb with A Couscous Salad

Preparation Time: 16 minutes
Cooking Time: 32 minutes
Servings: 3

Ingredients

- 75g couscous
- 1/2 chicken stock block, composed to 125ml
- 30g pack refreshing flat-leaf parsley, sliced
- 3 mint sprigs, leaves picked and sliced
- 1 tablespoon olive oil
- 200g pack suspended BBQ minted lamb leg beans, defrosted

- 200g lettuce berries, sliced
- 1/4 tsp, sliced
- 1 spring onion, sliced
- Pinch of ground cumin
- 1/2 lemon, zested and juiced
- 50g reduced-fat salad cheese

Directions:
1. Situate couscous into a heatproof bowl and then pour on the inventory. Cover and set aside for 10 mins, then mash with fork and stir in the herbs.
2. Brush little oil within the lamb steaks and season. Cook to package guidelines, then slit.
3. Blend tomatoes, cucumber and spring onion into the couscous with the oil, the cumin, and lemon juice and zest. Crumble on the salad and serve with the bunny.

Nutrition: 607 Calories 57g Fat 34g Protein

113. Garbanzo Kale Curry

Preparation Time: 18 minutes
Cooking Time: 41 minutes
Servings 8

Ingredients
- 4 cups dry garbanzo beans
- Curry Paste, but go low on the heat
- 1 cup sliced tomato
- 2 cups kale leaves
- 1/2 cup coconut milk

Directions
1. Put ingredients in the slow cooker. Close & cook on low for 8 hours.

Nutrition: 471 Calories 34g Fat 24g Protein

114. Buckwheat Kasha with Mushrooms and Onions

Preparation Time: 17 minutes
Cooking Time: 28 minutes
Servings: 3

Ingredients:
- Buckwheat, uncooked – 1 cup
- Olive oil, extra virgin – 3 tablespoons
- Vegetable broth – 2 cups
- Red onion, thinly sliced – 1
- Black ground pepper – .5 teaspoon
- Parsley, chopped – 3 tablespoons
- Walnuts, chopped – 3 tablespoons
- Peas, frozen – 1 cup

- Button mushrooms, sliced – 10 ounces
- Sea salt – 1.5 teaspoons

Directions:
1. On your stove set a medium-sized saucepan and pour the buckwheat and vegetable broth into it, stirring them together. Add in approximately half of the sea salt and black pepper.
2. Allow the broth to come to a boil over medium-high heat before reducing the heat to medium-low and covering the pot with a lid. Continue to cook until the buckwheat is tender. It should cook for an estimated ten minutes more.
3. Meanwhile, while the buckwheat cooks prepare the vegetables. Add the extra virgin olive oil into a favorite large skillet and sauté the onions until tender and slightly golden, about five minutes over medium heat.
4. Put the mushrooms into the hot skillet and continue to heat until the mushrooms are tender and begin to release their juices, about seven minutes. Stir in the peas and remaining seasoning, cooking until the peas are heated through, about three minutes.
5. Add the cooked buckwheat, parsley, and walnuts to the skillet, tossing it all together. Continue to cook the dish together until the flavors meld, about three additional minutes. Serve while warm.

Nutrition: 611 Calories 58g Fat 37g Protein

115. Sirtfood Cauliflower Couscous & Turkey Steak

Preparation Time: 14 minutes
Cooking Time: 52 minutes
Servings: 4

Ingredients
- 150g cauliflower, roughly chopped
- 1 garlic clove, finely chopped
- 40g red onion, finely chopped
- 1 bird's eye chili, finely chopped
- 1 tsp finely chopped fresh ginger
- 2 tbsp extra virgin olive oil
- 2 tsp ground turmeric
- 30g sun dried tomatoes, finely chopped
- 10g parsley
- 150g turkey steak

- 1 tsp dried sage
- Juice of ½ lemon
- 1 tbsp capers

Directions

1. Disintegrate the cauliflower using a food processor. Blend in 1-2 pulses
2. In a skillet, fry garlic, chili, ginger and red onion in olive oil for 2 minutes. Toss in the turmeric and cauliflower then cook for 1 minute. Remove from heat and add the tomatoes and roughly half the parsley.
3. Garnish the turkey steak with sage and dress with oil. With a skillet, over medium heat, cook turkey steak for 5 minutes. Drizzle lemon juice, capers and a dash of water. Side with the couscous.

Nutrition: 577 Calories 50g Fat 34g Protein

116. Turkey Escalope with Cauliflower Couscous

Preparation Time: 7 minutes
Cooking Time: 48 minutes
Servings 2

Ingredients

- 150g cauliflower, roughly chopped
- 1 clove of garlic, finely chopped
- 40g red onions, finely chopped
- 1 Thai chili, finely chopped
- 1 teaspoon chopped fresh ginger
- 2 tablespoons of extra virgin olive oil
- 2 teaspoons turmeric
- 30g dried tomatoes, finely chopped
- 10g parsley leaves
- 150g turkey escalope
- 1 teaspoon dried sage
- Juice of a 1/4 lemon
- 1 tablespoon capers

Directions

1. Mix the cauliflower in a food processor until the individual pieces are slightly smaller than a grain of rice.
2. Heat the garlic, onions, chili and ginger in a frying pan with a tablespoon of olive oil until they are slightly glazed. Add turmeric and cauliflower, mix well and heat for about 1 minute. Then remove from heat and add half of the parsley and all the tomatoes and mix well.

3. Mix the turkey escalope with the oil and sage. Put the rest of the oil in a pan and fry the scallops on both sides until they are ready. Then add the lemon juice, capers, remaining parsley and a tablespoon of water and warm it up again briefly. Serve with the cauliflower couscous.

Nutrition: 574 Calories 48g Fat 29g Protein

117. Tomato & Goat's Cheese Pizza

Preparation Time: 8 minutes
Cooking Time: 51 minutes
Servings 2

Ingredients

- 225g 8ozbuckwheat flour
- 2 teaspoons dried yeast
- Pinch of salt
- 150mls 5fl oz slightly water
- 1 teaspoon olive oil

For Topping:

- 75g 3ozfeta cheese, crumbled
- 75g 3ozpassata or tomato paste
- 1 tomato, sliced
- 1 red onion, finely chopped
- 25g 1oz rocket arugula leaves, chopped
- 562 calories per serving

Directions

1. Incorporate all the ingredients for the pizza dough then allow it to stand for 60 minutes
2. Roll the dough out to a size to suit you. Spoon the passata onto the base and add the rest of the toppings.
3. Bake at 400F for 18 minutes and serve.

Nutrition: 604 Calories 59g Fat 33g Protein

118. Roast Duck Legs with Red Wine Sauce

Preparation Time: 12 minutes
Cooking Time: 64 minutes
Servings: 3

Ingredients

- 1 bunch fresh rosemary, chopped
- 4 large garlic cloves
- 4 duck legs
- Salt to taste
- 1 teaspoon Chinese five-spice powder
- 1 ½ cups red wine
- 1 ½ tablespoons red currant jelly

Directions

1. Preheat an oven to 375 degrees.
2. Spread the rosemary sprigs and whole garlic cloves in a 9x13-inch baking dish.
3. Situate duck legs on top of the rosemary, and season with salt and five-spice powder. Bake for 1 hour.
4. Boil wine over medium-high heat. Once cooked, pour off and discard the fat. Drizzle the wine sauce over the duck legs and bake 17 minutes.

Nutrition: 607 Calories 54g Fat 31g Protein

119. Arugula-Stuffed Steak

Preparation Time: 13 minutes
Cooking Time: 72 minutes
Servings: 3

Ingredients

- 1 cup baby arugula
- 1 jar roasted red peppers
- 1 egg white
- ½ cup seasoned breadcrumbs
- ¼ cup Parmesan, grated
- ¼ cup sunflower seeds, toasted
- 1 garlic clove, minced
- Salt and pepper to taste
- 1 ½ -pound flank steak

Directions

1. Preheat oven to 350 degrees F.
2. Mix arugula with the roasted red peppers, egg white, breadcrumbs, Parmesan, sunflower seeds, minced garlic and salt and pepper to taste.
3. Cut the flank steak horizontally along the long edge to within ½" of the opposite edge.
4. Open your steak and use a meat mallet to flatten to ½" thickness.
5. Spread arugula mixture over the steak to within 1" of the edges.
6. Roll like a jelly roll, starting with a long side. Tie with some kitchen string and place in a greased 13-in. x 9-in. x 2-in. baking dish.
7. Cover and bake for 60 minutes
8. Uncover and bake for 42 minutes
9. Let stand for 13 minutes and cut into ½" slices to serve.

Nutrition: 551 Calories 53g Fat 30g Protein

120. Beef Stroganoff French Bread Toast

Preparation Time: 9 minutes
Cooking Time: 52 minutes
Servings: 3

Ingredient:

- Four tablespoons olive oil
- 1/2 cups mushrooms
- Two teaspoons salt, separated
- 1/2 teaspoon dark pepper
- Two tablespoons thyme
- Two tablespoons spread
- 1/2 cup onions, diced
- Two cloves garlic, minced
- 1-pound ground meat
- Three tablespoons generally useful flour
- Two teaspoons paprika
- 1/2 cups meat juices
- 1/2 cup sharp cream
- One teaspoon Dijon mustard

For the toasts:

- One portion French bread, inner parts dugout
- 2 cups mozzarella
- Three tablespoons cleaved Italian parsley

Directions:

1. Preheat stove to 350 degrees, and line a sheet container with material paper. Make the stroganoff: In a large Dutch grill or skillet, heat olive oil over medium warmth. Sauté mushrooms with one teaspoon salt and dark pepper. Include thyme.
2. Cook mushrooms until brilliant, roughly 4 minutes. Expel from a dish and put in a safe spot. Include margarine, onions and garlic to the container and sauté 2 minutes. Cook ground hamburger over medium warmth until dark-colored, roughly 4 minutes.
3. Add flour and paprika to cover uniformly. Include meat soup, sour cream and mustard. Blend entirely and include mushrooms back in. Round the emptied portion with stroganoff and top with mozzarella cheddar.
4. Spot on the readied heating sheet and prepare for 5 to 10 minutes until cheddar is

brilliant and softened. Head with parsley, cut and serve right away.

Nutrition: 615 Calories 61g Fat 37g Protein

121. Beef Burritos

Preparation Time: 12 minutes
Cooking Time: 23 minutes
Servings: 6

Ingredients:

- ¼ cup white onion, chopped
- ¼ cup green bell pepper, chopped
- 1-pound ground beef
- ¼ cup tomato puree, low-sodium
- ¼ teaspoon ground black pepper
- ¼ teaspoon ground cumin
- 6 flour tortillas, burrito size

Directions:

1. Take a skillet pan, place it over medium heat and when hot, add beef and cook for 5 to 8 minutes until browned.
2. Drain the excess fat, then transfer beef to a plate lined with paper towels and serve.
3. Return pan over medium heat, grease it with oil and when hot, add pepper and onion and cook for 4 minutes.
4. Switch to low heat, return beef to the pan, season with black pepper and cumin, pour in tomato puree, stir until mixed and cook for 5 minutes until done.
5. Lay beef mixture evenly on top of the tortilla, roll them in burrito style by folding both ends and then serve.

Nutrition: 265 Calories 9g Fat 15g Protein

122. Meatballs with Eggplant

Preparation Time: 17 minutes
Cooking Time: 63 minutes
Servings: 6

Ingredients:

- 1-pound ground beef
- ½ cup green bell pepper, chopped
- 2 medium eggplants, peeled and diced
- ½ teaspoon minced garlic
- 1 cup stewed tomatoes
- ½ cup white onion, diced
- 1/3 cup canola oil
- 1 teaspoon lemon and pepper seasoning, salt-free
- 1 teaspoon turmeric
- 1 teaspoon Mrs. Dash seasoning blend
- 2 cups of water

Directions:

1. Take a large skillet pan, place it over medium heat, add oil in it and when hot, add garlic and green bell pepper and cook for 4 minutes until sauté.
2. Transfer green pepper mixture to a plate, set aside until needed then eggplant pieces into the pan and cook for 8 minutes on both sides and set aside until needed.
3. Take a medium bowl, place beef in it, add onion, season with all the spices, stir then shape the mix into 30 small meatballs.
4. Place meatballs into the pan in a single layer and cook for 3 minutes, or until browned.
5. When done, place all the meatballs in the pan, add cooked bell pepper mixture in it along with eggplant, stir in water and tomatoes and simmer for 30 minutes at low heat setting until thoroughly cooked.
6. Serve straight away.

Nutrition: 265 Calories 18g Fat 17g Protein

123. Slow-Cooked Lemon Chicken

Preparation Time: 24 minutes
Cooking Time: 7 hours
Servings: 4

Ingredients:

- 1 teaspoon dried oregano
- ¼ teaspoon ground black pepper
- 2 tablespoons butter, unsalted
- 1-pound chicken breast, boneless, skinless
- ¼ cup chicken broth, low sodium
- ¼ cup water
- 1 tablespoon lemon juice
- 2 cloves garlic, minced
- 1 teaspoon fresh basil, chopped

Direction:

1. Blend oregano and ground black pepper. Brush mix over the chicken.
2. Cook butter in a medium-sized skillet at medium heat. Stir in chicken then transfer to the slow cooker.
3. Boil chicken broth, water, lemon juice and garlic in the skillet. Pour over the chicken.

4. Cover, adjust slow cooker at low for 5 hours.
5. Mix basil and baste chicken. Cover, cook at high for an additional 15–30 minutes

Nutrition: 197 Calories 9g Fat 26g Protein

124. Smothered Pork Chops and Sautéed Greens

Preparation Time: 23 minutes
Cooking Time: 61 minutes
Servings: 6

Ingredients:

Smothered Pork Chops:
- 6 pork loin chops
- 1 tbsp. black pepper
- 2 tsp. Paprika
- 2 tsp. granulated onion powder
- 2 tsp. granulated garlic powder
- 1 cup and 2 tbsp. flour
- ½ cup canola oil
- 2 cups low-sodium beef stock
- 1 ½ cups fresh onions, sliced
- ½ cup fresh scallions, sliced on the bias

Sautéed Greens:
- 8 cups fresh collard greens, chopped and blanched
- 2 tablespoons olive oil
- 1 tablespoon unsalted butter
- ¼ cup onions, finely diced
- 1 tablespoon fresh garlic, chopped
- 1 teaspoon crushed red pepper flakes
- 1 teaspoon black pepper
- 1 teaspoon vinegar (optional)

Direction:
1. Set oven to 350° F.

Pork Chops:
2. Incorporate black pepper, paprika, onion powder and garlic powder. With a half of mixture, rub with both sides of the pork chops then use the other half with 1 cup flour.
3. Set aside 2 tablespoons of flour mix.
4. Slightly coat pork chops with seasoned flour.
5. Cook oil in oven-ready sauté pan over medium-high.
6. Cook pork chops for 6 minutes on both sides. Take out from pan

7. Cook onions for 5 minutes. Mix 2 tablespoons of reserved flour with onions for about 1 minute.
8. Gradually, add beef stock and stir until thickened.
9. Place pork chops to pan and coat with sauce. Seal with foil and cook for 45 minutes at 350° F.
10. Take out from oven and cool for 8 minutes before serving.

Sautéed Greens:
11. To blanch greens, place greens to a boiling water for 30 seconds.
12. Drain boiling water off and quickly transfer in a bowl of ice and water.
13. Cool then drain and set aside.
14. In large sauté pan on medium-high heat, cook butter and oil together. Sauté onions and garlic for 6 minutes.
15. Cook collard greens and black and red pepper for 7 minutes on high heat.
16. Pull out from heat; stir in vinegar if desired.

Nutrition: 464 Calories 28g Fat 27g Protein

125. Pasta with Cheesy Meat Sauce

Preparation Time: 17 minutes
Cooking Time: 26 minutes
Servings: 6

Ingredients:
- ½ box large-shaped pasta
- 1-pound ground beef
- ½ cup onions
- 1 tbsp. onion flakes
- 1½ cups beef stock
- 1 tbsp. Better Than Bouillon® beef
- 1 tablespoon tomato sauce, no salt added
- ¾ cup Monterey or pepper jack cheese, shredded
- 8 ounces cream cheese, softened
- ½ teaspoon Italian seasoning
- ½ teaspoon ground black pepper
- 2 tablespoons French's® Worcestershire sauce, reduced sodium

Direction
1. Cook pasta noodles following the directions on the box.

2. In a sauté pan, fry ground beef, onions and onion flakes until the meat is browned.
3. Strain and add stock, bouillon and tomato sauce.
4. Simmer, stirring occasionally. Put in cooked pasta, turn off heat, and mix softened cream cheese, shredded cheese and seasonings. Stir pasta mixture.

Nutrition: 502 Calories 30g Fat 23g Protein

126. Aromatic Herbed Rice

Preparation Time: 14 minutes
Cooking Time: 18 minutes
Servings: 6

Ingredients:
- 2 tablespoons olive oil
- 3 cups cooked rice (don't overcook)
- 4–5 cloves fresh garlic, sliced thin
- 2 tablespoons fresh cilantro, chopped
- 2 tablespoons fresh oregano, chopped
- 2 tablespoons fresh chives, chopped
- ½ teaspoon red pepper flakes
- 1 teaspoon red wine vinegar

Directions:
1. In a large sauté pan, heat olive oil on medium-high heat and lightly sauté garlic. Add rice, herbs and red pepper flakes and continue to cook for 2–4 minutes or until well-mixed.
2. Turn off heat, add vinegar, mix well and serve.

Nutrition: 134 Calories 5g Fat 2g Protein

127. Herb-Crusted Roast Leg of Lamb

Preparation Time: 17 minutes
Cooking Time: 38 minutes
Servings: 12

Ingredients:
- 1 4-pound leg of lamb
- 3 tablespoons lemon juice
- 1 tablespoon curry powder
- 2 cloves garlic, minced
- ½ teaspoon ground black pepper
- 1 cup onions, sliced
- ½ cup dry vermouth

Direction:
1. Prep oven to 400° F.

2. Situate leg of lamb on a roasting pan. Drizzle 1 tsp. of lemon juice.
3. Blend 2 teaspoons of lemon juice and the rest of the spices. Brush paste onto the lamb.
4. Roast lamb at 400° F for 30 minutes.
5. Strain off fat and stir vermouth and onions.
6. Set heat to 325° F and cook for 2 hours. Baste leg of lamb frequently. Pull out from oven and rest 3 minutes before serving.

Nutrition: 292 Calories 20g Fat 24g Protein

128. Baked Potatoes with Spicy Chickpea

Preparation Time: 18 minutes
Cooking Time: 9 minutes
Servings: 5

Ingredients:
- 4-6 baking potatoes, pricked all over
- Two tablespoons olive oil
- Two red onions, finely chopped
- Four cloves garlic, grated or crushed
- 2cm ginger, grated
- Two tablespoons turmeric
- ½ -2 teaspoons of chili flakes (depending on how hot you like things)
- Two tablespoons cumin seeds
- Splash of water
- Two into 400g tins chopped tomatoes
- Two tablespoons unsweetened cocoa powder (or cacao)
- Two into 400g tins chickpeas (or kidney beans if you prefer) including the chickpea water
- Two yellow peppers (or whatever color you prefer!), chopped into bite size pieces
- Salt and pepper to taste (optional)
- Side salad (optional)

Directions:
1. Preheat the oven to 200C so you can make all the ingredients you need.
2. Put your baking potatoes in the oven when the oven is hot enough, and cook them for an hour or till they are cooked as you want them.
3. Put the olive oil and chopped red onion in a big broad saucepan once the potatoes are in the oven and cook gently with the lid

until the onions are soft but not brown for 5 minutes.

4. Remove the lid and add the garlic, cumin, ginger and chili. Cook on low heat for another minute, and then you add the turmeric and a tiny drizzle of water and cook for 3 minutes, keeping in minute not to let the saucepan get too dry.

5. Add cocoa (or cacao) powder, chickpeas (including chickpea water) and yellow pepper in the tomatoes. Boil it and simmer for 45 minutes at low heat until the sauce is thick and greasy (but don't let it burn!). Stew will be handled roughly at the same time as the potatoes.

6. At last, mix in the two tablespoons of parsley and some salt and pepper, if desired, and serve the stew over the baked potatoes, maybe with a small side salad.

Nutrition: 243 Calories 24g Fat 16g Protein

129. Buckwheat with Red Onion Dal

Preparation Time: 8 minutes
Cooking Time: 0 minutes
Servings: 4
Ingredients:

- One tablespoon olive oil
- One small red onion, sliced
- Three garlic cloves, grated or crushed
- One bird eye chili deseeded and finely chopped (more if you like things hot!)
- 2 cm ginger, grated
- Two teaspoons turmeric
- Two teaspoons graham masala
- 160g red lentils
- 200ml water
- 400ml coconut milk
- 160g buckwheat (or brown rice)
- 100g kale

Directions:

1. In a big, deep saucepan, put the olive oil and add the sliced onion. Cook at low pressure, with the lid on until softened for 5 minutes.

2. Add the garlic, chili and ginger and cook for 1 minute.

3. Add the turmeric, graham masala, sprinkle with water and cook for 1 minute.

4. Add the red lentils, coconut milk and 200 ml of water (fill the coconut milk with water and drop it into the casserole).

5. Thoroughly mix everything and cook over a gentle heat for 20 minutes with the lid on. If the dhal starts sticking, stir periodically and add a little more water.

6. After 20 minutes, add the Kale, whisk thoroughly and remove the lid and cook for another 5 minutes (1-2 minutes if spinach is used instead!)

7. Place the buckwheat in a medium saucepan about 15 minutes before the curry is ready, and put plenty of boiling water. Bring the water again to the boil and cook for 10 minutes

Nutrition: 234 Calories 19g fat 9g protein

130. Aromatic Chicken

Preparation Time: 19 minutes
Cooking Time: 13 minutes
Servings: 1
Ingredients:
For the salsa

- One large tomato
- One bird's eye chili, finely chopped
- 1tbsp capers, finely chopped
- 5g parsley, finely chopped
- Juice 1/2 lemon

For the chicken

- 120g skinless, boneless chicken breast
- 2tsp ground turmeric
- Juice 1/2 lemon
- 1tbsp extra virgin olive oil
- 50g kale, chopped
- 20g red onion, sliced
- 1tsp fresh ginger, finely chopped
- 50g buckwheat

Directions:

1. Heat the oven at 220oC/200oC fan/gas level 7

2. Cut the tomato thinly to make the salsa and make sure you hold as much of the liquid as possible. Mix with the chili, capers, lemon juice and parsley.

3. Marinate the chicken breast for 5-10 minutes with 1tsp of turmeric, lemon juice and half of the butter.

4. Heat the frying pan ovenproof; add the marinated chicken and cook each side for a minute until golden, then move to the oven for 8-10 minutes or until cooked through. Remove and cover with tape, then leave for 5 minutes to rest.
5. Then you cook the Kale in a 5-minutesute steamer. In the remaining oil, fry the onion and ginger until soft but not white, then put the cooked Kale and fry for one more minute.
6. Cook the buckwheat with the remaining turmeric as directed, and then serve.

Nutrition: 213 Calories 28g Fat 16g Protein

131. Fragrant Asian hotpot-Sirtfood

Preparation Time: 13 minutes
Cooking Time: 17 minutes
Servings: 2
Ingredients:
- 1 tsp tomato purée,
- 1-star anise, crushed (or 1/4 tsp ground anise),
- Small handful (10g) parsley, stalks finely chopped,
- Small handful (10g) coriander, stalks finely chopped,
- Juice of 1/2 lime,
- 500ml chicken stock, fresh or made with one cube
- 50 g broccoli, cut into small florets,
- 50 g beans sprout,
- 100g raw tiger prawns,
- 100g firm tofu, chopped,
- 50 g rice noodles, cooked according to packet directions,
- 50 g cooked water chestnuts, drained,
- 20 g sushi ginger, cut

Directions:
1. Stir in the cabbage, broccoli, prawns, tofu, noodles and water chestnuts and cook gently until the prawns are finished. Remove from heat and mix in the ginger sushi and the paste miso.
2. Serve sprinkled with the leaves of the parsley and coriander.

Nutrition: 185 calories 27g Fat 13g Protein

132. Buckwheat Bean Risotto

Preparation Time: 9 minutes
Cooking Time: 12 minutes
Servings: 2
Ingredients:
- 2 tbsp. of olive oil or butter,
- Two cloves of garlic, minced,
- 225g/8 of buckwheat,
- 400ml of hot water or vegetable stock,
- 225g/8 of frozen broad beans,
- 1/2 cup of sun-dried tomatoes in milk,
- Juice of half a lemon,
- 2 tbsp. of basil or coriander, chopped,
- 50g/2 oz. almonds, toasted, salt, and pepper,

Directions:
1. Cook olive oil in a frying pan. Cook the garlic for one minute.
2. Stir buckwheat to the saucepan and mix well to coat in the butter.
3. Add the stock or hot water. Cover for 10 minutes, and then simmer.
4. Stir in the beans. Cook until the beans are moist, for a few minutes.
5. Season well and stir sun-dried tomatoes, lemon juice, fresh herbs, and almonds.

Nutrition: 389 calories 19g Fat6g Protein

133. Butterbean and Vegetable

Preparation Time: 17 minutes
Cooking Time: 13 minutes
Servings: 2
Ingredients:
- 3 tbsp. of coconut oil or olive oil,
- One big onion, finely chopped,
- 2 tsp of root ginger, finely chopped,
- One clove of garlic, finely chopped,
- 1-2 tbsp. of curry powder,
- 200g/7 of green beans cut into 2 cm pieces,
- One cauliflower, cut into florets,
- Three sweet potatoes, peeled and chopped into large chunks,
- Two cans of butterbeans (or prepare your using 225g/8 of dried beans),
- 50-100g/2-4 of creamed coconut,

- 1 tbsp. Cook the onions until they are tender.

Directions:

1. Sauté garlic and ginger to the onions.
2. Then throw the green beans, cauliflower, and sweet potatoes into the curry powder and mix well to cover in the spices.
3. Attach the butter beans drained and rinsed, and enough hot water to cover the ingredients. Move some of the liquid from the pan into the bowl and dissolve the coconut cream inside. Remove this to the saucepan and cook for several minutes.
4. Just before serving, sprinkle over the fresh coriander.

Nutrition: 230 calories 31g fat 16g Protein

134. Lemon Paprika Chicken with Vegetable

Preparation Time: 18 minutes
Cooking Time: 9 minutes
Servings: 2

Ingredients:

- 3 tbsp. of olive oil,
- 2 tbsp. of paprika,
- Two carrots, chopped,
- 1/2 celeriac, peeled and chopped,
- Three turnips, peeled and chopped,
- 300 g of chicken wings,
- 1 pint of hot stock, Sprigs of rosemary and thyme,
- Two bay leaves, salt, and pepper,
- One lemon juice,
- A big bunch of kale, chopped,

Directions:

1. Cook oil in a big pan with a tight lid. Add the paprika, potatoes, celeriac, chicken and turnip wings to the pan and cook for a few minutes.
2. Stir in the pan the stock, spices, salt, pepper, and lemon juice and bring to the boil.
3. Turn the heat down, cover it with a lid, and gently simmer for 40 minutes.
4. Attach the kale and cook until the kale and the chicken are both cooked for a few more minutes.

Nutrition: 321 calories 30g Fat 24g Protein

135. Spicy Ras-El-Hanout Dressing

Preparation Time: 13 minutes
Cooking Time: 1 minute
Servings: 16

Ingredients:

- 125 ml Olive oil
- 1-piece Lemon (the juice)
- 2 teaspoons Honey
- 1 ½ teaspoons Ras el Hanout
- 1/2 pieces Red pepper

Directions:

1. Remove the seeds from the chili pepper.
2. Chop the chili pepper as finely as possible.
3. Place the pepper in a bowl with lemon juice, honey, and Ras-El-Hanout and whisk with a whisk.
4. Pour olive oil drop by drop while continuing to whisk.

Nutrition: 73 Calories 8g Fats 1g Carbohydrates

136. Broccoli & Mushroom Chicken

Preparation Time: 13 minutes
Cooking Time: 29 minutes
Servings: 5

Ingredients

- 3 tbsp. olive oil
- 1-pound chicken breast, cubed
- 1 medium onion
- 6 garlic cloves
- 2 cups fresh mushrooms
- 16 oz. broccoli florets
- ¼ cup water

Direction

1. Cook oil in a large wok over medium heat and fry chicken cubes for 4 minutes.
2. Situate chicken cubes onto a plate.
3. In the same wok, sauté onion for 4 minutes.
4. Cook mushrooms for 5 minutes.
5. Mix in the cooked chicken, broccoli, and water, and cook for 9 minutes, stirring occasionally.
6. Season well and remove from heat.

Nutrition: 196 Calories 11g Fat 21g Protein

137. Beef with Kale & Carrot

Preparation Time: 16 minutes

Cooking Time: 11 minutes

Servings: 4

Ingredients

- 2 tablespoons coconut oil
- 4 garlic cloves, minced
- 1-pound beef sirloin steak, cut into bite-sized pieces
- Ground black pepper, to taste
- 1½ cups carrots, peeled and cut into matchsticks
- 1½ cups fresh kale, tough ribs removed and chopped
- 3 tablespoons tamari

Direction

1. Melt the coconut oil in a wok over medium heat and sauté the garlic for about 1 minute.
2. Add the beef and black pepper and stir to combine.
3. Increase the heat to medium-high and cook for about 3–4 minutes or until browned from all sides.
4. Add the carrot, kale, and tamari, and cook for about 4–5 minutes.
5. Remove from the heat and serve hot.

Nutrition: 311 Calories 13.8g Fat 37g Protein

138. Lamb Chops with Kale

Preparation Time: 14 minutes

Cooking Time: 13 minutes

Servings: 4

Ingredients

- 1 garlic clove, minced
- 1 tablespoon fresh rosemary leaves, minced
- Salt and ground black pepper, to taste
- 4 lamb loin chops
- 4 cups fresh baby kale

Direction

1. Preheat the grill to high heat. Grease the grill grate.
2. In a bowl, add the garlic, rosemary, salt, and black pepper, and mix well.
3. Coat the lamb chops with the herb mixture generously.
4. Place the chops onto the hot side of grill and cook for about 2 minutes per side.
5. Now, move the chops onto the cooler side of the grill and cook for about 6–7 minutes.

6. Divide the kale onto serving plates and top each with 1 chop and serve.

Nutrition: 301 Calories 10g Fat 42g Protein

139. Chickpea with Swiss Chard

Preparation Time: 17 minutes

Cooking Time: 12 minutes

Servings: 4

Ingredients

- 2 tablespoon olive oil
- 2 garlic cloves, sliced thinly
- 1 large tomato, chopped finely
- 2 bunches fresh Swiss chard, trimmed
- 1 (18-ounce) can chickpeas, drained and rinsed
- Salt and ground black pepper, to taste
- ¼ cup water
- 1 tablespoon fresh lemon juice
- 2 tablespoons fresh parsley, chopped

Direction

1. Heat the oil in a big wok at medium heat and cook the garlic.
2. Add the tomato and cook for about 2–3 minutes, crushing with the back of spoon.
3. Cook remaining ingredients except lemon juice and parsley for 6 minutes.
4. Drizzle with the lemon juice and remove from the heat.
5. Serve hot with the garnishing of parsley.

Nutrition: 217 Calories 8.3g Fat 8.8g Protein

140. Tofu & Broccoli Curry

Preparation Time: 21 minutes

Cooking Time: 34 minutes

Servings: 5

Ingredients

- 1 (16-ounce) block firm tofu, drained, pressed, and cut into ½-inch cubes
- 2 tablespoons coconut oil
- 1 medium yellow onion, chopped
- 1½ tablespoons fresh ginger, minced
- 2 garlic cloves, minced
- 1 tablespoon curry powder
- Salt and ground black pepper, to taste
- 1 cup fresh mushrooms, sliced
- 1 cup carrots, peeled and sliced
- 1 (14-ounce) can unsweetened low-fat coconut milk

- ½ cup low-sodium vegetable broth
- 2 teaspoons light brown sugar
- 10 ounces broccoli florets
- 1 tablespoon fresh lime juice
- ¼ cup fresh basil leaves, sliced thinly

Direction

1. In a Dutch oven, cook oil over medium heat and sauté the onion, ginger and garlic for about 5 minutes.
2. Stir in the curry powder, salt, and black pepper, and cook for about 2 minutes, stirring occasionally.
3. Cook mushrooms and carrot for 4 minutes.
4. Stir in the coconut milk, broth, and brown sugar, and bring to a boil.
5. Add the tofu and broccoli and simmer for about 12–15 minutes, stirring occasionally.
6. Drizzle lime juice and remove from the heat.
7. Serve hot.

Nutrition: 184 Calories 11g Fat 10.5g Protein

141. Chicken & Veggies with Buckwheat Noodles

Preparation Time: 24 minutes
Cooking Time: 22 minutes
Servings: 2

Ingredients

- ½ cup broccoli florets
- ½ cup fresh green beans, trimmed and sliced
- 1 cup fresh kale, tough ribs removed and chopped
- 5 ounces buckwheat noodles
- 1 tablespoon coconut oil
- 1 brown onion, chopped finely
- 1 (6-ounce) boneless, skinless chicken breast, cubed
- 2 garlic cloves, chopped finely
- 3 tablespoons low-sodium soy sauce

Direction

1. In a medium pan of the boiling water, add the broccoli and green beans and cook for about 4–5 minutes.
2. Add the kale and cook for about 1–2 minutes.
3. Drain the vegetables and transfer into a large bowl. Set aside.

4. In another pan of the lightly salted boiling water, cook the soba noodles for about 5 minutes.
5. Drain the noodles well and then, rinse under cold running water. Set aside.
6. Meanwhile, in a large wok, melt the coconut oil over medium heat and sauté the onion for about 2–3 minutes.
7. Cook chicken cubes for 6 minutes.
8. Cook garlic, soy sauce and a little splash of water for 3 minutes, stirring frequently.
9. Add the cooked vegetables and noodles and cook for about 1–2 minutes, tossing frequently.
10. Serve hot with the garnishing of sesame seeds.

Nutrition: 463 Calories 11.7g Fat 22.5g Protein

142. Veggie Burgers

Preparation Time: 23 minutes
Cooking Time: 8 minutes
Servings: 4

Ingredients

- 1 cup water
- 1/3 cup dry couscous
- 1½ cups broccoli florets
- 2 teaspoons olive oil
- ½ cup onion, chopped
- ½ cup scallion, chopped
- 2 teaspoons ground cumin
- ¼ teaspoon ground turmeric
- 1 tablespoon sesame tahini
- 1 (15-ounce) can chickpeas, rinsed and drained
- ½ cup panko breadcrumbs
- 4 cups fresh kale, tough ribs removed and chopped

Direction

1. Preheat your oven to 400°F. Line a baking sheet with foil paper.
2. In a small pan, mix together water and couscous over medium heat and boil.
3. Pull out from heat and keep aside, covered for about 10 minutes
4. Meanwhile, in a pan of boiling water, arrange a steamer basket.
5. Place the broccoli in steamer basket and steam, covered for about 5–7 minutes.
6. Drain the broccoli well.

7. Using a wok, cook oil over medium heat and sauté the onion and scallion for 4 minutes.
8. Stir in the cumin and turmeric and remove from heat.
9. In a food processor, add the couscous, broccoli, onion mixture, tahini, and chickpeas, and pulse until well combined.
10. Transfer the mixture into a bowl.
11. Add the breadcrumbs and stir to combine.
12. Make equal-sized patties from mixture.
13. Arrange the patties onto the prepared baking sheet in a single layer.
14. Bake for about 50 minutes, flipping once halfway through.
15. Divide kale
16. Top with 1 patty and serve.

Nutrition: 321 Calories 7g Fat 12.8g Protein

143. Kale with Pine Nuts

Preparation Time: 13 minutes
Cooking Time: 14 minutes
Servings: 4

Ingredients

- 1 tablespoon olive oil
- 2 garlic cloves, minced
- 1½ pounds fresh kale, tough ribs removed and chopped
- ¼ cup water
- 3 teaspoons red wine vinegar
- Salt and ground black pepper, to taste
- 2 tablespoons pine nuts

Direction

1. Heat the olive oil in wok in medium heat and sauté the garlic.
2. Add kale and cook for about 3–4 minutes.
3. Add the water, vinegar, salt, and black pepper, and cook for 4–5 minutes.
4. Remove from heat and stir in the pine nuts.
5. Serve immediately.

Nutrition: 146 Calories 6.5g Fat 5.8g Protein

144. Bok Choy & Mushroom Stir Fry

Preparation Time: 17 minutes
Cooking Time: 9 minutes
Servings: 4

Ingredients

- 1-pound baby bok choy

- 4 teaspoons olive oil
- 1 teaspoon fresh ginger, minced
- 2 garlic cloves, chopped
- 5 ounces fresh mushrooms, sliced
- 2 tablespoons red wine
- 2 tablespoons soy sauce

Direction

1. Trim bases of bok choy and separate outer leaves from stalks, leaving the smallest inner leaves attached.
2. In a large cast-iron wok, heat the oil over medium-high heat and sauté the ginger and garlic for about 1 minute.
3. Cook mushrooms for 4 minutes, stirring frequently.
4. Stir in the bok choy leaves and stalks and cook for about 1 minute, tossing with tongs.
5. Stir in the wine, soy sauce, and black pepper, and cook for about 2–3 minutes, tossing occasionally.
6. Serve hot.

Nutrition: 77 Calories 5g Fat 3.5g Protein

145. Prawns with Asparagus

Preparation Time: 16 minutes
Cooking Time: 13 minutes
Servings: 4

Ingredients

- 3 tablespoons olive oil
- 1-pound prawns, peeled, and deveined
- 1-pound asparagus, trimmed
- Salt and ground black pepper, to taste
- 1 teaspoon garlic, minced
- 1 teaspoon fresh ginger, minced
- 1 tablespoon low-sodium soy sauce
- 2 tablespoons lemon juice

Direction

1. In a wok, pre-heat2 tablespoons of oil over medium-high heat and cook the prawns with salt and black pepper for about 3–4 minutes.
2. With a slotted spoon, situate prawns into a bowl. Set aside.
3. In the same wok, heat remaining 1 tablespoon of oil over medium-high heat and cook the asparagus, ginger, garlic, salt, and black pepper and sauté for about 6–8 minutes, stirring frequently.

4. Stir in the prawns and soy sauce and cook for about 1 minute.

5. Pour lemon juice and remove from the heat.

6. Serve hot.

Nutrition: 253 Calories 12.7g Fat 28.7g Protein

146. Eggplant Dipped Roasted Asparagus

Preparation Time: 14 minutes
Cooking Time: 35 minutes
Servings: 2
Ingredients
- 4 tbsp olive oil
- ½ pounds asparagus spears, trimmed
- Sea salt and black pepper to taste
- ½ tsp sweet paprika

For Eggplant Dip
- ½ pound eggplants
- 2 tsp olive oil
- ½ cup scallions, chopped
- 2 cloves garlic, minced
- 1 tbsp lemon juice
- ½ tsp chili pepper
- Salt and black pepper, to taste
- Fresh parsley, chopped for garnish

Directions
1. Line a parchment paper to a baking sheet. Add asparagus spears to the baking sheet. Toss with oil, sweet paprika, black pepper, and salt. Bake for 9 minutes at 390°F.
2. Add eggplants on a lined cookie sheet. Position under the broiler for about 20 minutes at 425°F; let the eggplants to cool. Peel them and discard the stems. Situate frying pan over medium-high heat and warm olive oil. Add in garlic and onion; sauté until tender.
3. Using a food processor, pulse together black pepper, roasted eggplants, salt, lemon juice, scallion mixture, and chili pepper to mix evenly.
4. Add parsley for garnishing. Serve alongside roasted asparagus spears.

Nutrition: 169 Calories 12g Fat 5g Protein

147. Steamed Asparagus & Grilled Cauliflower Steaks

Preparation Time: 13 minutes
Cooking Time: 21 minutes
Servings: 4
Ingredients
- 4 tbsp olive oil
- 1 head cauliflower, sliced into 'steaks'
- 1 red onion, sliced
- ¼ cup green chili sauce
- 1 tsp harissa powder
- Salt and black pepper to taste
- 1 lb. asparagus, trimmed
- Juice of 1 lemon
- 1 cup water
- Fresh parsley to garnish

Directions
1. Preheat the grill.
2. Blend olive oil, chili sauce, and harissa. Brush the cauliflower with the mixture. Situate steaks on the grill, and cook for 6 minutes. Flip the cauliflower, grill further for 6 minutes.
3. Boil water over high heat, place the asparagus in a sieve, and set over the steam from the boiling water. Cook for 6 minutes. After, remove to a bowl and toss with lemon juice. Remove the grilled cauliflower to a plate; sprinkle with salt, black pepper, red onion, and parsley. Serve with the steamed asparagus.

Nutrition: 118 Calories 9g Fat 2g Protein

148. Endive with Cheddar & Walnut Sauce

Preparation Time: 13 minutes
Cooking Time: 17 minutes
Serving: 2
Ingredients
- 1 endive heads, leaves separated
- 2 oz cheddar cheese, crumbled
- 1 cup heavy cream
- ½ tsp nutmeg
- Salt and black pepper to taste
- ½ cup toasted walnuts

Directions
1. Using a saucepan on medium heat, warm up heavy cream. Add in cheddar cheese, nutmeg, salt, and pepper and stir.
2. Remove to a bowl and whisk with a mixer until smooth. Let cool. Arrange the endive leaves on a serving plate.
3. Spoon the cheese mixture into the leaves and top with toasted walnuts to serve.

Nutrition: 360 Calories 23g Fat 12g Protein

149. Asian-Style Tofu Zucchini Kabobs

Preparation Time: 8 minutes
Cooking Time: 10 minutes
Serving: 2

Ingredient

- 8 oz extra firm tofu
- 1 medium zucchini, cut into 2-inch rounds
- 1 tbsp olive oil
- 2 tbsp freshly squeezed lemon juice
- 1 tsp smoked paprika
- 1 tsp cumin powder
- ½ tsp parsley dried
- 1 tsp garlic powder

Directions

1. Preheat a grill to medium heat.
2. Meanwhile, thread the tofu and zucchini alternately on the wooden skewers.
3. Scourge olive oil, lemon juice, paprika, parsley, cumin powder, and garlic powder.
4. Brush the skewers all around with the mixture and place on the grill grate. Cook on both sides for 5 minutes. Serve afterward.

Nutrition: 312 Calories 19g Fat18g Protein

150. Nutty Tofu Loaf

Preparation Time: 11 minutes
Cooking Time: 62 minutes
Serving: 4

Ingredients

- 2 tbsp olive oil + extra for brushing
- 2 red onions, finely chopped
- 4 garlic cloves, minced
- 1 lb. firm tofu, pressed and crumbled
- 2 tbsp soy sauce
- ¾ cup chopped walnuts
- ¼ cup buckwheat flakes
- 1 tbsp sesame seeds
- 1 cup chopped green bell peppers
- Salt and black pepper to taste
- 1 tbsp Italian seasoning
- ½ tsp brown sugar
- ½ cup tomato sauce

Directions

1. Prepare oven to 350 F and grease an 8 x 4-inch loaf pan with olive oil.
2. Cook 1 tbsp of olive oil in a small skillet and sauté the onion and garlic until softened and fragrant, 2 minutes. Situate onion mixture into a large bowl and mix with the tofu, soy sauce, walnuts, buckwheat flakes, sesame seeds, bell peppers, salt, black pepper, Italian seasoning, and brown sugar.
3. Spoon the mixture into the loaf pan, press to fit, and spread the tomato sauce on top. Bake the tofu loaf in the oven for 45 minutes.
4. Remove the loaf pan from the oven, invert the tofu loaf onto a chopping board, and cool for 5 minutes. Slice and serve warm.

Nutrition: 544 Calories 39g Fat 25g Protein

151. Chili Toasted Nuts

Preparation Time: 12 minutes
Cooking Time: 33 minutes
Serving: 4

Ingredients

- 1 cup walnuts nuts
- 1 tbsp extra-virgin olive oil, melted
- ¼ tsp hot sauce
- ¼ tsp garlic powder
- ¼ tsp onion powder

Directions

1. Set oven at 350 F and line a baking sheet with baking paper.
2. In a medium bowl, mix the nuts, olive oil, hot sauce, garlic powder, and onion powder. Lay mixture on the baking sheet and toast in the oven for 10 minutes.
3. Remove the sheet, allow complete cooling, and serve.

Nutrition: 267 Calories 25g Fat6g Protein

152. Creole Tofu Scramble with Kale

Preparation Time: 9 minutes
Cooking Time: 42 minutes
Serving: 2

Ingredients

- 2 tbsp extra-virgin olive oil, for frying
- 1 (14 oz) pack firm tofu, pressed and crumbled
- 4 green chilies, deseeded and chopped
- 1 tomato, finely chopped
- 2 tbsp chopped fresh green onions

- Salt and black pepper to taste
- 1 tsp turmeric powder
- 1 tsp Creole seasoning
- ½ cup chopped baby kale
- ¼ cup grated Parmesan cheese

Direction

1. Preheat olive oil in a huge skillet over medium heat and cook the tofu with occasional stirring until light golden brown. Make sure not to break the tofu into tiny bits but to have scrambled egg resemblance, 5 minutes.
2. Stir in the chilies, tomato, green onions, salt, black pepper, turmeric powder, and Creole seasoning. Sauté until the vegetables soften, 5 minutes.
3. Mix in the kale to wilt, 3 minutes, and then half of Parmesan cheese. Melt for 2 minutes and turn the heat off. Dish the food, top with the remaining cheese, and serve warm.

Nutrition: 258 Calories 16g Fat21g Protein

153. Vegetable Frittata with Red Onions & Green Chilies

Preparation Time: 13 minutes
Cooking Time: 27 minutes
Serving: 1

Ingredients

- 1 tbsp extra-virgin olive oil
- ½ small red onion, chopped
- 1 green chili pepper, chopped
- ½ carrot, chopped
- ½ zucchini, chopped
- 1 tsp turmeric
- 3 eggs
- Salt and black pepper to taste
- 1 tbsp fresh parsley, chopped

Directions

1. Preheat the oven to 350°F.
2. Warmup olive oil in a pan over medium heat. Stir in red onions and sauté for 3 minutes until tender. Pour in carrot, zucchini, and green chili, and cook for 4 minutes. Remove the mixture to a greased baking pan with cooking spray.
3. In a bowl, whisk the eggs with turmeric, salt, and pepper and pour over vegetables. Bake for 10-15 minutes until golden.

Drizzle with freshly chopped parsley and serve.

Nutrition: 288 Calories 23g Fat13g Protein

154. Sirtfood Frittata

Preparation Time: 8 minutes
Cooking Time: 16 minutes
Serving: 2

Ingredients

- 2 tsp olive oil
- 1 small red onion, chopped
- 2 garlic cloves, chopped
- 4 eggs, beaten
- 2 tomatoes, sliced
- 1 green chili, minced
- 2 tbsp fresh parsley, chopped
- Salt and black pepper, to taste

Directions

1. Set a pan over high heat and warm the olive oil. Sauté garlic and red onion until tender.
2. Whisk the eggs with yogurt. Pour into the pan and cook until eggs become puffy and brown to bottom. Add parsley, chili pepper and tomatoes to one side of the omelet. Season with black pepper and salt. Fold the omelet in half and slice into wedges.

Nutrition: 319 Calories 25g Fat14g Protein

155. Baby Arugula Stuffed Zucchini

Preparation Time: 11 minutes
Cooking Time: 42 minutes
Servings: 2

Ingredients

- 2 zucchinis, halved
- 4 tbsp olive oil
- 2 garlic cloves, minced
- 1½ oz baby arugula
- Salt and black pepper to taste
- 2 tbsp tomato sauce
- 1 cup Parmesan cheese, shredded

Directions

1. Scoop out the pulp of the zucchinis into a plate. Keep the flesh. Grease a baking sheet with cooking spray and place in the zucchini halves.
2. Preheat olive oil in a skillet at medium heat. Sauté the garlic until fragrant, about 1

minute. Add arugula and zucchini pulp. Cook until the arugula wilts; season with salt and pepper. Spoon the tomato sauce into the boats and spread to coat the bottom.

3. Spoon the arugula mixture into the zucchinis and sprinkle with the vegan parmesan cheese. Bake for 24 minutes at 370°F. Plate the zucchinis when ready, season with salt and black pepper.

Nutrition: 520 Calories 37g Fat20g Protein

156. Celery Buckwheat Croquettes

Preparation Time: 9 minutes
Cooking time: 25 minutes
Serving: 2

Ingredients

- ¾ cup buckwheat groats, cooked
- 3 tbsp extra-virgin olive oil
- ¼ cup minced red onion
- 1 celery stalk, chopped
- ¼ cup shredded carrots
- 1/3 cup buckwheat flour
- ¼ cup chopped fresh parsley
- Salt and black pepper to taste

Directions

1. Place the groats in a bowl. Cook 1 tbsp of oil in a skillet over medium heat. Place in onion, celery, and carrot and stir-fry for 5 minutes. Transfer to the buckwheat bowl.

2. Mix in flour, parsley, salt, and pepper. Place in the fridge for 20 minutes. Mold the mixture into cylinder-shaped balls. Warm up remaining oil in a skillet over medium heat. Fry the croquettes for 8 minutes, turning occasionally until golden.

Nutrition: 230 Calories 10g Fat6g Protein

157. Creole Tempeh & Black Bean Bowls

Preparation Time: 7 minutes
Cooking Time: 50 minutes
Servings: 4

Ingredients

- 2 tbsp olive oil
- 1 ½ cups crumbled tempeh
- 1 tsp Creole seasoning
- 2 red bell peppers, deseeded and sliced
- 2 cups vegetable broth
- Salt to taste
- 1 (8 oz) can black beans, drained and rinsed
- 2 chives, chopped
- 2 tbsp freshly chopped parsley

Direction

1. Cook olive oil in a medium pot and cook in the tempeh until golden brown, 5 minutes. Season with the Creole seasoning and stir in the bell peppers. Cook until the peppers slightly soften, 3 minutes.

2. Stir in the beans, vegetable broth, and salt. Cover and cook for 10 minutes. Stir in the chives and dish the food, garnished with the parsley.

Nutrition: 216 Calories 18g Fat21g Protein

158. Spicy Broccoli Pasta

Preparation Time: 6 minutes
Cooking Time: 24 minutes
Serving: 2

Ingredients

- 5 oz buckwheat fusilli
- 4 oz broccoli florets
- 1 tbsp extra-virgin olive oil
- 1 small red onion, finely sliced
- 1 garlic clove, finely sliced
- ½ tsp crushed chilies
- ½ tsp caraway seeds
- 1 large zucchini, coarsely grated
- 4 tbsp low-fat heavy milk
- ½ lemon, zested and juiced
- 3-4 ice cubes

Directions

1. Prepare the pasta according to package instructions. 4 minutes before the end, add in the broccoli to the pan. Drain and keep 3 tbsp of the pasta water.

2. Preheat oil in a huge skillet over a low heat. Add the onion and cook for 5 mins, then stir in the garlic, crushed chilies and caraway seeds. Cook 4-5 minutes more. Add the zucchini and season to taste. Fry until the zucchini is tender, 2 minutes.

3. Add the pasta, broccoli and reserved pasta water to the skillet. Take out from the heat and stir in the heavy cream and lemon juice. Serve warm.

Nutrition: 304 Calories 10g Fat11g Protein

159. Buckwheat Pilaf with Pine Nuts

Preparation Time: 13 minutes
Cooking time: 24 minutes
Serves: 2

Ingredients

- 1 cup buckwheat groats
- 2 cups vegetable stock
- ¼ cup walnuts
- 2 tbsp olive oil
- ½ red onion, chopped
- 1/3 cup chopped fresh parsley

Directions

1. Put the groats and vegetable stock in a pot. Bring to a boil, then lower the heat and simmer for 15 minutes. Heat a skillet over medium heat. Place in the pine nuts and toast for 2-3 minutes, shaking often. Heat the oil in the same skillet and sauté the onion for 3 minutes until translucent.
2. Once the groats are ready, fluff them using a fork. Mix in walnuts, onion, and parsley. Sprinkle with salt and pepper. Serve.

Nutrition: 277 Calories 19g Fat 5g Protein

160. Buckwheat Savoy Cabbage Rolls with Tofu

Preparation Time: 8 minutes
Cooking Time: 31 minutes
Serving: 2

Ingredients

- 2 tbsp extra-virgin olive oil
- 2 cups extra firm tofu, pressed and crumbled
- ½ medium red onion, finely chopped
- 2 garlic cloves, minced
- Salt and black pepper to taste
- 1 cup buckwheat groats
- 1 ¾ cups vegetable stock
- 1 bay leaf
- 2 tbsp chopped fresh cilantro + more for garnishing
- 1 head Savoy cabbage, leaves separated (scraps kept)
- 1 (23 oz) canned chopped tomatoes

Directions

1. Heat olive oil in a big skillet and cook the tofu until golden brown, 8 minutes. Cook onion and garlic for 3 minutes. Season with salt, black pepper and mix in the buckwheat, bay leaf, and vegetable stock.
2. Close the lid, allow boiling, and then simmer until all the liquid is absorbed. Open the lid; remove the bay leaf, adjust the taste with salt, black pepper, and mix in the cilantro.
3. Spread-out cabbage leaves on a flat surface and add 3 to 4 tablespoons of the cooked buckwheat onto each leaf. Roll the leaves to firmly secure the filling.
4. Pour the tomatoes with juices into a medium pot, season with a little salt, black pepper, and lay the cabbage rolls in the sauce. Cook over medium heat until the cabbage softens, 5 to 8 minutes. Turn the heat off and dish the food onto serving plates. Garnish with more cilantro and serve warm.

Nutrition: 598 Calories 28g Fat48g Protein

161. Potato and Chickpea Bake

Preparation Time: 18 minutes
Cooking Time: 42 minutes
Serving: 6

Ingredients:

- 1 large baking potato – pricked
- 1 teaspoon olive oil – extra virgin
- ½ red onion – chopped
- 1 garlic clove – mi9nced
- ½ teaspoon ginger – freshly grated
- Chili flakes to taste
- 1 teaspoon cumin seeds
- 1 teaspoon turmeric
- 1 cup tomatoes – tinned chopped
- ½ teaspoon cocoa powder – unsweetened
- 1 cup chickpeas with water
- 1 yellow pepper – chopped
- 1 tablespoon parsley
- Salt to taste

Directions:

1. Prep the oven to 425 degrees F. Once you place a potato in the oven, you will be baking for an hour or until the potato is

ready for your taste. Next, take a frying pan and add the olive oil.

2. Set the heat to low medium and add onions to the pan. Cover with the lid and cook on low heat for 5 minutes. When you remove the lid, add ginger, chili, cumin, and garlic. Cook for a minute then add a splash of water and turmeric.

3. Add tomatoes, cocoa, chickpeas, and yellow pepper. Bring the mixture to a simmer on low medium heat – you will be cooking the mixture between 30 and 40 minutes until the sauce thickens. Add salt to taste and parsley, and top the baked potato with the chickpeas sauce.

Nutrition: 268 Calories 4g Fat 9g Protein

162. Kale Dhal with Buckwheat

Preparation Time: 8 minutes
Cooking Time: 16 minutes
Serving: 5
Ingredients:

- 1 tablespoon extra-virgin olive oil
- 4 garlic cloves – minced
- 2cm piece ginger – grated
- 1 red onion – chopped
- 1 bird's eye chili – finely sliced
- 2 teaspoons garam masala
- 2 teaspoons turmeric
- 150 grams lentils – red
- 400 ml of coconut milk
- 100 grams kale
- 160 grams buckwheat
- 200 ml of water

Directions:

1. Take a deep skillet or a frying pan and add the oil. Heat up the pan then add the onions. Set on the low medium heat and cover the pan while the onion is cooking on low heat for 5 minutes. Remove the lid and add ginger, chili, and garlic.

2. Cook for another minute. Add masala and turmeric with a splash of water and cook for a minute. Blend coconut milk with 200 ml of water and add it to the pan. Add lentils and stir well to combine all ingredients in the pan then cook for 20

minutes with occasional stirring on low medium heat.

3. Place the lid on while cooking. Check for the dhal consistency and add more water if the mass is thickening. After 20 minutes, open lid and add kale.

4. Stir in to combine kale with the rest of the ingredients and cook on low heat for 5 minutes. 5 minutes after you start cooking the dhal with lentils, take a saucepan and add buckwheat with plenty of water.

5. Cook buckwheat for 10 minutes after bringing the water to a boil or until the buckwheat is soft enough to suit your taste. Serve dhal with buckwheat and enjoy your meal.

Nutrition: 209 Calories 6g Fat 10g Protein

163. Braised Puy Lentils

Preparation Time: 17 minutes
Cooking Time: 22 minutes
Serving: 6
Ingredients:

- 40 grams carrots – sliced
- 40 grams celery – sliced
- 75 grams Puy lentils
- 220 ml of vegetable stock
- 20 grams rocket salad
- 5 grams kale – chopped
- 1 tablespoon parsley – chopped
- 1 teaspoon thyme
- 1 teaspoon paprika
- 1 garlic clove – chopped
- 10 cherry tomatoes
- 2 tablespoons extra virgin olive oil
- 1 red onion - diced

Directions:

1. Prep the oven to 240 degrees F. Situate tomatoes on a small tin and bake for 35 to 40 minutes. As tomatoes are baking, set the stove on low-medium heat and add 1 tablespoon of olive oil, garlic, onion, celery, and carrots. Cook for 2 minutes with occasional stirring. Add paprika and thyme once the veggies are softened and stir in well to combine.

2. Wash and strain lentils then add them to the pan with the vegetable stock. Bring the

mixture to a simmer. Place the lid on and cook for 20 minutes on low heat.

3. Make sure to check the pan every 6 to 7 minutes and add water if necessary. Add kale and remove the lid.

4. Continue cook for 10 minutes then add parsley and tomatoes. Serve with rocket salad. Add the remaining olive oil to the rocket salad.

Nutrition: 213 Calories 16g Fat 23g Protein

164. Chicken Chili with Buckwheat

Preparation Time: 14 minutes
Cooking Time: 32 minutes
Serving: 5
Ingredients:

- 1 red onion – chopped
- 3 garlic cloves – chopped
- 2 bird's eye chili peppers – sliced
- 400 grams chicken – minced – you can choose thighs or breasts
- 150 ml red wine
- 1 red pepper – cored, deseeded and chopped
- 150 grams kidney beans – tinned
- 300 ml vegetable or chicken stock
- 400 grams tinned chopped tomatoes
- 1 tablespoon extra-virgin olive oil
- 1 tablespoon turmeric – ground
- 1 tablespoon cumin – ground
- 1 tablespoon tomato puree
- 1 tablespoon cocoa powder
- 5 grams parsley – chopped
- 160 grams buckwheat

Directions:

1. Take a skillet and add oil, set the heat to medium and add garlic, chili, and onion once the oil is heated. Cook for 2 minutes with occasional stirring. Add the spices from the in gradient list and cook for another minute. Stir in to combine then add the minced chicken and cook on high heat until the chicken is lightly browned and mixed with spices and onions.

2. Add the red wine. Cook until the wi9ne is reduced by half. Add kidney beans, tomatoes, puree, red pepper, cocoa, and stock. Simmer for one hour. You may need

to add water in the middle of cooking to achieve preferred consistency.

3. After the chili is cooked, add chopped herbs, stir in and serve with buckwheat. Cook the buckwheat according to direction on the package.

Nutrition: 226 Calories 8g Fat 19g Protein

165. Chickpea and Quinoa Curry

Preparation Time: 18 minutes
Cooking Time: 37 minutes
Serving: 4
Ingredients:

- 500 grams potatoes
- 3 garlic cloves – crushed
- 400 ml can coconut milk
- 400 grams chickpeas – canned
- 300 ml boiled water
- 180 grams quinoa
- 150 grams spinach
- 1 tablespoon tomato puree
- 3 teaspoons turmeric – ground
- 1 teaspoon coriander – ground
- 1 teaspoon ginger - ground
- 1 teaspoon chili flakes
- Salt to taste

Directions:

1. Place quartered potatoes in a pot filled with water, add a pinch of salt and bring the water to a boil. Cook for around 25 minutes after the boiling point until you can easily cut through potatoes with a knife.

2. Drain potatoes once cooked until no water is left. Transfer potatoes to a large pan then add turmeric, garlic, chili, ginger, coconut milk, coriander, tomato puree, and tomatoes and bring it all to boil and add salt. Mix well then add quinoa with 300 ml of boiled water. Set heat to low-medium and let the mixture simmer.

3. Cover the pan and allow the curry to cook for the next 30 minutes. Stir the curry every 5 minutes or so. Make sure that none of the ingredients are sticking to the bottom of the pan. After 15 minutes of cooking, add the chickpeas, stir in and cover the pot again.

4. When you are at the last 5 minutes of cooking, add spinach and stir in. You will know that the curry is ready when quinoa becomes soft instead of crunchy.

Nutrition: 333 Calories 12g Fat 14g Protein

166. Vegetable Chili

Preparation Time: 16 minutes
Cooking Time: 34 minutes
Serving: 4

Ingredients:

- ½ cup zucchini – fresh, chopped
- 50 grams Cremini mushrooms
- 2 cups tomatoes – diced
- 1 cup kidney beans – canned
- ½ cup red onion – chopped
- 1 tablespoon olive oil
- ½ cup red bell pepper – chopped
- 2 teaspoons cumin seeds – ground
- 1 teaspoon chili powder
- ½ bird's eye chili – sliced
- 1 garlic clove – minced

Directions:

1. Cook tablespoon of olive oil in a skillet over medium-high heat. Add the onions and garlic and sauté while occasionally stirring for a minute or two.
2. Add zucchini, peppers, and mushrooms. Sauté and stir for another 2 minutes or so, then add cumin and chili powder. After combining all the ingredients add the beans and tomatoes.
3. Bring the mixture to a boil. Adjust heat to medium and simmer for the next 20 to 30 minutes. Serve and enjoy.

Nutrition: 157 Calories 2g Fat 7g Protein

167. Lemon Splash Tofu

Preparation Time: 9 minutes
Cooking Time: 13 minutes
Serving: 3

Ingredients:

- 250 grams firm tofu – extra firm
- ½ teaspoon lemon zest – freshly grated
- ¼ lemon – peeled, fresh
- 1/8 cup sundried tomatoes
- 1 garlic clove
- ½ teaspoon ground fennel seeds
- 1 tablespoon extra-virgin olive oil

Direction:

1. Prepare the oven to 400 degrees F. Combine olive oil, tomatoes, fennel, crushed garlic, and lemon zest to make a marinade for the tofu. Lightly oil a baking dish then cut the tofu into four equal pieces.
2. Coat the top of the pieces with some of the marinade. Arrange the pieces in the baking dish. Bake for 13 minutes. Serve with the rest of the marinade and enjoy your dish.

Nutrition: 254 Calories 20g Fat 14g Protein

168. Veggie Stuffed Peppers

Preparation Time: 14 minutes
Cooking Time: 36 minutes
Serving: 6

Ingredients:

- 1 green pepper
- ¾ cup brown rice - cooked
- 2 tablespoons red onion – diced
- 2 tablespoons celery – diced
- ¼ cup tomato puree
- ½ bird's eye chili – finely sliced
- ½ teaspoon oregano - dry
- ½ teaspoon basil – dry
- ½ teaspoon thyme – ground
- 2 slices Mozzarella cheese
- 2 tablespoons olive oil

Directions:

1. Preheat skillet with a tablespoon of olive oil on medium heat. Add onions and celery and diced green pepper to the skillet. Sauté for one to two minutes.
2. Add tomato puree then cook for five minutes while simmering. Add the herbs and spices and stir in to combine. Add the brown rice and stir in to combine all the ingredients.
3. Take the whole pepper – top off and deseeded - and cut it in half across the length. Stuff each half with rice mixture. Situate one slice of cheese on each half then place in a lightly greased up baking dish. Bake over 350 degrees F for 23 minutes. Serve and enjoy!

Nutrition: 405 Calories 15g Fat 18g Protein

169. Veggie Jambalaya

Preparation Time: 12 minutes

Cooking Time: 29 minutes

Serving: 3

Ingredients:

- ¼ cup dark red beans – canned
- ¼ cup red onion – chop
- ¼ cup red bell pepper – chopped
- ¼ cup yellow pepper – chopped
- ¾ cups brown rice - cooked
- 1 garlic clove – minced
- 50 grams tomato paste – canned
- 25 grams silk five-grain tempeh
- ½ cup vegetable broth
- 1 bird's eye chili pepper
- 1 tablespoon extra-virgin olive oil
- Salt to taste

Directions:

1. Prep skillet on medium-high heat and add the oil. Add garlic and onion and sauté for a minute or two.
2. Reduce the heat to medium. Add sliced tempeh and peppers and cook until the veggies are softened to your preference. Add the spices and salt, broth, and tomato paste. Stir in to combine then bring the mixture to a simmer.
3. Once the jambalaya starts to simmer, add cooked brown rice and stir to combine. Serve while hot and enjoy your lunch.

Nutrition: 509 Calories 16g Fat 15g Protein

170. Veggie Stir Fry

Preparation Time: 9 minutes

Cooking Time: 24 minutes

Serving: 4

Ingredients:

- ¼ cup red onion – chopped
- ¼ cup broccoli – florets, chopped
- ¼ cup mushrooms – chopped
- ¼ cup red sweet pepper – chopped
- 1 bird's eye chili – sliced
- 1 tablespoon extra-virgin olive oil
- Salt to taste
- 1 tablespoon dark soy sauce

Directions:

1. Ready skillet on medium heat and add a tablespoon of oil. Once the oil is heated, add the veggies, sprinkling salt afterward.

2. Coat the veggies and cook the veggies. Add a tablespoon of soy sauce at the end, stir and serve hot.

Nutrition: 180 Calories 14g Fat 2g Protein

171. Buckwheat Pasta Salad

Preparation Time: 8 minutes

Cooking Time: 26 minutes

Serving: 2

Ingredients:

- 50 grams buckwheat pasta
- 50 grams rocket salad
- ½ avocado – peeled and diced
- 10 cherry tomatoes
- 10 olives
- 1 tablespoon extra-virgin olive oil
- 20 grams pine nuts

Directions:

1. Cook the buckwheat pasta as per to the instructions on the package. As the pasta is cooking, you will prepare the rest of the ingredients.
2. Drain the pasta and rinse it under the cold water. Combine all ingredients except the pine nuts. Top the salad with pine nuts.

Nutrition: 220 Calories 3g Fat 7g Protein

172. Greek Salad on a Stick

Preparation Time: 21 minutes

Cooking Time: 0 minute

Serving: 1

Ingredients:

- 2 skewers – wooden
- 8 black olives
- 1 red pepper – cut in 8 pieces
- 1 yellow pepper – cut in 8 pieces
- 100 grams cucumber – cut into cubes
- 100 grams feta cheese – cut into 8 pieces
- ½ red onion – cut into 8 pieces

Dressing:

- 1 tablespoon extra-virgin olive oil
- ½ lemon – juiced
- 1 teaspoon vinegar – balsamic
- 1 garlic clove – crushed
- Several leaves of basil - fresh
- Several leaves of oregano – fresh
- Salt to taste

Directions:

1. Submerge wooden skewers in warm water for 30 minutes before threading the ingredients. Prepare the Greek salad on skewers by threading all ingredients, previously preparing all the veggies and cheese for threading.
2. Thread the ingredients first threading olives, cherry tomatoes, cucumber, pepper, and feta cheese – repeat the process by threading ingredients in the same order.
3. Prepare the dressing by placing all ingredients from the dressing list in a bowl. Mix all ingredients then pour over the Greek salad on skewers.

Nutrition: 306 Calories 1g Fat 5g Protein

173. Tofu Curry

Preparation Time: 18 minutes
Cooking Time: 31 minutes
Serving: 5

Ingredients:

- 1-liter water
- 1 tablespoon grapeseed oil
- 1 red onion – chopped
- 1 bird's eye chili
- 4 garlic cloves – chopped
- 1 teaspoon paprika
- ¼ teaspoon cayenne pepper
- ½ teaspoon turmeric – ground
- 7cm piece of ginger – grated
- 1 teaspoon salt
- 250 grams red lentils – dry
- 50 grams edamame beans – frozen
- 200 grams tofu – firm, cubed
- 1 lime - juiced
- 200 grams kale
- 2 tomatoes - chopped

Directions:

1. Put stove to low medium heat and put the oil in a pan. Add onions and cook for 5 minutes with occasional stirring. After the onions are cooked, add ginger, garlic, and chili.
2. Cook for 2 more minutes then add cumin, salt, cayenne, paprika, and turmeric. Stir the ingredients to combine with the onion mixture then add the lentils. As you are preparing this base for your dish, take a large cooking pot and pour 1 liter of water.

3. Boil water then add the boiling water to the pan to bring the ingredients to simmer for 10 minutes. Set heat to low and allow the curry to cook for 20 to 30 minutes on low heat and until the consistency of the dish is porridge-like.
4. Add edamame beans, tofu, and tomatoes. Cook the curry for another 5 minutes after adding the three ingredients then add lime juice and kale. Cook until kale is softened. Serve warm and enjoy.

Nutrition: 342 Calories 5g Fat 28g Protein

174. Veggie and Buckwheat Stir

Preparation Time: 7 minutes
Cooking Time: 32 minutes
Serving: 4

Ingredients:

- ½ cup buckwheat
- 3 tablespoons extra virgin olive oil
- 1 cup of water
- 1 medium carrot
- 1 medium red onion
- 1 red bell pepper -diced, deseeded
- 1 yellow bell pepper – diced, deseeded
- 10 grams parsley - chopped

Directions:

1. Take a heavy bottom pan and add buckwheat. Cook for 5 minutes on medium-low with frequent stirring and with no oil or water. Buckwheat can easily burn, so make sure to stir while cooking for the first 5 minutes.
2. Cook 1 tablespoon of oil and stir in well. Mix and stir frequently until the oil is absorbed then add a cup of water.
3. Set heat to low, bring to a simmer, and cover with a lid. Cook for 20 minutes on low. Once you remove buckwheat from the heat don't open the lid but let it sit for another 20 minutes.
4. Pre-heat two tablespoons of oil in a skillet then add the onions, carrots, and peppers. Add some salt then stir to combine. Cook the veggies until softened.
5. Remove the lid from buckwheat then stir and add a sprinkle of salt. Add the sautéed veggies then stir to combine. Add parsley as a garnish and enjoy your meal.

Nutrition: 198 Calories 5g Fat 6g Protein

175. Sweet Pepper Mix

Preparation Time: 14 minutes
Cooking Time: 0 minute
Serving: 3
Ingredients:
- 1/8 cup green bell pepper
- ¼ cup red bell pepper
- 1/8 cup yellow pepper
- 1/8 cup red onion
- ¼ cup rocket salad
- 1 tablespoon parsley – chopped
- ¼ lemon - juiced

Directions:
1. Dice the bell peppers, onion, and parsley and combine with rocket salad. Mix to combine in a salad bowl then dress with lemon juice.

Nutrition: 34 Calories 0.1g Fat 0.5g Protein

176. Cottage Cheese Veggie Salad

Preparation Time: 14 minutes
Cooking Time: 0 minute
Servings: 2
Ingredients:
- 6 cherry tomatoes
- ½ cup cottage cheese
- 2 tbsps. scallion
- 2 green olives

Directions:
1. Slice five tomatoes into quarters; set aside remaining tomato for garnish.
2. Mix all ingredients except lettuce and garnish
3. Garnish with cheese mixture, and reserved cherry tomato.

Nutrition: 342 Calories 27g Fat 12g Protein

177. Arugula and Lemon Rice

Preparation Time: 7 minutes
Cooking Time: 37 minutes
Servings: 5
Ingredients:
- 1 red onion
- 1 cup mushrooms
- 2 cloves garlic
- 1 tbsp. olive oil
- 3 cup long-grain rice
- 10 oz. arugula
- 3 tbsp. lemon juice
- ¼ tsp. dill weed
- 1/3 cup feta cheese

Directions:
1. Set oven at 350°F. Cook onion, mushrooms and garlic in oil. Mix in the rice, arugula, lemon juice, dill and season well.
2. Set aside 1 tbsp. cheese and mix rest into skillet. Situate to greased 8-in. square baking dish. Drizzle with reserved cheese. Bake for 25 minutes.
3. Uncover then bake until heated through and cheese is melted.

Nutrition: 367 Calories 21g Fat 17g Protein

178. Spring Pesto Beans

Preparation time: 9 minutes
Cooking Time: 60 minutes
Servings: 3
Ingredients:
- 2 tbsp. Olive oil
- 2 tsp. Sweet paprika
- 1 lemon juice
- 2 tbsp. Basil pesto
- 1 lb. green beans
- ¼ tsp. black pepper
- 1 red onion

Direction:
1. Preheat pan with the oil at medium-high heat; cook onion for 5 minutes.
2. Cook beans and the rest of the ingredients for 11 minutes, then serve.

Nutrition: 312 Calories 26g Fat 8g Protein

179. Mung Sprouts Salsa

Preparation Time: 9 minutes
Cooking Time: 0 minute
Servings: 2
Ingredients:
- 1 red onion, chopped
- 2 c. mung beans, sprouted
- A pinch of red chili powder
- 1 green chili pepper, chopped
- 1 tomato, chopped
- 1 tsp. Chaat masala
- 1 tsp. lemon juice
- 1 tbsp. coriander, chopped

- Black pepper to the taste

Directions:
1. In a salad bowl, mix onion with mung sprouts, chili pepper, tomato, chili powder, Chaat masala, lemon juice, coriander and pepper, toss well, divide into small cups and serve.

Nutrition: 321 Calories 19g Fat 7g Protein

180. Honey Chili Squash

Preparation Time: 16 minutes
Cooking Time: 33 minutes
Servings: 2
Ingredients:

- 2 red onions, roughly chopped 2.5cm
- 1-inch chunk of ginger root, finely chopped
- 2 cloves garlic
- 2 bird's-eye chilies, finely chopped
- 1 butternut squash, peeled and chopped
- 100 ml (3½ fl. oz.) vegetable stock broth
- 1 tbsp. olive oil
- Juice of 1 orange
- Juice of 1 lime
- 2 tsps. honey

Directions:
1. Warm the oil into a pan and add in the red onions, squash chunks, chilies, garlic, ginger and honey. Cook for 3 minutes.
2. Squeeze in the lime and orange juice. Pour in the stock broth), orange and lime juice and cook for 15 minutes until tender.

Nutrition: 300 Calories 14g Fat 6g Protein

181. Salsa Bean Dip

Preparation Time: 9 minutes
Cooking Time: 22 minutes
Servings: 6
Ingredients:

- ½ c. salsa
- 2 c. canned white beans, no-salt-added, drained and rinsed
- 1 c. low-fat cheddar, shredded
- 2 tbsps. green onions, chopped

Directions:
1. Simmer beans with the green onions and salsa over medium heat for 20 minutes.
2. Mix cheese, until it melts, put off heat, set aside then serve.

Nutrition: 271 Calories 20g Fat 7g Protein

182. Roast Balsamic Vegetables

Preparation Time: 7 minutes
Cooking Time: 44 minutes
Servings: 2
Ingredients:

- 4 tomatoes, chopped
- 2 red onions, chopped
- 3 sweet potatoes, peeled and chopped
- 100g (3½ oz.) red chicory or if unavailable, use yellow
- 100g (3½ oz.) kale, finely chopped
- 300g (11 oz.) potatoes, peeled and chopped
- 5 stalks celery, chopped
- 1 bird's-eye chili, de-seeded and finely chopped
- 2 tbsps. fresh parsley, chopped
- 2 tbsps. fresh coriander cilantro chopped
- 3 tbsps. olive oil
- 2 tbsps. balsamic vinegar 1 teaspoon mustard
- Sea salt
- Freshly ground black pepper

Directions:
1. Place the olive oil, balsamic, mustard, parsley and coriander cilantro into a bowl and mix well.
2. Toss all the remaining ingredients into the dressing and season with salt and pepper. Transfer the vegetables to an ovenproof dish and cook in the oven at 200C/400F for 45 minutes.

Nutrition: 299 Calories 19g Fat 4g Protein

183. Courgette and Tomato Risotto

Preparation Time: 8 minutes
Cooking Time: 17 minutes
Servings: 9
Ingredients:

- 2 tbsp. olive oil
- 4 garlic cloves
- 1 ½ lb. Rice Arborio
- 6 tomatoes
- 2 tsp. chop rosemary
- 6 courgette
- 1 ¼ cup peas

- 12 cup hot vegetable stock

Directions:
1. Situate big, heavy-bottomed pan over medium heat then pour oil.
2. Once heated, sauté onion.
3. Cook the tomatoes then stir in the rice and rosemary. Cook half the stock
4. Cook remaining stock for 3 minutes.
5. Cook courgette and peas.
6. Season well.
7. Mix in the basil and set aside for 5 minutes.

Nutrition: 293 Calories 16g Fat 5g Protein

184. Black Bean Salsa

Preparation Time: 12 minutes
Cooking Time: 0 minute
Servings: 6

Ingredients:
- 1 tbsp. coconut aminos
- ½ tsp. cumin, ground
- 1 c. canned black beans, no-salt-added, drained and rinsed
- 1 c. salsa
- 6 c. romaine lettuce leaves, torn
- ½ c. avocado, peeled, pitted and cubed

Directions:
1. In a bowl, combine the beans with the aminos, cumin, salsa, lettuce and avocado, toss, divide into small bowls and serve as a snack.

Nutrition: 180 Calories 17g Fat 5g Protein

185. Brown Basmati Rice Pilaf

Preparation Time: 18 minutes
Cooking Time: 14 minutes
Servings: 2

Ingredients:
- ½ tbsp. vegan butter
- ½ c. mushrooms, chopped
- ½ c. brown basmati rice
- 3 tbsps. water
- 1/8 tsp. dried thyme
- Ground pepper to taste
- ½ tbsp. olive oil
- ¼ c. green onion, chopped
- 1 c. vegetable broth
- ¼ tsp. salt
- ¼ c. chopped, toasted pecans

Directions:

1. Place a saucepan over medium-low heat. Add butter and oil.
2. When it melts, add mushrooms and cook until slightly tender.
3. Stir in the green onion and brown rice. Cook for 3 minutes. Stir constantly.
4. Stir in the broth, water, salt and thyme.
5. When about to boil, reduce heat and cover with a lid. Simmer until rice is cooked.
6. Stir in the pecans and pepper.

Nutrition: 281 Calories 17g Fat 4g Protein

186. Crunchy Arugula with Apples

Preparation Time: 18 minutes
Cooking Time: 8 minutes
Servings: 3

Ingredients:
- 2 tbsp. olive oil
- 2 garlic cloves
- 2 tbsp. pine nuts
- 1 apple
- 10 ounces arugula

Directions:
1. Preheat olive oil in wok over low heat.
2. Cook the pine nuts, garlic and apple for 4 minutes
3. Adjust heat to medium and cook arugula for 4 minutes. Season it well.

Nutrition: 315 Calories 21g Fat 7g Protein

187. Cauliflower and Carrots Dip

Preparation Time: 17 minutes
Cooking Time: 32 minutes
Servings: 3

Ingredients:
- 1 cup carrots
- 2 cups cauliflower florets
- ½ cup cashews
- 2 ½ cup water
- 1 cup almond milk
- 1 tsp. garlic powder
- ¼ tsp. paprika

Direction:
1. Boil carrots with cauliflower, cashews and water at medium heat for 40 minutes, strain and place in the blender.
2. Blend almond milk, garlic powder and paprika, then serve

Nutrition: 289 Calories 21g Fat 8g Protein

188. Kale and Bean Casserole

Preparation Time: 7 minutes
Cooking time: 46 minutes
Servings: 3
Ingredients:

- 1 ½ cup milk
- 1 cup sour cream
- 1 cup mushrooms
- 2 cup green beans
- 2 cup kale
- ¼ cup capers
- ¼ cup walnuts

Direction:

1. Prepare oven to 375 degrees F then grease a casserole dish.
2. Scourge milk and sour cream.
3. Mix in mushrooms, green beans, kale, and capers. Fill into the casserole dish
4. Drizzle with the crushed walnuts.
5. Bake uncovered for 40 minutes.

Nutrition: 308 Calories 24g Fat 8g Protein

189. Red Coleslaw

Preparation Time: 11 minutes
Cooking Time: 0 minute
Servings: 4
Ingredients:

- 1 2/3 lbs. red cabbage
- 2 tbsps. ground caraway seeds
- 1 tbsp. whole grain mustard
- 1 1/4 c. mayonnaise, low fat, low sodium
- Salt and black pepper

Directions:

1. Cut the red cabbage into small slices.
2. Incorporate all the ingredients alongside cabbage.
3. Mix well, season with salt and pepper.
4. Serve!

Nutrition: 281 Calories 17g Fat 7g Protein

190. Balsamic Eggplant Salsa

Preparation Time: 18 minutes
Cooking Time: 9 minutes
Servings: 3
Ingredients:

- 1 ½ cup tomatoes
- 3 cup eggplant
- 2 tsp. capers
- 6 oz. green olives
- 4 garlic cloves
- 2 tsp. balsamic vinegar
- 1 tbsp. basil

Direction:

1. Pre-heat pan with the oil over medium-high heat, cook eggplant for 5 minutes.
2. Cook tomatoes, capers, olives, garlic, vinegar, basil and black pepper for 7 minutes then serve cold.

Nutrition: 284 Calories 18g Fat 11g Protein

191. Stir-Fried Prawn Noodles

Preparation Time: 19 minutes
Cooking Time: 22 minutes
Serving: 1

Ingredients:

- 5 ounce shelled raw king prawns, deveined
- 2 tsp tamari
- 2 tsp extra virgin olive oil
- soba (buckwheat noodles)
- 1 garlic clove, finely chopped
- 1 bird's eye chili, finely chopped
- 1 tsp finely chopped fresh ginger
- 1-ounce red onions, sliced
- 2-ounce celery, trimmed and sliced
- 3-ounce green beans, chopped
- 2-ounce kale, roughly chopped
- 100ml chicken stock
- 1-ounce lovage or celery leaves

Direction:

1. Warm-up frying pan over a high heat, then cook the prawns for 2–3 minutes in 1 teaspoon tamari and 1 teaspoon oil. Put the prawns onto a plate. Wipe the pan out with paper from the oven, because you would be using it again.
2. Cook the noodles 5–8 minutes in boiling water, or as directed on the packet. Drain and throw aside.
3. While, over medium-high heat, fry the garlic, chili and ginger, red onion, celery, beans and kale in the remaining oil for 2–3 minutes. Attach the stock and bring to the boil, then simmer for one to two minutes until the vegetables are cooked but crunchy.
4. Attach the prawns, noodles and leaves of lovage / celery to the oven, put back to the simmer, then reduce the heat and drink.

Nutrition: 317 Calories 24g Fat 9g Protein

192. Buckwheat Noodles and Shrimp

Preparation Time: 28 minutes
Cooking Time: 17 minutes
Serving: 1

Ingredients:

- 1/3-pound shelled whole jumbo shrimp, deveined tamari 2 teaspoons
- 2 Extra virgin olive oil Teaspoons
- 3 ounces soba
- 2 Nicely sliced garlic cloves
- 1 Finely minced Thai chili
- 1 tablespoon of beautifully minced fresh ginger
- 1/8 cup red onions
- 1/2 cup sliced celery including leaves
- 1/2 cup green beans, minced
- 3/4 cup kale, roughly chopped
- 1/2 cup chicken stock.

Direction

1. Heat a frying pan over high pressure, then cook the shrimp for 2 minutes in 1 teaspoon tamari and 1 teaspoon oil. Place the shrimp into a tray.
2. Cook the noodles for 7 minutes in boiling water. Drain and throw aside.
3. While, in the remaining tamari and oil over medium-high heat, fry the garlic, chili, ginger, red onion, celery, green beans, and kale for 2 min. Boil stock then simmer for a minute.
4. Attach the shrimp, pasta, and leaves of celery to the plate, bring back to a simmer, then remove and serve from fire.

Nutrition: 417 Calories 28g Fat 13g Protein

193. Prawn Arrabbiata

Preparation Time: 7 minutes
Cooking Time: 19 minutes
Serving: 1

Ingredients:

- 125-150 g Raw prawns
- 65 g Buckwheat pasta
- 1 tbsp Extra virgin olive oil

For arrabbiata sauce:

- 2-ounce Red onion, finely chopped
- 1 Garlic clove, finely chopped
- 2-ounce Celery, finely chopped
- 1 Bird's eye chili, finely chopped
- 1 tsp Dried mixed herbs
- 1 tsp Extra virgin olive oil
- 2 tbsp White wine (optional)

- 15-ounce Tinned chopped tomatoes
- 1 tbsp Chopped parsley

Direction:

1. Fry the onion, garlic, celery and chili over medium-low heat and dry herbs in the oil for 1–2 minutes. Set to medium heat then add the wine and cook 1 minute. Add the tomatoes and allow the sauce to steam for 20-30 minutes over medium-low heat
2. While cooking the sauce, bring a bowl of water to the boil and cook the pasta according to the Preparation packet. Once cooked, drain, toss with the olive oil and keep aside
3. Add the raw prawns to the sauce and cook for another 4 minutes then add the parsley and serve.
4. Mix in cooked pasta to the sauce and mix well but gently and serve.

Nutrition: 348 Calories 27g Fat 11g Protein

194. Salmon with Turmeric

Preparation Time: 19 minutes
Cooking Time: 27 minutes
Serving: 1

Ingredients:

- 10-ounce Skinned Salmon
- 1 tsp Extra virgin olive oil
- 1 tsp Ground turmeric
- 1/4 Juice of a lemon
- For the spicy celery
- 1 tsp Extra virgin olive oil
- 2-ounce Red onion, finely chopped
- 3-ounce Tinned green lentils
- 1 Garlic clove, finely chopped
- 1 cm Fresh ginger, finely chopped
- 1 Bier's eye chili, finely chopped
- 150 g Celery, cut into 2cm lengths
- 1 tsp Mild curry powder
- 6-ounce Tomato, cut into 8 wedges
- 100 ml Chicken or vegetable stock
- 1 tbsp Chopped parsley

Direction

1. Heat the oven to 200 C
2. Begin with the spicy celery. Heat over medium-low heat a frying pan, add olive oil, then onion, garlic, ginger, chili and celery. Cook gently for 2minutes, then

apply the curry powder and cook about a minute more.

3. Then introduce the tomatoes, stock and lentils and gently simmer for 10 minutes. Depending about how crunchy you want your celery you may want to increasing or decrease the cooking period.
4. In the meanwhile, bring together the turmeric, oil and lemon juice and spray over the salmon. Put on a baking tray and cook 8–10 minutes.
5. Stir the parsley through the celery to end, and serve with salmon.

Nutrition: 411 Calories 31g Fat 20g Protein

195. Salmon Fillet Pan-Fried

Preparation Time: 9 minutes
Cooking Time: 28 minutes
Serving: 1

Ingredients:

- 1/4 cup lemon parsley juice
- 1 Tbsp. capers
- 1 Clove of garlic, peeled roughly
- 1 tablespoon of extra virgin olive oil
- 1/4 avocado, peeled, stoned, and diced
- 2/3 cup cherry tomatoes, half
- 1/8 cup red onion, thinly sliced
- 13/4 ounces arugula
- 2 tablespoons celery leaves
- 1 x 5-ounce fillet of skinless salmon
- 2 Spoonful of brown sugar
- 1 Endive arm, roughly 21/2 ounces (70 g), halved in length

Direction:

1. Set oven to 220 ° C (425° F).
2. Situate parsley, lemon juice, capers, garlic, and 2 teaspoons of oil in a food processor or mixer for dressing and blend until smooth.
3. For the salad, combine the leaves of avocado, tomato, red onion, arugula, and celery.
4. Heat a fried casserole over high pressure. Roll the salmon in a little oil and sear for a minute or two in the hot pan to caramelize the fish's underside.
5. Switch to a baking tray and put in the oven for 5 to 6 minutes or until it is cooked;

decrease the cooking period by 2 minutes if you want the pink eaten inside of your cod.

6. Wipe the frying pan out meanwhile and put it back on high fire. Blend the brown sugar with the remaining oil tablespoon and pour it over the endive cut sides.

7. Put the cut-sides of the endive in the hot pan and cook for 2 to 3 minutes. In the sauce, mix the salad and eat with tuna, and endive.

Nutrition: 341Calories 29g Fat 13g Protein

196. Sirt Food Miso Marinated Cod

Preparation Time: 21 minutes
Cooking Time: 17 minutes
Serving: 1
Ingredients:

- 1-ounce miso
- 1 tbsp mirin
- 1 tbsp extra virgin olive oil
- 7-ounce skinless cod fillet
- 1-ounce red onion, sliced
- 2-ounce celery, sliced
- 1 garlic clove, finely chopped
- 1 bird's eye chili, finely chopped
- 1 tsp finely chopped fresh ginger
- 3-ounce green beans
- 3-ounce kale, roughly chopped
- 1 tsp sesame seeds
- 1-ounce parsley, roughly chopped
- 1 tbsp tamari
- 2-ounce buckwheat
- 1 tsp ground turmeric

Direction

1. Incorporate miso, mirin and 1 teaspoon of the oil. Rub all over the cod and marinate for 30 minutes. Heat the oven to a temperature of 220C.

2. Bake the cod for about 10 minutes.

3. Preheat wok with the remaining oil. Sauté onion then add the celery, garlic, chili, ginger, green beans and kale.

4. Cook the buckwheat according to the package instruction: with the turmeric for 3 minutes.

5. Add the sesame seed, the parsley and the tamari to the stir-fry and serve with the greens and the fish.

Nutrition: 407 Calories 21g Fat 13g Protein

197. Smoked Salmon Omelet

Preparation Time: 19 minutes
Cooking Time: 11 minutes
Serving: 1
Ingredients:

- 2 Medium eggs
- 100 g Smoked salmon, sliced
- 1/2 tsp Capers
- 10 g Rocket, chopped
- 1 tsp Parsley, chopped
- 1 tsp Extra virgin olive oil

Direction:

1. Beat eggs. Add the salmon, the capers, the rocket and the Persil.

2. Pre-heat olive oil in a non-stick frying pan. Pour egg mixture and spread around the pan evenly.

3. Reduce heat and let the omelet cook. Slide the spatula along the sides and roll up or split the omelet in half to eat.

Nutrition: 499 Calories 34g Fat 14g Protein

198. Seafood Salad

Preparation Time: 22 minutes
Cooking Time: 0 minute
Serving: 1
Ingredients:

- 3-ounce rocket
- 3-ounce chicory leaves
- 4-ounce smoked salmon slices
- 4-ounce avocado, peeled, stoned and sliced
- 2-ounce celery, sliced
- 1-ounce red onion, sliced
- 11-ounce walnuts, chopped
- 1 tbs capers
- 1 large Medjool date, pitted and chopped
- 1 tbs extra-virgin olive oil
- Juice ¼ lemon
- 1-ounce parsley, chopped
- 1-ounce lovage or celery leaves, chopped

Direction

1. Prepare the salad leaves in a plate. Incorporate all the remaining ingredients together and situate on top of the leaves.

Nutrition: 351 Calories 23g Fat 7g Protein

199. Salmon Pasta Smoked with Chili/Arugula

Preparation Time: 17 minutes
Cooking Time: 26 minutes
Serving: 4

Ingredients:

- 2 Spoonful of extra virgin olive oil
- 1 Orange, finely diced onion
- 2 Teaspoons of garlic, finely minced
- 2 Thai, finely minced chilies
- 1 cup cherry tomatoes
- 1/2 cup (100ml) white wine with half
- Buckwheat pasta: 9 to 11 ounces
- 9 Ounces Smoked Salmon
- 2 Teaspoons capers
- 1/2 lemon juice
- 2 ounces of arugula
- 1/4 cup of minced parsley

Direction

1. In a frying pan flame 1 tablespoon of the oil over medium heat. Stir in the cabbage, garlic, chili and cook until smooth but not dark.
2. Attach the tomatoes and require to cook for one or two minutes. To rising by half, add the white wine and bubble.
3. Boil pasta with 1 tablespoon of oil and water for 9 minutes, then rinse.
4. Break the salmon into pieces and add the capers, lemon juice, arugula and parsley to the tomato saucepan. Attach the sauce, blend together and eat right away. Drizzle some oil left on hand.

Nutrition: 427 Calories 28g Fat 14g Protein

200. Minty Salmon Salad

Preparation Time: 13 minutes
Cooking time: 19 minutes
Serving: 1

Ingredients:

- 1 salmon fillet (12 ounce)
- 2-ounce mixed salad leaves
- 2-ounce young spinach leaves
- 2 radishes, trimmed and thinly sliced
- 5cm piece cucumber, cut into chunks
- 2 spring onions, trimmed and sliced
- 1 small handful parsley, roughly chopped

For the dressing:

- 1 tsp low-fat mayonnaise
- 1 tbsp natural yogurt
- 1 tbsp rice vinegar
- 2 leaves mint, finely chopped
- Salt and freshly ground black pepper

Direction

1. Pre - heat to 200 ° C (180 ° C fan / Gas 6).
2. Situate salmon filet on a baking tray and bake through for 17 minutes. Take out from the oven.
3. Mix the mayonnaise, mustard, rice wine vinegar, mint leaves then season and leave to stand for at least 5 minutes to allow the aromas to form.
4. Arrange the salad leaves and spinach with cucumber, radishes, spring onions and parsley.
5. Put cooked salmon over the salad and sprinkle over the dressing.

Nutrition: 328 Calories 27g Fat 13g Protein

201. Stir-Fry Shrimp and Buckwheat

Preparation Time: 18 minutes
Cooking Time: 24 minutes
Serving: 1

Ingredients

- Shelled raw jumbo shrimp, deveined 1/3 pound (150g)
- Tamari 2 teaspoons
- Extra virgin olive oil 2 teaspoons
- Soba (buckwheat noodles) 3 ounces (75g)
- Garlic cloves, finely sliced 2
- Thai chili, finely sliced 1
- Teaspoon finely sliced fresh ginger 1
- Red onions, sliced 1/8 cup (20g)
- Celery 1/2 cup (45g)
- Green beans, chopped 1/2 cup (75g)
- Kale, roughly chopped 3/4 cup (50g)
- Chicken stock 1/2 cup

Direction

1. Steam a deep fryer over high temperature, then cook the shrimp for two or three minutes in 1 tablespoon tamari and one teaspoon oil. Put the shrimp into a tray. Flush the skillet out with a towel of paper, as you will be using it again.

2. Bake the noodles for five to eight minutes in boiling water, or as indicated on the box. Flush and put away.
3. Elsewhere, in the leftover tamari and oil over medium-high heat, cook the garlic, ginger, chili, celery, red onion, (but not the leaves), kale and green beans for two to three min. Remove the stocks and bring to a simmer, then steam for a couple of minutes until baked and yet crunchy.
4. Add the shrimp, pasta, and foliage of celery to the bowl, bring to a simmer, turn off the heat and drink.

Nutrition: 417 Calories 28g Fat 13g Protein

202. Pan-Fried Salmon Fillet with Leafy Salad

Preparation Time: 14 minutes
Cooking time: 19 minutes
Serving: 1

Ingredients

- Parsley 1/4 cup
- Juice of lemon ¼
- Capers 1 tablespoon
- Clove garlic, roughly chopped 1
- Extra-virgin olive oil 1 tablespoon
- Avocado 1/4
- Cherry tomatoes, 2/3 cup
- Red onion, thinly sliced 1/8 cup
- Arugula 1 3/4 ounces
- Celery leaves 2 tablespoons
- Skinless salmon fillet 1 x 5-ounce
- Brown sugar 2 teaspoons
- Head of endive 1

Direction

1. Heat the oven up to 220 ° C (425oF).
2. Put the parsley, garlic, lemon juice, capers, and two teaspoons of oil in a mixing bowl or blender for dressing and mix until thick and creamy.
3. For the salad, combine the leaves of red onion, tomato, arugula, avocado and celery.
4. Warm a frying casserole over high temperature. Massage the salmon in a little oil and sear for a moment or so in the frying skillet to caramelize the exterior. Exchange to a small bowl and bake in the oven for four to six minutes or until it is finished cooking; decrease the heating

process by two minutes if you like the pink presented inside of your fish.
5. Wash the saucepan out afterwards and put everything back on high fire. Mix the brown sugar with the remaining oil teaspoon and sprinkle it over the endive cut sides.
6. Position the sides of the endive cut into the skillet and cook for two or three minutes, trying to turn frequently, until tender and perfectly golden brown. In the sauce, mix the salad and top with tuna, and endive.

Nutrition: 371 Calories 28g Fat 7g Protein

203. Miso-Marinated Baked Cod

Preparation time: 17 minutes
Cooking Time: 29 minutes
Serving: 1

Ingredients

- Miso 3 1/2 teaspoons
- Mirin 1 tablespoon
- Extra-virgin olive oil 1 tablespoon
- Skinless cod fillet 1 x 7-ounce
- Red onion, sliced 1/8 cup
- Celery, sliced 3/8 cup
- Garlic cloves, finely sliced 2
- Thai chili, finely sliced 1
- Finely sliced fresh ginger 1 teaspoon
- Green beans 3/8 cup
- Kale, roughly chopped 3/4 cup
- Sesame seeds 1 teaspoon
- Parsley, roughly chopped 2 tablespoons
- Tamari 1 tablespoon
- Buckwheat 1/4 cup
- Ground turmeric 1 teaspoon

Direction

1. Blend the oil with the mirin, miso and 1 teaspoon. Massage the cod all over and consider leaving for thirty min to marinate. Heat the oven up to 220 ° C (425oF).
2. Cook the cod for ten minutes.
3. In the meantime, heat the residual oil to a large skillet or wok. Stir-fry the onion for another few minutes, then bring the celery, chili, garlic, ginger, green beans, and kale. Toss and roast till the kale is roasted through and crispy. To help the frying

process you might have to bring a little water to the skillet.

4. Fry the buckwheat along with the turmeric as per the manufacturer's guidelines.
5. To the stir-fry insert the parsley, sesame seeds, and tamari and represent with buckwheat and salmon.

Nutrition: 331 Calories 21g Fat 17g Protein

204. Superfood Salad

Preparation Time: 19 minutes
Cooking Time: 0 minutes
Serving: 2

Ingredients

- Arugula 1 3/4 ounces
- Endive leaves 1 3/4 ounces
- Smoked salmon slices 3 1/2 ounces
- Avocado, peeled, stoned, and sliced 1/2 cup
- Celery including leaves, sliced 1/2 cup
- Red onion, sliced 1/8 cup
- Walnuts, chopped 1/8 cups
- Capers 1 tablespoon
- Large Medjool date, pitted and chopped 1
- Extra-virgin olive oil 1 tablespoon
- Juice of lemon ¼
- Parsley, chopped 1/4 cup

Direction

1. Position the leaf of salad on a tray, or in a plastic bucket. Blend all the rest of the ingredients and represent over the foliage.

Nutrition: 307 Calories 17g Fat 6g Protein

205. Smoked Salmon Pasta

Preparation Time: 14 minutes
Cooking Time: 23 minutes
Serving: 4

Ingredients

- Extra virgin olive oil 2 tablespoons
- Red onion, finely sliced 1
- Garlic cloves, finely sliced 2
- Thai chilies, finely sliced 2
- Cherry tomatoes, cut in half 1 cup
- White wine 1/2 cup
- Buckwheat pasta 9 to 11 ounces
- Smoked salmon 9 ounces
- Capers 2 tablespoons
- Juice of lemon ½
- Arugula 2 ounces

- Parsley, chopped 1/4 cup

Direction

1. In a broiler pan start cooking one teaspoon of the oil over moderate flame. Stir in the onion, garlic, chili, and fry till smooth but not dark brown.
2. Start adding the tomatoes and permit to bake for one or two minutes. To minimize by half, append the white wine and bubble.
3. Bake the pasta in hot water with one tablespoon of oil for eight to ten minutes based on whether you like it to serve, then rinse.
4. Split the salmon into pieces and apply the capers, lemon juice, arugula, parsley, and the tomato into saucepan. Insert the sauce, blend together, and eat straight away. Sprinkle some oil over top.

Nutrition: 334 Calories 21g Fat 13g Protein

206. Vietnamese Turmeric Fish with Herbs & Mango Sauce

Preparation Time: 23 minutes
Cooking time: 34 minutes
Serving: 4

Ingredients

- Fresh cod fish 1 ¼ lbs.
- Coconut oil in pan and fry the fish 2 tablespoons
- Sea salt to taste

Fish marinade

- Turmeric powder 1 tablespoon
- Sea salt 1 teaspoon
- Chinese cooking wine 1 tablespoon
- Minced ginger 2 teaspoons
- Olive oil 2 tablespoons

Infused Scallion and Dill Oil

- Scallions 2 cups
- Fresh dill 2 cups
- Sea salt to taste

Mango dipping sauce

- Medium sized ripe mango 1
- Rice vinegar 2 tablespoons
- Juice of lime ½
- Garlic clove 1
- Dry red chili pepper 1 teaspoon

Direction

1. Marinate the fish for one hour or as long as it is overnight.
2. Add all ingredients in a mixing bowl under "Mango Dipping Sauce," and combine until quality is obtained.

For the Fish:

3. Cook 2 tablespoons of coconut oil at high temperature in a big, nonstick skillet. Add the pre-marinated fish if hot
4. A loud sizzle should be heard, upon which you can reduce the heat to moderate heat.
5. Do not turn or relocate the fish till after, about 5 minutes. Top with a tablespoon of sea salt.
6. When the fish is in golden brown, move the fish gently on the other side on cook. Transmit onto a large plate once it's accomplished.

For Scallion and Dill Infused Oil:

7. Just use rest of the oil over medium to high heat in the frying pan, stir in 2 cups of scallions and 2 cups of dill. Remove from the heat once the scallions and dill are introduced. Start giving them a delicate flip, about fifteen seconds, till the scallions and dill simmered. Season with a sprinkle of salt at sea.
8. Plop the scallion, dill and infused oil over the fish and represent fresh cilantro, lime, and nuts with mango sauce.

Nutrition: 471 Calories 31g Fat 21g Protein

207. Salmon Sirt Super Salad

Preparation Time: 13 minutes
Cooking Time: 0 minute
Serving: 2

Ingredients

- Rocket 50g
- Chicory leaves 50g
- Smoked salmon slices 100g
- Avocado 80g
- Celery 40g
- Red onion 20g
- Walnuts, finely sliced 15g
- Capers 1 tbs
- Large Medjool date 1
- Extra-virgin olive oil 1 tbs
- Juice of lemon ¼
- Parsley, finely sliced 10g

- Celery leaves or lovage, finely sliced 10g

Direction

1. Organize the leaves of the salad over a serving dish. Blend all the rest of the ingredients and represent over the leaves.

Nutrition: 349 Calories 26g Fat 13g Protein

208. Smoke Salmon with Egg

Preparation Time: 17 minutes
Cooking Time: 8 minutes
Serving: 1

Ingredients

- 2 medium eggs
- 100 g / 3.5 oz of smoked salmon, sliced
- 1/2 teaspoon capers
- 10 g / 0.35 oz of chopped rocket
- 1 teaspoon minced parsley
- 1 teaspoon of extra virgin olive oil

Direction

1. Crack eggs and beat well. Add salmon, capers, arugula and parsley.
2. Cook olive oil in a non-stick pan until it is hot but not smoking. Fill egg mix and lay it out around the pan equally.
3. Reduce the heat and let the omelet cook. Fold the tortilla in half to serve.
4. Heat an ovenproof skillet until hot, then add the marinated chicken and cook for 2 minutes on both sides, until lightly browned, then transfer to the oven for 8-10 minutes. Take out from the oven, wrap with foil and let rest for 5 minutes before serving.
5. Meanwhile, cook the black cabbage in a steamer for 5 minutes. Fry the red onions and ginger in a little oil until soft but not colored, then add the cooked cabbage and fry for another minute.

Nutrition: 291Calories 19g Fat 6g Protein

209. Stir-Fried Greens, Sesame & Cod

Preparation time: 16 minutes
Cooking Time: 11 minutes
Serving: 2

Ingredients:

- 20 g / 0.70 oz miso
- 1 tbsp mirin
- 1 tbsp extra virgin olive oil
- 200 g / 7 oz skinless cod fillet

- 20 g / 0.70 oz red onion, sliced
- 40 g / 1.4 oz celery, sliced
- 1 garlic clove, finely chopped
- 1 bird's eye chili, finely chopped
- 1 tsp finely chopped fresh ginger
- 60 g / 2.1 oz green beans
- 50 g / 1.7 oz kale, roughly chopped
- 1 tsp sesame seeds
- 5g / 1 tsp parsley, roughly chopped
- 1 tbsp tamari
- 30 g / 1 oz buckwheat
- 1 tsp ground turmeric

Direction

1. Blend miso, mirin, and 1 teaspoon of the oil. Brush all over the cod and marinate for 30 minutes. Set oven to 220°C/gas 7.
2. Bake the cod for 10 minutes.
3. Prep a frying pan with the remaining oil. Cook onion then mix celery, garlic, chili, ginger, green beans, and kale.
4. Cook the buckwheat following the packet's instructions for 3 minutes and sprinkle turmeric
5. Stir the sesame seeds, parsley, and tamari to the stir-fry and serve with the greens and fish.

Nutrition: 321 Calories 19g Fat 9g Protein

210. Turmeric Baked Salmon

Preparation time: 23 minutes

Cooking time: 14 minutes

Serving: 2

Ingredients

- 125-150 g / 4.5- 5.5 oz Skinned Salmon
- 1 tsp Extra virgin olive oil
- 1 tsp ground turmeric
- ¼ Juice of a lemon
- For the spicy celery
- 1 tsp Extra virgin olive oil
- 40 g / 1.4 oz Red onion, finely chopped
- 60 g / 2 oz Tinned green lentils
- 1 Garlic clove, finely chopped
- 1 cm fresh ginger, finely chopped
- 1 Bird's eye chili, finely chopped
- 150 g / 1.7 oz Celery, cut into 2cm lengths
- 1 tsp Mild curry powder
- 130 g / 4.5 oz Tomato, cut into eight wedges
- 100 ml / ½ cup Chicken or vegetable stock
- 1 tbsp Chopped parsley

Direction

1. Heat oven to 200 ° C.
2. Start with hot celery. Pre-heat frying pan over medium-low heat, add the olive oil, then the onion, garlic, ginger, chili and celery. Fry for 2 minutes, then add the curry powder and cook for another minute.
3. Add the tomatoes, then the broth and lentils and simmer for 10 minutes.
4. Blend turmeric, oil, and lemon juice and rub the salmon. Situate on a baking sheet and cook for 9 minutes.
5. Combine parsley through the celery and serve with the salmon.

Nutrition: 328 Calories 21g Fat 13g Protein

211. Potato Carrot Salad

Preparation Time: 17 minutes
Cooking Time: 11 minutes
Servings: 6
Ingredients:

- Water
- Six potatoes, sliced into cubes
- Three carrots, sliced into cubes
- One tablespoon milk
- One tablespoon Dijon mustard
- ¼ cup mayonnaise
- Pepper to taste
- Two teaspoons fresh thyme, chopped
- One stalk celery, chopped
- Two scallions, chopped
- One slice turkey bacon, cooked crispy and crumbled

Directions:

1. Fill your pot with water.
2. Place it over medium-high heat.
3. Boil the potatoes and carrots for 10 to 15 minutes or until tender.
4. Drain and let cool.
5. In a bowl, mix the milk mustard, mayo, pepper, and thyme.
6. Stir in the potatoes, carrots, and celery.
7. Coat evenly with the sauce.
8. Cover and refrigerate for 4 hours.
9. Top with the scallions and turkey bacon bits before serving.

Nutrition: 106 Calories 5.3g Fat 2g Protein

212. High Protein Salad

Preparation Time: 6 minutes
Cooking Time: 7 minutes
Servings: 4
Ingredients:
Salad:

- One 15-oz can green kidney beans
- 2 4 tbsp capers
- 3 4 handfuls arugula
- 4 15-oz can lentils

Dressing:

- 5 1 tbsp caper brine
- 6 1 tbsp tamari
- 7 1 tbsp balsamic vinegar
- 8 2 tbsp peanut butter
- 9 2 tbsp hot sauce
- 10 1 tbsp tahini

Directions:
For the dressing:

1. In a bowl, stir together all the materials until they come together to form a smooth dressing.

For the salad:

2. Mix the beans, arugula, capers, and lentils. Top with the dressing and serve.

Nutrition: 205 Calories 2g Fat 13g Protein

213. Vegan Wrap with Apples and Spicy Hummus

Preparation Time: 12 minutes
Cooking Time: 0 minutes
Servings: 2
Ingredients:

- One tortilla
- 6-7 tbsp Spicy Hummus (mix it with a few tbsp of salsa)
- Only some leaves of fresh spinach or romaine lettuce
- 1 tsp fresh lemon juice
- 1½ cups broccoli slaw
- ½ apple, sliced thin
- 4 tsp dairy-free plain unsweetened yogurt
- Salt and pepper

Directions:

1. Mix the yogurt and the lemon juice with the broccoli slaw. Add the salt and a dash of pepper for taste. Mix well and set aside.
2. Lay the tortilla flat.
3. Spread the spicy hummus over the tortilla.
4. Lay the lettuce down on the hummus.
5. On one half, pile the broccoli slaw on the lettuce.
6. Place the apple slices on the slaw.
7. Fold the sides of the tortilla up, starting with the end that has the apple and the slaw. Roll tightly.
8. Cut it in half and serve.

Nutrition: 205 Calories 2g Fat 12g Protein

214. Rice and Veggie Bowl

Preparation Time: 7 minutes
Cooking Time: 12 minutes

Servings: 6

Ingredients:
- 2 tbsp coconut oil
- 1 tsp ground cumin
- 1 tsp ground turmeric
- 1 tsp chili powder
- One red bell pepper, chopped
- 1 tsp tomato paste
- One bunch of broccolis, cut into bite-sized florets with short stems
- 1 tsp salt, to taste
- One large red onion, sliced
- Two garlic cloves, minced
- One head of cauliflower, sliced into bite-sized florets
- 2 cups cooked rice
- Newly ground black pepper to taste

Directions:
1. Heat the coconut grease over medium-high heat in a large pan
2. Wait until the oil is hot, stir in the turmeric, cumin, chili powder, salt, and tomato paste.
3. Cook the content for 1 minute. Stir repeatedly until the spices are fragrant.
4. Add the garlic and onion. Sauté for 3 minutes.
5. Add the broccoli, cauliflower, and bell pepper. Cover the pot. Cook for 3 to 4 minutes and stir occasionally.
6. Add the cooked rice. Stir so it will combine well with the vegetables—Cook for 2 to 3 minutes. Stir until the rice is warmed through.
7. Check the seasoning. And make adjustments to taste if desired.
8. Decrease heat and cook on low for 2 to 3 more minutes so the flavors will meld.
9. Serve with freshly ground black pepper.

Nutrition: 260 Calories 9g Fat 9g Protein

215. Cucumber Tomato Chopped Salad

Preparation Time: 18 minutes
Cooking Time: 0 minutes
Servings: 6

Ingredients:
- ½ cup light mayonnaise
- One tablespoon lemon juice
- One tablespoon fresh dill, chopped
- One tablespoon chive, chopped
- ½ cup feta cheese, crumbled
- Salt and pepper to taste
- One red onion, chopped
- One cucumber, diced
- One radish, diced
- Three tomatoes, diced
- Chives, chopped

Directions:
1. Combine the mayo, lemon juice, fresh dill, chives, feta cheese, salt, and pepper in a bowl.
2. Mix well.
3. Stir in the onion, cucumber, radish, and tomatoes.
4. Coat evenly.
5. Garnish with the chopped chives.

Nutrition: 187 Calories 16.7g Fat 3.3g Protein

216. Zucchini Pasta Salad

Preparation Time: 6 minutes
Cooking Time: 0 minutes
Servings: 15

Ingredients:
- Five tablespoons olive oil
- Two teaspoons Dijon mustard
- Three tablespoons red-wine vinegar
- One clove garlic, grated
- Two tablespoons fresh oregano, chopped
- One shallot, chopped
- ¼ teaspoon red pepper flakes
- 16 oz. zucchini noodles
- ¼ cup Kalamata olives pitted
- 3 cups cherry tomatoes, sliced in half
- ¾ cup Parmesan cheese shaved

Directions:
1. Mix the olive oil, Dijon mustard, red wine vinegar, garlic, and oregano, shallot, and red pepper flakes in a bowl.
2. Stir in the zucchini noodles.
3. Sprinkle on top the olives, tomatoes, and Parmesan cheese.

Nutrition: 299 Calories 27g Fat 7g Protein

217. Egg Avocado Salad

Preparation Time: 14 minutes
Cooking Time: 0 minutes
Servings: 4

Ingredients:

- One avocado
- Six hard-boiled eggs, peeled and chopped
- One tablespoon mayonnaise
- Two tablespoons freshly squeezed lemon juice
- ¼ cup celery, chopped
- Two tablespoons chives, chopped
- Salt and pepper to taste

Directions:
1. Add the avocado to a large bowl.
2. Mash the avocado using a fork.
3. Stir in the egg and mash the eggs.
4. Add the mayo, lemon juice, celery, chives, salt, and pepper.
5. Chill in the refrigerator. Wait for at least 30 minutes before serving.

Nutrition: 224 Calories 19g Fat 10.6g Protein

218. Arugula Salad

Preparation Time: 17 minutes
Cooking Time: 0 minutes
Servings: 4

Ingredients:
- 6 cups fresh arugula leaves
- 2 cups radicchio, chopped
- ¼ cup low-fat balsamic vinaigrette
- ¼ cup pine nuts, toasted and chopped

Directions:
1. Arrange the arugula leaves in a serving bowl.
2. Sprinkle the radicchio on top.
3. Drizzle with the vinaigrette.
4. Sprinkle the pine nuts on top.

Nutrition: 85 Calories 6.6g Fat 2.2g Protein

219. Sautéed Cabbage

Preparation Time: 9 minutes
Cooking Time: 14 minutes
Servings: 8

Ingredients:
- ¼ cup butter
- One onion, sliced thinly
- One head cabbage, sliced into wedges
- Salt and pepper to taste
- Crumbled crispy bacon bits

Directions:
1. Cook butter to a pan over medium-high heat.
2. Cook the onion for 1 minute, stirring frequently.

3. Season with the salt and pepper.
4. Add the cabbage then stir it for 12 minutes.
5. Sprinkle with the crispy bacon bits.

Nutrition: 77 Calories 5.9g Fat 1.3g Protein

220. Cucumber Edamame Salad

Preparation Time: 6 minutes
Cooking Time: 9 minutes
Servings: 2

Ingredients:
- 3 tbsp. Avocado oil
- 1 cup cucumber, sliced into thin rounds
- ½ cup fresh sugar snap peas cut up or whole
- ½ cup fresh edamame
- ¼ cup radish, sliced
- One large avocado, peeled, pitted, sliced
- One nori sheet, crumbled
- 2 tsp. Roasted sesame seeds
- 1 tsp. Salt

Directions:
1. Make a medium-sized pot filled halfway with water to a boil over medium-high heat.
2. Add the sugar snaps and cook them for about 2 minutes.
3. Remove the pot off the heat, drain the excess water, transfer the sugar snaps to a medium-sized bowl, and set aside.
4. Fill the pot with water again, add the teaspoon of salt and bring to a boil over medium-high heat.
5. Add the edamame to the pot and let them cook for about 6 minutes.
6. Take the pot off the heat, drain the excess water, transfer the soybeans to the bowl with sugar snaps, and cool down for about 5 minutes.
7. Combine all ingredients, except for the nori crumbs and roasted sesame seeds, in a medium-sized bowl.
8. Delicately stir, using a spoon, until all ingredients are evenly coated in oil.
9. Top the salad along with the nori crumbs and roasted sesame seeds.
10. Shift the bowl to the fridge and allow the salad to cool for at least 30 minutes.

11. Serve chilled and enjoy!

Nutrition: 409 Calories 39g Fats 7.6g Protein

221. Garden Patch Sandwiches on Multigrain Bread

Preparation Time: 17 minutes
Cooking Time: 0 minutes
Servings: 4

Ingredients:

- 1pound extra-firm tofu drained and patted dry
- One medium red bell pepper, finely chopped
- One celery rib, finely chopped
- Three green onions, minced
- A quarter cup shelled sunflower seeds
- A half cup vegan mayonnaise, homemade or store-bought
- A half teaspoon salt
- A half teaspoon celery salt
- A quarter teaspoon freshly ground black pepper
- Eight slices whole grain bread
- 4 (1/4-inch) slices ripe tomato
- Four lettuce leaves

Directions:

1. Grind the tofu put it in a large bowl. Add the bell pepper, celery, green onions, and sunflower seeds. Stir in the mayonnaise, salt, celery salt, and pepper and mix until well combined.
2. Toast the bread, if desired. Spread the mixture evenly onto four slices of the bread. Top each with a tomato slice, lettuce leaf, and the remaining bread. Chop the sandwiches diagonally in half and serve.

Nutrition: 9g Protein 25g Fats 399 Calories

222. Garden Salad Wraps

Preparation Time: 18 minutes
Cooking Time: 12 minutes
Servings: 4

Ingredients:

- Six tablespoons olive oil
- 1-pound extra-firm tofu, drained, patted dry, and cut into 1/2-inch strips
- One tablespoon soy sauce
- A quarter cup apple cider vinegar

- One teaspoon yellow or spicy brown mustard
- A half teaspoon salt
- A quarter teaspoon freshly ground black pepper
- 3 cups shredded romaine lettuce
- Three ripe Roma tomatoes, finely chopped
- One large carrot, shredded
- One medium English cucumber, peeled and chopped
- 1/3 cup minced red onion
- A quarter cup sliced pitted green olives
- 4 (10-inch) whole-grain flour tortillas or lavash flatbread

Directions:

1. In a large frypan, heat two tablespoons of the oil over medium heat. Add the tofu. Cook it until golden brown, about 10 minutes. Sprinkle with soy sauce and set aside to cool. Combine the vinegar, mustard, salt, and pepper with the remaining four tablespoons oil, stirring to blend well. Set aside. Mix the lettuce, tomatoes, carrot, cucumber, onion, and olives. Pour on the dressing and flip to coat.
2. To assemble wraps, place one tortilla on a work surface and spread with about one-quarter of the salad. Place a few strips of tofu on the tortilla and roll up tightly. Slice in half

Nutrition: 89 Calories 8g Fat 4g Protein

223. Marinated Mushroom Wraps

Preparation Time: 14 minutes
Cooking Time: 0 minutes
Servings: 2

Ingredients:

- Three tablespoons soy sauce
- Three tablespoons fresh lemon juice
- 1A half tablespoons toasted sesame oil
- Two portobello mushroom caps
- One ripe Hass avocado pitted and peeled
- 2 cups fresh baby spinach leaves
- One medium red bell pepper
- One ripe tomato, chopped
- Salt and freshly ground black pepper

Directions;

1. Combine the soy sauce, two tablespoons of the lemon juice, and the oil. Add the portobello strips, toss to combine, and marinate for 1 hour or overnight. Drain the mushrooms and set aside.
2. Mash the avocado with the remaining one tablespoon of lemon juice.
3. To assemble wraps, place one tortilla on a work surface and spread with some of the mashed avocados. Topmost with a layer of baby spinach leaves.
4. In the lower third of each tortilla, arrange strips of the soaked mushrooms and some bell pepper strips. Sprinkle with the tomato and salt and black pepper to taste. Roll up tightly and cut in half diagonally. Repeat with the remaining ingredients and serve.

Nutrition: 89 Calories 8g Fat 4g Protein

224. Tamari Toasted Almonds

Preparation Time: 3 minutes
Cooking Time: 9 minutes
Servings: 2

Ingredients:

- ½ cup raw almonds, or sunflower seeds
- Two tablespoons tamari or soy sauce
- One teaspoon toasted sesame oil

Directions:

1. Preparing the ingredients.
2. Preheat dry skillet at medium-high heat, and then add the almonds, stirring very frequently to keep them from burning. Once the almonds are toasted, 7 to 8 minutes for almonds, or 3 to 4 minutes for sunflower seeds, pour the tamari and sesame oil into the hot skillet and stir to coat.
3. You can turn off the heat, and as the almonds cool, the tamari mixture will stick to and dry on the nuts.

Nutrition: 89 Calories 8g Fat 4g Protein

225. Peppers and Hummus

Preparation Time: 18 minutes
Cooking Time: 0 minutes
Servings: 4

Ingredients:

- One 15-ounce can chickpeas, drained and rinsed

- Juice of 1 lemon or one tablespoon prepared lemon juice
- ¼ cup tahini
- Three tablespoons olive oil
- ½ teaspoon ground cumin
- One tablespoon water
- ¼ teaspoon paprika
- One red bell pepper, sliced
- One green bell pepper, sliced
- One orange bell pepper, sliced

Directions:

1. In a food processor, mix chickpeas, lemon juice, tahini, two tablespoons of olive oil, cumin, and water.
2. A process on high speed until blended, about 30 seconds: scoop the hummus into a bowl and pour the remaining tablespoon of olive oil. Sprinkle with paprika. If desires, serve with sliced bell peppers.

Nutrition: 89 Calories 8g Fat 4g Protein

226. Baby Spinach Snack

Preparation Time: 12 minutes
Cooking Time: 13 minutes
Servings: 3

Ingredients:

- 2 cups baby spinach, washed
- A pinch of black pepper
- ½ tablespoon olive oil
- ½ teaspoon garlic powder

Directions:

1. Spread the baby spinach on a lined baking sheet, add oil, black pepper and garlic powder, toss a bit, introduce in the oven, bake at 350 degrees F for 10 minutes, divide into bowls and serve as a snack.

Nutrition: 125 calories 4g fat 2g protein

227. Bacon Potato Bites

Preparation Time: 17 minutes
Cooking Time: 22 minutes
Servings: 5

Ingredients:

- 1 potato
- 2 bacon slices
- 1 small avocado

Directions:

1. Spread potato slices on a lined baking sheet, spray with cooking oil, situate in the oven at 350 degrees F, bake for 20

minutes, arrange on a platter, top each slice with avocado and crumbled bacon and serve as a snack.

Nutrition: 187 calories 14g fat 16g protein

228. Dill Bell Pepper Snack Bowls

Preparation Time: 14 minutes
Cooking Time: 0 minutes
Servings: 4

Ingredients:
- 2 tablespoons dill, chopped
- 1 yellow onion, chopped
- 1 pound multi colored bell peppers
- 3 tablespoons olive oil
- 2 and ½ tablespoons white vinegar
- Black pepper to the taste

Directions:
1. In a salad bowl, mix bell peppers with onion, dill, pepper, oil and vinegar, toss to coat, divide into small bowls and serve as a snack.

Nutrition: 120 calories 3g fat 3g protein

229. Spicy Pumpkin Seeds Bowls

Preparation Time: 13 minutes
Cooking Time: 8 minutes
Servings: 6

Ingredients:
- ½ tablespoon chili powder
- ½ teaspoon cayenne pepper
- 2 cups pumpkin seeds
- 2 teaspoons lime juice

Directions:
1. Spread pumpkin seeds on a lined baking sheet, add lime juice, cayenne and chili powder, toss well, introduce in the oven, roast at 275 degrees F for 20 minutes, divide into small bowls and serve as a snack.

Nutrition: 170 calories 2g fat 6g protein

230. Apple and Pecans Bowls

Preparation Time: 14 minutes
Cooking Time: 0 minutes
Servings: 4

Ingredients:
- 4 big apples, cored, peeled and cubed
- 2 teaspoons lemon juice
- ¼ cup pecans, chopped

Directions:
1. Incorporate apples with lemon juice and pecans, toss, divide into small bowls and serve as a snack.

Nutrition: 120 calories 4g fat 3g protein

231. Zucchini Bowls

Preparation Time: 12 minutes
Cooking Time: 23 minutes
Servings: 12

Ingredients:
- Cooking spray
- ½ cup dill, chopped
- 1 egg
- ½ cup whole wheat flour
- Black pepper to the taste
- 1 yellow onion, chopped
- 2 garlic cloves, minced
- 3 zucchinis, grated

Directions:
1. In a bowl, mix zucchinis with garlic, onion, flour, pepper, egg and dill, stir well, shape small bowls out of this mix, arrange them on a lined baking sheet, grease them with some cooking spray, bake at 400 degrees F for 20 minutes, flipping them halfway, divide them into bowls and serve as a snack.

Nutrition: 120 calories 1g fat 6g protein

232. Cheesy Mushrooms Caps

Preparation Time: 14 minutes
Cooking time: 31 minutes
Servings: 20

Ingredients:
- 20 white mushroom caps
- 1 garlic clove, minced
- 3 tablespoons parsley, chopped
- 2 yellow onions, chopped
- Black pepper to the taste
- ½ cup low-fat parmesan, grated
- ¼ cup low-fat mozzarella, grated
- A drizzle of olive oil
- 2 tablespoons non-fat yogurt

Directions:
1. Pre-heat pan with some oil over medium heat, add garlic and onion, stir, cook for 10 minutes and transfer to a bowl.

2. Add black pepper, garlic, parsley, mozzarella, parmesan and yogurt, stir well, stuff the mushroom caps with this mix, arrange them on a lined baking sheet, bake in the oven at 400 degrees F for 20 minutes and serve them as an appetizer.

Nutrition: 120 calories 1g fat 7g protein

233. Mozzarella Cauliflower Bars

Preparation Time: 12 minutes
Cooking Time: 41 minutes
Servings: 12

Ingredients:
- 1 big cauliflower head, riced
- ½ cup low-fat mozzarella cheese, shredded
- ¼ cup egg whites
- 1 teaspoon Italian seasoning
- Black pepper to the taste

Directions:
1. Spread the cauliflower rice on a lined baking sheet, cook in the oven at 375 degrees F for 20 minutes, transfer to a bowl, add black pepper, cheese, seasoning and egg whites, stir well, spread into a rectangle pan and press well on the bottom.
2. Introduce in the oven at 375 degrees F, bake for 20 minutes, cut into 12 bars and serve as a snack.

Nutrition: 140 calories 1g fat 6g protein

234. Garlic Lovers Hummus

Preparation Time: 2 minutes
Cooking Time: 0 minute
Servings: 12

Ingredients:
- 3 tbsps. Freshly squeezed lemon juice
- All-purpose salt-free seasoning
- 3 tbsps. Sesame tahini
- 4 garlic cloves
- 15 oz. no-salt-added garbanzo beans
- 2 tbsps. Olive oil

Directions:
1. Drain garbanzo beans and rinse well.
2. Situate all the ingredients in a food processor and pulse until smooth.
3. Serve immediately or cover and refrigerate until serving.

Nutrition: 103 Calories 5g Fat: 4g Protein

235. Spinach and Kale Mix

Preparation Time: 5 minutes
Cooking Time: 0 minute
Servings: 4

Ingredients:
- 2 chopped shallots
- 1 c. no-salt-added and chopped canned tomatoes
- 2 c. baby spinach
- 2 minced garlic cloves
- 5 c. torn kale
- 1 tbsp. olive oil

Direction:
1. Warmup a pan with the oil over medium-high heat, add the shallots, stir and sauté for 5 minutes.
2. Add the spinach, kale and the other ingredients, toss, cook for 10 minutes more, divide between plates and serve.

Nutrition: 89 Calories 3.7g Fat 3.6g Protein

236. Turmeric Carrots

Preparation Time: 11 minutes
Cooking Time: 41 minutes
Servings: 4

Ingredients:
- 1-pound baby carrots, peeled
- 1 tablespoon olive oil
- 2 spring onions, chopped
- 2 tablespoons balsamic vinegar
- 2 garlic cloves, minced
- 1 teaspoon turmeric powder
- 1 tablespoon chives, chopped
- ¼ teaspoon cayenne pepper
- A pinch of salt and black pepper

Directions:
1. Arrange carrots in a baking sheet with parchment paper, toss oil, spring onions and the other ingredients, then bake at 380 degrees F for 40 minutes. Serve

Nutrition: 79 calories 3.8g fat 1g protein

237. Spinach Mix

Preparation Time: 13 minutes
Cooking Time: 14 minutes
Servings: 4

Ingredients:
- 1-pound baby spinach
- 1 yellow onion, chopped

- 1 tablespoon olive oil
- 1 tablespoon lemon juice
- 2 garlic cloves, minced
- A pinch of cayenne pepper
- ¼ teaspoon smoked paprika
- A pinch of salt and black pepper

Directions:
1. Preheat pan with the oil over medium-high heat, cook onion and the garlic for 2 minutes.
2. Add the spinach and the other ingredients, toss, cook over medium heat for 10 minutes, divide between plates and serve as a side dish.

Nutrition: 71 calories 4g fat 3.7g protein

238. Orange Carrots
Preparation Time: 7 minutes
Cooking Time: 22 minutes
Servings: 4

Ingredients:
- 1-pound carrots, peeled and roughly sliced
- 1 yellow onion, chopped
- 1 tablespoon olive oil
- Zest of 1 orange, grated
- Juice of 1 orange
- 1 orange, peeled and cut into segments
- 1 tablespoon rosemary, chopped
- A pinch of salt and black pepper

Direction:
1. Warmup a pan with the oil over medium-high heat, add the onion and sauté for 5 minutes.
2. Add the carrots, the orange zest and the other ingredients, toss, cook over medium heat for 20 minutes more, divide between plates and serve.

Nutrition: 140 calories 3.9g fat 2.1g protein

239. Zucchini Pan
Preparation Time: 4 minutes
Cooking Time: 23 minutes
Servings: 4

Ingredients:
- 1-pound zucchinis, sliced
- 1 yellow onion, chopped
- 2 tablespoons olive oil
- 2 apples, peeled, cored and cubed
- 1 tomato, cubed

- 1 tablespoon rosemary, chopped
- 1 tablespoon chives, chopped

Direction:
1. With a pan, preheat oil on medium heat, cook onion for 3 minutes.
2. Cook zucchinis and the other ingredients at medium heat for 17 minutes then serve.

Nutrition: 170 calories 5g fat 7g protein

240. Stir-Fried Mushroom with Ginger
Preparation Time: 14 minutes
Cooking time: 27 minutes
Servings: 3

Ingredients:
- 1-lb. mushrooms
- 1-piece yellow onion
- 1 tbsp. ginger
- 1 tbsp. olive oil
- 2 tbsp. balsamic vinegar
- 2 garlic cloves
- 0.25 cup lime juice
- 2 tbsp. walnuts

Directions:
1. In a pan, cook oil over medium-high heat, sauté onion and ginger for 5 minutes.
2. Cook mushrooms and the other ingredients, at medium heat for 15 minutes more and serve.

Nutrition: 123 calories 3g fat 6g protein

241. Polenta Bake
Preparation Time: 7 minutes
Cooking Time: 27 minutes
Serving: 6

Ingredients
- One tablespoon of olive oil
- ½ diced medium-sized eggplant (if allergic, use mushrooms)
- ½ diced small sized zucchini
- ¼ teaspoon of salt
- ¼ cup of water
- ¼ teaspoon of freshly grounded pepper
- 5 ounces of baby spinach
- 1 cup of prepared marinara sauce
- ¼ cup of chopped fresh basil
- 7 ounces of prepared polenta
- 1 cup of shredded part-skim mozzarella
- Six tablespoons of cheese

Direction:

1. Preheat your oven to 232 C
2. Coat your baking dish with some cooking spray
3. Place a large nonstick skillet on medium-high heat.
4. Then add your diced eggplants, zucchini, salt, and pepper.
5. Allow the ingredients cook, but make sure you occasionally stir until the vegetables are soft and about to turn brown. This process should last 4-6 minutes. Don't let the vegetables burn.
6. Add your baby spinach. Let the spinach cook for about 3 minutes until it wilts. Stir only once.
7. Add your marinara sauce into the vegetables and stir. Let it heat for a minute or two,
8. Turn off the heat and stir in your basil.
9. Put polenta slices in your baking dish. Place them in a single layer. You can trim the slices to fit in the dish if necessary.
10. Sprinkle your cheese on the polenta
11. Top polenta with eggplant mixture. You can add more cheese.
12. Bake for 12-15 minutes until it's bubbling and the cheese has melted. Leave it for 5 minutes after baking before you serve.

Nutrition 2.7g Fats 4.1g Protein 201 Calories

242. Raw Carrot and Almond Loaf

Preparation Time: 18 minutes
Cooking Time: 7 minutes
Serving: 4

Ingredients

- 6-8 medium-sized fresh carrots
- Juice of ½ medium-sized lemon
- ½ cup of almonds
- Fresh and chopped Parsley
- Four tablespoons of tahini
- 40g plain flour (optional)
- 30g Coconut sugar or as much as you wish (optional)
- ¼ teaspoon of baking powder (optional)

Direction

1. Grate your carrots properly
2. Put the grated carrots in a food processor with an S blade.

3. Blend carrots and lemon in the food processor. Let them whizz properly.
4. Transfer the mixture into a bowl.
5. Whizz up almond into the processor. Almonds must be well-grounded.
6. Then, add the blended almonds and carrot mixture together.
7. Add your parsley and tahini and blend them all.
8. Transfer your mixture into a loaf thin. Bake for 7 minutes.
9. Cut into slices to serve. Serve as an appetizer.
10. If you wish to add flour, sugar, and baking powder, you should cover the mixture with foil and leave it to bake for up to 45 minutes.
11. Carrot and almond loaf can be served with cream cheese icing topping. But be careful; you don't want to take too much sugar.
12. For cream cheese toppings, mix one tablespoon of low-fat yogurt, 20g cream cheese, lemon juice, and sugar in a bowl. Put it in a refrigerator to freeze. Then serve when the baked loaf is ready.

Nutrition 7g Fats 6.5g Protein 103 Calories

243. Kale and Red Onion Dhal with Bucket Wheat

Preparation Time: 17 minutes
Cooking Time: 21 minutes
Serving: 5

Ingredients

- 160g of bucket wheat
- 100g of kale
- 200ml of water
- 160g of red lentils
- 400ml of coconut milk
- 2 cm of grated ginger cloves
- Two teaspoons of turmeric
- One seedless and finely chopped birds eye chili
- Three grated garlic cloves
- Two teaspoons of garam masala
- One sliced red onion

Direction

1. Place a deep saucepan on low heat. Add your olive oil and onions and allow it to

cook for 5 minutes. Your onions should soften and not turn brown.

2. Then, add your ginger, chili, and garlic.

3. Add turmeric, garam masala, and just a splash of water. Let it cook for another minute.

4. Next, you add lentils, coconut milk, and 200ml of water. To get the right measurement for your water, you can just pour water into the coconut milk can and then into the pan.

5. Mix your ingredients properly. Cook for 23 minutes more.

6. Then, add your kale, stir and cover it to cook for 5 minutes.

7. Cook your buckwheat in a medium-sized saucepan separately for 10 minutes before curry is ready. You can do this 15minutes before the curry is ready.

8. Serve bucket wheat and curry on a plate when they are ready.

Nutrition 12g Fats 3.4g Proteins 458 Calories

244. Kale with Lemon Tahini Dressing

Preparation Time: 18 minutes
Cooking Time: 0 minutes
Serving: 6

Ingredients

For your salad

- 250- 275g of curly kale
- one tablespoon of squeezed lemon juice
- ½ tablespoon of olive oil
- ½ tablespoon of toasted sesame oil
- one medium-sized carrot
- ½ tablespoon of pure maple syrup
- one medium-sized beet
- 2-3 tablespoons of pumpkin seeds.
- one tablespoon of hemp seeds (optional)
- A pinch of salt

For dressing

- three tablespoons of tahini
- one minced garlic clove
- three tablespoons of olive oil
- 80ml of squeezed lemon juice
- Salt and pepper

Direction

1. Remove the large stems from the curly kale. You can use Tuscan kale if you wish.

2. Squeeze your lemon juice separately. Make sure you pick out all the seeds. Since you will need lemon juice for dressing, you should get more than one lemon.

3. Make sure your carrot and beet are peeled and grated.

4. Begin preparation. Pour your kale into a large salad bowl. Add lemon juice, oil, maple syrup, salt, and garlic.

5. Massage the mixture gently with your hand. Continue massaging until kale is soft and wilting. This process should last for 3-5 minutes.

6. Give kale extra time to soften by setting the mixture aside to marinate for 15-20 minutes.

7. Prepare your dressing. In a smaller bowl, add tahini, lemon juice, garlic, olive oil, salt, and pepper. Whisk the mixture properly. Taste and adjust seasoning as you desire. Then set aside.

8. When the kale is ready, pour the dressing over the kale. Toss the salad until it is evenly coated.

9. Add grated carrot and beet and toss it again until it has mixed well. If you are using hemp seeds, make sure they are hulled and sprinkle them over the salad.

Nutrition 20g Fats 10g Protein 189 Calories

245. Broccoli and Kale Green Soup

Preparation Time: 18 minutes
Cooking Time: 31 minutes
Serving: 4

Ingredients

- 1 liter of stock
- one tablespoon of sunflower oil
- four sliced garlic cloves
- two thumb-sized ginger
- one teaspoon of ground coriander
- two pieces of fresh turmeric root
- ½ teaspoon of Himalayan salt
- 400g of roughly sliced courgette
- 170g of broccoli
- 200g of chopped kale
- A pack of parsley for garnish; don't cut all
- two limes, zest, and juice

Direction

1. Put your sunflower oil in a deep pan. Add garlic, coriander, ginger, turmeric, and salt. Then, fry for 2 minutes on medium heat. Stir so it doesn't burn.
2. Then add three tablespoons of water, so the spices don't get too dry,
3. Add courgette and mix well. Make sure you mix the courgette into the spices thoroughly. Allow it to coat well and cook for 3 minutes.
4. Add 400ml stock and allow it to simmer for 3 minutes. You can make stock by mixing two tablespoons of bouillon powder into boiling water.
5. Then, add your broccoli, lime juice, kale, and the remaining stock into the soup. Allow it to cook for 3-4 minutes.
6. Turn off the heat and add your roughly chopped parsley. Leave some whole leaves for garnish.
7. Fill your soup into a blender and blend on high speed.
8. Serve into four plates. Garnish with zest lime and whole parsley.

Nutrition 8g Fats 10g Protein 182 Calories

246. Butter Bean and Vegetable Korma

Preparation Time: 9 minutes
Cooking Time: 34 minutes
Serving: 4

Ingredients

- three normal-size cloves of garlic
- one onion
- one fresh chili
- ½ piece of fresh ginger, thumb size
- 750g sweet potatoes
- one medium tomato
- 250g frozen peas
- 100g green sugar snaps/beans
- 2 tbsp. oil
- 400g large leek
- 400ml water
- one tin (400ml) coconut milk
- 3 tbsp. soy sauce/tamari
- 1 tbsp. honey
- 2 tsp. ground cumin
- Juice of a lemon
- 2 tsp. ground coriander
- 1 tsp. ground turmeric
- 2 tsp. salt
- 4 tsp. medium curry powder
- ½ tsp. freshly ground black pepper
- Bunch of fresh coriander
- one tin (400g) butterbeans

Direction

1. Pour two tablespoons of oil into a huge saucepan. Chop the tomato, red onion and put them into the pan
2. Add the grated ginger, chili chopped garlic into the pan and have it cooked for about five minutes.
3. Prepare the leeks and sweet potato. Do not forget to include the leafy bits
4. Add the ground cumin, curry powder, turmeric, ground coriander, and black pepper to the pan.
5. Next, add 400 ml of water, one tin of coconut milk, two teaspoons of salt, the juice of 1 lemon, 1tablespoons of liquid sweetener, and three tablespoons of tamari (or soy sauce)
6. Add the leeks, sweet potato, and beans and have the mixture stewed until the sweet potatoes are cooked or for about 20 minutes.
7. Save a few peas for the purpose of garnishing and the rest of it inside. Also, add sugar snap peas. Serve!

Nutrition: 417 calories 19g fats 8g protein

247. Courgette Tortilla

Preparation Time: 8 minutes
Cooking Time: 21 minutes
Serving: 2

Ingredients

- 1 tbsp. olive oil
- one large coarsely grated courgette
- 1 tsp. harissa
- four large eggs
- 3 tbsps. reduced-fat hummus
- one large red pepper, torn into strips
- three pitted queen olives, quartered
- Handful coriander

Direction

1. Cook oil in a 20cm non-stick frying pan. Put the courgette and let it cook for some

minute while stirring it periodically until it softens.

2. Beat the eggs with the harissa and pour them into the pan.
3. Proceed to cook gently. Stir to let the egg that is uncooked flow onto the base of the pan.
4. When more than half has been cooked, do not touch it for about two minutes. Place a plate, then take back to the pan, facing the uncooked part down, to have the cooking completed.
5. Tip on top of a board and spread using the hummus to serve.
6. Scatter with the coriander, olives, and pepper.
7. Cut into quarters and eat cold or warm.

Nutrition: 317 calories 21g fat 13g protein

248. Almond Butter and Alfalfa Wraps

Preparation Time: 7 minutes
Cooking Time: 0 minutes
Servings: 1
Ingredients

- Juice of 1 lemon
- 4 tbsp. of almond nut butter
- three finely sliced radishes
- 2-3 carrots grated
- 1 cup of alfalfa sprouts
- Nori sheets or lettuce leaves
- Pepper and salt

Direction

1. Combine the almond butter with a sufficient amount of water and an ample amount of lemon juice so you will have a paste with your desired level of thickness.
2. Next, have the alfalfa sprouts and grated carrot mixed inside a bowl. Sprinkle with the remaining lemon juice that was set aside. Proceed to the season with pepper and salt to taste.
3. Using the almond butter, smear the nori sheets or lettuce leaves, depending on the one you are using. Top the resulting mixture with the alfalfa sprout mixture and carrot. Roll it up and serve. Enjoy!

Nutrition: 409 calories 17g fat 6g protein

249. Buckwheat Bean and Tomato Risotto

Preparation Time: 11 minutes
Cooking Time: 23 minutes
Servings: 4
Ingredients

- 2 tbsp. of butter or olive oil
- two cloves of chopped garlic
- eight ounces/225g buckwheat
- 400ml of vegetable stock or hot water
- eight ounces/225g broad beans
- ½ cup of sun-dried tomatoes inside an oil
- Juice of half a lemon
- 2 tbsp. of chopped coriander or basil
- two ounces/50g of toasted almonds
- Pepper and salt

Direction

1. Heat the butter or olive oil inside a frying pan. Include the garlic and allow it to cook for a period of one minute.
2. Next, place the buckwheat into the pan and have it stirred thoroughly. This is to allow the buckwheat to be coated in the oil.
3. After that, add the stock or hot water. Then close the frying pan and let it simmer for 10 minutes.
4. When you are done simmering, stir the broad beans in. Then proceed to cook until the beans are just tender, which should be for a few minutes.
5. After that, add the fresh herbs, lemon juice, sun-dried tomatoes, and almonds. Season with pepper and salt to taste. Serve and enjoy your meal!

Nutrition: 358 calories 21g fat 14g protein

250. Vegetable Curry with Tofu

Preparation Time: 14 minutes
Cooking Time: 20 minutes
Serving: 3
Ingredients

- ½ tbsp. rapeseed oil
- One large onion, chopped
- three cloves garlic, peeled and grated
- One large thumb (7cm) fresh ginger, peeled and grated
- One red chili, deseeded and thinly sliced

- ¼ tsp ground turmeric
- ¼ tsp cayenne pepper
- ½ tsp paprika
- ¼ tsp ground cumin
- ½ tsp salt
- 150g dried red lentils
- ½ -liter boiling water
- 30g frozen soya edamame beans
- 100g firm tofu, chopped into cubes
- a tomato, roughly chopped
- Juice of 1 lime
- 100g kale leaves stalk removed and torn

Direction
1. Put the oil over low-medium heat in a heavy-bottom pan. Add the turmeric, cayenne, cumin, paprika, and oil. Remove and mix again before adding the red lentils.
2. Pour in the boiling water and cook for 10 minutes until the curry has a thick' porridge' consistency, then reduce the heat and cook for another 20-30 minutes.
3. Add soya beans, tofu, and tomatoes and continue to cook for another 5 minutes. Add the juice of lime and kale leaves and cook until the kale is tender.

Nutrition 342 Calories 5g Fat 28g Protein

251. Sirt Food Mushroom Scramble Eggs

Preparation Time: 6 minutes
Cooking Time: 9 minutes
Serving: 4

Ingredients
- two eggs
- 1 tsp ground turmeric
- 1 tsp mellow curry powder
- 20g kale, generally slashed
- 1 tsp additional virgin olive oil
- ½ superior bean stews, daintily cut
- Bunch of catch mushrooms, meagerly cut
- 5g parsley, finely slashed

Direction
1. Blend the turmeric and curry powder and include a little water until you have accomplished light glue.
2. Steam the kale for 2–3 minutes.
3. Preheat oil in a skillet at medium heat and fry the bean stew and mushrooms for 2 minutes.
4. Include the eggs and flavor glue and cook over medium warmth at that point, add the kale and keep on cooking over medium heat for a further moment. At long last, include the parsley, blend well and serve.

Nutrition 158 Calories 9.96g Protein 10.9g Fat

252. Green Salad Skewers

Preparation Time: 17 minutes
Cooking Time: 0 minutes
Serving: 6

Ingredients
- Eight large black olives
- Eight cherry tomatoes
- One yellow pepper
- ½ red onion, chopped
- 100g cucumber, sliced
- 100g feta, chopped into 8
- Ingredients for the dressing
- two wooden skewers
- eight cherry tomatoes
- one tablespoon of extra virgin olive oil
- ½ lemons
- one teaspoon of balsamic vinegar
- ½ clove garlic, peeled and crushed
- Few basil leaves, finely chopped
- Few leaves oregano, finely chopped
- Salt
- Freshly ground black pepper

Direction
1. Let the wooden skewers get soaked for 30 minutes with water
2. The skewers then need to be filled with the salad ingredients.
3. Mix all the dressing ingredients in a bowl, then pour over the skewers.

Nutrition 236 Calories 46g Fat 7g Protein

253. Baked Potatoes with Spicy Chickpea Stew

Preparation Time: 9 minutes
Cooking Time: 38 minutes
Serving: 4

Ingredients
- One red onion, nicely chopped
- Two cloves- grated

- Grated ginger (1cm)
- One tablespoon, chili-flakes
- Turmeric one -tablespoon
- A sprinkle of water
- Nicely chopped tomatoes (2×200g)
- Cocoa powder (unsweetened) 1tbs
- Two tin of chickpeas (200g each ×2)
- Nicely chopped pepper in smaller sizes
- Parsley with garnish (one tablespoon)
- Salt
- Pepper

Direction

1. Get all ingredients ready.
2. Preheat oven, over an average heat/preferably 200 degree).
3. When heated to a desired extent, place baking potatoes and cooked to your desired satisfaction, preferably for one hour: to fifteen minutes.
4. Get a saucepan and placed in your olive oil alongside the chopped onion, and cooked till onions are soft.
5. Cook more for five minutes over average heat, adding your garlic, chili, and ginger with it.
6. Add water (a little splash), turmeric, and cook for some minutes (preferably 4-5 minutes).
7. At this stage, the tomatoes, pepper, (yellow), and cocoa powder will be added and cooked for 35 minutes over an average heat till its sauce and thick to an extent.
8. Add salt (a pinch of it), parsley (two tablespoons), and pepper (optional) when the stew is almost ready.
9. Stir and serve on potatoes (Baked).

Nutrition: 391 calories 27g fat 14g protein

254. Buckwheat Garden Salad

Preparation Time: 19 minutes
Cooking Time: 0 minutes
Serving: 3

Ingredients

- One cup of buckwheat
- Water, two cups
- Salt, half teaspoon
- Half cherry Lotte nicely diced
- Green olives, 12 preferably large
- Two nicely diced (yellow pepper)

- Smoothly chopped broccoli florets, one cup
- 50gram of walnuts, chopped
- Half cup of fresh dill, smoothly chopped
- One lime of juice
- Olive oil, one tablespoon
- Half teaspoon of black pepper

Direction

1. Get a saucepan, medium-size, and fill with small water to boil.
2. Salt, buckwheat groats will be added to the boiling water to cook till it absorbed the ingredients.
3. Allow the cooked buckwheat to cool for an hour before adding green olive, cherry Lotte, yellow bell pepper (diced), red onions, florets, chopped broccoli, and walnuts in a fitted bowl for thorough mixing.
4. Serve meal immediately after mixing or reserved for hours in a refrigerator.

Nutrition: 417 calories 29g fat 15g protein

255. Cucumber, Pineapple, Parsley, And Lemon Smoothie

Preparation Time: 7 minutes
Cooking Time: 0 minutes
Serving: 2

Ingredients

- A bunch of leaf parsley nicely chopped.
- Coconut water 3/4 cup.
- Half cucumber, nicely chopped.
- Two cups of frozen pineapple.
- A drip of liquid stevia (5 drops preferably)
- Ginger.

Direction

1. Ensure the ingredients are ready.
2. Get a blender, preferably a bigger blender.
3. Place ingredients in one at a time to blend all.
4. Blend ingredients over extremely high heat for three minutes till it's super creamy and smooth to serve.

Nutrition: 98 calories 11g fat 3g protein

256. Buckwheat Meatballs

Preparation Time: 14 minutes
Cooking Time: 18 minutes
Serving: 4

Ingredients:

- 100 grams of buckwheat;
- 1 whole egg;
- a clove of garlic;
- a bunch of parsley;
- nutmeg;
- breadcrumbs;
- salt and pepper.

Directions

1. Wash the buckwheat and transfer it to a pot. Let it toast for a few seconds, after which add about 250/300 ml of cold water, sprinkle salt, and cook for 23 minutes.
2. Chop a clove of garlic and put it in a pan with a drizzle of oil, add the buckwheat well drained from the remaining cooking water and let it flavor together for a few minutes. Transfer everything into a bowl and let it cool.
3. When the wheat is warm, add the slightly beaten egg, nutmeg, finely chopped parsley, a pinch of pepper, and mix well.
4. Now form some balls with the help of a spoon and roll them in breadcrumbs. Compact the meatballs by squeezing them between the palms of your hands and, at the same time, flatten them slightly at the poles.
5. Grease a pan with oil and cook the meatballs on both sides until they are golden brown. Serve them hot buckwheat meatballs accompanied by vegetables to taste.

Nutrition: 471 calories 16g fats 7g protein

257. Cabbage and Buckwheat Fritters

Preparation Time: 11 minutes
Cooking Time: 4 minutes
Serving: 3

Ingredients:

- 20 g grated cheese
- 50 g cabbage tops
- 1 egg
- 1 tablespoon Flour 00
- 1/2 shallot
- Extra virgin olive oil
- Salt

Directions

1. Clean the cabbage and choose the florets. Finely cut the shallot and situate in the pressure cooker with 1 tablespoon of oil and the cabbage florets.
2. Brown gently, add the buckwheat and twice as much saltwater or vegetable broth. Close the pan and cook for 15 minutes from the start of the hiss.
3. Open the pot and let the mixture cool down. Add the egg and add enough flour to obtain a homogeneous mixture with a moderately firm consistency.
4. If necessary, add salt to taste. With floured hands, form round meatballs and then crush them slightly to flatten them.
5. Place them in a baking tray and brush them with a drizzle of oil. Bake them in the oven for 15 minutes at about 200 °C (392 °F)

Nutrition: 391 calories 12g fat 6g protein

258. Buckwheat Salad with Artichokes

Preparation Time: 18 minutes
Cooking Time: 6 minutes
Serving: 4

Ingredients:

- 300 g buckwheat
- 200 g cherry tomatoes
- 5 artichokes
- 1 clove of garlic
- 1/2 cup large green olives
- fresh marjoram
- 5 tablespoons extra virgin olive oil
- salt
- 1 lemon

Directions

1. Using non-stick pan, toast the buckwheat grains, always stirring for 3 minutes, then boil salted water for 11 minutes. Drain and set aside.
2. Clean the artichokes: remove the outer leaves, trim them and remove the beard, cut them into segments, and throw them away as they are cleaned in water acidulated with lemon juice, so that they do not blacken.
3. In the meantime, brown the clove of garlic dressed lightly crushed in two tablespoons of oil.

4. When the artichokes are all hulled and cut, drain them and put them in the pan. Brown them without burning, then lower the heat and cook until they have softened a bit; they must remain al dente. Remove the garlic clove and sprinkle with a little fresh marjoram.
5. Put the buckwheat in the pan with the artichokes, stir well, and cook for a couple of minutes to make it taste good. Turn off and set aside.
6. Rinse and chop the cherry tomatoes in 2, leaving them a little in a colander to drain the vegetation water.
7. Slice olives in half and remove the stone.
8. Incorporate the cherry tomatoes and olives with buckwheat, add more marjoram leaves, stir and let them flavor well covered, over low heat.

Nutrition: 341 calories 21g fat 15g protein

259. Pasta with Rocket Salad and Linseed

Preparation Time: 21 minutes
Cooking Time: 21 minutes
Serving: 4
Ingredients:
- 400 gr of whole meal pasta
- 1 bunch of washed and dried Rocket
- 1 tablespoon of peeled almonds
- 1 tablespoon Linseed
- 1/2 clove of Garlic
- 4 spoons of extra virgin olive oil
- 3 tablespoons of water (if necessary)
- A few drops of lemon juice
- Salt
- Pepper

Directions
1. First, wash the arugula and put it to dry on a kitchen cloth, then boil water and throw the dough;
2. In a mixer, add 1 tablespoon of linseed, 1 tablespoon of almonds, half a clove of garlic (without the sprout) and 4 tablespoons of oil;
3. Cut everything for a few minutes, if necessary, add a little water to make the pesto more fluid;

4. At this point add the rocket, a few drops of lemon juice, a pinch of salt and turn the mixer again for a few seconds, then add salt and pepper, and your pesto is ready;
5. Before draining the pasta, set aside some cooking water so that it can be used later, in case the pesto is too thick;
6. Once drained, put the pasta on the pot, season it with the pesto, and, if necessary, add a little cooking water previously-stored; continuing to stir for about a minute, and now your dish is ready to taste!

Nutrition: 401 calories 29g fat 17g protein

260. Sirt Yogurt

Preparation Time: 7 minutes
Cooking Time: 0 minutes
Serving: 1
Ingredients
- 125g mixed berries
- 150g Greek yogurt
- 25g of chopped walnuts
- 10g of dark chocolate (85 percent cocoa) grated

Directions
1. Put your favorite berries in a bowl and pour yogurt on top. Sprinkle them with nuts and chocolate.
2. For a vegan alternative, you can replace Greek yogurt with soy or coconut milk.

Nutrition: 297 calories 27g fat 11g protein

261. Sirt Pita Bread

Preparation Time: 14 minutes
Cooking Time: 17 minutes
Serving: 4
Ingredients
- 1 c. warm water
- 2 tsp. active dry yeast
- 1 tsp. granulated sugar
- 3 c. all-purpose flour, divided
- 1 tbsp. extra-virgin olive oil
- 1 1/2 tsp. kosher salt

Direction
1. Situate pizza stone or large cast iron skillet in your oven and preheat to 500 F. Mix warm water, yeast, and sugar until dissolved. Stir in ½ cup flour and set aside for 15 minutes

2. Combine oil, salt, and 2 cups flour (reserving ½ cup) until a shaggy mass form. Sprinkle clean surface with some of reserved flour and knead for 7 minutes.
3. Situate dough in a clean large bowl and wrap with plastic. Keep aside in warm place for 1 hour.
4. Slightly dust a clean surface with flour. Press down dough and turn it out onto surface. Portion dough into 8 pieces and roll into balls. Seal with a towel for 10 minutes.
5. Working one simultaneously, roll each round into a ¼"-thick circle about 8" wide, dust dough with extra flour if it starts to stick.
6. Situate as many pitas that will fit on your skillet then bake 5 minutes. Repeat
7. Wrap baked pitas with a clean kitchen towel to keep warm.

Nutrition: 487 calories 26g fat 13g protein

262. Red Bean Sauce with Baked Potato

Preparation Time: 21 minutes
Cooking Time: 15 minutes
Serving: 1
Ingredients:
- 40g red onion, finely chopped
- 1 teaspoon of fresh ginger, finely chopped
- 1 clove of garlic, finely chopped
- 1 Bird's Eye chili pepper, finely chopped
- 1 teaspoon of extra virgin olive oil
- 1 teaspoon of turmeric powder
- 1 teaspoon of cumin powder
- 1 pinch of powdered cloves
- 1 pinch of cinnamon powder
- 1 medium potato 190g peeled
- 1 teaspoon of brown sugar
- 50g red pepper, stripped of stalks and seeds and coarsely chopped
- 150ml vegetable stock
- 1 tablespoon of cocoa powder
- 1 teaspoon of sesame seeds
- 2 teaspoons of peanut butter
- 150g canned red beans
- 5g chopped parsley

Directions

1. Set oven to 200 °C (392 °F).
2. Fry the onion, ginger, garlic, and chili pepper in oil in a medium pan over medium heat for about 12 minutes. Cook spices for 2 minutes.
3. Place the potato on a baking tray, put it in the hot oven and cook for 45-60 minutes
4. Add the peeled tomatoes, sugar, peppers, stock, cocoa powder, sesame seeds, peanut butter, and beans; and simmer for 45-60 minutes.
5. Finally, sprinkle with parsley.

Nutrition: 491 calories 31g fat 16g protein

263. Curly Kale with Sweet Potatoes

Preparation Time: 23 minutes
Cooking Time: 19 minutes
Serving: 1
Ingredients:
- 50g Curly Kale
- 200 g Sweet potatoes
- Red onion
- 1 teaspoon bird's eye chili pepper
- 2 tablespoons extra virgin olive oil
- Salt

Directions

1. Slice sweet potatoes into small cubes and put them in a pan with a drizzle of oil and the onion into small pieces.
2. Add salt. Once cooked, add the cut kale and chili pepper. Turn well until the kale is well withered. Continue cooking for another 5 minutes, always stirring with a ladle!

Nutrition: 391 calories 24g fat 9g protein

264. Buckwheat Pasta with Zucchini and Cherry Tomatoes

Preparation Time: 9 minutes
Cooking Time: 29 minutes
Serving: 2
Ingredients:
- 160 g buckwheat pasta
- 2 zucchinis
- 6 cherry tomatoes
- 1/2 red onion
- extra virgin olive oil

- halls
- bird's-eye chili

Directions
1. Fry the oil in a pan with the sliced onion and chili pepper.
2. When the onion has taken a little color, add the cherry tomatoes and zucchini slices; turn well and let cook with a lid on medium heat for about 10 minutes, turning occasionally.
3. Boil the salted water for the pasta, then drain the pasta.
4. Throw it directly into the sauce and fry everything in a pan for about a minute.

Nutrition: 458 calories 23g fats 18g protein

265. Pasta with Red Chicory and Walnuts

Preparation Time: 9 minutes
Cooking Time: 32 minutes
Serving: 1

Ingredients:
- 70 g buckwheat pasta
- 100 g red chicory
- 10 g extra virgin olive oil
- 20 g walnuts
- 30 g bacon cut into strips
- 10g Bird's eye chili minced
- Salt

Directions
1. Stew the red chicory in a saucepan with oil, and when it is cooked, add the walnut grains that you have previously browned with bacon cut into strips.
2. Cook pasta in salted water, strain it and add it to the mixture of red chicory and walnuts and sauté for a few seconds; finally, a sprinkling of chili.

Nutrition: 319 calories 15g fat 9g protein

266. Cabbage and Red Chicory Flan

Preparation Time: 13 minutes
Cooking Time: 18 minutes
Serving: 4

Ingredients:
- 800g cabbage
- 250g red chicory
- 100g red onions 100 g

- 3 tablespoons Extra virgin olive oil
- Salt
- Pepper
- 2 tablespoon breadcrumbs
- 60g walnuts

Directions
1. Clean the cauliflower by eliminating the green leaves and the central core, and always with the help of a smooth blade knife, detach all the tops, dividing in half the bigger ones. Transfer the cleaned buds into a colander and rinse them under cold water.
2. Situate saucepan full of water on the fire and as soon as it boils, dip the cauliflower tops, cooking them for about 10 minutes; the consistency will have to remain rather al dente, since it will be sautéed in the pan; then continue with the cooking in the oven. Drain the cauliflower into a bowl and leave it aside.
3. Heat a drizzle of oil in a large pan, add the onion and sauté over low heat. Once golden, add the cauliflower, salt, and pepper to taste. Stir and let everything season for about 5-6 minutes.
4. In the meantime, clean the red chicory by removing the central core, slice it thinly and mix to the pan with the cauliflower; stir, and fry for a few seconds so as not to wither too much.
5. Put out the fire and set aside. Chop the nuts.
6. Heat the oven to 200 °C in static mode. Grease 4 bowls with a diameter of about 11 cm and fill them with cauliflower and red chicory, sprinkle on the surface a pinch of breadcrumbs and walnut grains.
7. Bake for about 15 minutes, gratinating the last minutes of cooking with the grill to brown the surface. Remove from the oven and serve hot.

Nutrition: 429 calories 31g fats 27g protein

267. Red Chicory and Kale Salad

Preparation Time: 18 minutes
Cooking Time: 0 minutes
Serving: 4

Ingredients:

- 200 g of canned chickpeas
- 1 kale
- 1 red chicory
- 1 red onion
- 40g extra virgin olive oil
- Salt
- Lemon juice
- Walnuts
- Rocket salad

Directions

1. Clean the kale leaves and cut them into strips. Let them wither with finely chopped red onion in a non-stick pan with two tablespoons of extra virgin olive oil.
2. When the kale is cooked, mix it with the chickpeas, drained from their preserving liquid, in a salad bowl. The ingredient that will give that bitters' touch to the dish will be the red chicory, to be used raw.
3. Mix the various components and then season with fine salt, good extra virgin olive oil, and a splash of lemon, which will give acidity to the dish. Add the walnuts and some arugula leaves!

Nutrition: 427 calories 26g fat 14g protein

268. Egg Scramble with Kale

Preparation Time: 17 minutes
Cooking Time: 4 minutes
Serving: 3

Ingredients

- 4 eggs
- 1/8 teaspoon ground turmeric
- Salt and ground black pepper, to taste
- 1 tablespoon water
- 2 teaspoons olive oil
- 1 cup fresh kale, tough ribs removed and chopped

Direction

1. Beat eggs, turmeric, salt, black pepper, and water until foamy.
2. In a wok, heat the oil over medium heat.
3. Add the egg mixture and stir to combine.
4. Decrease heat to medium-low and cook for a minute.
5. Mix in the kale and cook for about 3–4 minutes, stirring frequently.
6. Remove from the heat and serve immediately.

Nutrition 183 Calories 13g Fat 12g Protein

269. Buckwheat Porridge

Preparation Time: 9 minutes
Cooking Time: 19 minutes
Servings: 2

Ingredients

- 1 cup buckwheat, rinsed
- 1 cup unsweetened almond milk
- 1 cup water
- ½ teaspoon ground cinnamon
- ½ teaspoon vanilla extract
- 1–2 tablespoons raw honey
- ¼ cup fresh blueberries

Direction

1. Mix all the ingredients (except blueberries and honey) on medium-high heat and boil.
2. Now, reduce the heat to low and simmer, covered for about 10 minutes.
3. Drizzle honey and remove from the heat.
4. Set aside, covered, for about 5 minutes.
5. With a fork, fluff the mixture, and transfer into serving bowls.
6. Top with blueberries and serve.

Nutrition 358 Calories 4.7g Fat 12g Protein

270. Eggs with Kale

Preparation Time: 13 minutes
Cooking Time: 28 minutes
Servings: 4

Ingredients

- 2 tablespoons olive oil
- 1 yellow onion, chopped
- 2 garlic cloves, minced
- 1 cup tomatoes, chopped
- ½ pound fresh kale, tough ribs removed and chopped
- 1 teaspoon ground cumin
- ¼ teaspoon red pepper flakes, crushed
- Salt and ground black pepper, to taste
- 4 eggs
- 2 tablespoons fresh parsley, chopped

Direction

1. Cook oil in a large wok over medium heat and sauté the onion for about 4–5 minutes.
2. Sauté garlic for a minute.
3. Add the tomatoes, spices, salt, and black pepper, and cook for about 2–3 minutes, stirring frequently.

4. Cook kale for 4 minutes.
5. Carefully, crack eggs on top of kale mixture.
6. With the lid, cover the wok and cook for about 10 minutes, or until desired doneness of eggs.
7. Serve hot with the garnishing of parsley.

Nutrition 175 Calories 11.7g Fat 8.2g Protein

271. Miso Soup

Preparation Time: 11 minutes
Cooking time: 31 minutes
Serving: 3

Ingredients:

- 10 g wakame
- 1 liter of water
- 5 g (1 sachet) instant dashi granules
- 100 g tofu, chopped into cubes
- 1 heaping tablespoon (25 g) white miso paste
- 2 spring onions, cut and chopped

Direction

1. Place the wakame in a small bowl or cup and cover generously with water. Leave on for a few minutes.
2. Bring the 1-liter water to a boil in a large saucepan. Stir in the instant dashi powder until it has dissolved.
3. Turn down heat to simmer and stir the tofu. Add the wakame to the soup by discarding the water.
4. Let simmer for 2 minutes. Situate miso paste in a bowl and add a tablespoon of the dashi broth at a time.
5. Stir until the miso has dissolved and you have a smooth, thick sauce. Take the pan off the stove and stir in the miso. Try the soup and add a little more miso if desired.
6. Serve in two bowls and sprinkle the chopped green onion evenly over each dish.

Nutrition: 318 calories 24g fat 11g protein

272. Mexican Chicken Soup

Preparation Time: 13 minutes
Cooking time: 1 hour
Serving: 4

Ingredients:

- 4 chicken legs
- 2 shallots, peeled and roughly chopped
- 1 carrot, peeled and roughly chopped
- 1 liter of water
- 400 g of chopped tomatoes
- 300 ml passata
- 1 green pepper, deseeded and chopped
- 1 red chili, pitted and finely chopped
- 2 cloves of garlic, peeled and chopped
- 1 teaspoon dried mixed herbs
- 1 teaspoon paprika
- 1 teaspoon smoked paprika
- ½ teaspoon ground turmeric
- ½ teaspoon ground cumin
- 1 teaspoon mild chili powder
- 400 g canned black beans, drained
- 400 g canned kidney beans, drained
- 30 g (very large handful) parsley, chopped
- Salt and freshly ground black pepper

Direction

1. Place the chicken drumsticks, shallots, and carrots in a large saucepan. Pour over the water and bring to a boil.
2. Cook for 20 minutes, then remove the chicken drumsticks with a slotted spoon and set aside to cool.
3. Add the chopped tomatoes, passata, green pepper, chili and garlic and bring them back to boiling point.
4. Add the dried herbs, paprika, smoked paprika, turmeric, cumin and chili powder and simmer gently for 30 minutes.
5. Pull skin out from the chicken drumsticks and pull as much chicken off the bone as possible.
6. Cut the chicken and add it to the pan along with the black beans and kidney beans for the last 5 minutes.
7. Take out from heat and sprinkle parsley. Season generously.

Nutrition: 361 calories 35g fat 21g protein

273. Thai Spinach Soup

Preparation Time: 13 minutes
Cooking Time: 17 minutes
Serving: 4

Ingredients:

- 1 teaspoon olive oil
- 2 shallots, peeled and chopped
- ½ teaspoon ground cumin
- 1 thumb (5 cm) fresh ginger, peeled and grated
- 1 stick lemongrass
- 1 red chilies, deseeded, chopped
- Zest and juice of 1 lime

- 1 liter of boiling water
- 400 g coconut milk
- 250 g fresh spinach
- 1 tbsp Thai Green Curry Paste
- Large handful (20 g) parsley
- Large handful (20 g) of coriander

Direction:
1. In a large saucepan, cook olive oil slightly and fry the shallots for 5 minutes until they soften.
2. Add the cumin, fresh ginger, lemongrass, chili, and lime zest. Stir thoroughly, then pour in the water.
3. Bring to a boil, then add the coconut milk, simmer again slightly and cook for another 10 minutes.
4. Add the spinach and curry paste and simmer gently until the spinach is cooked through.
5. Remove from heat and throw away the lemongrass stick. Stir in parsley, coriander and lime juice.

Nutrition: 226 calories 21g protein 17g fat

274. Savoy Cabbage and Bacon Soup

Preparation Time: 12 minutes
Cooking Time: 37 minutes
Serving: 6

Ingredients:
- 200 g bacon or pancetta, roughly chopped
- 2 shallots, peeled and chopped
- 2 cloves of garlic, peeled and sliced
- 200 g white potatoes, peeled and roughly chopped
- 1.2 liters of boiling water
- 500 ml chicken broth, fresh or made with 1 cube
- 1 tsp English mustard
- 800 g savoy cabbage stalk removed and chopped
- 200 ml crème fraiche
- Large handful (30 g) parsley, roughly chopped

Direction:
1. Prep large saucepan over high heat and toss in the bacon. Fry for 3–5 minutes, turning regularly, until brown and crispy. Pull out with a slotted spoon and set aside.

Add the shallots, stir and turn the heat on low.
2. Let the shallots cook for 5 minutes. Add the garlic and potato, sauté them for a few minutes then add the boiling water, chicken broth and mustard. Boil and simmer for 10 minutes. Stir the cabbage, return to the boil and cook for another 6 minutes.
3. Put in a blender in two batches and stir until smooth. Put the bacon back in and carefully heat the soup in the pan. Add the crème fraiche with a light fizz and cook for another 2 minutes before serving.

Nutrition: 296 calories 28g fat 16g protein

275. Edamame Beans Pesto Soup

Preparation Time: 13 minutes
Cooking Time: 41 minutes
Serving: 2

Ingredients:
- 1 teaspoon olive oil
- 1 leek, cut and sliced
- 1 clove of garlic, peeled and sliced
- 100 g white potatoes, peeled and diced
- 200 g fresh or frozen soy / edamame beans
- 3-4 basil leaves, torn
- 750 ml vegetable stock, fresh or prepared
- 50 g baby leaf spinach, shredded
- 1 tbsp pesto

Direction:
1. Cook oil in a large saucepan and gently fry the leek and garlic for 10 minutes. Add the potato, three quarters of the soybeans and the basil.
2. Boil broth, and simmer gently for 20 minutes. 2 Put the soup in a blender and stir until smooth. Situate soup to the pan and let it simmer gently. Stir in the remaining soybeans, spinach and pesto and heat for another 5 minutes.

Nutrition: 272 calories 26g protein 11g fat

276. Spicy Butternut Squash and Kale Soup

Preparation Time: 14 minutes
Cooking Time: 22 minutes
Serving: 4

Ingredients:

- 1 tbsp olive oil
- 2 shallots, peeled and chopped
- 1 clove of garlic, peeled and sliced
- 200 g sweet potato, peeled and diced
- 800 g (1 small) butternut squash, pitted, peeled and diced
- 1 red chili, pitted and chopped
- 1 teaspoon smoked paprika
- ½ teaspoon paprika
- 1 teaspoon ground turmeric
- 1 teaspoon salt
- 500 ml vegetable stock, fresh or prepared
- 1 liter of boiling water
- 1 tbsp whole grain mustard
- 20 g parmesan, finely grated
- 200 g of kale leaves, removed stems and roughly chopped
- 200 ml crème fraiche

Direction:
1. Cook oil in a large, thick-bottomed saucepan. Add shallots and garlic and stir-fry for 5 minutes.
2. Add the sweet potato and butternut squash. Stir, cover and cook gently for 10 minutes.
3. Stir in the chili, paprika, turmeric and salt. Boil stock and water. Let simmer for 20 minutes.
4. Put in a blender in two batches and stir until smooth. Return to the pan and gently heat it.
5. Add the mustard, parmesan and kale. Cook for 6 minutes. Add the crème fraiche, bring back to temperature and serve.

Nutrition: 234 calories 28g fat 11g protein

277. Kale Stilton Soup
Preparation Time: 13 minutes
Cooking Time: 31 minutes
Serving: 4
Ingredients:
- 1 tbsp olive oil
- 2 shallots, peeled and diced
- 2 leeks, cut and sliced
- 150 g white potatoes, peeled and diced
- 500 ml vegetable stock, fresh
- 500 ml of boiling water

- 400 g kale leaves, stems removed and roughly chopped
- 2 tbsp (30 ml)
- Sherry 200 ml skimmed milk
- 2 tbsp (30 ml) double cream (45% fat)
- 50 g Stilton, crumbled
- Large handful (20 g) parsley, roughly chopped
- Salt and freshly ground black pepper

Direction:
1. Cook oil in a large saucepan and gently fry the shallots and leeks for 10 minutes until tender.
2. Stir in the potato then add the stock and the boiling water. Boil, then reduce the heat and simmer lightly for 15 minutes.
3. Use a potato masher to mash the potatoes in the pan - or mix them in a blender if you prefer.
4. Add the kale, let it simmer gently, and cook for 4 minutes until the kale is just tender.
5. Add the sherry, milk, cream and half of the stilton.
6. Let simmer until the stilton has dissolved. Season generously with salt and pepper.
7. Divide into four bowls and serve with parsley sprinkled with Stilton.

Nutrition: 232 calories 24g fat 11g protein

278. Curry Broth
Preparation Time: 11 minutes
Cooking Time: 25 minutes
Serving: 4
Ingredients:
- 1 tbsp olive oil
- 2 shallots
- 1 clove of garlic
- 2 green chilies, pitted and finely chopped
- 1 teaspoon mild chili powder
- 1 teaspoon ground turmeric
- ¼ teaspoon cloves
- ¼ teaspoon ground cinnamon
- 1 teaspoon salt
- 150 g broccoli, cut into small florets
- 200 g kale leaves, stems removed and roughly chopped
- 400 ml chicken or vegetable stock, fresh
- 1 liter of boiling water

- 250 g tofu, cut into small cubes
- 2 spring onions, cut and chopped
- 20 g coriander, chopped

Direction:

1. Using large saucepan with a thick bottom, cook oil over low heat.
2. Add the shallots and sauté them for 5 minutes, until they just start to soften.
3. Add the garlic, green chilies, spices, and salt. Stir then add the broccoli and kale.
4. Fry for 2-3 minutes. Stir the stock and water and bring to a boil.
5. Let simmer gently for 15 minutes.
6. Add the tofu, spring onions, and coriander and cook for a few more minutes until it warms up.

Nutrition: 232 calories 23g fat 15g protein

279. Walnut Soup

Preparation Time: 16 minutes
Cooking Time: 1 hour
Serving: 1

Ingredients:

- 2 teaspoons of native olive oil
- 30g heard red onion
- 30 grams of heard celery
- 1 clove of heard garlic
- 1 teaspoon dried thyme
- 75 g canned or homemade white beans such as cannellini or haricot
- 500 ml vegetable broth
- 50 g kale, roughly chopped
- 4 chopped walnut halves

Direction:

1. Over medium saucepan, cook 1 teaspoon of olive oil over medium heat and fry the red onions, celery and garlic for 2-3 minutes. When soft, add the thyme, beans, and broth and bring to a boil.
2. Simmer at low heat for 25 minutes then stir the kale and cook for another 10 minutes. When all of the vegetables are cooked through, blend the mixture until smooth.
3. Prep your oven to 160 ° C / Gas 3 and roast your walnuts for 10-15 minutes. Serve with the remaining teaspoon of olive oil and topped with the roasted walnuts.

Nutrition 22g Fat 12g Protein 260 Calories

280. Spicy Lentils Vegetable Soup

Preparation Time: 13 minutes
Cooking Time: 31 minutes
Serving: 3

Ingredients:

- 1 teaspoon extra virgin olive oil plus
- 30 g red onion
- 30 g celery
- 30 g carrot
- 1 Birds Eye Chili
- 1 clove of garlic
- 1 teaspoon ground turmeric
- 1 tsp curry powder
- 500 ml vegetable broth
- 50 g red lentils
- 1 teaspoon chopped parsley

Direction:

1. With a small saucepan, heat the olive oil over low to medium heat and fry the onion, celery and carrot for 2-3 minutes until soft. Add the chili, garlic and spices and cook for another minute. Stir vegetable stock and lentils and bring to a boil. Simmer gently for 30 minutes and stir from time to time so that nothing sticks to the bottom.
2. Once the lentils have broken down and they have a nice soupy consistency, stir in the parsley and serve with a dash of extra virgin olive oil.

Nutrition 7g Fat 8g Protein 120 Calories

281. Watercress Soup

Preparation Time: 11 minutes
Cooking Time: 12 minutes
Serving: 2

Ingredients:

- 2 teaspoons of native olive oil
- 30 g of celery, smaller ties
- 30 g white onion, smaller rights
- 200 ml vegetable broth
- 50 g canned or homemade white beans such as cannellini or haricot
- 75 g watercress
- 1 tbsp chopped parsley

Direction:

1. Fill 1 teaspoon of olive oil in a small saucepan and cook the celery and onion gently for 2 minutes. Fill stock and beans, bring to a boil and cook over medium heat for 10 minutes.
2. Chop roughly the watercress and parsley, add to the pan and cook for 1 minute.
3. Remove from heat and stir until smooth. Serve the soup drizzled with the remaining teaspoon of olive oil.

Nutrition 11g Fat 5g Protein 130 Calories

282. Curry and Rice Stew

Preparation Time: 12 minutes
Cooking Time: 17 minutes
Serving: 4

Ingredients:

- 2 teaspoons of rapeseed oil
- 225 g paneer, cut into cubes
- Salt and freshly ground black pepper
- 1 red onion, sliced
- 1 thumb (5 cm) fresh ginger, peeled and grated
- 2 cloves of garlic, peeled and grated
- 2 fingers of chili peppers, heads removed and finely chopped
- ½ teaspoon aniseed
- 250 g cooked brown rice
- 250 g ready-to-eat or cooked Puy lentils
- 100 g frozen soy / edamame beans
- ½ teaspoon salt
- ½ teaspoon ground turmeric
- ½ teaspoon ground cumin
- ½ teaspoon ground coriander
- 1 teaspoon mild chili powder
- 2 tomatoes, chopped
- 50g baby spinach leaves
- Large handful (20g) parsley, chopped

Direction:

1. Cook oil in a large pan over high heat and add the paneer. Season generously with salt and pepper.
2. Cook the paneer, stirring frequently, until golden brown all over. Pull out and set aside.
3. Add the onion and reduce the heat in the pan to low. Before adding the ginger, garlic, chili peppers and anise, cook for 2 minutes and cook slowly for another 5 minutes.
4. Put the rice and lentils in a large bowl and mix gently, breaking up any lumps and separating the grains.
5. If the soybeans are frozen or need to be cooked, cook them according to the directions in the package. Add the salt, ground spices and chili powder to the pan and stir. Add the rice and lentil mixture, soybeans and tomatoes to the pan.
6. Stir very well and cook hot. Finally add the spinach and parsley and return the paneer to the pan.
7. Stir to combine and serve immediately. After cooling down completely, all spare servings can be chilled and served cold the next day.

Nutrition 19g Fat 24g Protein 347 Calories

283. Chinese Style with Pak Choi

Preparation Time: 17 minutes
Cooking Time: 1 hour
Serving: 4

Ingredients:

- 400 g firm tofu, cut into large cubes
- 1 tbsp corn flour
- 1 tbsp water
- 125 ml chicken stock
- 1 tbsp rice wine
- 1 tbsp tomato paste
- 1 teaspoon brown sugar
- 1 tbsp soy sauce
- 1 clove of garlic, peeled and chopped
- 1 thumb (5 cm) fresh ginger, peeled and grated
- 1 tbsp rapeseed oil 100 g shiitake mushrooms, sliced
- 1 shallot, peeled and sliced
- 200 g Pak choy
- 400 g minced pork (10% fat)
- 100 g sprouts
- Large handful (20 g) parsley, chopped

Direction:

1. Wrap tofu on kitchen paper, and set aside.
2. In a small bowl, mix the cornmeal and water and remove any lumps.

3. Add the chicken broth, rice wine, tomato paste, brown sugar and soy sauce.
4. Mix crushed garlic and ginger. Cook oil to a high temperature in a wok or large pan.
5. Add the shiitake mushrooms and sauté them for 2-3 minutes until cooked and shiny.
6. Take mushrooms from the pan with a slotted spoon and set aside.
7. Situate tofu in the pan and fry until golden brown on all sides.
8. Put the shallot and Pak choy in the wok, stir-fry for 2 minutes and then add the minced meat. Cook until cooked through, then add the sauce, reduce the heat by one notch, and let the sauce bubble around the meat for a minute or two.
9. Put the sprouts, shiitake mushrooms and tofu in the pan and warm through.
10. Take away from heat, sprinkle parsley and serve immediately.

Nutrition 19g Fat 36g Protein 347 Calories

284. Cauliflower Kale Curry

Preparation Time: 13 minutes
Cooking Time: 32 minutes
Serving: 4
Ingredients:

- 200 g buckwheat
- 2 tbsp ground turmeric
- 1 red onion, chopped
- 3 cloves of garlic, minced
- 2.5 cm piece of fresh ginger, chopped
- 1–2 chili peppers, chopped
- 1 tbsp coconut oil
- 1 tbsp mild curry powder
- 1 tbsp ground cumin
- 2 × 400 g cans of chopped tomatoes
- 300 ml vegetable broth
- 200 g kale, roughly chopped
- 300 g cauliflower, chopped
- 1 × 400 g can of butter beans, drained
- 2 tomatoes, cut into wedges
- 2 tbsp chopped coriander

Direction:

1. Cook the buckwheat following to the instructions on the package and add 1 tablespoon of turmeric to the water.

2. In the meantime, cook the onion, garlic, ginger and chili peppers in the coconut oil over medium heat for 2-3 minutes.
3. Add the seasonings, including the remaining tablespoon of turmeric and continue cooking over low to medium heat for 1–2 minutes.
4. Add the canned tomatoes and the broth and bring to a boil then simmer for 10 minutes.
5. Add the kale, cauliflower and butter beans and cook for 10 minutes.
6. Add the tomato wedges and coriander and cook for another minute.
7. Then serve them with the buckwheat.

Nutrition 17g Fat 8g Protein 270 Calories

285. Sirt Chicken Korma

Preparation Time: 16 minutes
Cooking Time: 51 minutes
Serving: 4
Ingredients:

- 350 ml chicken stock
- 30 g Medjool date, chopped
- 2 cinnamon sticks
- 4–5 cardamom pods, slightly split
- 250 ml coconut milk
- 8 boneless, skinless chicken thighs
- 1 tbsp ground turmeric
- 200 g buckwheat
- 150 ml of Greek yogurt
- 50 g of ground walnuts
- 2 tbsp chopped coriander

For the curry paste

- 1 large red onion, quartered
- 3 cloves of garlic
- 2 cm piece of fresh ginger
- 1 tbsp mild curry powder
- 1 teaspoon ground cumin
- 1 tbsp ground turmeric
- 1 tbsp coconut oil

Direction:

1. Situate ingredients for the curry paste in a food processor and flash for about a minute until you have a nice paste.
2. Fry the paste in a heavy pan over medium heat for 1-2 minutes then add the broth, date, cinnamon, cardamom pods, and coconut milk.

3. Bring to a boil then add the chicken legs. Reduce the heat, cover the pan with a lid, and simmer for 45 minutes.
4. Boil water and stir in the turmeric.
5. Add the buckwheat and cook according to the directions on the package. As soon as the chicken is tender, stir in the yogurt and cook the walnuts over low heat for a few more minutes.
6. Add the coriander and serve with the buckwheat.

Nutrition 16g Fat 32g Protein 330 Calories

286. Cauliflower Soup

Preparation Time: 12 minutes
Cooking Time: 47 minutes
Servings: 4

Ingredients:

- 3 pounds cauliflower, florets separated
- 1 yellow onion, chopped
- 1 tablespoon coconut oil
- Black pepper to the taste
- 2 garlic cloves, minced
- 2 carrots, chopped
- 2 cups beef stock
- 1 cup water
- ½ cup coconut milk
- 1 teaspoon olive oil
- 2 tablespoons parsley, chopped

Directions:

1. Heat a pot with the coconut oil over medium-high heat, add carrots, onion, and garlic, stir, and cook for 5 minutes.
2. Add cauliflower, water, and stock, stir, bring to a boil, cover, and cook for 45 minutes.
3. Transfer soup to your blender and pulse well, add coconut milk, pulse well again, ladle into bowls, drizzle the olive oil over the soup, sprinkle parsley and serve for lunch.

Nutrition: 190 Calories 2g Fat 4g Protein

287. Broccoli Soup

Preparation Time: 13 minutes
Cooking Time: 1 hour
Servings: 4

Ingredients:

- 2 pounds broccoli, florets separated
- 1 yellow onion, chopped
- 1 tablespoon olive oil
- Black pepper to the taste
- 1 cup celery, chopped   2 carrots, chopped
- 3 and ½ cups low-sodium chicken stock
- 1 tablespoon cilantro chopped

Directions:

1. Heat a pot with the oil over medium-high heat, add the onion, celery, and carrots, stir, and cook for 5 minutes.   Add broccoli, black pepper, and stock, stir, and cook over medium heat for 1 hour.
2. Pulse using an immersion blender, add cilantro, stir the soup

Nutrition: 170 Calories 2g Fat 3g Fiber

288. Shrimp Soup

Preparation Time: 12 minutes
Cooking Time: 15 minutes
Servings: 6

Ingredients:

- 46 ounces low-sodium chicken stock
- 3 cups shrimp, peeled and deveined
- A pinch of black pepper
- 2 tablespoons green onions, chopped
- 1 teaspoon dill, chopped

Directions:

1. Put the stock in a pot, bring to a simmer over medium heat, add black pepper, onion, and shrimp, stir and simmer for 8-10 minutes.
2. Add dill, stir, cook for 5 minutes more, ladle into bowls and serve.

Nutrition: 190 Calories 7g Fat 8g Protein

289. Parmesan Tomato Soup

Preparation Time: 11 minutes
Cooking Time: 24 minutes
Servings: 4

Ingredients:

- ½ cup tomatoes, chopped
- 1 tablespoon tomato paste
- 1 teaspoon garlic, diced
- 2 cups beef broth
- 1 teaspoon chili pepper
- 2 oz Parmesan, grated
- 1/3 cup fresh cilantro, chopped
- 2 potatoes, chopped

Directions:

1. Mix up together tomatoes and tomato paste and transfer the mixture in the pan.
2. Add garlic and beef broth.
3. Add chopped potatoes and chili pepper.
4. Boil the ingredients for 15 minutes or until potato is soft.
5. Then blend the mixture with the help of the hand blender or in the food processor.
6. Add chopped cilantro and simmer the soup for 5 minutes.
7. Ladle the cooked soup in the serving bowls and top every bowl with Parmesan generously.

Nutrition: 148 Calories 3.9g Fat 9.2g Protein

290. Meatball Soup

Preparation Time: 13 minutes
Cooking Time: 28 minutes
Servings: 4
Ingredients:
- 1 cup ground beef
- 1 tablespoon semolina
- ½ teaspoon salt
- 1 egg yolk
- ½ teaspoon ground black pepper
- 4 cups chicken stock
- 1 carrot, chopped
- 1 yellow onion, diced
- 1 tablespoon butter
- ½ teaspoon turmeric
- ½ teaspoon garlic powder

Directions:
1. Toss butter in the skillet and heat it until it is melted.
2. Add onion and cook it until light brown.
3. Meanwhile, pour chicken stock in the pan.
4. Add garlic powder and turmeric.
5. Bring the liquid to boil. Add chopped carrot and boil it for 10 minutes.
6. In the mixing bowl, mix up together ground beef, semolina, salt, egg yolk, and ground black pepper.
7. Make the small sized meatballs.
8. Put the meatballs in the chicken stock.
9. Add cooked onion.
10. Cook the soup for 15 minutes over the medium-low heat.

Nutrition: 143 Calories 8.8g Fat 8.8g Protein

291. Eggplant Soup

Preparation Time: 12 minutes
Cooking Time: 31 minutes
Servings: 4
Ingredients:
- ½ cup tomatoes, chopped
- 2 eggplants, trimmed
- ¼ cup fresh parsley, chopped
- ¼ cup fresh cilantro, chopped
- 1 yellow onion, diced
- ½ teaspoon ground cumin
- ½ teaspoon cayenne pepper
- 1 celery stalk, chopped
- 1 tablespoon olive oil
- 1 teaspoon salt
- 1 garlic clove, peeled
- 1 teaspoon butter
- 4 cups chicken stock

Directions:
1. Peel eggplants and sprinkle them with olive oil and salt.
2. Preheat the oven to 360F.
3. Put the eggplants in the tray and transfer it in the preheated oven.
4. Bake the vegetables for 25 minutes.
5. Meanwhile, pour chicken stock in the pan.
6. Add chopped tomatoes, parsley, cilantro, ground cumin, cayenne pepper, celery stalk, and diced garlic clove.
7. Simmer the mixture for 5 minutes.
8. Meanwhile, heat the butter in the skillet.
9. Add onion and roast it until translucent.
10. Add the onion in the boiled chicken stock mixture.
11. When the eggplants are cooked, transfer them in the food processor and blend until smooth.
12. After this, put the blended eggplants in the chicken stock mixture.
13. Blend the soup until you get a creamy texture.
14. Simmer the soup for 5 minutes.

Nutrition: 137 Calories 5.7g Fat 4.2g Protein

292. Lemon Lamb Soup

Preparation Time: 12 minutes
Cooking Time: 51 minutes
Servings: 8
Ingredients:

- 1 ½-pound lamb bone in
- 4 eggs, beaten
- 2 cups lettuce, chopped
- 1 tablespoon chives, chopped
- ½ cup fresh dill, chopped
- ½ cup lemon juice
- 1 teaspoon salt
- ½ teaspoon white pepper
- 2 tablespoons avocado oil
- 5 cups of water

Directions:
1. Chop the lamb roughly and place in the pan.
2. Add avocado oil and roast the meat for 10 minutes over the medium heat. Stir it with the help of spatula from time to time.
3. Then sprinkle the meat with white pepper and salt. Fill water and bring the mixture to boil.
4. Scourge eggs and lemon juice.
5. Add a ½ cup of boiling water from the pan and whisk the egg mixture until smooth.
6. Add dill, chives, and lettuce in the soup. Stir well.
7. Cook the soup for 30 minutes over the medium-high heat.
8. Then add egg mixture and stir it fast to make the homogenous texture of the soup.
9. Cook it for 3 minutes more.

Nutrition: 360 Calories 22.9g Fat 33.6g Protein

293. Mushroom and Cheese Soup

Preparation Time: 14 minutes
Cooking Time: 18 minutes
Servings: 2
Ingredients:
- 1 cup cremini mushrooms, chopped
- 1 cup Cheddar cheese, shredded
- 2 cups of water
- ½ teaspoon salt
- 1 teaspoon dried thyme
- ½ teaspoon dried oregano
- 1 tablespoon fresh parsley, chopped
- 1 tablespoon olive oil
- 1 bell pepper, chopped

Directions:
1. Pour olive oil in the pan.

2. Add mushrooms and bell pepper. Roast the vegetables for 5 minutes over the medium heat.
3. Then sprinkle them with salt, thyme, and dried oregano.
4. Add parsley and water. Stir the soup well.
5. Cook the soup for 10 minutes.
6. After this, blend the soup until it is smooth and simmer it for 5 minutes more.
7. Stir in cheese until cheese is melted.
8. Ladle the cooked soup into the bowls. It is recommended to serve soup hot.

Nutrition: 320 Calories 26g Fat 15.7g Protein

294. Eggplant Stew

Preparation Time: 14 minutes
Cooking Time: 19 minutes
Servings: 4
Ingredients:
- ½ teaspoon cumin seeds
- 1 tablespoon coriander seeds
- ½ teaspoon mustard seeds
- 1 tablespoon olive oil
- 1 tablespoon ginger, grated
- 2 garlic cloves, minced
- 1 green chili pepper, chopped
- A pinch of cinnamon powder
- ½ teaspoon cardamom, ground
- ½ teaspoon turmeric powder
- 1 teaspoon lime juice
- 4 baby eggplants, cubed
- 1 cup low-sodium veggie stock
- 1 tablespoon cilantro, chopped

Directions:
1. Heat a pot with the oil over medium-high heat, add cumin, coriander, and mustard seeds, stir, and cook them for 5 minutes.
2. Add ginger, garlic, chili, cinnamon, cardamom, and turmeric, stir, and cook for 5 minutes more.
3. Add lime juice, eggplants, and stock, stir, cover, and cook over medium heat for 15 minutes. Add cilantro, stir, divide into bowls, and serve for lunch.

Nutrition: 270 Calories 4g Fat 9g Protein

295. Leeks Soup

Preparation Time: 12 minutes
Cooking Time: 75 minutes
Servings: 6

Ingredients:

- 2 gold potatoes, chopped
- 1 cup cauliflower florets
- Black pepper to the taste
- 5 leeks, chopped
- 4 garlic cloves, minced
- 1 yellow onion, chopped
- 3 tablespoons olive oil
- A handful parsley, chopped
- 4 cups low-sodium chicken stock

Directions:

1. Heat a pot with the oil over medium-high heat, add onion and garlic, stir, and cook for 5 minutes.
2. Add potatoes, cauliflower, black pepper, leeks, and stock, stir, bring to a simmer, cook over medium heat for 30 minutes, blend using an immersion blender, add parsley, stir, ladle into bowls, and serve.

Nutrition: 150 Calories 8g Fat 8g Protein

296. Pea Stew

Preparation Time: 19 minutes
Cooking Time: 23 minutes
Servings: 3

Ingredients:

- 1 carrot, cubed
- 1 yellow onion, chopped
- 1 and ½ tablespoons olive oil
- 1 celery stick, chopped
- 5 garlic cloves, minced
- 2 cups yellow peas
- 1 and ½ teaspoons cumin, ground
- 1 teaspoon sweet paprika
- ¼ teaspoon chili powder
- A pinch of black pepper
- ¼ teaspoon cinnamon powder
- ½ cup tomatoes, chopped
- Juice of ½ lemon
- 1-quart low-sodium veggie stock
- 1 tablespoon chives, chopped

Directions:

1. Heat a pot with the oil over medium heat, add carrots, onion, and celery, stir, and cook for 5-6 minutes.
2. Add garlic, peas, cumin, paprika, chili powder, pepper, cinnamon, tomatoes, lemon juice, peas, and stock, stir, bring to a

simmer, cook over medium heat for 20 minutes, add chives, toss, divide into bowls and serve.

Nutrition: 272 Calories 6g Fat 9g Protein

297. Chicken Leek Soup

Preparation Time: 12 minutes
Cooking Time: 35 minutes
Servings: 4

Ingredients:

- 1 cup cabbage, shredded
- 6 oz leek, chopped
- ½ yellow onion, diced
- 1-pound chicken breast, skinless, boneless
- 1 tablespoon butter
- 1 teaspoon salt
- ½ teaspoon dried oregano
- ½ teaspoon dried thyme
- 1 tablespoon canola oil
- 4 cups of water

Directions:

1. Chop the chicken breast into the cubes and place in the pan.
2. Add butter and canola oil.
3. Cook the chicken for 5 minutes. Stir it from time to time.
4. After this, add yellow onion and chopped leek.
5. Add salt, dried oregano, and thyme. Mix up the ingredients well and sauté for 5 minutes.
6. Then add water and cabbage.
7. Close the lid and cook soup over the medium heat for 25 minutes.

Nutrition: 222 Calories 9.4g Fat 25g Protein

298. Carrot Soup

Preparation Time: 14 minutes
Cooking Time: 31 minutes
Servings: 6

Ingredients:

- 5 cups beef broth
- 4 carrots, peeled
- 1 teaspoon dried thyme
- ½ teaspoon ground cumin
- 1 teaspoon salt
- 1 ½ cup potatoes, chopped
- 1 tablespoon olive oil
- ½ teaspoon ground black pepper

- 1 tablespoon lemon juice
- 1/3 cup fresh parsley, chopped
- 1 chili pepper, chopped
- 1 tablespoon tomato paste
- 1 tablespoon sour cream

Directions:
1. Line the baking tray with baking paper.
2. Put sweet potatoes and carrot on the tray and sprinkle with olive oil and salt.
3. Bake the vegetables for 25 minutes at 365F.
4. Meanwhile, pour the beef broth in the pan and bring it to boil.
5. Add dried thyme, ground cumin, chopped chili pepper, and tomato paste.
6. When the vegetables are cooked, add them in the pan.
7. Boil the vegetables until they are soft.
8. Then blend the mixture with the help of the blender until smooth.
9. Simmer it for 2 minutes and add lemon juice. Stir well.
10. Then add sour cream and chopped parsley. Stir well.
11. Simmer the soup for 3 minutes more.

Nutrition: 123 Calories 4.1g Fat 5.3g Protein

299. Chickpeas Stew

Preparation Time: 13 minutes
Cooking Time: 41 minutes
Servings: 4

Ingredients:
- 1 teaspoon olive oil
- 1 cup chickpeas
- 4 garlic cloves, minced
- 1 yellow onion, chopped
- 1 green chili pepper, chopped
- 1 teaspoon coriander, ground
- ½ teaspoon cumin, ground
- ½ teaspoon sweet paprika

- 2 tomatoes, chopped
- 1 and ½ cups low-sodium veggie stock
- A pinch of black pepper
- 3 cups spinach leaves
- 1 tablespoon lemon juice

Directions:
1. Heat a pot with the oil over medium heat, add garlic, onion, and chili pepper, stir, and cook for 5 minutes.
2. Add coriander, cumin, paprika and black pepper, stir and cook for 5 minutes more.
3. Add chickpeas, tomatoes, stock, and lemon juice, stir, cover the pot, cook over medium heat for 25 minutes, add spinach, cook for 5 minutes more, divide into bowls, and serve.

Nutrition: 270 Calories 7g Fat 9g Protein

300. Green Beans Stew

Preparation Time: 13 minutes
Cooking Time: 22 minutes
Servings: 4

Ingredients:
- 2 tablespoons olive oil
- 2 carrots, chopped
- 1 yellow onion, chopped
- 20 ounces green beans
- 2 garlic cloves, minced
- 7 ounces canned tomatoes, chopped
- 5 cups low-sodium veggie stock
- 1 tablespoon parsley, chopped

Directions:
1. Heat a pot with the oil, over medium heat, add onion, stir, and cook for 5 minutes.
2. Add carrots, green beans, garlic, tomatoes, black pepper, and stock, stir, cover, and simmer over medium heat for 20 minutes.
3. Add parsley, divide into bowls, and serve for lunch.

Nutrition: 281 Calories 5g Fat 11g Protein

301. Walnut Chocolate Cupcakes

Preparation Time: 9 minutes
Cooking Time: 40 minutes
Serving: 6

Ingredients:
- Buckwheat flour, 1 ½ cup
- Sugar, 2 cups
- Cocoa powder, 1 cup
- Salt, ½ tsp
- Almond milk, 1 ½ cup
- Vanilla extract, ½ tsp
- Coconut oil, ½ cup
- Walnuts, 2 tbsp
- Baking powder, 1 tsp

Direction:
1. Preheat your oven to 180 °C. Lay baking paper on the bottom of a cupcake pan.
2. Mix in flour, cocoa, and sugar and mix through. Mix in the vanilla extract, almond milk, coconut oil, walnuts, and baking powder and mix until it turns into a batter. Add boiling water and beat until it's evenly mixed in with the batter.
3. Pour in the batter evenly across cake cases, filling up to ¾ of each case. Bake for up to 18 minutes and let cool.
4. Optionally, you can add vegan icing.

Nutrition: 411 calories 21g fats 19g protein

302. Sirtfood Kale Smoothie

Preparation Time: 6 minutes
Cooking Time: 0 minutes
Serving: 1

Ingredients:
- Kale, finely chopped, 2 cups
- Raw honey, 2 tsp
- 1 banana
- 1 apple
- Fresh ginger, chopped, 1 tsp
- Half a glass of water, if needed

Direction:
1. Blend all the ingredients together and enjoy!

Nutrition: 107 calories 11g fats 6g protein

303. Fruity Matcha Smoothie

Preparation Time: 8 minutes
Cooking Time: 0 minutes
Serving: 2

Ingredients:
- Matcha powder, 2 tsp
- Milk, 1 ½ cup
- Raw honey, 2 tsp
- Melon, chopped, two cups
- Mint leaves, fresh, 2-3 pieces
- Lemon or lime juice, 1-2 tbsp

Direction:
1. Mix all the ingredients into a blender, starting from the liquids to melon, and top with milk, spices, and lemon/lime juice. Blend all together and enjoy!

Nutrition: 174 calories 17g fat 6g protein

304. Fresh SirtFruit Compote

Preparation Time: 19 minutes
Cooking Time: 0 minutes
Serving: 4

Ingredients:
- Green tea, fresh, ½ cup
- 1 lemon, halved
- 1 chopped apple
- Red grapes, seedless, 1 cup
- Strawberries, 2 cups
- Raw honey, 1 tsp

Directions:
1. Cook fresh green tea and 1 tsp of raw honey. Add the juice from ½ lemon and let cool.
2. Pour the grapes and strawberries into a bowl and pour the tea over the fruit. Serve after a couple of minutes.

Nutrition: 211 calories 14g fat 4g protein

305. Spicy Sirtfood Ricotta

Preparation Time: 11 minutes
Cooking Time: 34 minutes
Serving: 5

Ingredients:
- Extra virgin olive oil, 2 tsp
- Unsalted ricotta cheese, 200 g
- 1 chopped red onion
- 1 tsp of fresh ginger

- 1 finely sliced garlic clove
- 1 finely sliced green chili
- 1 cup diced cherry tomatoes
- ½ tsp ground cumin
- ½ tsp ground coriander
- ½ tsp mild chili powder
- Chopped parsley, ½ cup
- Fresh spinach leaves, 2 cups

Direction:

1. Heat olive oil in a lidded pan over high heat. Toss in the ricotta cheese, seasoning it with pepper and sea salt. Fry until it turns golden and removes from the pan.
2. Add the onion to the pan and reduce the heat. Fry the onion with chili, ginger, and garlic for around eight minutes and add the chopped tomatoes. Close lid and cook for another five minutes.
3. Add the remaining spices and sea salt to the cheese, put the cheese back into the pan and stir, adding spinach, coriander, and parsley. Cover and cook for 3 minutes.

Nutrition: 388 calories 27g fat 13g protein

306. Sirtfood Baked Potatoes

Preparation Time: 12 minutes

Cooking Time: 42 minutes

Serving: 8

Ingredients:

- Potatoes, 5 pieces
- Extra virgin olive oil, 2 tbsp
- Organic red wine, 1 tbsp
- 2 finely chopped red onions
- 4 finely chopped garlic cloves
- Finely chopped ginger, 1 tsp
- 1 chopped Bird's eye chili pepper
- Powdered cumin, 1 tbsp
- Ground turmeric, 1 tbsp
- Water, 1 tbsp
- Tomatoes, 2 small cans
- Cocoa powder, 2 tbsp
- Parsley, 2 tbsp
- A pinch of salt
- A pinch of pepper

Direction:

1. Ready oven to 200 °C. Bake potatoes for one hour. In the meantime, fry onions in olive oil for five minutes until they're soft.

Add chili, garlic, cumin, and ginger and cook for another minute on low heat.

2. Add a tablespoon of water to prevent dryness. Mix in the tomato, chickpeas, pepper, and cocoa powder and let simmer for 45 minutes until the sauce becomes thick. Add parsley, salt, and pepper and serve with potatoes.

Nutrition: 391 calories 22g fat 14g protein

307. Spicy Quinoa with Kale

Preparation Time: 17 minutes

Cooking Time: 32 minutes

Serving: 4

Ingredients:

- Canned quinoa, 1 can
- Extra virgin olive oil, 1 tbsp
- 1 sliced red onion
- 3 finely chopped garlic cloves
- 1 finely chopped bird's eye chili
- Turmeric, 2 tsp
- Coconut milk, 2 cups
- Water, 1 cup
- Kale, chopped, 1 cup
- Buckwheat, 2 cups

Direction:

1. Fry the onions for five minutes in olive oil. Add ginger, garlic, and chili, and fry for another five minutes. Toss in the turmeric and wait for another minute. Then add in the quinoa and coconut milk, pour in a glass of water, and cook for 20 minutes. Cook kale for another five minutes.
2. Halfway through cooking the quinoa, fry the buckwheat in water for ten minutes. Drain and serve with the quinoa.

Nutrition: 401 calories 29g fat 17g protein

308. Mediterranean Sirtfood Quinoa

Preparation Time: 16 minutes

Cooking Time: 29 minutes

Serving: 5

Ingredients:

- Quinoa, 2 cups
- Extra virgin olive oil, 1 tbsp
- Finely chopped garlic cloves, 1 tbsp
- Fresh ginger, chopped, 1 tsp
- 1 sliced bird's eye chili

- 1 sliced red bell pepper
- Ground turmeric, ½ tsp
- Ground cumin, 1 tsp
- A pinch of salt
- A pinch of pepper
- Chopped kale, 1 cup
- Lemon juice, 2 tbsp

Direction:
1. Start off by cooking the quinoa. Pour into a pot, cover with two parts water, and bring to a boil. Let it boil for up to thirty minutes.
2. During the last five minutes, pan-fry the vegetables except kale in olive oil for up to five minutes. Once the vegetables have softened, add cumin, paprika, turmeric, salt, and pepper.
3. Stir through and insert quinoa. Stir again, add vegetable stock, and pan-fry until the excess liquid vapors out. Serve and enjoy!

Nutrition: 487 calories 31g fats 24g protein

309. Eggplant and Potatoes in Red Wine

Preparation Time: 8 minutes
Cooking Time: 43 minutes
Serving: 6
Ingredients:
- 1 large diced potato
- Finely chopped parsley, 2 tsp
- 1 sliced red onion
- Sliced kale, 1 cup
- 1 finely chopped garlic clove
- Sliced eggplant, 2 cups
- Vegetable stock, 1 ½ cup
- Tomato sauce, 1 tsp
- Extra virgin olive oil, 1 tbsp

Direction:
1. Preheat your oven to 220 °C.
2. Boil the potatoes for 6 minutes, strain, and roast in the oven for 45 minutes on 1 tsp of extra virgin olive oil. Turn potatoes over every ten minutes so that they cook evenly. Add chopped parsley once the potatoes are done.
3. Stir-fry the garlic, onions, and eggplant on olive oil for up to five minutes. Add the vegetable stock and tomato sauce, bring to

a boil, and let simmer up to 15 minutes on low medium heat.
4. Serve with potatoes.

Nutrition: 491 calories 32g fats 16g protein

310. Potatoes with Onion Rings in Red Wine

Preparation Time: 11 minutes
Cooking Time: 32 minutes
Serving: 4
Ingredients:
- Diced potatoes, 3 cups
- Extra virgin olive oil, 1 tbsp
- Finely chopped parsley, ½ tbsp
- Red wine, 1 tbsp
- Vegetable stock, 150ml
- Tomato sauce, 1 tsp
- 1 sliced red onion
- Kale, sliced, 1 cup
- A pinch of salt
- A pinch of pepper
- 1 chopped bird's eye chili

Direction:
1. Boil the potatoes for up to five minutes and drain. Roast at 22o °C for 45 minutes. Add the parsley after taking the potatoes out of the oven.
2. Fry the onions for up to seven minutes in 1 tsp of olive oil and add kale and garlic. Add vegetable stock and let boil for up to two minutes. Serve alongside potatoes.

Nutrition: 341 calories 19g fats 8g protein

311. Sweet Potatoes with Grilled Tofu and Mushrooms

Preparation Time: 9 minutes
Cooking Time: 28 minutes
Serving: 4
Ingredients:
- Tofu, 14 oz
- Chicken stock, 1 cup
- Buckwheat flour, 1 tbsp
- Water, 1 tbsp
- Red wine, 1 tbsp
- Brown sugar, 1 tsp
- Tomato sauce, 1 tbsp
- Soy sauce, 1 tbsp

- 1 finely chopped garlic clove
- Ginger, finely chopped, 1 tsp
- Extra virgin olive oil, 1 tbsp
- Mushrooms, sliced, 1 cup
- 1 sliced red onion
- Kale, chopped, 2 cups
- Sweet potato, diced, 400 g
- Buckwheat, 1 cup
- Chopped parsley, 2 tbsp
- Vegetable stock, 2 cups

Direction:

1. Drain tofu by wrapping it in kitchen paper as you prepare other ingredients.
2. Cook buckwheat in vegetable stock. Add red wine, the tomato sauce, soy sauce, brown sugar, ginger, and garlic.
3. Stir-fry mushrooms for up to three minutes until cooked through. Add tofu and stir fry until the cheese turns golden. Remove from the pan and set aside.
4. Add the onions and stir fry for two minutes, upon which you'll add the diced sweet potatoes.
5. Pour more water or vegetable stock if needed, and add the sauce a minute or two before finishing. Combine the remaining ingredients and serve.

Nutrition: 361 calories 27g fat 18g protein

312. Buckwheat Stew

Preparation Time: 24 minutes
Cooking Time: 29 minutes
Serving: 5

Ingredients:

- 1 finely chopped red onion
- 1 finely chopped large carrot
- 1 finely chopped garlic clove
- Finely chopped celery, 3 tbsp
- Extra virgin olive oil, 1 tbsp
- 1 finely chopped garlic clove
- 1 finely chopped bird's eye chili
- Vegetable stock, 2 cups
- Rosemary, ½ tsp
- Basil, ½ tsp
- Dill, ½ tsp
- Celery, finely chopped, 1 tbsp
- Canned tomatoes, 400 g
- Buckwheat, 2 cups

- Kale, chopped, ½ cup
- Parsley, chopped, 1 tbsp

Direction:

1. Fry the onions, garlic, chili, celery, carrot, and spice herbs in olive oil on low heat. Once the onion turns soft, add the vegetable stock and tomato sauce.
2. Once the stock boils, add the buckwheat and let simmer for another half an hour. Add kale and parsley during the last five minutes.

Nutrition: 394 calories 24g fats 17g protein

313. Sirtfood Curry

Preparation Time: 13 minutes
Cooking Time: 27 minutes
Serving: 4

Ingredients:

- Skim milk
- Quinoa, 2 cups
- Chickpeas, 4 cups
- Potatoes, 14 oz
- Spinach, 1 ½ cup
- Tomato sauce, 1 tbsp
- 3 crushed garlic cloves
- Ground ginger, 1 tsp
- Ground turmeric, 3 tsp
- Ground coriander, 1 tsp
- Bird's eye chili powder, 1 tsp
- A pinch of salt
- A pinch of pepper

Direction:

1. Cook the potatoes for up to 30 minutes and drain. Move to a large pan and add all the ingredients except quinoa and bring to a boil.
2. Once the mixture has boiled, add the quinoa and chickpeas, and up to 1 ½ cup of water if needed. Decrease heat and simmer for 30 minutes while mixing regularly.

Nutrition: 374 calories 26g protein 14g fats

314. Onion Mushroom Salsa

Preparation Time: 9 minutes
Cooking Time: 14 minutes
Serving: 3

Ingredients:

- Mushrooms, 1 1/5 cups

- Ground turmeric, 2 tsp
- Lime juice, 1 tbsp
- Chopped Kale, 1 cup
- 1 sliced red onion
- Arugula, 1 cup
- Fresh ginger, chopped, 1 tsp

Direction:

1. Fry the mushrooms on a thin layer of extra virgin olive oil for up to five minutes, while stirring and making sure they're cooking evenly. As you fry, sprinkle turmeric over the mushrooms. Add kale half-way through, letting it soften only lightly. Prepare a plate and lay out fresh arugula.
2. Incorporate remaining ingredients together to make a salsa. Serve one dish next to another and enjoy!

Nutrition: 214 calories 1g fats 6g protein

315. Sirtfood Tofu Sesame Salad

Preparation Time: 14 minutes
Cooking Time: 4 minutes
Serving: 4
Ingredients:

- Sesame seeds, 1 tbsp
- 1 sliced cucumber
- Kale, chopped, 1 cup
- Arugula, 1 cup
- 1 fine sliced red onion
- Chopped parsley, ¼ cup
- Grilled tofu, diced, 2 cups
- Extra virgin olive oil, 2 tbsp
- Lime juice, 2 tbsp
- Soy sauce, 2 tbsp
- Raw honey, 1 tsp

Direction:

1. First, start by roasting sesame seeds for up to two minutes. Set aside to cool. If you've bought raw tofu, grill briefly on a thin layer of olive oil. Leave the remaining oil for salad dressing.
2. Mix vegetables and spices into a bowl. Toss in the chopped grilled tofu and sesame seeds, and mix to distribute evenly throughout the salad. To finish off, drizzle with lime juice and olive oil.

Nutrition: 451 calories 28g fat 14g protein

316. Cucumber Rolls on Cauliflower Salad

Preparation Time: 27 minutes
Cooking Time: 4 minutes
Serving: 4

Ingredients

- 600 g small cucumber (2 small cucumbers)
- 1 carrot
- ½ orange bell pepper
- 1 stick celery
- 1 avocado
- 2 tbsp sprouts
- salt
- pepper
- 1 cauliflower
- 50 g raisins
- 3 tbsp olive oil
- 3 tbsp lemon juice
- 1 ground cumin
- 1 pinch cinnamon
- chili flakes
- 4 stems parsley

Direction

1. Clean and wash the cucumbers and cut or cut lengthways into thin slices; cut the cut of the cucumber into narrow long strips.
2. Peel the carrot. Halve, core, and wash the peppers. Clean and wash the celery stick. Cut everything into thin finger-length strips.
3. Halve the avocado, remove the core, lift the pulp from the skin and cut into small slices. Wash the sprouts thoroughly and let them drain. Bundle some vegetable strips each and wrap them with a few sprouts in 1 cucumber slice, season with salt and pepper. Chill until served.
4. Clean, wash, and divide the cauliflower into small florets. Cook cauliflower in boiling salted water for about 5 minutes. Then drain, quench and let cool. Finely chop the cauliflower, mix with the raisins and oil. Season the cabbage with lemon juice, salt, pepper, cumin, cinnamon, and chili flakes.
5. Wash the parsley, shake dry and chop the leaves. Spread the cauliflower on a plate.

Put 2–3 cucumber rolls and parsley on each.
Nutrition: 481 calories 26g fat 13g protein

317. Sweet Potato Salad with Spinach, Apple and Quinoa

Preparation Time: 23 minutes
Cooking Time: 14 minutes
Serving: 4

Ingredients

- 450 g large sweet potatoes (1 large sweet potato)
- salt
- pepper
- 1 map. curry powder
- 3 tbsp olive oil
- 200 g baby spinach
- 1 lemon
- 30 g walnut kernels (2 tbsp)
- 1 green apple
- 1 tsp maple syrup
- 2 tbsp vegetable broth
- 15 g puffed quinoa (4 tbsp)
- 5 g chive blossom (1 handful)

Direction

1. Skin sweet potato and cut it into bite-size pieces. Mix with salt, pepper, 1 pinch of curry and 1 tablespoon of oil and place on a baking sheet lined with baking paper.
2. Cook the sweet potato in a prep oven at 200 ° C (180 ° C fan oven; gas: setting 3), turning it bite-proof in 20 minutes, turning occasionally. Pullout and let cool for 10 minutes.
3. In the meantime, clean, wash and shake spinach dry. Drizzle lemon juice. Roughly chop walnuts. Clean, wash, quarter, core the apple, cut into small pieces and drizzle with half of the lemon juice.
4. Mix the remaining lemon juice with maple syrup, salt, pepper and remaining oil into a dressing.
5. Combine ingredients with the dressing in a bowl and divide into 4 bowls. Sprinkle the salad with quinoa and chive flowers.

Nutrition: 391 calories 26g fat 14g protein

318. Avocado and Mozzarella Salad Bowl

Preparation Time: 19 minutes
Cooking Time: 0 minutes
Serving: 4

Ingredients

- 60 g avocado
- Tomato 50 g
- Mozzarella cheese 40g
- Endive salad 20 g
- Raw lamb lettuce 10 g
- 2 tablespoons olive oil
- 1 fresh basil
- Sea salt 1 pinch
- Black pepper 1 pinch

Direction

1. Wash the lettuce leaves, drain well, then chop them into small bowls.
2. Wash and slice the tomatoes.
3. Slice mozzarella cheese. Wash the basil, shake to dry, and peel the leaves.
4. Remove the core by halving the avocado.
5. Take out avocado pulp from the skin and cut it into strips.
6. Add avocado, tomato, mozzarella, and basil to the salad.
7. Sprinkle with olive oil and season with a teaspoon of salt and pepper in a salad bowl.

Nutrition: 358 calories 21g fat 17g protein

319. Chicory and Orange Salad

Preparation Time: 39 minutes
Cooking Time: 0 minutes
Serving: 4

Ingredients

- 2 chicory
- 2 oranges
- 1 tsp honey
- 1 tbsp white balsamic vinegar
- 2 tablespoons of walnut oil
- Salt and pepper
- at will walnut kernels

Direction

1. Wash the chicory and cut into rough strips.
2. Fillets of 1.5 oranges, squeeze out the remaining half of the orange.
3. Mix the orange juice, honey, vinegar, oil, salt, and pepper well.
4. Add chicory and orange fillets and let steep for half an hour. Sprinkle with chopped walnut kernels as desired.

Nutrition: 314 calories 21g fats 14g protein

320. Mango and Avocado Salad with Watercress

Preparation Time: 14 minutes
Cooking Time: 0 minutes
Serving: 3

Ingredients

Salad:

- 3 handfuls of watercress
- 1 mango
- 1 avocado
- 1 spring onion
- 2 tbsp coriander leaves
- A little lime juices

Dressing:

- 2 cloves of garlic, finely diced
- 2/3 tsp ginger, finely diced
- 3 tbsp light sesame oil
- 1 tablespoon of rice vinegar
- Salt and pepper
- Some brown sugar
- 1 chili pepper without seeds
- a little dark sesame oil

Direction

Salad:

1. Clean, wash, spin dry watercress and cut it into bite-size pieces.
2. Peel the mango and avocado, remove the stones and cut the pulp into wedges. Immediately drizzle the avocado with a little lime juice so that it doesn't turn brown.
3. Rinse and slice spring onions into thin rings.
4. Pluck coriander leaves a little smaller depending on the size.

Dressing:

5. Sweat the garlic and ginger in half a tablespoon of heated light sesame oil, place in a bowl and let cool.
6. Mix in the vinegar, salt, pepper, and sugar.
7. Fold in the remaining light oil.
8. Add the chili to taste.

9. Season with the dark sesame oil.

Nutrition: 361 calories 28g fats 16g protein

321. Coconut Pancakes with Kiwi Salad

Preparation Time: 13 minutes
Cooking Time: 4 minutes
Serving: 4

Ingredients

Kiwi Salad

- 4 kiwi fruits
- 4 tbsp maple syrup
- 2 tbsp lemon juice

Pancakes

- 250 g flour
- 3 level teaspoons of baking powder
- 1.5 tablespoons of sugar
- salt
- 4 eggs
- 200 ml of coconut milk
- clarified butter

Direction

Kiwi Salad

1. Peel and dice the kiwi fruit. Then mix with the maple syrup and lemon juice.

Pancakes

2. Mix the flour, baking powder, sugar and 1 pinch of salt in a bowl.
3. Add the eggs and coconut milk and mix everything with the whisk to a smooth dough.
4. Heat a coated pan and melt approx. 1/2 tbsp clarified butter in it.
5. Put the dough in tablespoon-sized portions in the pan and bake for 4 minutes on each side.
6. Process the rest of the dough as well, adding a little clarified butter if necessary.
7. Serve the pancakes with the kiwi salad.

Nutrition: 391 calories 29g fats 12g protein

322. Salads with Oranges

Preparation Time: 13 minutes
Cooking Time: 0 minutes
Serving: 4

Ingredients

- 1 small red cabbage
- 2 teaspoons of salt
- 2 carrots
- 2 oranges
- 1 bunch of spring onions
- 1/2 bunch of parsley
- 3 tablespoons of balsamic vinegar
- 4 spoons of olive oil
- 1/2 tablespoon of mustard
- 1 pinch of Ceylon cinnamon powder
- black pepper, freshly ground
- 15 g of butter
- 2 spoons of honey
- 100 g of walnuts

Direction

1. Remove the wilted leaves from the red cabbage and cut it into quarters. Remove the stem.
2. Now cut the red cabbage into skinny strips or plan with the food processor.
3. Mix in a bowl with the salt and knead vigorously for 5 minutes so that everything mixes well.
4. Peel the oranges and peel off the white skin with a knife. Get the juice. Then cut the oranges into slices.
5. Mix vinegar, mustard, cinnamon, a little pepper, olive oil and orange juice and pour over the red cabbage. Let it go well.
6. Coarsely chop almost all the nuts, set aside only a few halves for decoration.
7. Heat the butter in a pan: first brown the decorative walnuts, then lightly brown the chopped walnuts. Chopped walnuts don't take long, so start with the halves.
8. Now add the honey to the nuts and mix well. Now immediately distribute the nuts on a plate and let them cool, otherwise they will join together.
9. Peel the carrots and coarsely grate them.
10. Squeeze the parsley and finely chop it.
11. Rinse spring onions and cut them into slices. Set aside some onions for decoration.

Nutrition: 341 calories 21g fats 18g protein

323. Autumn Salad

Preparation Time: 11 minutes
Cooking Time: 12 minutes
Serving: 4

Ingredients

- 150 g of corn salad
- 2 pears

- 60g of pink grapes
- 2 tbsp lemon juice
- 12 kernels of walnuts
- 2 spoons of honey
- 1 roll of goat cheese
- 2 spoons of butter
- 4 spoons of balsamic vinegar
- 6 spoons of water
- Salt and pepper from the mill
- 4 tablespoons of walnut or olive oil

Direction

1. Read the lamb's lettuce, clean, wash and spin dry.
2. The pear wash, cut into quarters and remove the seeds. Cut the quarters lengthways into narrow slits and immediately turn them into lemon juice.
3. Wash the grapes, pluck them from the stems, cut them in half and, if necessary, remove the stones.
4. Slice walnuts and roast them in a pan without fat until they smell slightly, then take them out.
5. Cut the goat cheese into finger-thick slices and grill briefly in the oven on a baking sheet (under baking paper).
6. Clean the pan and melt the butter in it. Sauté the pear slices in it, turning once. Add the honey and swirl everything well.
7. Deglaze with vinegar and water and bring to the boil briefly.
8. Remove from the heat, let the pear slices cool lukewarm in the brew, then remove from the brew.
9. Season the broth well, then stir in the oil vigorously.
10. Mix the lamb's lettuce in a bowl with the dressing and grapes, fold in the pear slices.
11. Sprinkle with walnuts and arrange the goat cheese on the plate.

Nutrition: 464 calories 31g fat 17g protein

324. Creamy Salmon Salad

Preparation Time: 16 minutes
Cooking Time: 32 minutes
Serving: 4

Ingredients

- 1 salmon fillet (130g)
- 40g mixed lettuce leaves

- 40g young spinach leaves
- 2 radishes, edged and thinly chopped
- Cucumber 5 cm (50 g), cut into pieces
- 2 spring onions, peeled and cut into slices
- 1 small handful (10 g) of parsley, coarsely chopped

For dressing:

- 1 teaspoon low-fat mayonnaise
- 1 tablespoon of natural yogurt
- 1 tablespoon rice vinegar
- 2 mint leaves, finely chopped
- Salt and freshly ground black pepper

Direction

1. Oven preheats to 200 ° C (180 ° C fan / Gas 6).
2. Situate salmon filet on a baking tray and bake for 18 minutes. Remove, and set aside from the oven. The salmon in the salad is equally lovely and hot or cold. If your salmon has skin, just cook the skin side down and remove the salmon from the skin after frying, using a slice of bread. When cooked, it should slide off easily.
3. Mix mayonnaise, yogurt, rice wine vinegar, mint leaves and salt and pepper then put aside for 7 minutes.
4. Situate the salad leaves and spinach with the radishes, cucumber, spring onions and parsley in a plate and top with salmon then sprinkle over the dressing.

Nutrition: 366 calories 27g fat 14g protein

325. May Beet Salad with Cucumber

Preparation Time: 19 minutes
Cooking Time: 10 minutes
Serving: 4

Ingredients

- 3 may turnips
- 1 cucumber
- 1 spring onion
- 2 stems parsley
- 150 g Greek yogurt
- 1 tbsp apple cider vinegar
- 1 tsp honey
- 1 tsp mustard
- sea-salt
- cayenne pepper

- pepper

Direction

1. Clean, peel and slice the turnips. Clean and wash the cucumber and also slicer. Rinse and cut the spring onions into rings. Put everything in a salad bowl and mix.
2. Wash parsley, shake dry and chop finely. Mix a dressing with yoghurt, apple cider vinegar, honey, mustard and 2–3 tbsp water. Season with salt and cayenne pepper.
3. Combine salad dressing with the mayonnaise and cucumber and let it steep for about 10 minutes, then grind it with pepper and serve.

Nutrition: 369 calories 19g fat 8g protein

326. Lentil Salad with Spinach, Rhubarb and Asparagus

Preparation Time: 14 minutes
Cooking Time: 0 minutes
Serving: 5

Ingredients

- 100 g beluga lentils
- 2 tbsp olive oil
- salt
- 250 g white asparagus
- 100 g rhubarb
- 1 tsp honey
- 50 g baby spinach (2 handfuls)
- 20 g pumpkin seeds

Direction

1. Bring the beluga lentils to the boil with three times the amount of water. Cook over medium heat for about 25 minutes. Drain, rinse and drain. Mix with 1 tablespoon of olive oil and a pinch of salt. In the meantime, wash, clean, peel and cut asparagus into pieces. Wash, clean and cut the rhubarb into pieces.
2. Heat 1 tablespoon of olive oil in a pan and fry the asparagus in it for about 8 minutes over medium heat, turning occasionally. Then add rhubarb and honey and fry and salt for another 5 minutes. Wash spinach and spin dry. Roughly chop the pumpkin seeds.
3. Arrange spinach with lentils, asparagus, and rhubarb on two plates and serve sprinkled with pumpkin seeds.

Nutrition: 381 calories 30g fat 16g protein

327. Spicy Onion Meatballs with Potato Salad

Preparation Time: 14 minutes
Cooking Time: 28 minutes
Serving: 4

Ingredients

- 400 g small potatoes
- 1 bunch radish
- 1 cucumber
- 1 bunch chives
- 2nd small onions
- 400 g beef steak or beef
- 1 egg
- 2 tbsp oatmeal
- 1 tbsp low-fat quark
- pepper
- salt
- 2 tsp rapeseed oil
- 250 ml classic vegetable broth
- 1 tbsp herbal vinegar

Direction

1. Wash the potatoes thoroughly, put them in a saucepan, cover with water and bring to a boil. Cover and cook for about 20 minutes.
2. In the meantime, wash, clean and slice radishes.
3. Peel and halve the cucumber with a peeler, halve the halves lengthways and remove the seeds with a spoon. Slice the cucumber.
4. Wash the chives, shake dry and cut the stalks into rolls.
5. Peel the onions and grate them in a bowl.
6. Add the mince, egg, oatmeal and quark. Season with pepper, knead well and form 4 meatballs with moistened hands.
7. Slowly fry brown on both sides in the hot oil in a coated pan over low heat. Heat the broth in a small saucepan.
8. Drain the potatoes, quench under cold water. Peel potatoes. It is best to impale it with a fork and remove the bowl with a small knife. Cut the potatoes into slices directly over a bowl and pour the hot broth over them.

9. Pour vinegar over the potatoes as well. Mix in the cucumber slices, radishes and chive rolls. Salt, pepper and serve with the meatballs.

Nutrition: 488 calories 34g fats 28g protein

328. Tomato and Zucchini Salad with Feta

Preparation Time: 13 minutes
Cooking Time: 0 minutes
Serving: 4

Ingredients
- 2 zucchinis
- 4 tbsp olive oil
- salt
- pepper
- 400 g tomatoes
- 200 g cherry tomatoes
- 3 spring onions
- 1 bunch basil (20 g)
- 2 tbsp apple cider vinegar
- 100 g feta (45% fat in dry matter)

Direction
1. Clean, wash, and cut zucchini. Heat 1 tablespoon of oil in a pan, fry the zucchini in it over medium heat for 5 minutes. Season with salt and pepper.
2. Clean, wash, and chop tomatoes. Wash and halve cherry tomatoes. Wash the spring onions and cut them into rings. Wash the basil, shake dry and pick the leaves.
3. Mix zucchini, tomatoes, cherry tomatoes, and basil. Add the remaining oil and apple cider vinegar, mix, and season with salt and pepper. Crumble the feta. Serve the salad sprinkled with feta.

Nutrition 355 calories 21g fat 13g protein

329. Cucumber and Radish Salad with Feta

Preparation Time: 13 minutes
Cooking Time: 0 minutes
Serving: 4

Ingredients
- 1½ cucumbers
- 1 bunch radish
- 1 bunch rocket (80 g)
- 4th gherkins
- 200 g feta

- 4 tbsp olive oil
- 3 tbsp lemon juice
- 1 tsp mustard
- 1 tsp honey
- salt
- pepper

Direction
1. Clean, wash, and cut cucumber and radishes into thin slices. Wash the rocket and shake it dry. Halve the pickled gherkins lengthways and cut into slices. Crumble the feta.
2. Whisk for the dressing oil with lemon juice, mustard, and honey, season with salt and pepper. Mix the cucumber, radish, and pickled cucumber slices and mix with the dressing. Place on a plate and sprinkle with the feta and rocket.

Nutrition: 264 calories 18g fat 8g protein

330. Baked Salmon Salad with Creamy Mint Dressing

Preparation Time: 16 minutes
Cooking Time: 28 minutes
Serving: 4

Ingredients
- 1 salmon fillet (130g)
- 40g mixed lettuce leaves
- 40g young spinach leaves
- 2 radishes, edged and thinly chopped
- Cucumber 5 cm (50 g), cut into pieces
- 2 spring onions, peeled and cut into slices
- 1 small handful (10 g) of parsley, coarsely chopped

For dressing:
- 1 teaspoon low-fat mayonnaise
- 1 tablespoon of natural yogurt
- 1 tablespoon rice vinegar
- 2 mint leaves, finely chopped
- Salt and freshly ground black pepper

Direction
1. Oven preheats to 200 ° C
2. Position salmon filet on a baking tray then bake for 16minutes. Pull it out, and keep aside from the oven.
3. Mix mayonnaise, mint leaves, yogurt, rice wine vinegar, and season well. Set aside for 5 minutes.

4. Arrange the salad leaves and spinach with the radishes, cucumber, spring onions and parsley. Situate salmon over the salad and drizzle the dressing.

Nutrition: 361 calories 22g fat 14g protein

331. Green Juice Salad

Preparation Time: 12 minutes
Cooking Time: 0 minutes
Servings: 1

Ingredients:

- 2 handfuls of chopped kale
- 1 handful of chopped arugulas
- 1 tablespoon chopped parsley
- 2 stalks of celery, sliced into bite-sized pieces
- ½ green apple, chopped into bite-sized pieces
- 6 walnuts, crushed
- 1 tablespoon olive oil
- ½ lemon, juiced
- 1 tsp grated ginger
- A pinch of salt and pepper

Directions:

1. Mix the juice of the lemon, ginger, seasonings, and olive oil into a small jar or small Tupperware container. Set aside until you are ready to eat.
2. In a large bowl or large Tupperware container, add your kale, arugula, parsley, celery, apple, and walnut. Mix it up until well combined and set aside until you are ready to eat.
3. When you are ready to eat it, shake up your dressing, then add it to the bowl and mix thoroughly.

Nutrition: 23g fat 12g protein 14 Calories

332. Strawberry Buckwheat Salad

Preparation Time: 21 minutes
Cooking time: 0 minutes
Servings: 2

Ingredients:

- 2/3 cup buckwheat
- 2 tablespoon turmeric powder
- 1 whole avocado, diced
- 1 whole tomato, diced
- ¼ cup diced red onion

- ¼ cup diced and pitted dates
- 2 tablespoon capers
- 1 ½ cups roughly chopped parsley
- 1 1/3 cups sliced strawberries
- Juice from 1 lemon
- Two cups of chopped arugula

Directions:

1. Cook your buckwheat with the turmeric powder added. Make sure that you follow the instructions that came on the package. When it is done, drain it and set it aside until it has completely cooled off
2. Mix all of your chopped ingredients together, keeping the arugula separate. Add the lemon and oil. Place all ingredients on top of the arugula and serve.

Nutrition: 122 Calories 13g Fat 9g Protein

333. Salmon Salad

Preparation Time: 23 minutes
Cooking Time: 0 minutes
Servings: 3

Ingredients:

- 3 cups of arugula
- 3 cups of chicory leaves
- ½ cup sliced smoked salmon
- ½ of an avocado, peeled and sliced
- 6 walnuts, crushed,
- 1 tablespoon capers
- 1 large Medjool date, pitted and chopped
- 1 tablespoon of olive oil
- ¼ lemon, juiced
- 10 sprigs of parsley, chopped
- 1 medium stalk of celery, chopped
- ½ cup thinly sliced red onion

Directions:

1. Chop and prepare all ingredients
2. Place salad leaves into a large bowl
3. Mix the remaining ingredients together in another bowl and pour on top of the leaves. Serve.

Nutrition: 188 Calories 26g Protein 6.2g fat

334. Chicken Sirtfood Salad

Preparation Time: 27 minutes
Cooking Time: 0 minutes
Servings: 1

Ingredients:

- ¼ cup plain Greek yogurt

- ¼ lemon, juiced
- 1 tsp cilantro, finely chopped
- 1 tsp turmeric powder
- ½ tsp curry powder (more to taste if you prefer it spicy)
- ¾ cup cooked chicken breast in bite-sized pieces
- 3 whole walnuts, crushed
- 1 Medjool date, pitted and diced
- 1/8 cup diced red onion
- 1 bird's eye chili, diced (remove seeds if you do not want it to be too spicy)
- cups roughly chopped arugula

Directions:
1. In a medium-sized bowl, combine your Greek yogurt, the juice from the lemon, your cilantro, and the curry and turmeric powders. Combine well.
2. Add in your chicken, walnuts, date, onion, and chili and mix together thoroughly.
3. Add to the top of the arugula. Serve.

Nutrition: 370 Calories 14g Protein 33g Fat

335. Sirtfood Pesto Buckwheat Salad

Preparation Time: 22 minutes
Cooking Time: 0 minutes
Servings: 4
Ingredients:

- 4 cups of parsley
- 1 tsp minced garlic
- 1 lemon, juiced
- ½ cup of walnuts
- 3 bird's eye chilies'—remove the seeds if you do not like spicy food
- ½ cup cauliflower, broken down
- 2 tablespoon parmesan cheese, freshly shredded
- 2 tablespoons extra virgin olive oil
- 2 tablespoon water
- Salt and pepper to taste
- 2 cups diced chicken breast, cooked
- 8 oz buckwheat pasta (dry weight), cooked

Directions:
1. Prepare your chicken and pasta, and set aside in a large bowl.
2. In a food processor, combine all ingredients aside from chicken and pasta.

Blend until the consistency of pesto. Stop and scrape down walls from time to time to mix well.
3. Add 1 cup of pesto to the pasta and mix. If still dry, add more pesto to taste and mix well. Store in the fridge until ready to eat. This serves 4.

Nutrition: 379 calories 9.3g fat 4g protein

336. Kale Tofu Stir Fry

Preparation Time: 14 minutes
Cooking Time: 0 minutes
Ingredients:
For the tofu:

- 1 block of firm tofu
- 3 teaspoon curry powder
- 2 tablespoon soy sauce

For the stir fry:

- 3 large kale leaves, chopped
- 3 large arugula leaves, chopped
- ½ of a red cabbage
- 2 carrots, sliced
- 2 minced cloves of garlic
- 2 inches of minced ginger
- 4 tablespoon soy sauce
- 4 servings of buckwheat noodles

Directions:
1. Start by cutting up your tofu. It should be in bite-sized pieces. Then, mix in the soy sauce and the curry powder for the tofu and create a paste, which you will use to coat the tofu cubes. Set aside.
2. Cook your buckwheat noodles according to the package. Set aside when they are done.
3. Prepare all of your vegetables.
4. Prepare two frying pans with oil and turn them up to high. Put the tofu in one pan and cook until golden on all sides.
5. Add your garlic and ginger to the other pan and sauté for one minute
6. Add the kale, arugula, and cabbage to the garlic and ginger and cook until it begins to wilt. Then, add in the carrots and soy sauce. Cook for another two minutes.
7. Serve with pasta on the bottom, stir fry in the middle, and tofu on top, or store with pasta and stir fry in one container with the tofu in a separate one.

Nutrition: 232 Calories 8g Fat 10g Carbohydrate

337. Greek Stuffed Portobello Mushrooms

Preparation Time: 1 hour
Cooking Time: 42 minutes
Servings: 4

Ingredients:

- 3 tablespoons extra-virgin olive oil, divided
- ½ teaspoon ground pepper, divided
- 1 cup chopped spinach
- ½ cup quartered cherry tomatoes
- 1 clove garlic, minced
- ¼ teaspoon salt
- 2 tablespoons pitted and sliced Kalamata olives
- 4 Portobello mushrooms
- 1/3 cup crumbled feta cheese
- 1 tablespoon chopped fresh oregano

Directions:

1. Firstly, Preheat oven to 400 degrees F.
2. Mix 2 tablespoons oil, garlic, 1/4 teaspoon pepper and salt in a small bowl. Using a silicone brush, coat mushrooms all over with the oil mixture. Place on a large rimmed baking sheet and bake until the mushrooms are mostly soft, 8 to 10 minutes.
3. In the meantime, combine spinach, tomatoes, feta, olives, oregano and the remaining 1 tablespoon oil in a medium bowl. Once the mushrooms have softened, remove from the oven and fill with the spinach mixture. Bake until the tomatoes have wilted, about 10 minutes.

Nutrition: 345 Calories 54g Fat 6g Protein

338. Turmeric Sautéed Greens

Preparation Time: 3 minutes
Cooking Time: 0 minutes
Servings: 3

Ingredients:

- 1 tablespoon olive oil
- 1 2-inch piece fresh turmeric
- 1/4 teaspoon kosher salt
- 3 garlic cloves, minced
- 2 tablespoons water
- 2 bunches kale, spinach, or Swiss chard, thinly sliced

Directions:

1. Firstly, heat oil in a large sauce pan by using medium heat.
2. Now, add garlic and turmeric and sauté for 30 seconds.
3. Further, add kale and salt and sauté for 1 minute.
4. At the last add water to the pan and cook stirring until the greens are just wilted and serve.

Nutrition: 87 Calories 56g Protein 28g fat

339. Sautéed Collard Greens

Preparation Time: 21 minutes
Cooking Time: 17 minutes
Servings: 4

Ingredients:

- 1 slice thick-cut bacon, diced
- 1 bunch collard greens
- 2 garlic cloves, minced
- 1/2 teaspoon kosher salt

Directions:

1. Firstly, Put the bacon in a sauté pan over medium-low heat and cook for 5 minutes to render as much fat as possible.
2. While the bacon is cooking, remove the stems from the collard greens, and thinly slice the leaves across.
3. Now, add the garlic to the pan and cook for 1 minute. Add the greens and salt, stir well to coat the greens with the bacon fat, reduce heat to low, and cook for 5 minutes, until wilted, stirring occasionally. If you like them softer, cook for 10 minutes.

Nutrition: 87 Calories 10g Fat 56g Protein

340. Brussels Sprouts With Turmeric and Mustard Seeds

Preparation Time: 31 minutes
Cooking Time: 18 minutes
Servings: 2

Ingredients:

- 1 teaspoon oil
- 1/2 teaspoon (0.5 tsp) black mustard seeds
- 1/4 teaspoon (0.25 tsp) turmeric
- 3 cloves of garlic finely chopped
- 2 teaspoon or more sesame seeds
- 2 cups (176 g) Brussels sprouts
- 1/2 teaspoon (0.5 tsp) coriander powder

- 1 green chili finely chopped
- 1/2 teaspoon (0.5 tsp) cumin seeds
- 6 to 8 fresh or frozen curry leaves optional
- 1/2 teaspoon (0.5 tsp) garam masala optional
- cayenne to taste
- 1/2 teaspoon (0.5 tsp) salt or to taste
- 1/4 cup (62.5 ml) water
- cilantro and lemon for garnish

Directions:

1. First of all, heat oil in a large skillet over medium heat., When hot, put cumin and mustard seeds and cook until they change color or start to pop. Further, put curry leaves, garlic and chili carefully. Cook for a minute.
2. Now, add Brussels sprouts and toss well. Cook for 4 to 5 minutes until some edges get golden brown. Stir once or twice in between.
3. Put sesame seeds, mix in and cook for a minute. Mix in ground spices, salt and mix in and cook for a minute.
4. Add 1/4 cup or more water. Cover and cook for 7 to 9 minutes. This will steam the sprouts.
5. Finely, taste and adjust salt and heat. Add a dash of lemon and cilantro and serve.

Nutrition: 321 Calories 22g Fat 22g Protein

341. Sirt Salad

Preparation Time: 13 minutes
Cooking Time: 0 minutes
Servings: 1
Ingredients:

- 1 3/4 ounces (50g) arugula
- 1 3/4 ounces (50g) endive leaves
- 3 1/2 ounces (100g) smoked salmon cuts
- 1/2 cup (80g) avocado, stripped, stoned, and cut
- 1/2 cup (50g) celery including leaves, cut
- 1/8 cup (20g) red onion, cut
- 1/8 cups (15g) pecans, hacked
- 1 tablespoon tricks
- 1 huge Medjool date, hollowed and hacked
- 1 tablespoon additional virgin olive oil
- juice of 1/4 lemon
- 1/4 cup (10g) parsley, slashed

Directions:

1. Spot the serving of mixed greens leaves on a plate or in a huge bowl.
2. Combine all the rest of the fixings and serve on the leaves.

Nutrition: 108 Calories 33g Fat 44g Protein

342. Buckwheat Tabbouleh and Strawberry

Preparation Time: 43 minutes
Cooking Time: 23 minutes
Servings: 1
Ingredients:

- 1/3 cup (50g) buckwheat
- 1 tablespoon ground turmeric
- 1/2 cup (80g) avocado
- 3/8 cup (65g) tomato
- 1/8 cup (20g) red onion
- 1/8 cup (25g) Medjool dates, pitted
- 1 tablespoon escapades
- 3/4 cup (30g) parsley
- 2/3 cup (100g) strawberries, hulled
- 1 tablespoon additional virgin olive oil
- juice of 1/2 lemon
- 1-ounce (30g) arugula

Directions:

1. Cook the buckwheat with the turmeric as per the bundle directions.
2. Channel and put aside to cool.
3. Finely hack the avocado, tomato, red onion, dates, tricks, and parsley and blend in with the cool buckwheat.
4. Cut the strawberries and tenderly blend into the serving of mixed greens with the oil and lemon juice. Serve on a bed of arugula.

Nutrition: 234 Calories 3h Fat 6g Protein

343. Smoked-Tender Salmon Sirt Salad

Preparation Time: 24 minutes
Cooking Time: 0 minutes
Servings:4
Ingredients:

- 1 cup, or ¼ package if large of smoked salmon slices
- 1 avocado, pitted, sliced, and scooped out
- 10 walnuts, chopped
- 5 lovage or celery leaves), chopped

- 2 celery stalks, chopped or sliced thinly
- ½ small red onion, sliced thinly
- 1 Medjool pitted date, chopped
- 1 tbsp. capers
- 1 tbsp. extra virgin olive oil
- 1/4 of a lemon, juiced
- 5 sprigs of parsley, chopped

Directions:
1. Wash and dry salad makings and vegetables, top with salmon.

Nutrition: 214 Calories 2g Protein 9g Fat

344. Coronation Chicken Salad

Preparation Time: 28 minutes
Cooking time: 0 minutes
Servings: 1

Ingredients:
- 75 g Natural yoghurt
- Juice of 1/4 of a lemon
- 1 tsp Coriander, chopped
- 1 tsp Ground turmeric
- 1/2 tsp Mild curry powder
- 100 g Cooked chicken breast, cut into bite-sized pieces
- 6 Walnut halves, finely chopped
- 1 Medjool date, finely chopped
- 20 g Red onion, diced
- 1 Bird's eye chili
- 2-ounce Rocket, to serve

Direction
1. Blend the yoghurt, lemon juice, coriander and spices together in a bowl. Add all the remaining Ingredients and serve on a bed of the rocket.

Nutrition: 122 Calories 13g Fat 9g Protein

345. Salad Buckwheat Pasta

Preparation Time: 26 minutes
Cooking Time: 22 minutes
Serving: 1

Ingredient
- 2 ounces of buckwheat pasta, cooked according to the directions for packaging
- Big pound of rye
- Tiny pound of basil leaves
- 8 Halved cherry tomatoes
- 1/2 Avocado
- 10 olives diced

- 1 Tablespoon of extra virgin olive oil
- 21/2 spoonful of pine nuts

Direction
1. Combine all the ingredients, except the pine nuts, gently and place them on a tray, then spread the nuts over the edges.

Nutrition: 322 Calories 17g Fat 8g Protein

346. Cucumber & Onion Salad

Preparation Time: 19 minutes
Cooking Time: 0 minutes
Servings: 2

Ingredients:
- 3 large cucumbers, sliced thinly
- ½ cup red onion, sliced
- 2 tablespoons olive oil
- 1 tablespoon fresh apple cider vinegar
- Sea salt, to taste
- ¼ cup fresh parsley, chopped

Directions:
1. In a salad bowl, place all the ingredients and toss to coat well. Serve immediately.

Nutrition: 81 Calories 5.8g Fat 1.3g Protein

347. Citrus Fruit Salad

Preparation Time: 16 minutes
Cooking Time: 0 minutes
Servings: 2

Ingredients:
For Salad:
- 3 cups fresh kale, tough ribs removed and torn
- 1 orange, peeled and segmented
- 1 grapefruit, peeled and segmented
- 2 tablespoons unsweetened dried cranberries

For Dressing:
- 2 tablespoons extra-virgin olive oil
- 2 tablespoons fresh orange juice
- 1 teaspoon Dijon mustard
- ½ teaspoon raw honey
- Salt and ground black pepper, as required

Directions:
1. For salad: in a salad bowl, place all ingredients and mix.
2. For dressing: place all ingredients in another bowl and beat until well combined.
3. Place dressing on top of salad and toss to coat well. Serve immediately.

Nutrition: 256 Calories 14.5g Fat 4.6g Protein

348. Mixed Berries Salad

Preparation Time: 17 minutes
Cooking Time: 0 Minutes
Servings: 4

Ingredients:

- 1 cup fresh strawberries
- ½ cup blackberries
- ½ cup blueberries
- ½ cup raspberries
- 6 cups arugula
- 2 tablespoons olive oil

Directions:

1. Toss all the ingredients to coat well.

Nutrition: 105 Calories 7.6g Fat 1.6g Protein

349. Orange and Beet Salad

Preparation Time: 18 minutes
Cooking Time: 0 minutes
Servings: 4

Ingredients:

- 3 large oranges, peeled, seeded and sectioned
- 2 beets, trimmed, peeled and sliced
- 6 cups fresh rocket
- ¼ cup walnuts, chopped
- 3 tablespoons olive oil
- Pinch of salt

Directions:

1. In a salad bowl, place all ingredients and gently, toss to coat.
2. Serve immediately.

Nutrition: 233 Calories 15.6g Fat 4.8g Protein

350. Strawberry, Apple & Arugula Salad

Preparation Time: 18 minutes
Cooking Time: 0 minutes
Servings: 4

Ingredients:

- 4 cups fresh baby arugula
- 2 apples, cored and sliced
- 1 cup fresh strawberries, hulled and sliced
- ¼ cup walnuts, chopped
- 4 tablespoons olive oil
- Salt and ground black pepper, as required

Directions:

1. For the salad, place all the ingredients in a large bowl and mix well.

2. For the dressing, place all the ingredients in a bowl and beat until well combined.
3. Pour the dressing over the salad and toss it all to coat well.
4. Serve immediately.

Nutrition: 243 Calories 19g Fat 2.9g Protein

351. Shrimp Salad

Preparation Time: 15 minutes
Cooking Time: 7 minutes
Servings: 6

Ingredients:

For Shrimp:

- 1 tablespoon olive oil
- 1 garlic clove, crushed
- 2 tablespoons fresh rosemary, chopped
- 1-pound raw shrimp, peeled and deveined
- ¼ teaspoon red pepper flakes, crushed
- Salt and ground black pepper, as required

For Salad:

- 8 cups fresh arugula
- 3 tablespoons olive oil
- 2 tablespoons fresh lime juice
- Salt and ground black pepper, as required

Directions:

1. In a large wok, heat oil over medium heat and sauté 1 garlic clove for about 1 minute. Add the shrimp with red pepper flakes, salt and black pepper and cook for about 4-5 minutes.
2. Remove the wok of shrimp from heat and set aside to cool. In a large bowl, add the shrimp, arugula, oil, lime juice, salt and black pepper and gently, toss to coat. Serve immediately.

Nutrition: 182 Calories 11g Fat 18g Protein

352. Smoked Salmon Sirt Salad

Preparation Time: 19 minutes
Cooking Time: 44 minutes
Servings: 3

Ingredients:

- 1 cup or ¼ package if large of smoked salmon slices no cooking needed!
- 1 avocado, pitted, sliced, and scooped out
- 10 walnuts, chopped
- 5 Lovage or celery leaves), chopped
- 2 celery stalks, chopped or sliced thinly

- ½ small red onion, sliced thinly
- 1 Medjool pitted date, chopped
- 1 tbsp. capers
- 1 tbsp. extra virgin olive oil
- 1/4 of a lemon, juiced
- 5 sprigs of parsley, chopped

Directions:
1. Wash and dry salad makings and vegetables, top with salmon.

Nutrition: 192 Calories 11g Fat 18g Protein

353. Waldorf Salad

Preparation Time: 12 minutes
Cooking Time: 0 minutes
Servings: 4

Ingredients:
- 250 gr of celeriac
- 250 gr of apples
- 70 gr of walnuts
- 150 gr of mayonnaise
- 200 gr of yogurt (thick)
- 1 tbsp. honey
- 1 lemon

Directions:
1. To prepare the Waldorf salad, start cleaning the celeriac, peel it by cutting the peel with a knife, wash it and cut it into slices and then into strips.
2. Bring the salted water to a boil and blanch the celeriac for 2-3 minutes, then drain and pat dry with a tea towel. Now move on to cleaning the apples, wash them, peel them and cut them into slices and then into strips.
3. Then dip the apples in water acidulated with lemon juice to prevent it from turning black (keep aside 1 tablespoon of lemon juice which you will need for dressing).
4. For the dressing, combine the mayonnaise, yogurt, a spoonful of lemon juice and honey, salt and pepper in a bowl, mix everything and add celery and apples.
5. Season the fruit and vegetables with the prepared dressing and add the coarsely chopped walnuts.

Nutrition: 243 Calories 20g Fat 2g Protein

354. Brown Rice Salad with Octopus

Preparation Time: 16 minutes
Cooking Time: 61 minutes
Servings: 6

Ingredients:
- 500 gr of octopus
- 250 gr of brown rice
- 2courgette
- 1 clove of garlic
- 1 potato
- 1 egg

Directions:
1. First clean the octopus, then put it in a saucepan, cover it with cold water and put on the fire: cook for about 50 minutes after the boiling begins. Finally drain and let cool.
2. In the meantime, cook the rice, in abundant salted water, for the time indicated on the package, then drain it and let it cool too.
3. Cook the egg for 8 minutes from boiling to make it hard and boil the potato.
4. Wash and peel the courgette cut them into cubes and sauté them in a pan with a little oil and garlic. When they begin to soften, while remaining a little crunchy, add salt and pepper and let cool.
5. Cut the octopus into chunks, season it with salt, pepper, oil and parsley and add it to the courgette.
6. Also add the rice, the potato and the egg into chunks and gently mix everything.
7. Add potatoes and eggs.
8. Mix well.
9. Leave to rest in the fridge for 1 hour, and then serve your brown rice salad with octopus on the table.

Nutrition: 154 Calories 7.6g Fat 2.9g Protein

355. Exotic Rice Salad

Preparation Time: 8 minutes
Cooking Time: 21 minutes
Servings: 4

Ingredients:
- 250 gr of basmati rice
- 1 pineapple
- 200 gr of shrimp
- 150 gr of peas
- 50 gr of pecans
- 1/2 lime

- EVO oil

Directions:
1. Rinse the rice under running water several times until the water has become transparent.
2. Cook the basmati rice in a saucepan with plenty of salted water for the time reported in the package.
3. Once cooked, drain, and put the rice to cool
4. Cook basmati rice.
5. Sauté the shrimp and boiled peas in a pan with a spoonful of oil then cool prawns and peas.
6. Cut a pineapple in half lengthwise and empty it of the pulp, leaving in each half shell a border of a few millimeters.
7. Cut the flesh of the pineapple into cubes.
8. In a bowl put the rice; add the pineapple, peas and shrimp, season with the lime juice and a spoonful of oil.
9. Then add a handful of pecans and mix.
10. Put the exotic rice salad in the fridge for ½ hr. and serve.

Nutrition: 529 Calorie 10g Fat 9.5g Protein

356. Light Tuna and Bread Salad

Preparation Time: 17 minutes
Cooking Time: 8 minutes
Servings: 4

Ingredients:
- 4-5 slices of bread cut not too thin
- 3 boxes of natural tuna
- 4-5 not too ripe tomatoes for salad
- Salt and pepper
- 4 spoons of olive oil
- a pinch of oregano

Directions:
1. Heat a non-stick pan and in the meantime cut the slices of bread into coarse cubes. Add the bread to the pan, leaving it toasted well from all sides and then turning it often.
2. As soon as the bread is ready, let it cool.
3. In a salad bowl, or in four smaller bowls, put the bread, drain the tuna and distribute it on the bread, add a pinch of oregano.
4. We cut the tomatoes into not too regular cubes and put them in the salad.

5. At this point we can choose to season the salad with oil, salt and pepper and mix well, or use the condiments separately.

Nutrition: 180 Calories 10g Fat 11g Protein

357. Spicy Avocado Salad

Preparation Time: 7 minutes
Cooking Time: 0 minutes
Servings: 1

Ingredients:
- 1 avocado
- Few leaves of iceberg salad
- 2 green tomatoes
- Two tablespoons of mayonnaise
- Spoonful of ketchup
- Zest and juice of half a lime
- Small hot pepper
- Salt and pepper
- Extra virgin olive oil
- White vinegar a few drops

Directions:
1. Empty the avocado pulp and put it in a bowl by squeezing it
2. Add the green tomatoes cut into small cubes
3. Finely cut the chili pepper after removing the seeds
4. Cut the leaves of the iceberg salad into strips and add them to the rest
5. Put salt and pepper. Combine ketchup and mayonnaise, add the oil, the juice and the zest of the lime, the vinegar and mix everything
6. Use the avocado peel as a container.

Nutrition: 460 Calories 31g Fat 10g Protein

358. Hot Chicory & Nut Salad

Preparation Time: 8 minutes
Cooking Time: 42 minutes
Servings: 2

Ingredients:
For the salad:
- 100g 3½ oz. green beans
- 100g 3½ oz. red chicory
- 100g 3½ oz. celery, chopped
- 25g 1 oz. macadamia nuts, chopped
- 25g 1 oz. walnuts, chopped
- 25g 1 oz. plain peanuts, chopped
- 2 tomatoes, chopped

- 1 tablespoon olive oil

For the dressing:

- 2 tablespoons fresh parsley, finely chopped
- ½ teaspoon turmeric
- ½ teaspoon mustard
- 1 tablespoon olive oil
- 25mls 1fl oz. red wine vinegar

Directions:

1. Mix together the ingredients for the dressing then set them aside. Heat a tablespoon of olive oil in a frying pan then add the green beans, chicory and celery.

2. Cook until the vegetables have softened then add in the chopped tomatoes and cook for 2 minutes. Add the prepared dressing, and thoroughly coat all of the vegetables. Serve onto plates and sprinkle the mixture of nuts over the top. Eat immediately.

Nutrition: 438 calories 31g Fat 18g Protein

359. Tuna, Egg & Caper Salad

Preparation Time: 8 minutes
Cooking Time: 21 minutes
Servings: 2

Ingredients:

- 100g 3 ½ oz. red chicory or yellow if not available
- 150g 5 oz. tinned tuna flakes in brine, drained
- 100g 3 ½ oz. cucumber
- 25g 1 oz. rocket arugula
- 6 pitted black olives
- 2 hard-boiled eggs, peeled and quartered
- 2 tomatoes, chopped
- 2 tablespoons fresh parsley, chopped
- 1 red onion, chopped
- 1 stalk of celery

- 1 tablespoon capers
- 2 tablespoons garlic vinaigrette

Directions:

1. Place the tuna, cucumber, olives, tomatoes, onion, chicory, celery, and parsley and rocket arugula into a bowl. Pour in the vinaigrette and toss the salad in the dressing.

2. Serve onto plates and scatter the eggs and capers on top.

Nutrition: 340 calories 31g Fat 12g Protein

360. Nutty Fruit Granola

Preparation Time: 7 minutes
Cooking Time: 52 minutes
Servings: 2

Ingredients:

- 200g 7 oz. oats
- 250g 9 oz. buckwheat flakes
- 100g 3½ oz. walnuts, chopped
- 100g 3½ oz. almonds, chopped
- 100g 3½ oz. dried strawberries
- 1½ teaspoons ground ginger
- 1½ teaspoons ground cinnamon
- 120mls 4fl oz. olive oil
- 2 tablespoon honey

Directions:

1. Combine the oats, buckwheat flakes, nuts, ginger and cinnamon. In a saucepan, warm the oil and honey. Stir until the honey has melted.

2. Pour the warm oil into the dry ingredients and mix well. Lay out mixture out on a large baking tray then bake at 150C for 50 minutes. Allow it to cool. Add in the dried berries.

Nutrition: 220 Calories 2.5g Fat 6g Protein

361. Snow-Flakes

Preparation Time: 9 minutes
Cooking Time: 8 minutes
Servings: 5

Ingredients:

- Won ton wrappers
- Oil to frying
- Powdered-sugar

Directions:

1. Cut won ton wrappers just like you'd a snow-flake
2. Heat oil when hot add won-ton, fry for approximately 30 seconds then reverse over.
3. Drain on a paper towel with powdered sugar.

Nutrition: 10g Carbohydrates 5g Fat 4g Protein

362. Lemon Ricotta Cookies with Lemon Glaze

Preparation Time: 12 minutes
Cooking Time: 19 minutes
Servings: 12

Ingredients:

- 2 1/2 cups all-purpose flour
- 1 tsp. baking powder
- 1 tsp. salt
- 1 tbsp. unsalted butter softened
- 2 cups of sugar
- 2 capsules
- 1 teaspoon (15-ounce) container whole-milk ricotta cheese
- 3 tbsp. lemon juice
- 1 lemon

Glaze:

- 11/2 cups powdered sugar
- 3 tbsp. lemon juice
- 1 lemon

Directions:

1. Pre heat the oven to 375 degrees F.
2. In a medium bowl combine the flour, baking powder, and salt. Set-aside.
3. Mix butter and the sugar levels. Using electric mixer beat the sugar and butter for minutes. Put eggs1 at a time, beating until incorporated.

4. Blend ricotta cheese, lemon juice and lemon zest. Stir in the dry skin.
5. Line two baking sheets with parchment paper. Spoon the dough on the baking sheets. Bake for fifteen minutes. Take it out and cool for 20 minutes.
6. Combine the powdered sugar lemon juice and lemon peel in a small bowl. Spoon 1/2-tsp on each cookie and flatten it. Allow glaze harden for approximately two hours. Pack the biscuits to a decorative jar.

Nutrition: 24.5g Carbohydrates 13.4g Protein 2g Fat

363. Homemade Marshmallow Fluff

Preparation Time: 7 minutes
Cooking Time: 17 minutes
Servings: 3

Ingredients:

- 3/4 cup sugar
- 1/2 cup light corn syrup
- 1/4 cup water
- 1/8 tbsp. salt
- 3 little egg whites egg whites
- 1/4 tsp. cream of tartar
- 1 teaspoon 1/2 tsp. vanilla infusion

Directions:

1. In a little pan, mix together sugar, corn syrup, salt and water. Attach a candy thermometer into the side of this pan, which makes sure it will not touch the underside of the pan. Set aside.
2. From the bowl of a stand mixer, combine egg whites and cream of tartar. Begin to whip on medium speed with the whisk attachment.
3. Meanwhile, turn burner on top and place the pan with the sugar mix onto heat. Allow mix into a boil and heat to 240 degrees, stirring periodically.
4. The aim is to find the egg whites whipped to soft peaks and also the sugar heated to 240 degrees at near the same moment. Simply stop stirring the egg whites once they hit soft peaks.
5. Once the sugar has already reached 240 amounts, turn noodle onto reduce. Insert a

little quantity of the popular sugar mix and let it mix. Insert still another little sum of the sugar mix. Carry on adding and mixing slowly that means you never scramble the egg whites.

6. After all of the sugar was added into the egg whites, then turn the rate of this mixer and also keep overcoming concoction for around 79 minutes until the fluff remains glossy and stiff. In roughly the 5-minute mark, then add vanilla extract.

7. Use fluff immediately or store in an airtight container in the fridge for around two weeks.

Nutrition: 0.2g Carbohydrates 5g Fat 3.8g Protein

364. Banana Ice-Cream
Preparation Time: 6 minutes
Cooking Time: 11 minutes
Servings: 3
Ingredients:
- 3 quite ripe banana - peeled and rooted
- Couple of chocolate chips
- Two tbsp. skim milk

Directions:
1. Throw all ingredients into a food processor and blend until creamy.
2. Eat freeze and appreciate afterwards.

Nutrition: 0.3g Fat 23g Carbohydrates 3g Protein

365. Perfect Little Snack Balls
Preparation Time: 7 minutes
Cooking Time: 9 minutes
Servings: 4
Ingredients:
- 1/2 cup chunky peanut butter
- 3 tbsp. flax seeds
- 3 tbsp. wheat germ
- 1 tbsp. honey or agave
- 1/4 cup powder

Directions:
1. Blend dry ingredients and adding from the honey and peanut butter.
2. Mix well and roll into chunks and then conclude by rolling into wheat germ.

Nutrition: 3.1g fat 3.3g Carbohydrates 2g Protein

366. Loaded Chocolate Pretzel Cookies
Preparation Time: 7 minutes
Cooking Time: 14 minutes

Servings: 12
Ingredients:
- 1 cup yoghurt
- 1/2 tsp. baking soda
- 1/4 teaspoon salt
- 1/4 tsp. cinnamon
- 4 tbsp. butter softened
- 1/3 cup brown sugar
- 1 egg
- 1/2 tsp. vanilla
- 1/2 cup dark chocolate chips
- 1/2 cup pretzels tsp. chopped

Directions:
1. Pre heat oven to 350 degrees.
2. At a medium bowl whisk together the sugar, butter, vanilla and egg.
3. In another bowl stir together the flour, baking soda and salt.
4. Stir the bread mixture in using all the moist components, along with the chocolate chips and pretzels until just blended.
5. Drop a large spoonful of dough on an unlined baking sheet.
6. Bake for 15-17 minutes, or until the bottoms are somewhat all crispy
7. Allow to cool on a wire rack.

Nutrition: 40g Carbohydrates 8g Protein 288 Calories

367. Mascarpone Cheesecake with Almond Crust
Preparation Time: 12 minutes
Cooking Time: 21 minutes
Servings: 3
Ingredients:
Crust
- 1/2 cup slivered almonds
- 8 tsp. -- or 2/3 cup graham cracker crumbs
- 2 tbsp. sugar
- 1 tbsp. salted butter melted

Filling
- 1 (8-ounce) packages cream cheese, room temperature
- 1 (8-ounce) container mascarpone cheese, room temperature
- 3/4 cup sugar
- 1 tsp. fresh lemon juice (or imitation lemon-juice)

- 1 tsp. vanilla infusion
- 2 large eggs, room temperature

Directions:

1. For the crust: Set oven to 350 degrees. Blend almonds, cracker crumbs sugar in a food processor. Mix in butter.
2. Press the almond mixture on the base of the pan. Bake for 3 minutes. Cool. Decrease the oven temperature to 325 degrees f.
3. For your filling: with an electric mixer, beat the cream cheese, mascarpone cheese, and sugar. Stir in the lemon juice and vanilla. Add the eggs1 at a time, beating until combined after each addition.
4. Fill cheese mixture on the crust from the pan. Situate the pan into Pyrex dish fill enough hot water to the pan. Bake for 60 minutes. Transfer the cake to a stand for 1 hour. Refrigerate before cheesecake is cold, at least eight hours.
5. Use melted chocolate to decorate the cake!

Nutrition: 5g Carbohydrates 25g Fat 5g Protein

368. Marshmallow Popcorn Balls

Preparation Time: 7 minutes
Cooking time: 17 minutes
Servings: 12
Ingredients:

- 2 bags of microwave popcorn
- 1 12.6 ounces. Tote M&M's
- 3 cups honey roasted peanuts
- 1 pkg. 16 ounce. Massive marshmallows
- 1 cup butter, cubed

Directions:

1. In a bowl, blend the popcorn, peanuts and M&M's.
2. In a big pot, combine marshmallows and butter.
3. Cook medium-low warmth.
4. Insert popcorn mix, blend nicely
5. Spray muffin tins with nonstop cooking spray.
6. When cool enough to handle, spray hands together with non-stick cooking spray and then shape into chunks and put into the muffin tin to carry contour.
7. Add Popsicle stick into each chunk and then let cool.

8. Wrap each person in vinyl when chilled.

Nutrition: 1.1g Fat 3.2g Fiber 4g Protein

369. Homemade Ice-Cream Drumsticks

Preparation Time: 8 minutes
Cooking Time: 13 minutes
Serving: 4
Ingredients:

- Vanilla ice cream
- Two hazelnut chunks
- Magical shell - out chocolate
- Sugar levels
- Nuts

Directions:

1. Soften ice cream and mixing topping
2. Fill underside of sugar with magic and nuts shell and top with ice-cream.
3. Wrap parchment paper round cone and then fill cone over about 1.5 inches across the cap of the cone (the newspaper can help to carry its shape).
4. Shirt with magical nuts and shell.
5. Freeze for about 20 minutes, before ice cream is business.

Nutrition: 7g Fat 3g Protein 199 Calories

370. Ultimate Chocolate Chip Cookie Fudge Brownie Bar

Preparation Time: 11 minutes
Cooking Time: 13 minutes
Servings: 12
Ingredients:

- 1 cup (2 sticks) butter, softened
- 1 cup granulated sugar
- 3/4 cup light brown sugar
- Two big eggs
- 1 tablespoon pure vanilla extract
- Two 1/2 cups all-purpose flour
- 1 tsp. baking soda
- 1 tsp. lemon
- 2 cups (12 oz.) milk chocolate chips
- Inch kg double stuffed Oreos
- Inch family-size (9×1 3) brownie mixture
- 1/4 cup hot fudge topping

Directions:

1. Pre heat oven to 350 degrees f.

2. Cream the butter and sugars in a large bowl using an electric mixer at medium speed for 35 minutes.
3. Add the vanilla and eggs and mix well to thoroughly combine. In another bowl whisk together the flour, baking soda and salt, and slowly incorporate in the mixer till the bread is simply combined.
4. Stir in chocolate chips.
5. Spread the cookie dough at the bottom of a 9×1-3 baking dish that is wrapped with wax paper and then coated with cooking spray.
6. Shirt with a coating of Oreos. Mix together brownie mix, adding an optional 1/4 cup of hot fudge directly into the mixture.
7. Twist the brownie batter within the cookie-dough and Oreos.
8. Cover with foil and bake at 350 degrees f for half an hour.
9. Remove foil and continue baking for another 15 25 minutes.
10. Let cool before cutting on brownies might nevertheless be gooey at the midst while warm, but will also place up perfectly once chilled.

Nutrition: 7g Fat 25g Carbohydrates 3g Protein

371. Matcha Apple & Green Juice

Preparation Time: 13 minutes
Cooking Time: 0 minutes
Servings: 2
Ingredients:

- 5 ounces fresh kale
- 2 ounces fresh arugula
- ¼ cup fresh parsley
- 4 celery stalks
- 1 green apple, cored and chopped
- 1 (1-inch) piece fresh ginger, peeled
- 1 lemon, peeled
- ½ teaspoon Matcha green tea

Directions:
1. Mix all ingredients into a juicer and extract the juice following the manufacturer's method.
2. Split into two glasses and serve immediately.

Nutrition: 113 Calories 0.6g Fat 2.8g Protein

372. Apple, Cucumber & Celery Juice

Preparation Time: 14 minutes
Cooking Time: 0 minutes
Servings: 2
Ingredients:

- 3 large apples, cored and sliced
- 2 large cucumbers, sliced
- 4 celery stalks
- 1 (1-inch) piece fresh ginger, peeled
- 1 lemon, peeled

Directions:
1. Situate all ingredients into a juicer and extract it as per the manufacturer's method.
2. Divide into two glasses and serve.

Nutrition: 230 Calories 1.1g Total Fat 3.3g Protein

373. Lemony Apple & Kale Juice

Preparation Time: 11 minutes
Cooking Time: 0 minutes
Servings: 2
Ingredients:

- 2 large green apples, cored and sliced
- 4 cups fresh kale leaves
- 4 tablespoons fresh parsley leaves
- 1 tablespoon fresh ginger, peeled
- 1 lemon, peeled
- ½ cup of filtered water

Directions:
1. Place all ingredients in a blender and pulse until well combined.
2. Through a fine mesh strainer, strain the juice and transfer into two glasses.
3. Serve immediately.

Nutrition: 196 Calories 0.6g Fat 5.2g Protein

374. Watermelon Juice

Preparation Time: 7 minutes
Cooking Time: 0 minutes
Servings: 1
Ingredients:

- 20g of young kale leaves
- 250g of watermelon chunks
- 4 mint leaves
- ½ cucumber

Directions:

1. Remove the stalks from the kale and roughly chop it.
2. Peel the cucumber, if preferred, and then halve it and seed it.
3. Place all ingredients in a blender or juicer and process until you achieve a desired consistency. Serve immediately.

Nutrition: 0.6g Protein 7.6g Carbohydrates 0.2g Fat

375. Apple Muffins

Preparation Time: 13 minutes
Cooking Time: 14 minutes
Servings: 5

Ingredients:

- 2 eggs
- 1 cup oat flour
- ½ teaspoon salt
- 2 tablespoon stevia
- 3 apples, washed and peeled
- ½ cup skim milk
- 1 tablespoon olive oil
- ½ teaspoon baking soda
- 1 teaspoon apple cider vinegar

Directions:

1. Beat the eggs in the mixing bowl and whisk them well.
2. Add the skim milk, salt, baking soda, stevia, and apple cider vinegar.
3. Stir the mixture carefully. Grate the apples and add the grated mixture in the egg mixture.
4. Stir it carefully and add the oat flour.
5. Add the olive oil and blend into a smooth batter. Preheat the oven to 350 F.
6. Fill each muffin from halfway with the batter and place the muffins in the oven.
7. Cook the dish for 15 minutes.
8. Remove the cooked muffins from the oven.
9. Cool the cooked muffins well and serve them.

Nutrition: 200 Calories 6g Fat 11.7g Protein

376. Dark Chocolate Terrine

Preparation Time: 57 minutes
Cooking Time: 6 minutes
Servings: 10

Ingredients:

- For lubing the dish use vegetable oil

- 1/2 pound (2 sticks) unsalted spread
- 12 ounces ambivalent chocolate
- One teaspoon moment espresso powder
- 1 cup filtered confectioners' sugar
- 1/3 cup unsweetened cocoa powder
- Eight extra-huge egg yolks, at room temperature
- One tablespoon Cognac or liquor
- Touch of genuine salt
- Three extra-huge egg whites, at room temperature
- One tablespoon granulated sugar
- 1/2 cup cold overwhelming cream
- One teaspoon unadulterated vanilla concentrate
- Orange Sauce, formula follows
- Newly ground orange pizzazz, for serving
- Fleur de sel, for serving

Orange Sauce:

- Four extra-enormous egg yolks, at room temperature
- 1/2 cup sugar
- One teaspoon cornstarch
- 1 3/4 cups burnt entire milk
- One teaspoon unadulterated vanilla concentrate
- 1/2 teaspoons Cognac or liquor
- One tablespoon Grand Marnier alcohol
- 1/4 teaspoon ground orange pizzazz

Directions:

1. Softly oil an eight 1/2-by-4 1/2-by-2-inch portion skillet and line it as perfectly as conceivable with cling wrap, permitting the finishes to wrap over the sides. (I lay two bits of saran wrap transversely in the skillet, covering in the middle.) Place the container in the cooler.
2. Spot an enormous heatproof bowl over a dish of stewing water. Spot the margarine in the bowl, at that point the chocolate and espresso powder and warmth until simply softened, mixing once in a while with a flexible spatula. When the chocolate and margarine are dissolved, take the bowl off the warmth and speed in, each in turn, and all together, first the confectioners' sugar, at that point the cocoa powder, egg yolks,

Cognac and salt. Put the bowl in a safe spot for 15 minutes to cool.

3. Spot the egg whites and granulated sugar in the bowl of an electric blender fitted with the whisk connection and beat on fast until the white's structure firm however not dry pinnacles. Overlay the whites into the cooled chocolate blend with an elastic spatula.

4. Without cleaning the bowl or whisk connection, empty the cream and vanilla into the bowl and beat on fast until it frames firm pinnacles. Overlay the cream cautiously, however entirely into the chocolate blend. Fill the readied portion skillet, smooth the top, overlap the saran wrap over the top and chill for 4 hours or overnight.

5. To serve, turn the terrine out of shape and open it up. Spoon a puddle of Orange Sauce in every pastry plate and spot a cut of the terrine in the center. Sprinkle each serving delicately with orange pizzazz and fleur de sel.

For Orange Sauce:

6. Beat the egg yolks and sugar in the bowl of an electric blender fitted with the oar connection on medium-fast for 3 minutes, until exceptionally thick. Diminish to low speed and blend in the cornstarch.

7. With the blender still on low, gradually empty the hot milk into the egg blend (I utilize a fluid estimating cup for pouring). Empty the blend into a perfect, little, profound pot and cook over medium-low warmth, mixing continually with a wooden spoon, until it arrives at 180 degrees F on a treats thermometer and thickens to the consistency of overwhelming cream. The blend will cover the spoon. Try not to cook it over 180 degrees F, or the eggs will scramble! Promptly (it will continue cooking in the pan), pour the sauce through a fine-work sifter into a bowl, and mix in the vanilla, Cognac, Grand Marnier, and orange pizzazz. Spread and chill.

Nutrition: 175 Calories 7g Fat 3g Protein

377. Dark Chocolate Oatmeal

Preparation Time: 16 minutes
Cooking Time: 23 minutes

Servings: 4

Ingredients:

- 1/2 cups antiquated oats
- 1/4 cup unsweetened cocoa powder
- One teaspoon vanilla concentrate
- 1/2 teaspoon salt
- 1/3 cup nectar
- 1/2 cup cleaved toasted pecans
- Two bananas, cut into coins
- 1/2 cup dried fruits, plumped in warm water

Directions:

1. Heat 3 cups of water to the point of boiling in an enormous pot over medium warmth. Include the oats, cocoa powder, vanilla, and salt and cook, usually blending until thickened, 5 to 7 minutes. Mood killer the warmth and mix in the nectar. Spread and let represent 2 minutes.

2. Top each presenting with two tablespoons cleaved pecans, half of a cut banana and two tablespoons fruits. Serve right away.

Nutrition: 130 Calories 5g Fat 2g Protein

378. Dark Chocolate Nut Bars

Preparation Time: 75 minutes
Cooking Time: 22 minutes
Servings: 16

Ingredients:

- Two teaspoons virgin coconut oil
- 1 cup unsweetened coconut chips
- 1/2 cup hacked hazelnuts
- 1/2 cup hacked pecans
- 1/2 cup hacked cashews
- 1/2 cup trail blend (nuts as it were)
- One tablespoon ground flaxseed
- 1/2 cup maple syrup
- 1/3 cup nectar
- Legitimate salt
- 1/2 cup dull chocolate chips

Directions:

1. Special equipment: a candy thermometer
2. Preheat the broiler to 350 degrees F. Brush an 8-by-8-inch dish with one teaspoon of the coconut oil and put it in a safe spot.
3. Join the coconut chips, hazelnuts, pecans, cashews, trail blend, and flaxseed and spread into an even layer on a preparing

sheet. Toast until daintily brilliant, 10 to 12 minutes, at that point move to a large heatproof bowl. Put in a safe spot.

4. In a little pan, consolidate the maple syrup, nectar, and 1/2 teaspoon salt and heat to the point of boiling over medium-high warmth. Cook, sometimes mixing, until the temperature on a treat's thermometer peruses 260 degrees F, around 5 minutes. Promptly pour over the nut blend and mix to cover.

5. Utilize a flexible spatula to press the blend into the readied dish and let cool until set, around 30 minutes.

6. To make the chocolate sprinkle, consolidate the chocolate chips and staying one teaspoon coconut oil in a medium heatproof bowl and spot over a little pot of stewing water. Warmth, blending, until softened and smooth.

7. Shower the chocolate over the blend. At the point when set, cut into bars and serve.

Nutrition: 180 Calories 9g Fat 4g Protein

379. Dark Chocolate Martini

Preparation Time: 6 minutes
Cooking Time: 0 minutes
Servings: 1
Ingredients:

- Sugar
- Cleaved dull chocolate
- Vodka
- Coffee
- Orange

Directions:

1. Blend 2 tablespoons every raw sugar and finely cleaved dull chocolate on a plate. Consolidate 2 ounces every chocolate alcohol and vodka, 1-ounce chilled coffee, 1/2 teaspoon new squeezed orange, and a piece of orange get-up-and-go in a mixed drink shaker with ice; mix well.

2. Saturate the edge of a chilled martini glass and plunge it in the sugar-chocolate blend. Strain the mixed drink into the glass and trimmed with an orange wedge.

Nutrition: 405 Calories 39g Carbohydrates 8g Protein

380. Dark Chocolate Brownies

Preparation Time: 27 minutes

Cooking Time: 23 minutes
Servings: 24
Ingredients:

- 8 ounces ambivalent chocolate, coarsely cleaved
- Two tablespoons unsalted spread
- 1 cup entire grain cake flour*
- 1/4 cup unsweetened ordinary cocoa powder
- 1/4 teaspoon salt
- 1/4 teaspoon preparing pop
- Four huge eggs
- 1 cup stuffed light earthy colored sugar
- 1/2 cup plain low-fat yogurt
- 1/4 cup canola oil
- Two teaspoons vanilla concentrate
- 3/4 cup hacked pecans (discretionary)

Directions:

1. Preheat the stove to 350 degrees. Coat a 9 x 13inch preparing dish with cooking shower.

2. Dissolve the chocolate and spread in a twofold evaporator or heatproof bowl set over a pot of scarcely stewing water, blending every so often.

3. In a medium bowl, whisk together the flour, cocoa, salt, and preparing pop.

4. In an enormous bowl, whisk the eggs and sugar until smooth. Include the yogurt, oil, and vanilla, and race to consolidate.

5. Include the chocolate-spread blend and rush until mixed. Include the flour blend and blend until just soaked.

6. Move the blend to the readied container and sprinkle with nuts if utilizing. Heat for 20-25 minutes, until a wooden toothpick embedded in the middle comes out with a couple of sodden pieces. Cool totally in the skillet on a wire rack. Cut into 24 squares.

Nutrition: 140 Calories 3g Fat 2g Protein

381. Dark-Choco Mousse

Preparation Time: 22 minutes
Cooking Time: 1 hour
Servings: 5
Ingredients:

- 1 (12.3-ounce) bundle luxurious tofu, depleted

- 3 ounces great mixed chocolate, finely cleaved
- 1/4 cup unsweetened cocoa powder, ideally Dutch-prepared
- 1/4 cup water
- One tablespoon liquor
- 1/2 cup in addition to 1/2 teaspoon superfine sugar
- 1/4 cup substantial cream
- 1/4 teaspoons shaved chocolate

Directions:
1. In a blender or food processor, puree the tofu until it is smooth.
2. Put the slashed chocolate, cocoa powder, 1/4 cup water, and liquor in a pot or warmth proof bowl fitted over a pot containing 1-inch scarcely stewing water. Mix now and again, until liquefied and smooth. Expel from heat. Blend in 1/2 cup of sugar, a little at once, until smooth.
3. Add the chocolate blend to the tofu and puree until smooth and all-around mixed. Spoon the mousse into serving dishes, cover, and refrigerate for at any rate 60 minutes.
4. Whip the cream with a mixer. At the point when the cream is whipped, include the staying 1/2 teaspoon of sugar and get done with whipping.
5. Top each presenting with a bit of whipped cream and a sprinkle of chocolate shavings and serve.

Nutrition: 100 Calories 0.1g Fat 3g Protein

382. Strawberry Buckwheat Pancakes

Preparation Time: 7 minutes
Cooking Time: 42 minutes
Servings: 2

Ingredients:
- 100g 3½oz strawberries, chopped
- 100g 3½ oz. buckwheat flour
- 1 egg
- 250mls 8fl oz. milk
- 1 teaspoon olive oil
- 1 teaspoon olive oil for frying
- Freshly squeezed juice of 1 orange

Directions:

1. Pour the milk. Mix in the egg and olive oil. Sift in the flour to the liquid mixture. Heat a little oil in a pan and pour in a quarter of the mixture or to the size you prefer.
2. Sprinkle in a quarter of the strawberries into the batter. Cook for around 2 minutes on each side. Serve hot with a drizzle of orange juice.

Nutrition: 175 Calories 35g Fat 21g Protein

383. Strawberry & Nut Granola

Preparation Time: 7 minutes
Cooking Time: 51 minutes
Servings: 2

Ingredients:
- 200g 7oz oats
- 250g 9oz buckwheat flakes
- 100g 3½ oz. walnuts, chopped
- 100g 3½ oz. almonds, chopped
- 100g 3½ oz. dried strawberries
- 1½ teaspoons ground ginger
- 1½ teaspoons ground cinnamon
- 120mls 4fl oz. olive oil
- 2 tablespoon honey

Directions:
1. Combine the oats, buckwheat flakes, nuts, ginger and cinnamon.
2. In a saucepan, warm the oil and honey. Stir until the honey has melted.
3. Pour the warm oil into the dry ingredients and mix well.
4. Fill mixture out on a big baking tray and bake at 300F until the granola is golden.
5. Allow it to cool. Add in the dried berries. Store in an airtight container until ready to use.

Nutrition: 360 Calories 28g Fat 19g Protein

384. Chilled Strawberry & Walnut Porridge

Preparation Time: 8 minutes
Cooking Time: 53 minutes
Servings: 2

Ingredients:
- 100g 3½ oz. strawberries
- 50g 2oz rolled oats
- 4 walnut halves, chopped
- 1 teaspoon chia seeds

- 200 ml 7fl oz. unsweetened soya milk
- 100 ml 3½ fl. oz. water

Directions:

1. Place the strawberries, oats, soya milk and water into a blender and process until smooth. Stir in the chia seeds and mix well. Chill in the fridge overnight and serve.

Nutrition: 268 Calories 31g Fat 21g Protein

385. Sweet Oatmeal

Preparation Time: 8 minutes
Cooking Time: 11 minutes
Servings: 3

Ingredients:

- 1 cup oatmeal
- 5 apricots
- 1 tablespoon honey
- 1 cup coconut milk, unsweetened
- 1 teaspoon cashew butter
- ¼ teaspoon salt
- ½ cup of water

Directions:

1. Combine the coconut milk and oatmeal together in the saucepan and stir the mixture.
2. Add the water and stir it again. Sprinkle the mixture with the salt and close the lid.
3. Cook the oatmeal on medium heat for 10 minutes.
4. Meanwhile, chop the apricots into tiny pieces and combine the chopped fruit with the honey. When the oatmeal is cooked, add cashew butter and fruit mixture. Stir and serve.

Nutrition: 336 Calories 21.2g Fat 6.2g Protein

386. Watergate Salad Recipe

Preparation Time: 62 minutes
Cooking time: 0
Servings: 1

Ingredients:

- 2 (8-ounce) jars squashed pineapple in juice, undrained
- 1 (3.4-ounce) bundle pistachio moment pudding
- 1 (8-ounce) tub solidified whipped beating, defrosted
- 1 cup smaller than usual marshmallows
- 1/2 cup toasted walnuts, hacked

Directions:

1. In a medium bowl, mix together the full substance of the pineapple jars and the pudding blend until smooth.
2. Overlay in whipped fixing and marshmallows. Cover and refrigerate in any event 60 minutes. Sprinkle walnuts on top before serving.

Nutrition: 150 Calories 2g Fat 7g Carbohydrates

387. Moroccan Leeks Snack

Preparation Time: 13 minutes
Cooking time: 0 minute
Serving: 4

Ingredients:

- 1 bunch radish, sliced
- 3 cups leeks, chopped
- 1 ½ cups olives, pitted and sliced
- Pinch turmeric powder
- 2 tablespoons essential olive oil
- 1 cup cilantro, chopped

Directions:

1. Take a bowl and mix in radishes, leeks, olives and cilantro.
2. Mix well.
3. Season with pepper, oil, turmeric and toss well.
4. Serve and enjoy!

Nutrition: 130 Calories 4g Protein 3g Fats

388. Strawberry Pretzel Salad

Preparation Time: 46 minutes
Cooking time: 11 minutes
Servings: 4

Ingredients:

Pretzel Crust

- 3 1/2 cups pretzels, squashed
- 1/4 cup sugar
- 1/2 cup unsalted spread, dissolved

Cream Cheese Filling

- 8 Oz cream cheddar, mellowed
- 1/2 cup sugar
- 8 Oz cool whip, or whipped cream (solidly whipped)
- Strawberry Jell-O Topping
- 1 lbs. new strawberries, hulled and cut
- 2 cups bubbling water
- 6 Oz strawberry jelly powder

Directions:

1. Preheat stove to 350°F. Put aside a 9x13 inch glass preparing dish. Spot pretzels in a

Ziplock sack, seal and pound with a moving pin to smash daintily. In a medium bowl, mix together the liquefied margarine and sugar.

2. Include the squashed pretzels and blend to cover. Press the pretzel blend into the preparing dish, and afterward heat for 10 minutes. Expel from broiler. In a medium bowl, consolidate jelly powder with bubbling water.

3. Mix gradually for one moment until broke down and put in a safe spot. In a huge bowl, beat the cream cheddar and sugar until soft. Utilizing a huge spatula, crease in the cool whip until equitably mixed.

4. When the prepared pretzels are cool, spread the cream cheddar blend equitably on top until level over the dish. At that point, chill for at any rate 30 minutes. While chilling, you can wash, body and cut the strawberries.

5. Tenderly spot the cut strawberries onto the filling in a solitary layer. Include any residual strawberries top as a fractional second layer. When the Jell-O blend is room temperature, spill over the strawberries utilizing the rear of a spoon for even dispersion. Chill for in any event two hours. Serve and appreciate it!

Nutrition: 200 Calories 9g Carbohydrates 2g Fats

389. Sheet Pan Apple Pie Bake

Preparation Time: 22 minutes
Cooking Time: 16 minutes
Servings: 1
Ingredients:

- 8 flour tortillas, 8 inches
- 4 tbsp unsalted spread
- 8 Granny Smith apples, stripped, cored and cleaved
- 3/4 cup sugar, partitioned
- 3 tsp cinnamon, partitioned
- 1 tbsp lemon juice, new pressed
- Serving thoughts - discretionary
- whipped cream
- frozen yogurt
- caramel sauce

Directions:

1. Preheat stove to 400°F. Put aside a medium preparing sheet. On a medium

preparing sheet, orchestrate 6 tortillas in a blossom petal design with a few creeps outside the dish and a few crawls of cover.

2. Spot a seventh tortilla in the center. Spot an enormous skillet on medium-high warmth. Include spread, slashed apples, 1/2 cup sugar and 2 tsp cinnamon. Sauté the apples for 8-10 minutes until they begin to relax, mixing normally with a wooden spoon.

3. Spoon apple blend from skillet over tortillas on prepared sheet. Spread out to make an even layer. Overlay the folds of tortilla outside the dish over the apples. Spot the eighth tortilla in the center to cover the hole.

4. Blend staying 1/4 cup sugar with 1 tsp cinnamon. Sprinkle equally over the tortillas. Spot another preparing dish on top to hold the tortillas set up and heat for 20 minutes. Expel from the stove and permit to cool for 5-10 minutes.

5. Present with discretionary frozen yogurt, whipped cream and caramel sauce. Appreciate!

Nutrition: 250 Calories 2g Fats 4g Carbohydrates

390. Heaven on Earth Cake

Preparation Time: 24 minutes
Cooking Time: 0
Serving: 1
Ingredients:

- 1 box Angel nourishment cake
- 1 bundle (3.4 ounces) moment vanilla pudding
- 1/2 cups milk
- 1 cup harsh cream
- 1 can (21 ounces) cherry pie filling
- 1 tub (8 ounces) Cool Whip
- 1 tablespoon almond bits, toasted

Directions:

1. Heat fluffy cake as indicated by bundle's bearings. Permit to cool and cut into 3D shapes. In a bowl, consolidate pudding blend, milk, and acrid cream and beat until smooth.

2. Put in a safe spot. In a 9x13 preparing dish, organize 1/2 of cake solid shapes layer. Spoon 2/3 of cherry over cake. Spot the staying 1/2 of the cake over pie filling.

3. Spoon pudding over cake and spread equally. Spoon and spread whipped besting over the pudding layer. Embellishment cake with the rest of the pie filling and toasted almonds. Chill for around 4 to 5 hours.

Nutrition: 250 Calories 1g Fats 5g Carbohydrates

391. Strawberry Upside-Down Cake

Preparation Time: 14 minutes
Cooking Time: 43 minutes
Serving: 1
Ingredients:

- 2 c. new strawberries squashed
- 2 3 Oz strawberry Jell-O
- 3 c. little marshmallows
- 18.25 oz. strawberry cake blend + fixings to get ready cake blend
- Cool Whip

Directions:

1. Take your two cups of strawberries and pound them with a fork. Fill a lubed 9x13 in cake container. Sprinkle strawberry Jell-O over the highest point of the strawberries. At that point, sprinkle the marshmallows over the Jell-O.
2. Plan cake blend, as indicated by bundle headings. Pour over the marshmallows. Heat at 350 degrees for 40-50 minutes or until cake tests are done.
3. Let sit for around 15 minutes and afterward, run a blade around the outside of the cake. Flip onto a serving plate. Refrigerate. Present with Cool Whip. Store scraps in the fridge.

Nutrition: 250 Calories 2g Fiber 1g Fats

392. Lemon Blueberry Poke Cake

Preparation Time: 31 minutes
Cooking Time: 63 minutes
Serving: 1
Ingredients:

- 1 box vanilla cake blend, in addition to fixings called for on box
- 2 1/2 c. Blueberries
- Juice of 1/2 lemon
- 1 tbsp. Granulated sugar
- 1/2 c. Whipped besting

For the frosting and topping:

- 1 c. (2 sticks) spread, relaxed
- 2 (8-oz.) Squares cream cheddar, mellowed
- 2 1/4 c. Powdered sugar
- Get-up-and-go of 1 lemon
- Juice of 1/2 lemon
- 1 tsp. Unadulterated vanilla concentrate
- Blueberries, for decorate

Directions:

1. Preheat stove to 350°. Line a 9"- x-13" dish with material paper and oil with cooking shower. Prepare cake as indicated by bundle guidelines. Let cool totally.
2. Make the blueberry sauce: In a little pan over medium warmth, join blueberries, lemon squeeze, and sugar. Bring to a stew and cook for 7 minutes. Expel from warm and fill a medium bowl.
3. Let cool for 15 minutes, at that point overlay in whipped beating. Make icing: In a huge bowl utilizing a hand blender, beat the spread and cream cheddar. Include powdered sugar, lemon get-up-and-go and squeeze, and vanilla and beat until smooth and soft.
4. Utilizing the rear of a wooden spoon, jab openings all over cooled cake at that point pour blueberry blend on top. Spread icing on top at that point embellish cake with more blueberries.

Nutrition: 235 Calories 2g Fats 5g Carbohydrates

393. Easy No-Churn Funfetti Ice Cream Cake

Preparation Time: 23 minutes
Cooking Time: 11 minutes
Serving: 6
Ingredients:

- 2 cups heavy whipping cream, well chilled
- Two teaspoons vanilla extract
- ¼ teaspoon salt
- 14 Oz sweetened condensed milk
- 2 Tablespoons unsalted butter, melted and cooled
- 1/2 cup rainbow sprinkles

For the frosting:

- 1 cup semi-sweet chocolate chips
- 1 cup butter

Directions:

1. Place a large bowl or whisk attachment into the freezer to chill for about 10 minutes. Carefully pour condensed milk and melted butter into the bowl, then gently fold into the whipped cream.
2. Then quickly fold in the sprinkles. Spread the ice cream in the prepared pan and freeze for several hours, or until firm.

Nutrition: 260 Calories 5g Fats 9g Carbohydrates

394. Lemon Tofu Cheesecake

Preparation Time: 44 minutes
Cooking Time: 0
Servings:8

Ingredients:
- Silk tofu, drained – 24 ounces
- Almond butter – 1.5 tablespoons
- Date sugar – 1 cup
- Lemon zest – 1 teaspoon
- Sea salt .5 teaspoon
- Vanilla extract - .5 teaspoon
- Lemon juice - 2 tablespoons
- Cornstarch – 1.5 tablespoons
- Crust, 8-inch – 1 (optional)

Directions:
1. Preheat the oven to Fahrenheit three-hundred and fifty degrees. If you are preparing the lemon tofu cheesecake without a crust, I recommend preparing eight individual ramekins to divide the filling between. Otherwise, prepare an eight-inch crust of your choice.
2. Whisk together the lemon juice with the cornstarch to form a slurry.
3. In a food processor or blender, combine the cornstarch slurry and remaining ingredients until fully combined, smooth, and creamy. You don't want any lumps.
4. Pour the lemon tofu cheesecake filling into the prepared crust or ramekins. If baking with the crust, allow the cheesecake to cook until set, about thirty minutes.
5. Allow the cheesecake to cool to room temperature, and then transfer it to the fridge until completely chilled through.

Nutrition: 174 Calorie 2g Fat 7g Carbohydrates

395. Blueberry Walnut Crisp

Preparation Time: 43 minutes
Cooking Time: 38 minutes

Servings: 6
Ingredients:
- Walnuts, chopped - .25 cup
- Rolled oats - .5 cup
- Date sugar – 2 tablespoons
- Cinnamon, ground - .5 teaspoon
- Sea salt - .25 teaspoon
- Butter, cut into cubes – 2 tablespoons
- Blueberries – 4 cups
- Cornstarch – 1 tablespoon
- Date sugar – 2 tablespoons
- Lemon zest - .5 teaspoon
- Vanilla extract – 1 teaspoon

Directions:
1. Begin by preheating your oven to Fahrenheit three-hundred and fifty degrees and preparing six individual ramekins with non-stick cooking spray. Set the ramekins on a baking sheet to avoid spilling.
2. In a bowl, toss together the blueberries with the cornstarch, date sugar, lemon zest, and vanilla. Once combined, divide the blueberries between the ramekins.
3. To make the crispy topping combine the remaining ingredients with a fork or pastry cutter. It will be crumbly. Top the blueberries in the ramekins with the crumble.
4. Set the baking sheet of ramekins in the oven and bake until golden-brown, about twenty-five to thirty minutes. Remove the blueberry walnut crisp from the oven and allow the crisps to cool slightly before serving.

Nutrition: 211 Calories 2g Fats 5g Carbohydrates

396. Red Wine Poached Pears

Preparation Time: 37 minutes
Cooking Time: 0
Servings: 6

Ingredients:
- Bosc pears – 6
- Cherries, pitted - .5 cup (optional)
- Red wine – 2 cups
- Orange juice - .5 cup
- Vanilla extract – 2 teaspoons
- Date sugar - .5 cup
- Cinnamon stick – 1

- Cloves, whole – 8
- Orange zest - .5 teaspoon

Directions:
1. Add all of your red wine poached pear ingredients, except for the Bosc pears, into a large Dutch oven. You need a pot large enough to fit all six whole hears.
2. Allow the wine mixture to reach a simmer in the pot while stirring to dissolve the date sugar.
3. Wait until the poaching liquid has reached a simmer and then peel the pears. Place the pears into the poaching liquid, arranging them so that they are submerged.
4. Allow the pears to continue simmering on medium-low for about twenty to twenty-five minutes. But while the pears poach rearrange and rotate them every five minutes.
5. Once the pears are done poaching, keep the pears upright in the wine mixture. Remove the pot from the heat of the stove, and allow both the pears and poaching liquid to cool down together.
6. While you can serve the poached pears once cooled to room temperature
7. When chilling the pears in the fridge, keep them stored in the liquid.
8. Once you are ready to serve the pears, remove them from the liquid and set them on serving dishes. Meanwhile, add the poaching liquid into a saucepan and allow it to simmer to heat until it forms a slightly thickened syrup.
9. Pour the red wine syrup over the cold pears and serve.

Nutrition: 266 Calories 6g Carbohydrates 4g Fat

397. Dark Chocolate Walnut No-Bake Cookies

Preparation Time: 24 minutes
Cooking Time: 0 minutes
Servings: 24
Ingredients:
- Walnuts, chopped - .25 cups
- Coconut oil – 3 tablespoons
- Cocoa powder - .25 cup
- Dark chocolate chips - .5 cup
- Shredded coconut, unsweetened – 2 cups
- Almond butter - .5 cup

- Honey - .33 cup
- Vanilla extract – 1 teaspoon
- Sea salt - .25 teaspoon

Directions:
1. Prepare an aluminum baking sheet by covering it with kitchen parchment, wax coated paper, or a silicone mat.
2. Melt the coconut oil with the almond butter and honey over low heat in a saucepan. Once melted, stir in the remaining ingredients.
3. Use a tablespoon to scoop out portions of the chocolate walnut dough and roll each portion into a ball in your hands. Place the dark chocolate walnut no-bake cookie balls on the prepared baking sheet.
4. Freeze the cookies for ten minutes to set up. Enjoy immediately, or store the leftovers in a container in the freezer.

Nutrition: 139 Calories 14g Carbohydrates 4g Fats

398. No-Bake Triple Berry Mini Tarts

Preparation time: 12 minutes
Cooking time: 46 minutes
Serving: 4
Ingredients:
- Frozen mixed berries, defrosted – 1 cup
- Honey - .5 cup
- Cacao butter, melted – 5 tablespoons
- Coconut cream - .33 cup
- Walnuts, raw – 2 cups
- Dates – 1 cup

Directions:
1. In a food processor, combine the walnuts with the dates until it forms a crumbly mixture that can hold together when you press it. Scrape down the sides as needed.
2. Prepare a mini muffin tin for the crust to make the mini-tarts. Spray the pan with non-stick cooking spray.
3. Press the prepared crust into the mini muffin tin, forming mini tarts with crust pressed both on the bottom and on the sides of the muffin cups.
4. In a blender, mix the berries and other remaining ingredients until completely smooth. Divide the berry mixture between the crusts.

5. Place the filled muffin tin in the fridge and allow it to chill for six hours, or until set.

6. Use a kitchen knife to run around the edges of each tart to release them from the pan. Use a fork and take each tart out of the pan. Serve or store in a container in the fridge or freezer.

Nutrition: 239 Calories 7g Protein 27g Fats

399. Mocha Buckwheat Pudding

Preparation Time: 14 minutes
Cooking time: 33 minutes
Serving: 4

Ingredients:

- Buckwheat groats - .5 cup
- Cocoa powder – 3 tablespoon s
- Chocolate soy protein powder – 2 scoops
- Instant espresso powder – 1 teaspoon
- Almond butter – 2 tablespoons
- Soymilk, unsweetened - .5 cup
- Banana – 1
- Dates, pitted – 2

Directions:

1. Cover the buckwheat groats in water and allow them to soak overnight to soften. Rinse it well.

2. Add the prepared buckwheat and the remaining ingredients all into a blender together, and blend on high speed until completely smooth.

3. Serve the pudding immediately or allow it to chill first.

Nutrition: 110 Calories 3g Protein 1g Fats

400. Loaded Chocolate Fudge

Preparation Time: 13 minutes
Cooking time: 42 minutes
Serving: 4

Ingredients:

- 1 cup Medjool dates, chopped
- 2 tablespoons coconut oil, melted
- 1/2 cup peanut butter
- ¼ cup of unsweetened cocoa powder
- ½ cup walnuts
- 1 teaspoon vanilla

Directions:

1. Soak the dates in warm water for 20 – 30 minutes

2. Lightly grease an 8" square baking pan with coconut oil.

3. Add dates, peanut butter, cocoa powder and vanilla to a food processer and blend until smooth.

4. Fold in walnuts.

5. Pack into the greased baking pan and put in your freezer for 1 hour

6. Cut into 16 or more bite-sized squares and store in semi-airtight container in the refrigerator.

Nutrition: 120 Calories 4g Protein 3g Fats

CONCLUSION

Thanks for making it to the end of sirtfood diet cookbook. Sirtfood diet plan is a great plan that like all plans need to be implemented with a great deal of effort, discipline and determination. Sirtfood diet can help you lose weight if you fully implement it into your life and make it a habit.

As stated above this diet is not supposed to be a short-term plan but a long-term lifestyle goal. You cannot implement this diet and then revert to your normal eating habits. You need to adopt lifestyle changes. If you wish to lose weight and stay fit, then you need to do something about it.

It is suggested to eat sirtfood diet recipes every day. The future benefits of sirtfood diet will overcome any initial discomfort you might feel during the beginning phases of the diet. If you wish to make this diet successful, then you need to believe in it.

I hope you have enjoyed reading Sirtfood Diet Plan.

Good luck on your sirtfood journey!